FINANCIAL SECTOR
GOVERNANCE

THE WORLD BANK GROUP

THE INTERNATIONAL MONETARY FUND

THE BROOKINGS INSTITUTION

This book is based on a conference entitled Building the Pillars of Financial Sector Governance, held on April 16–19, 2001, in New York City. The conference was jointly sponsored by the World Bank Group, the International Monetary Fund, and the Brookings Institution.

The previous volumes in this series are available from the Brookings Institution Press:

Financial Markets and Development: The Crisis in Emerging Markets (1999)

Managing Financial and Corporate Distress: Lessons from Asia (2000)

*Open Doors: Foreign Participation in Financial Systems
in Developing Countries* (2001)

ROBERT E. LITAN
MICHAEL POMERLEANO
V. SUNDARARAJAN
Editors

FINANCIAL SECTOR GOVERNANCE

The Roles of the Public and Private Sectors

BROOKINGS INSTITUTION PRESS
Washington, D.C.

ABOUT BROOKINGS

The Brookings Institution is a private nonprofit organization devoted to research, education, and publication on important issues of domestic and foreign policy. Its principal purpose is to bring knowledge to bear on current and emerging policy problems. The Institution maintains a position of neutrality on issues of public policy. Interpretations or conclusions in Brookings publications should be understood to be solely those of the authors.

Library of Congress Cataloging-in-Publication data available

ISBN 0-8157-5289-x (alk. paper)

9 8 7 6 5 4 3 2 1

The paper used in this publication meets minimum requirements of the American National Standard for Information Sciences—Permanence of Paper for Printed Library Materials, ANSI Z39.48-1992.

Typeset in Adobe Garamond

Composition by R. Lynn Rivenbark
Macon, Georgia

Printed by Victor Graphics
Baltimore, Maryland

Contents

PART FIVE
Summaries of Breakout Sessions

Foreword

SUDDEN FINANCIAL CRISES are a recurring and disturbing feature of globalization. Emerging market economies are especially at risk. Understanding this phenomenon requires not just reactive analysis in the wake of each outbreak but a regular forum in which experts from a variety of disciplines and perspectives can study the problem and develop solutions over time. To that end, the World Bank Group, the International Monetary Fund, and the Brookings Institution have collaborated since 1998 on a series of annual conferences designed to be of interest to investors, analysts, and policymakers throughout the world with the objective of stimulating policy dialogue and sharing global experiences.

This year's program was held in April 2002 in New York and concentrated on governance in the financial sectors of emerging markets. The conference brought together individuals from a variety of disciplines and sectors, including senior policymakers from developed market countries, practitioners from the financial services industry, officials of multilateral organizations, government officials and private sector participants from emerging market countries, and selected academicians. Many individuals contributed to the success of the conference and to this volume, including the formal discussants and authors of the papers contained here.

Special thanks are also owed to Colleen Mascenik at the World Bank, who along with the editors, helped organize the conference. In addition,

Alicia Jones and Sandip Sukhtankar at Brookings provided valuable assistance throughout the planning and organizing of the conference. We also acknowledge the editorial, proofreading, and indexing assistance of Marty Gottron, Carlotta Ribar, and Julia Petrakis.

Funds for the conference were generously supplied by the World Bank Group, the International Monetary Fund, and the Brookings Institution.

STROBE TALBOTT
President, Brookings Institution

Washington, D.C.
September 2002

FINANCIAL SECTOR
GOVERNANCE

ROBERT E. LITAN
MICHAEL POMERLEANO
V. SUNDARARAJAN

1

Strengthening Financial Sector Governance in Emerging Markets

POLICYMAKERS AND ANALYSTS are still sifting through the wreckage of the Asian financial crisis of 1997 and the subsequent crises in Argentina, Russia, and Turkey to discern key lessons so similar crises will not recur. Some lessons are by now well understood and have been acted upon. Pegged exchange rates can encourage excessive borrowing and expose countries to financial collapse when foreign exchange reserves run dry. By and large, rates that were formerly fixed are now more or less flexible. Inadequate disclosures by both private companies and central banks also can create dangers of financial collapse. More transparency is now found in most of the emerging markets where the financial system did indeed collapse. And the laxity in the supervision and regulation of financial institutions in these markets that aggravated their financial crises has, to a significant degree, been corrected.

One problem, however, has received too little attention thus far: the extent to which financial crises have resulted from a failure in "governance"—broadly defined to include the efficient and effective management of public institutions and private firms. When countries and firms borrow excessively and mismanage their financial affairs, then almost by definition, they are not being governed well. Governance problems in the financial sectors of crisis-affected countries proved to be of special concern.

Among the problems: uninformed investors who were too ready to invest in debt and equity without gathering adequate information; inadequate provision of information by firms and governments that issued these securities; poor regulation of banks and capital markets; ill-defined incentives to avoid excessive risks in private and state-owned financial institutions and companies; the lack of clearly defined and enforced property rights; and insolvency regimes that, after the crises occurred, did not protect creditors.

This volume has been assembled to improve understanding of these particular problems of the financial sector. The papers that follow were commissioned as part of the fourth annual conference on emerging markets finance sponsored by the World Bank Group, the International Monetary Fund, and the Brookings Institution, which was held in New York in April 2002. As in previous years, the 2002 conference brought together a distinguished group of senior public officials, private sector participants, and academic experts to debate and examine the new research commissioned by the sponsors and presented at the conference. In this initial chapter, we summarize some of the highlights of the papers presented at the conference, as well as the discussion by the participants and authors about the subjects raised in the papers. Although this summary does not follow the sequence of the papers contained in the volume, the narrative nonetheless provides a framework within which the papers can be read.

What Is Governance?

In its broadest sense, *governance* refers to the range of institutions and practices by which authority is exercised. As authors of several of the papers in this volume point out, the term is typically used in a governmental context and includes the mechanisms for selecting, monitoring, and replacing officials performing governmental duties, as well as the institutions that create and deliver public goods to citizens.

For the private sector, and specifically for corporations, governance also includes institutions and practices designed to ensure that those running companies serve the interests of those who own them. Solving what has come to be known as the principal-agent problem is not an issue for privately held companies, where the managers are the owners or represent dominant shareholders, and it may be less of a problem, at least in principle, where ownership is highly concentrated in one or a few owners who then have significant incentives to monitor the behavior of managers (but who also then have greater incentives and opportunity to loot the corporation). Where ownership is more widely dispersed, or where minority shareholders' and other stakeholders' interests need to be protected, however, various other institutions—including disclosure requirements, legal protections of the rights of minority shareholders, fiduciary obligations imposed on officers and directors, market conduct rules, an active corporate takeover market, and incentive contracts for managers—have been developed in advanced economies (especially the United States) to ensure that the interests of corporate agents (managers) are closely aligned with their principals (shareholders), and other stakeholders.

The Importance of Financial Sector Governance

This volume focuses specifically on governance in the *financial sector* in emerging markets, in both public and private contexts. Special emphasis is given to this sector because of the unique character of financial intermediaries and the added complexity of standard governance problems among financial institutions. For example, questions of transparency, incentive conflicts, and agency conflicts in the corporate sector are compounded by greater opacity, government ownership, and regulation of financial institutions, banks in particular. In addition, the costs of poor governance in the financial sector are much more widespread than are those of individual corporations. Because financial intermediaries are the repositories of household wealth, their losses or failures can lead to large systemic and social costs.

Governance in the financial sector has both a public and a private dimension. On the public side, governments typically regulate financial institutions and markets and in many countries also own and operate financial institutions directly. In the private context, financial sector governance refers not only to the control financial institutions can and do exercise over borrowers, but also to the institutions and practices, including the governance of regulators, designed to ensure the soundness of financial institutions themselves. The capital markets also provide a means of governance of both financial and nonfinancial firms.

Financial sector governance is important for several clear and obvious reasons. One critical reason is to avoid financial crises—the failures of large numbers of financial institutions or the sudden and sharp collapse of prices of financial instruments traded on capital markets. Financial institutions must function effectively, because they operate the payments system and store much of the wealth in any society. Likewise, capital markets are instrumental in enabling companies to raise funds and investors to hold or access their wealth. In a very real sense, therefore, financial sectors are the functional equivalent of circulatory systems in human beings. Just as humans can be killed or severely impaired if they suffer a heart attack, the real sectors of economies can be crippled if the financial system becomes dysfunctional.

Every one of the major economic crises in emerging market countries in recent years—in East Asia, Argentina, Brazil, Russia, and Turkey—was accompanied or triggered by a crisis in its financial sector, and the citizens of these countries suffered deep pain in the process. In the case of Indonesia, which was hit hardest during the Asian financial crisis, the fiscal costs alone of having the government step in to make good on the obligations of the privately held banks exceeded 100 percent of the country's gross domestic product (GDP). Financial crises also typically entail large social and economic costs, which are visited not only on the wealthy who have something to lose, but also on entire populations of countries where employment opportunities dwindle and wages collapse when GDP drops sharply and currency values plummet.

The costs of financial crises are not the only reasons for being interested in the governance of the financial sector, however. Poor governance is typically associated with corruption, which not only corrodes the trust individuals have in their private and public institutions, but also acts as a significant deterrent to foreign direct investment (FDI). In chapter 3, Shang-Jin Wei of the IMF and Brookings estimates that corruption currently imposes the equivalent of a tax on FDI in excess of 20 percent in many emerging market countries. This "corruption premium" depresses the total amount of FDI—in some countries, by more than 50 percent; it also shifts the composition of incoming foreign capital toward bank lending and shorter-term portfolio flows, both of which make countries more vulnerable to financial crises if confidence in the economy (or its government) is suddenly shattered.

More broadly, Daniel Kaufmann from the World Bank explores in chapter 4 the linkage between governance in the public and private sectors. Based on extensive empirical studies on various governance indicators, Kaufmann notes that "control of corruption" as an aspect of good governance is strongly and positively correlated with the soundness of financial systems. His paper presents evidence showing that elite financial firms in the private sector often play a strong hand in shaping rules and institutions in the public financial sector and that regulatory capture by firms is more widespread in the financial sector than in other regulated sectors. He also emphasizes that regulatory capture by firms calls for a multipronged strategy to foster good governance. Instead of the conventional policy advice geared at public sector officials, Kaufmann recommends a systemwide approach to reform that focuses on building transparency, improving incentives, and preventing corruption on both the public and private sector sides.

Poorly governed financial institutions are liabilities to the financial system: first, because, as Kaufmann demonstrates, they exert a distorting influence on public sector rules and institutions, and second, because they lend to the wrong borrowers and in excessive amounts. Channeling the scarce savings of a country's society to wasteful borrowers deprives sound companies of credit and thus acts as a drag on economic growth. Excessive lending, meanwhile, can lay the foundation for a future financial crisis when an economic shock renders many borrowers unable to repay.

Governance of Banks

Banks are the principal financial intermediary in emerging markets (but less so in developed countries, especially the United States). Banks are funded mainly by depositors; thus bank failures can adversely affect household wealth while possibly leading to systemic losses. The development of new technologies, major industry consolidation, globalization, and deregulation have placed the banking industry at a strategic crossroads. Therefore, banks face a more competitive, volatile global environment than other types of corporations.

Gerald Caprio and Ross Levine explain in chapter 2 why banks pose a special governance problem that is different from ordinary corporations. First, banks' activities are more opaque and thus more difficult for shareholders and creditors to monitor. Second, because governments heavily regulate banks, ownership may be dispersed by mandate (as it is in 79 of the 107 countries for which the authors had data) and thus takeovers may be impeded, directly or through prohibitions on bank ownership by certain kinds of companies. Third, the protection of bank deposits by government deposit insurance programs can undercut incentives for depositors to monitor management, thus shifting responsibility for governance of banks to other parties or institutions. Accordingly, the authors encourage more public reporting of banks' financial conditions, greater entry by foreign banks into emerging markets (which enhances competition and brings greater technical expertise to local banking markets), more market discipline to counteract the disincentive effects of deposit insurance (through, for example, subordinated debt requirements), and perhaps enhanced fiduciary obligations imposed on bank managers and directors. The authors also argue that the need for such additional countervailing measures is especially great in emerging market countries, where information is scarce and less reliable than in industrial countries, where economies are more likely to be dominated by a few family-owned conglomerates, and where state ownership of financial institutions is more pronounced.

A number of the conference participants were not as confident as Caprio and Levine about the benefits of greater foreign ownership of banking systems, especially in small open economies, where if domestic banks were wiped out, foreign banks would have too ample an opportunity to cherry-pick the best customers and leave much of the country underserved. Several participants questioned whether concentrated ownership—a frequently mentioned solution to the principal-agent problem for corporations generally—is appropriate for banks, which can be more easily looted (directly or indirectly, by channeling funds to companies owned by their shareholders).

Meanwhile, despite a wave of privatization around the world in the past two decades, 40 percent of the world's population still resides in countries where most bank assets are controlled by state-owned institutions. State-owned banks pose special governance problems. Government ownership thwarts competitive forces, limits the effectiveness of government supervision in the financial sector, and tends to increase the opacity of banks' operations. Governments can use their state-owned institutions to support excessive government spending and to favor less-than-creditworthy borrowers. All of these tendencies can dampen overall economic growth. In addition, governments often operate their institutions, or the regulatory processes that govern them, in ways that discourage the development of vibrant private sector competitors.

For all of these reasons, there was support voiced at the conference for efforts by governments that continue to own banks to privatize them. But reservations were expressed at the same time. In particular, Y. V. Reddy, deputy governor of the Reserve Bank of India, argues in a case study that governance structures need to be improved before widespread privatizations take place in order to prevent small groups from benefiting from interconnected lending.

The experiences of the Hong Kong Monetary Authority (HKMA) and the Monetary Authority of Singapore (MAS) provide some useful lessons in financial sector governance. For example, increasing the contestability of markets, especially by opening the financial sector to foreign investment, decreases the reliance on family or conglomerate relationships. Legal and bankruptcy frameworks are critical to putting the right incentives in place for a competitive financial sector. To promote transparency and independent audits of financial institutions, HKMA issued a guideline in May 2000 requiring the board of each bank to establish an audit committee made up of nonexecutive directors, the majority of whom should be independent; furthermore, the members must have written terms of reference specifying their authorities and duties. MAS takes another approach to strengthening governance of banks, requiring banks to separate financial and nonfinancial businesses and to change their audit firms every five years.

Governance of Investment Companies

Collective investment schemes—which enable investors to own proportionate shares of a pool of financial assets—have become increasingly important financial institutions in developed countries. The governance structures of these institutions vary widely. Corporate-style mutual funds, found mostly in the United States and a few emerging markets, dominate in terms of value of assets. Contractual and trust-type structures dominate in terms of the number of funds and are found mostly in countries where joint stock company laws do not permit firms to issue and redeem their own shares continuously or where liquid markets to manage open-ended schemes may not be well developed.

Sally Buxton and Mark St. Giles argue in chapter 9, however, that the governance structure is irrelevant for the conduct and performance of collective investment funds. The key to their sound performance lies in effective market discipline underpinned by strong disclosure. They stress the importance of reputational risk in disciplining fund managers and propose a three-pronged approach resting on competition, disclosure, and the ability to exit funds.

The lack of transparency and disclosure by collective investment funds in emerging market countries, in particular, inhibits their performance.

Indeed, the authors report that it is difficult in many emerging markets even to locate a list of the investment funds that are available. Accordingly, they recommend that emerging markets set and enforce disclosure standards for investment vehicles (including a requirement that net asset values be published regularly), while educating the public—through the media— about their risks and rewards.

Asset management companies, or AMCs, a very specialized type of investment vehicle, were created by East Asian governments to hold and ultimately sell troubled assets (often loans) that were formerly on the books of weak or insolvent financial institutions. In countries where banking problems have been severe, AMCs have become major financial institutions in their own right. For example, the Indonesian Bank Restructuring Agency controls 70 percent of the financial sector assets in Indonesia. Clearly, therefore, as the case study by David Cooke illustrates, the governance for these institutions has critical implications for the pace of problem resolution and the costs involved.

The East Asian AMCs are modeled to a large extent on similar institutions that were established in the aftermath of financial crisis in many industrial and emerging market countries in the 1970s and 1980s. Perhaps the best known—and most successful—AMC was the Resolution Trust Corporation (RTC), created in the United States in 1990 to dispose of assets held by hundreds of insolvent savings and loan institutions. The RTC disposed of its assets quickly, placing them in the hands of private sector managers who found alternative uses for them.

The conference participants discussed the experiences of the AMCs created following the Asian financial crisis. They generally agreed that many of these institutions faced conflicting objectives, that their responsibilities were poorly defined, and that oversight committees were not sufficiently separated from management. Looking ahead, possible solutions are to articulate explicit missions for the AMCs; to provide for independent and informed oversight committees, which would articulate the policy objectives and review AMC performance; and to create independent operating boards with authority to manage AMC activities.

Pension Funds

As the population of the world ages, pension funds—both public and private—assume greater importance, both for the individuals covered and for the development of the financial systems to which the funds belong. At this point in time, according to data provided by Gregorio Impavido in chapter 11, almost half of the world's labor force is covered by mandatory, publicly managed, defined-benefit pension plans that are funded on a pay-as-you-go basis. Another 32 percent is covered by partially funded public pension systems. Just 10–15 percent of the world's labor force is covered by public or private defined-contribution pension funds.

The governance of pension funds is critically important, since the quality and performance of fund management can determine the income flows to which retirees are entitled, as well as the level of government funding of any shortfall between what the plans may promise (if they are defined-benefit) and what they are capable of delivering. Impavido provides evidence of poor performance by many publicly managed pension systems and demonstrates that this poor performance is highly correlated with measures of (poor) governance, including government-imposed restrictions on investments and the absence of pension board authority to govern investment decisions. Impavido recommends that public pension programs be given a clear mandate—to maximize the returns for retirees—and not be assigned collateral social objectives; that the boards be insulated, to the maximum extent possible, from political influence; that the members of the board meet rigorous qualifications for serving and that they understand and avoid any conflicts of interest when administering these plans; and that the performance of the plans be disclosed regularly so that boards can be held accountable to beneficiaries.

The Role of Capital Markets in Exerting Governance

Achieving good corporate governance generally has been more challenging for emerging market countries than for advanced economies (notwithstanding the failure of Enron in the United States) for several reasons: corporate ownership in emerging market economies tends to be highly concentrated, often in a few families, with only limited ownership by minority shareholders; takeover markets are thin or nonexistent; and judicial enforcement through formal government sanctions or class action suits also is not widely used or available. Various ideas for improving corporate governance in these circumstances were suggested at the conference.

One improvement might be a requirement that certain kinds of corporate transactions, especially those involving controlling shareholders, be approved by a majority of the minority shareholders. Another participant suggested having specialized courts with expertise in corporate law. Some participants thought high listing standards on exchanges, such as those now used in Germany and Brazil, would strengthen corporate governance, but others questioned whether there was enough demand by companies to satisfy those standards. Another possibility would be to limit investments of pension funds in local companies only to those firms that meet certain minimum, but high, corporate governance standards. The participants broadly endorsed the implementation of internationally endorsed best practice guidelines for corporate governance, especially enforcement of rules on disclosure.

An important lesson that emerged from the papers and from comparison of various countries' experiences was that the changes to capital markets are not a "silver bullet" to facilitate better governance. Moreover, capital markets cannot be viewed in isolation, but instead must be seen as institutions that are inextricably linked to a constellation of legal practices, other institutions, and corporate governance structures. As a result, policymakers and regulators need to tailor their approaches to governance to the institutions and practices that have grown up in specific countries.

For example, the fear of hostile takeover, which is a strong disciplinary force in U.S. markets, relies on a rather well-developed, high-yield bond market that has been a source of funding for acquiring firms. However, this blunt instrument of corporate governance that wrenches out corporate inefficiencies in many advanced economies is simply not relevant in emerging markets or some developed economies, where takeovers are not prevalent. As a result, participants and authors at the conference agreed that it would be a mistake to assume that what may be an effective governance device in developed economies can easily be transplanted to any emerging market economy.

One area of continuing controversy in academic circles about corporate governance is whether Anglo-American common law, where rules are developed over time on a case-by-case basis, does a better or worse job in fostering the development of financial markets than European "civil law," where the rules are set forth in statutes and tend to be less changeable over time. In examining this controversy in chapter 10, Cally Jordan and Mike Lubrano of the World Bank Group agree that legal traditions and systems fundamentally shape the feasibility of various corporate governance mechanisms. But as they highlight in their paper, the debate over the superiority of Anglo-American or European civil law obscures the very important governance role played by *private* rules, whether by contract, often underpinned by voluntary codes of conduct and thus adopted ex ante, or by ex post enforcement through contractual dispute resolution, including arbitration, or through market discipline. Drawing on recently published work, Jordan and Lubrano make the case that private law has been especially important in the development of markets for derivatives instruments. The effectiveness of private rules that rely on voluntary codes of good conduct to promote good governance very much depends, however, upon how they interact with and complement the public rules that underpin governance.

Public Sector Governance of the Financial Sector

Finally, given the economic importance of the financial sector and the dangers when it functions poorly, it is not surprising that governments in both developed and emerging market countries alike take a keen interest in regulating and supervising financial institutions and markets. Jeff Carmichael, chairman of the Australian Prudential Regulation Authority, points out in chapter 5 that the public sector has a close and complex relationship with the financial sector in most economies, often playing several roles simultaneously: the regulator of financial institutions; an owner of financial institutions; a market participant; a fiduciary agent; and sometimes an agent that directly intervenes in the operations of the market. Carmichael outlines a number of principles for effective public sector regulation and oversight. These principles were further analyzed in both normal times and crisis periods in chapter 6 by Udaibir Das and Marc Quintyn of the IMF.

First, perhaps the most important financial public sector governance principle is to ensure the independence of financial regulators, matched by appropriate accountability arrangements. Regulators must be protected against both capricious dismissal and damage suits for performing their regulatory duties.

Second, government agencies (whether financial or not) should have transparent objectives and operational processes, both supported by adequate reporting to the public.

Third, arrangements should be in place to ensure the integrity of the regulatory agency. For example, it is useful to maintain and enforce codes of conduct to govern the staff of regulatory bodies, including a mechanism for judicial review of agency decisions. Carmichael also reinforced the importance of preventing corruption from infecting public oversight of financial institutions and markets.

Das and Quintyn emphasize that incentives for good corporate governance can be distorted in situations of financial distress and crisis and that the scope of regulatory governance has to be reinforced through new institutional structures with enhanced transparency and greater accountability.

The IMF and World Bank are working jointly to assess adherence to financial sector standards as part of a broader assessment of stability and development needs in the Financial Sector Assessment Program (FSAP). Since the inception of the FSAP in 1999, nearly eighty countries have participated or agreed to participate in the program. FSAPs typically have assessed country practices against various internationally accepted standards in supervision, transparency, and market infrastructure (in particular, the IMF Code of Good Practices on Transparency in Monetary and Financial Policies), as well as international standards for the supervision of banks, securities firms, insurance companies and payments systems. As stressed in the Carmichael and Das-Quintyn chapters, these standards give primary emphasis to the importance of independence of regulatory agencies from political influence as a threshold indicator of good public sector governance.

Based on their review of the findings of the FSAPs, Das and Quintyn report that securities regulators score highest of all financial sector regulators on the scale of governance, with banking regulators falling right behind. Banking regulators score as high as they do because in many countries banking supervision is carried out by the nation's central bank, which is more than likely to be strong institutionally, adequately funded, and independent of much of the rest of the government. Insurance regulators face the greatest challenges in adhering to international standards.

Another key indicator of good public sector governance is the degree of transparency of the regulatory objectives and operations, including the regulators' relationships with other agencies. By this measure, the FSAP process reveals that developing countries as a whole, including transition economies, lag behind advanced countries. On the positive side, however, even in developing countries, banking and payments systems supervisors—again, often central banks—score reasonably high.

Looking ahead, the FSAP process is designed to identify and highlight key policy reforms that hold the best prospects for improving financial sector governance practices. Enhancing the independence and accountability of financial regulators, supported by the appropriate degree of transparency of regulatory actions, can greatly add to financial stability and help the public to determine whether financial regulations are serving the public interest.

Summary and Conclusions

Public and private financial sector governance cannot be addressed in isolation without considering the institutional setting. Differences across countries in the degree of rule of law, competition, and the effectiveness of the takeover market shape the effectiveness of governance measures. With respect to governance in the financial sector in particular, policymakers must recognize and take account of the unique institutional and legal climates in various countries. For example, it is useless to threaten litigation as an instrument for enforcing governance in a country that lacks the legal institutions or cultural tradition for lawsuits. Likewise, policymakers cannot expect that market discipline or reputational risk will rein in financial managers when the necessary market mechanisms—transparency, ability to enter and exit markets, and competition—are lacking.

As a result, there is no single, universally applicable remedy to governance challenges in the financial sector. Instead, the collection of papers and discussion at the conference suggest a two-pronged effort, with each element reinforcing the other: one that works to strengthen regulatory oversight on the one hand, while enhancing informational transparency, contestability of markets, foreign access, shareholder participation—in effect, greasing the wheels of the market—on the other.

PART I

Governance of
the Financial Sector:
A Conceptual Framework
and Measurement Issues

GERARD CAPRIO JR.
ROSS LEVINE

2

Corporate Governance in Finance: Concepts and International Observations

JUST AS CORPORATE governance influences the efficiency of firm production at the corporate level, so does the effectiveness of a nation's corporate governance system shape economic performance at the country
level. Standard agency theory defines the corporate governance problem in
terms of how holders of equity and debt influence managers to act in the
best interests of the providers of capital. To the extent that shareholders and
creditors induce managers to maximize firm value, the efficiency with
which firms allocate resources will improve. In the Berle and Means con-
ception of the firm, diffuse shareholders exert corporate governance
through voting rights and the election of boards of directors and diffuse
debt holders limit managerial discretion through bond covenants.[1] These
mechanisms, however, do not always work well around the world. Small
investors have a difficult time exercising corporate governance because of
informational asymmetries and poor legal, bankruptcy, and regulatory systems. In their comprehensive review of the corporate governance literature, Shleifer and Vishny conclude that outside of the United States and

Xin Chen provided helpful research assistance. We thank Luc Laeven for very helpful discussions.
Michael Pomerleano, Bob Litan, and Raj Singh gave helpful feedback on an earlier draft but are in no
way implicated here. The findings do not necessarily represent the opinions of the World Bank, its
management, the Executive Directors, or the countries they represent.
    1. Berle and Means (1932).

the United Kingdom, small investors play very little role in exerting corporate control.[2] Instead, large investors—large equity holders and large banks—are the primary sources of corporate governance.

If the world is to rely on banks—and other financial intermediaries—to exert effective corporate governance, then the managers of financial institutions must themselves face sound corporate governance. If bank managers face sound incentives, they will be more likely to allocate capital efficiently and then implement effective corporate governance over the firms in which they invest. If bank managers have enormous discretion to act in their own interests, however, rather than in the interests of the bank's equity and debt holders, then corporate governance will be adversely affected. In particular, banks will allocate capital less efficiently, and bank managers may actually induce firm managers to behave in ways that favor the interests of bank managers but hurt overall firm performance. Thus, the corporate governance of banks and other financial intermediaries is crucial for shaping capital allocation both at the firm level and at the country level. Nevertheless, the financial sector has generally received far less attention in the corporate governance literature than seems warranted by its central role in a nation's corporate governance system.

To correct this imbalance, this paper uses standard theories of corporate governance to highlight the special problems facing corporate governance of financial intermediaries and combines this theoretical perspective with international observations to make policy recommendations. As corporations that issue equity and debt, financial intermediaries face standard corporate governance problems. We argue, however, that banks and nonbank financial intermediaries are different from the standard corporation. Financial intermediaries—banks in particular—have special attributes that intensify standard corporate governance problems, and pervasive government involvement raises new impediments to effective corporate control. While this paper's theoretical framework holds for both banks and nonbank financial intermediaries, we focus primarily on banks because we have detailed international information on the regulation and supervision of commercial banks and because banks constitute the largest financial intermediaries around the world and especially in emerging markets. Except in some obvious exceptions, such as the discussion of deposit insurance, the points noted for banks apply to all financial intermediaries. In some cases, we discuss particular characteristics of pension funds and insurance companies.

2. Shleifer and Vishny (1997).

The paper first presents a general description of the corporate governance problem and examines the roles of various sources of governance: equity holders, debt holders, the competitive discipline of output markets, and governments. We then reexamine how each of these governance channels is affected by the special problems facing banks and other intermediaries, especially those in developing countries. We conclude with some policy recommendations.

This paper represents an opening salvo in our research on corporate governance of financial intermediaries. We have initiated a series of microeconomic studies in which we use international evidence to explore how the corporate governance structure of commercial banks influences corporate financing decisions and investment decisions at the firm level.

Corporate Governance: A Generic Model

This section describes the corporate governance structure of a generic firm. We follow Shleifer and Vishny's comprehensive survey of corporate governance and take an agency perspective that focuses on the separation of ownership and control.[3] How do the suppliers of capital influence managers to act in the best interests of capitalists? We examine how equity and debt holders—diffuse and concentrated holders of debt and equity—attempt to exert corporate governance and the impediments that exist. In our "generic model," we also consider the government. First, governments construct the basic legal system underpinning corporate governance. Second, governments may influence the flow of corporate finance by restricting corporate activities and insuring corporate finance in the case of banks and occasionally other intermediaries.[4] We consider each of these stakeholders and also discuss the market for corporate control.

Equity: Minority Shareholders

In the standard Berle and Means firm, diffuse shareholders exert corporate governance by voting directly on crucial issues, such as mergers, liquidation, and fundamental changes in business strategy, and by electing the

3. Shleifer and Vishny (1997).

4. For example, Indian authorities in the 1990s provided guarantees for holders of the largest mutual funds, and banks in several countries (such as Israel in the 1980s) effectively extended their own safety net by attempting to provide minimum prices for shares of underwritten issues.

boards of directors to represent the interests of the owners and oversee the myriad of managerial decisions. Incentive contracts are a common mechanism for aligning the interests of managers with those of shareholders. The board of directors may negotiate managerial compensation contracts that link compensation with the achievement of particular results. These contracts may include share ownership, stock options, and other contingent compensation mechanisms. In this setup, diffuse shareholders obtain the benefits of holding a diversified portfolio of assets while exerting corporate governance through their voting rights and the board of directors.

Several factors, however, keep diffuse shareholders from effectively exerting corporate control. Informational asymmetries between managers and small shareholders are large. Small shareholders frequently lack the expertise and incentives (that is, they do not have sufficient money on the line) to close the information gap substantially and monitor managers. Also, the board of directors often does not represent the interests of the minority shareholders and instead may be captured by management. To the extent that management captures the board, the probability that incentive contracts will solve the corporate governance problem is lowered. Indeed, incentive contracts "create enormous opportunities for self-dealing for the managers, especially if these contracts are negotiated with poorly motivated boards of directors rather than with large investors."[5] Also, voting rights are not generally effective because managers have enormous discretion over the flow of information. Furthermore, many countries have no laws protecting the rights of minority shareholders, and many of those that do have such laws on the books do not enforce them, a problem that further hinders corporate governance by minority shareholders. These forces work to provide managers with significant discretion over the control of corporate assets.

Equity: Concentrated Ownership

One corporate governance mechanism for preventing managers from deviating too far from the interests of owners is concentrated ownership. Large investors have the incentives to acquire information, monitor managers, and exert corporate government over managerial decisions. Furthermore,

---

5. Shleifer and Vishny (1997, p. 745). Jensen and Murphy (1990) show that compensation incentives are inefficient to induce managers to act in investors' interests relative to the personal benefits of managerial control.

large shareholders can elect their representatives to the board of directors and thwart managerial control of the board of directors. Large shareholders will also be more effective at exercising their voting rights than an ownership structure dominated by small, comparatively uninformed investors. Nor does concentrated ownership rely as much on the legal system. An owner with 51 percent of the equity does not need elaborate legal support to exert his ownership rights. Furthermore, large shareholders can more effectively negotiate managerial incentive contracts that avoid self-dealing and align investor and manager interests than can a diffuse group of shareholders whose representatives—the board of directors—can be manipulated by management. As ownership becomes more diffuse, managers can more easily manipulate information, form alliances with different groups, and capture control of the firm. Thus, outside of a very few countries, such as the United States and the United Kingdom, concentrated ownership is the standard mechanism for exerting corporate control.[6]

Concentrated ownership raises new corporate governance problems, however. Besides the fact that concentrated ownership implies that wealthy investors are not diversified, concentrated owners may benefit themselves at the expense of minority shareholders, debt holders, and other stakeholders in the firm, with adverse effects on corporate finance and resource allocation. Large investors may pay themselves special dividends, exploit business relationships with other firms they own that profit the investors at the expense of the corporation, and in general maximize the private benefits of control at the expense of minority shareholders.[7] Furthermore, large equity owners may seek to shift the assets of the firm to higher-risk activities since shareholders benefit on the upside, while debt holders share the costs of failure.[8] Finally, Shleifer and Summers show that large investors might have greater incentives than managers to expropriate resources from employees. While concentrated ownership is a common mechanism for confronting the corporate governance issue, it has its drawbacks. Again, the legal system's ability to thwart insider arrangements that exploit small shareholders and labor has important implications for the effectiveness of corporate governance and hence resource allocation and economic efficiency.

6. La Porta, Lopez-de-Silanes, and Shleifer (1999). Note, it can be argued that concentrated ownership is stimulated by and simultaneously encourages a weak legal system and poor information.

7. DeAngelo and DeAngelo (1988); Zingales (1994).

8. Jensen (1988).

Debt: Diffuse

Debt purchasers provide finance in return for a promised stream of payments and a variety of other covenants pertaining to corporate behavior, such as the value and risk of corporate assets. If the corporation violates these covenants or defaults on the payments, then debt holders typically obtain the rights to repossess collateral, throw the corporation into bankruptcy proceedings, vote in the decision to reorganize, and vote on removing managers. Since the legal obligation of the corporation is to each debt holder, creditors do not need to coordinate to take action against a delinquent firm.[9] Because that factor tends to make debt renegotiation much more difficult, corporate governance may be more severe with diffuse debt holdings than with concentrated debt. Clearly, the effective exertion of corporate control with diffuse debt depends on the efficiency of the legal and bankruptcy systems.[10]

There are barriers, however, that prevent diffuse debt holders from effectively exerting corporate governance. The legal system in many countries gives companies the right of an automatic stay on assets, and managers frequently remain in place pending a decision by the bankruptcy court. This makes repossession of assets difficult even for secured creditors and reduces the governance power of debt holders. Furthermore, inefficient bankruptcy proceedings frequently take years to complete even in the most developed economies, which further erodes the corporate governance role of diffuse debt. Thus, around the world, legal protection of diffuse debt holders seems insufficient to protect the rights of investors and limit managerial discretion.

Debt: Concentrated

As with large equity holders, concentrated debt can ameliorate some of the problems with diffuse debt. For many companies, banks typically are the large creditors. A bank's corporate governance power derives from its legal rights in the event that firms default or violate covenants; the short matu-

9. Shleifer and Vishny (1997, pp. 763–64).
10. Nevertheless, since the legal rights of debt holders are more clearly specified in debt contracts than is the corresponding case for equity contracts, violations of debt covenants and payments are easier to verify than violations of equity commitments where the rights are typically couched in terms of the general fiduciary responsibility of management. For instance, equity is not promised any payments and does not have a claim on any particular asset of the corporation.

rity of its loans, so corporations must return regularly; and its frequent dual role as both debt holder and the voter of substantial equity shares (either its own shares or those of other investors). Concentrated debt holders can also renegotiate the terms of the loan, which may avoid inefficient bankruptcies. Thus, large creditors can frequently exert substantial control rights over firms as well as exercise important cash flow power.

Nevertheless, large creditors face important obstacles to exerting sound corporate governance in many countries. First, the effectiveness of large creditors relies importantly on the legal and bankruptcy systems. It is by using—and by threatening to use—legal means that creditors exert influence over management. If the legal system does not efficiently identify the violation of covenants and payments and provide the means to bankrupt and reorganize firms, then creditors lose a crucial mechanism for exerting corporate governance. Outside of a small number of countries, legal systems around the world are demonstrably inefficient at protecting outside investors. Also, with poor legal and bankruptcy systems, the flexibility to renegotiate debt arrangements with large creditors may lead to inefficient renegotiation, the continuation of unprofitable enterprises, and impediments to corporate finance since the balance of power in those renegotiations shifts markedly toward debtors.[11]

Second, large creditors—like large shareholders—may attempt to shift the activities of the corporation to reflect their own preferences. For instance, large creditors may induce the company to forgo good investments and take on too little risk because the creditor bears some of the cost but will not share the benefits.[12] More generally, large creditors may seek to manipulate the corporation's activities for personal gain rather than maximize the profits of the firm. These features suggest that large creditors do not fully resolve the problem of aligning managers' incentives to maximize profits.

Third, large creditors may not be independent. In cases where a single family controls both a bank and a nonfinancial firm, it would be surprising to see much discipline by the former on the latter. Where relatively few families control a large portion of an economy, only foreign creditors may be independent, and this group may suffer from particularly large informational asymmetries and an inability to enforce contracts.[13]

11. Gertner, Scharfstein, and Stein (1994).
12. Myers (1977).
13. For the case of East Asian firms, see Claessens, Djankov, and Lang (1999).

Competition

Instead of focusing on the legal mechanisms through which equity and debt holders seek to exert corporate control, Alchian and Stigler stress competition.[14] According to this view, market competition forces firms to minimize costs, including the adoption of corporate control mechanisms that minimize the cost of raising external finance. In their extensive survey of corporate governance, Shleifer and Vishny argue that although "product market competition is probably the most powerful force toward economic efficiency in the world, we are skeptical that it alone can solve the problem of corporate governance."[15] They stress that labor and capital are highly firm specific and cannot be rented in spot markets throughout the day. Thus, people advance capital, and firm managers have discretion over the allocation of those resources. While product market competition constrains firm managers, it does not prevent them from exploiting firm resources for private gains, and this is the core of the corporate governance problem.

A second form of competition may also address governance problems: takeovers. Poorly performing firms may receive a tender offer from another firm, and the shareholders can decide whether they wish to accept the offer. If they accept, the acquiring firm may fire the managers of the target firm. A fluid takeover market would thus create incentives for managers to act in the best interests of the shareholders to avoid being fired in a takeover. Jensen argues that takeovers are a crucial and effective corporate governance device in the United States.[16]

Countervailing evidence, however, questions the efficacy of takeovers as a corporate governance mechanism. First, the bidder must engage in extensive and costly research of many firms to identify a worthy target. Then, the bidder pushes up the price of the shares as it tenders its offer and attempts to gain control of the firm. That reduces the bidder's profits and hence its incentives for researching firms and managers. Second, takeovers may not reflect the failure of management in the target firm, but rather the breakdown of corporate control in the takeover firm. Specifically, the takeover firm's managers may be maximizing the private benefits of their corporate empires, rather than maximizing firm value. Third, an active

14. Alchian (1950); Stigler (1958).
15. Shleifer and Vishny (1997, p. 738).
16. Jensen (1988, 1993).

takeover market requires a large, liquid capital market that can provide bidders with enormous amounts of capital quickly if they identify a worthy target. Outside of a couple of countries, we do not observe such well-developed capital markets. (We recognize that especially for large firms, national boundaries for capital markets are fast becoming the exception.) Finally, powerful managers will work to thwart hostile takeovers through poison pills and antitakeover legislation.[17] Given the political power of managers and the scarcity of large, liquid capital markets, it is not surprising that takeovers are essentially nonexistent as a corporate governance mechanism outside the United States and the United Kingdom.[18]

Government

Government plays a key role in corporate governance by defining the legal environment and sometimes by directly influencing managerial decisions. As emphasized above, the efficiency of the bankruptcy system and the degree to which managers maintain control through the bankruptcy process help determine whether the threat of bankruptcy influences managerial decisions. Similarly, the extent to which equity and bond holders can exert corporate governance depends on the ability to write and then enforce contracts, to oblige management to provide accurate and comprehensive information before shareholders vote on important issues, to enforce the obligations of the boards of directors, to specify and have managerial incentive contracts enforced, and to have confidence in the full range of contractual arrangements that define the firm in modern corporations. Moreover, the forces of political economy that produce the laws, enforcement mechanisms, and bankruptcy processes, and the ability of powerful managers to influence legislation all profoundly shape corporate governance.

Beyond defining the rules of the game, the government may directly influence corporate governance. At one extreme, the government may own the firm, so the government is charged with monitoring managerial decisions and limiting the ability of managers to maximize private benefits at the cost of society. At a less extreme level, governments regulate corporations. Specifically, governments regulate the activities and asset allocations of corporations and may even insure corporate liabilities in favored industries, even in countries that traditionally tend to disavow such support

17. Jensen (1993).
18. Shleifer and Vishy (1997).

(take, for example, the Chrysler bailout in the United States). In theory governments regulate to maximize social welfare, limit adverse externalities, exploit positive ones, deal with monopoly power, and directly prohibit managers from undertaking socially adverse actions.[19] Glaeser and Shleifer argue that governments tend to use regulations instead of the threat of legal sanctions when the legal system does not effectively dissuade managers from taking socially costly actions.[20] Thus, regulations that work ex ante may be optimal in situations where the use of ex post legal penalties is ineffective.

The problem with using state ownership and regulation of corporate activities to resolve the corporate governance problem is that it places control rights in the hands of government bureaucrats who almost certainly do not have the same incentives as a private owner. Thus, these government bureaucrats are unlikely to induce managers to maximize firm value. Rather, politicians frequently use state enterprises for personal gain by placing cronies in positions of corporate power, catering to special interest groups, or supporting politically influential unions that help politicians to retain power.[21] Indeed, the evidence suggests that public enterprises are extremely inefficient producers and that they frequently disregard social objectives, as evidenced by the finding that state enterprises are worse polluters than private firms.[22]

Discussion and Tentative Lessons

The discussion of the corporate governance problem in a generic firm highlights key ingredients that influence the effectiveness of various corporate control mechanisms. While we recognize that each of these tentative lessons is subject to many qualifications, a broad reading of the literature tends to point in the direction of these lessons even if allowances are needed for special circumstances. First, huge informational asymmetries between the providers of capital and controllers of capital (managers) tend to create more severe corporate governance problems for equity and debt

19. Laffont and Tirole (1993).
20. Glaeser and Shleifer (2002).
21. Shleifer and Vishny (1994).
22. See Boycko, Shleifer, and Vishny (1995) on the efficiency of public enterprises; see Grossman and Krueger (1993) on pollution.

holders than an environment where information is more transparent. Indeed, informational asymmetries lie at the core of the agency problem.[23]

Second, very competitive environments—both in the product market and in the takeover market—tend to reduce the corporate governance problem more than an environment dominated by entrenched monopolies. Substantial differences across industries and countries in the degree of competition and in the effectiveness of the takeover market tend to shape the effectiveness of corporate control. Third, the legal and bankruptcy systems fundamentally shape the feasibility of various corporate governance mechanisms. Whether it is the fiduciary responsibility of managers, the voting rights of owners, the board of directors, incentive contracts, debt covenants, bankruptcy, reorganization, self-dealing, or the ability to have a large, liquid capital market, all of these are defined and made more or less effective by the legal and bankruptcy system. Fourth, government regulation and ownership are key. Do regulations work to thwart market power and ameliorate market imperfections? Or do government actions protect political cronies, empower state discretion over the allocation of resources, and limit the competitive environment? The effectiveness of government actions may differ both across industries and across the globe. It seems clear, however, that government policies play a central role in shaping the effectiveness of various corporate governance mechanisms.

Governance in Finance

This section discusses special characteristics of banks and nonbank financial intermediaries that intensify the corporate governance problem and reviews empirical evidence. Other financial intermediaries, such as contractual savings institutions and insurance companies, experience many of the same issues. Although we discuss these other financial intermediaries, we focus on commercial banks because we have detailed cross-country information on bank regulation and supervision and because banks are the largest financial intermediaries internationally.

---

23. This does not imply that a marginal decrease in informational asymmetries will everywhere and always induce better outcomes. But it certainly does suggest that industries with enormous informational gaps between owners and managers will almost certainly face a bigger corporate governance problem than industries with very small informational asymmetries.

In particular, we examine three interrelated characteristics of financial intermediaries and the ways these traits affect corporate governance. First, banks and other intermediaries are more opaque than nonfinancial firms, a fact that fundamentally intensifies the agency problem. Because of the greater information asymmetries between insiders and outside investors in banking, it is more difficult for equity and debt holders to monitor managers and use incentive contracts, and easier for managers and large investors to exploit the private benefits of control, rather than maximize value. It is also unlikely that potential outside bidders with poor information will generate a sufficiently effective takeover threat to improve governance substantially. A more monopolistic sector is likely to ensue, one that will generate less corporate governance through product market competition, compared with an industry with fewer informational asymmetries.

Second, banks, like most intermediaries, are heavily regulated, a characteristic that frequently impedes natural corporate governance mechanisms. For instance, deposit insurance reduces monitoring by insured depositors, reduces the desirability of banks to raise capital from large, uninsured creditors with incentives to monitor, and increases incentives for shifting bank assets to more risky investments. Regulatory restrictions on the concentration of ownership interfere with one of the main mechanisms for exerting corporate governance around the world: concentrated ownership; and regulatory restrictions on entry, takeovers, and bank activities reduce competition, which in turn reduces market pressures on managers to maximize profits. Moreover, bank regulators and supervisors frequently have their own incentives in influencing bank managers that do not coincide with value maximization.

Finally, government ownership of banks fundamentally alters the corporate governance equation. State ownership of banks is widespread in many countries, making corporate governance of the banking industry very different from other industries. We now discuss the special corporate governance problems facing banks in more detail.

The same information problems—except for the particular complications induced by explicit deposit insurance that pertain only to banks—affect nonbank intermediaries. Indeed, pensions and insurance are areas that have seen a government backstop in particular countries (although it is rarely explicit). Pensions and insurance, usually the main other nonbank intermediaries in emerging markets, also are areas that are especially heavily regulated or controlled outright by public bodies.

Banks Are Opaque

Although information asymmetries plague all sectors, many assert that this informational asymmetry is larger with financial intermediaries. In product or other service markets, purchasers part with their money in exchange for something now. In finance, money now is exchanged for a "promise to pay" in the future. Also, in many product or service markets, if the object sold—from a car to a haircut—is defective, the buyers often find out relatively soon. However, loan quality is not readily observable for quite some time and can be hidden for extensive periods. Moreover, banks and nonbank financial intermediaries can also alter the risk composition of their assets more quickly than most nonfinancial industries, and banks can readily hide problems by extending loans to clients to cover previous debt obligations they cannot service.

This type of opacity—the difficulty of assessing the ongoing performance of a corporation—is particularly acute in banking, where loans are generally not traded in liquid, efficient secondary markets. The opacity problem is eased for pension funds and insurance companies to the extent that they hold assets that are traded in efficient markets. Insurance liabilities, however, typically suffer from the same information problems as loans, and indeed the information problem can be compounded by the long time lapse between taking out a policy and any payout.[24] Also, many countries do not have efficient securities markets. Like banks, therefore, pension fund and insurance companies frequently suffer from severe informational asymmetries.

Although views are not unanimous, substantial empirical evidence suggests that banks are considerably more opaque than other industries.[25] The observation that a single trader can cripple or bring down a large bank seems to be a recurrent fact, with the more egregious examples being Barings in the 1990s and AIB/Allfirst in 2002. Both incidents nicely demonstrate that information problems affect senior bank managers in their own institutions as well.[26] Similarly, some may view the recent

24. Conversely, insurance companies more often insure particular classes of risk (although they may custom-design large individual risks), which can render their activities more observable than banks making a number of disparate commercial and industrial loans to firms on which information may be more limited.

25. See Bentsen (1999), for example.

26. In both cases, "rogue" traders were disguising heavy losses, and in the case of Allied Irish Bank, this state of affairs apparently continued for five years.

collapse of Enron as a counterexample because it was an energy company whose sudden collapse surprised virtually all observers. Yet Enron collapsed not because of its energy business, but because of its financial intermediation activities, in particular the trading of complex financial products. That conglomerates can be brought down by financial subsidiaries is fully consistent with the contention that banks are generally more opaque than nonfinancial enterprises.

More systematically, Morgan finds that bond analysts disagree more over the bonds issued by banks than by nonfinancial firms. Moreover, using call report data, he shows that disparity in views increases with the size of bank loans relative to total assets.[27] Conversely, holding greater capital tends to reduce the discrepancy between bond analysts' views.[28] Thus, loan-making banks tend to be more opaque than nonfinancial firms.[29]

IMPLICATIONS FOR EQUITY AND DEBT FINANCIERS. The greater informational asymmetries between insiders and outsiders in banking make it very difficult for diffuse equity and debt holders to monitor bank managers or to use incentive contracts to align managers' interests with their own. Lower transparency makes it easier for controlling owners and managers to exploit other claimants, whether through risk-taking behavior or outright looting.[30] When outcomes are difficult to measure and easy to manipulate in the short run, managers will find it easier to construct a variety of "compensation" packages that allow managers to benefit at the expense of the long-run health of the financial institution. In many cases

---

27. Morgan (forthcoming). Interestingly, Morgan finds that disagreement is greater for banks with more cash on their balance sheets, but in addition to possible nervousness (Myers-Rajan, 1998) caused by buildups of cash (what does the bank know about its portfolio, or what complex trade is it about to undertake, which may be interpreted by the market as providing a buffer for an event of which the market is unaware) is the fact that "cash" in bank balance sheets can include a number of IOUs. Banks with a larger fraction of assets in their premises see less variation in bond analysts' views.

28. True, Flannery, Kwan, and Nimalendran (1998) found that investment bank analysts disagreed less about banks than about nonfinancial enterprises and even forecast future earnings more accurately. However, Flannery, Kwan, and Nimalendran focus on the views of investment bankers, while Morgan (forthcoming), focuses on bond analysts, who are likely to have fewer conflicts of interest than investment bankers.

29. There are no comparable studies (that the authors could find) on pension or insurance company opacity. However, the well-known collapse of the Orange County pension funds because of a public manager's gambling in derivatives markets (Jorion, 1995) bears eerie similarity to the failures of Barings Bank and the AIB-Allfirst fiasco, suggesting that the same opacity problem is present in both branches of financial intermediation.

30. Akerlof and Romer (1993).

bankers who are interested in boosting their own compensation in the short run can give a high-interest loan to a borrower in trouble, thereby boosting interest income.[31] And by controlling significant pools of resources, bankers can move asset prices. Thus if a few banks in a market with a high degree of concentration (the norm in developing countries, as noted below) become "bullish" or otherwise want to book more assets in certain sectors, the consequent increase in asset prices will make those interested in more prudent management look like Jeremiahs. Even knowledgeable outside owners will find monitoring difficult in these circumstances, and diffused shareholders will have a much greater problem.

Information problems have potentially dire implications for those who provide funds to intermediaries in the form of debt contracts. Debt holders do not enjoy any upside potential from risk taking but do bear the costs when the risks are so great that the bank's ability to service its debt is impaired. Yet the fact that opacity makes it easier to loot or engage in excessive risk taking in banking is precisely what gives large creditors (including large depositors) an incentive to monitor closely. Not only does anecdotal evidence suggest that large creditors tend to run first, but empirical evidence provides some support for their ability to do so. For example, Calomiris and Powell show that Argentine banks in the late 1990s with low levels of subordinated (uninsured) debt were also those banks with comparatively high nonperforming loan ratios. Creditors with good information and their money at risk got out.[32]

Opaqueness also facilitates the ability of insiders to exploit outside investors and the government. In most developing countries, the presence of conglomerates and the domination of large sectors of the economy by relatively few families make insider abuses more likely, most often at the expense of outside equity investors; smaller creditors, including depositors; and ultimately taxpayers. For example, the staggering losses in the Indonesian crisis of the late 1990s are difficult to understand in a relatively undeveloped economy with a high dependence on agriculture—and in the absence of a massive crop failure.[33] Tabalujan documents that at the end of 1996, some banks had lent as much as 85–345 percent of their capital to

31. In the same vein, insurers can inflate their incomes by lowering underwriting standards, or pension managers with compensation contracts based on return alone might take larger risks with their portfolios than is optimal for their clients.

32. Calomiris and Powell (2000).

33. The authors are indebted to Millard Long for this observation.

bank insiders.[34] Such loans, never to be repaid, are the most convenient way to loot banks.

Similarly, La Porta, Lopez-de-Silanes, and Zamarripa find high rates of connected lending in Mexico.[35] They find that 20 percent of total loans go to parties with some relationship to the bank. These loans benefited from interest rates that were about 415–420 basis points below those to unrelated parties, after accounting for various borrower characteristics, such as size, profitability, and leverage. Related borrowers also benefited from longer maturities, were significantly less likely to have to post guarantees or collateral, and were 33 percent less likely to pay back; moreover, the recovery rates on these loans were massively less (78 cents on the dollar lower) than on loans to unrelated parties. The authors conclude that systematic looting was occurring.

Finally, Laeven presents evidence that insiders in Russian banks benefit not so much from more favorable interest rates as from much higher loan volumes.[36] Since 71 percent of all such loans were not repaid (and since interest rates were more controlled or observed at the time), the author reasonably concludes that there was not much point for Russian insiders to haggle over terms!

IMPLICATIONS FOR GOVERNANCE BY COMPETITION. The opacity of banks can weaken competitive forces that in other industries help discipline managers through the threat of takeover as well as through competitive product markets. Takeovers are likely to be less effective when insiders have much better information than potential purchasers do. Although there are no data pertaining to the incidence of hostile takeovers in emerging market banking, an informal survey of World Bank financial sector experts revealed amazingly few such events, apart from takeovers following bank failure. Even in industrialized countries, hostile takeovers tend to be rare in banking, although in recent years merger activity has been on the upswing.[37] Indeed, long delays in the regulatory approval process associated with bank purchases make hostile takeovers in banking extremely rare. Anderson and Campbell find little such activity in Japanese banks up to 1996, notwithstanding the serious problems there.[38] They also found little

34. Tabalujan (2001).
35. La Porta, Lopez-de-Silanes, and Zamarripa (2001).
36. Laeven (2001).
37. See Prowse (1997) on hostile takeovers in banking; Berger, Demsetz, and Strahan (2001) on merger activity.
38. Anderson and Campbell (2000).

relation between bank performance and executive turnover in this case. Since their sample period ended, merger and downsizing finally appear to be occurring there. To be clear, the possibility of takeover in normal times because bank managers are not performing well could be a channel for exerting corporate governance, but it appears generally to be rare, especially in emerging market banking. Takeover after a bank failure, which is happening with greater frequency, does not affect managerial incentives almost by definition.

Furthermore, the absence of active, efficient securities markets can reduce the usefulness of the takeover threat in particular and corporate governance of financial intermediaries more generally. If potential corporate raiders cannot raise capital quickly and efficiently, the effectiveness of the takeover threat as a corporate control device is diminished. Similarly, if bank shares do not trade actively in efficient equity markets, takeovers lose some of their effectiveness as a mechanism for exerting corporate control over banks. Moreover, the absence of well-developed securities markets means that many types of financial instruments that might be used to limit managerial discretion in banks and nonbank financial intermediaries (such as debentures and subordinated debt) do not exist. Thus, many of the prerequisites for corporate control through market competition do not function in many countries.

Product market competition also is less common in banks, especially in developing economies. Information asymmetries should lead to less competition in banking, as bankers overcome information barriers by developing relationships with their clients. A variety of indicators are consistent with little competition in low- and middle-income countries, as seen in table 2-1, where countries are grouped into four income groups. In terms of basic concentration data, the major difference is between the two higher- and the two lower-income groups. With family domination it is not surprising that entry barriers would be higher, as suggested by higher fractions of entry applications denied, and in particular by less entry by foreigners, who might be expected to be less reluctant, compared with other domestic residents, to compete aggressively for business against powerful domestic banks. As noted below, greater state ownership in lower-income countries also likely limits competitive forces. Thus it appears that actual competition "on the ground" is likely to be less in lower-income countries.

Limited competition is also the rule for nonbank financial intermediaries. In addition to information problems, the small size of developing country markets usually limits the insurance market drastically, aided in

Table 2-1. *Bank Regulations across Countries, by Income Group*

Regulation	Income group			
	Low	Low-middle	Upper-middle	Upper
Bank concentration				
Total deposits in five largest banks (percent)	0.72	0.72	0.62	0.62
Entry applications denied (percent)	0.45	0.37	0.12	0.05
Foreign entry applications denied (percent)	0.51	0.31	0.04	0.05
Commercial banks that are foreign owned (percent)[a]	0.33	0.26	0.29	0.18
Are there limits on foreign ownership? (yes=1; no=0)	0.13	0.26	0.40	0.23
Are there limits on foreign entry (yes=1; no=0)	0.25	0.21	0.13	0.08
Commercial banks that are state-owned (percent)	0.33	0.31	0.16	0.14
Is a certified audit required? (yes=1)	0.85	0.95	1.00	0.94
Ten largest banks rated by international credit rating (percent)	0.10	0.10	0.35	0.39
Indexes				
Bank accounting transparency[b]	2.25	2.52	2.85	2.55
No deposit insurance[c]	0.60	0.33	0.15	0.29
Private monitoring index[d]	4.85	5.76	6.30	6.52
Number of countries	20	21	20	31

Source: World Bank Database on Bank Regulation and Supervision.

a. Percentage of banking system assets in banks that are more than 50 percent foreign owned.

b. This index adds one for each of the following affirmative answers: (a) the income statement does not include accrued though unpaid interest or principal on nonperforming loans, (b) banks are required to produce consolidated financial statements, and (c) bank directors are legally liable for erroneous information disclosed publicly.

c. Equals one if there is not an explicit deposit insurance scheme and if depositors were not compensated the last time a bank failed.

d. This index variable adds one for each of the following affirmative answers: (a) there is a compulsory external audit by a licensed or certified auditor, (b) 100 percent of the top ten banks are rated by international credit rating agencies, (c) there is no explicit deposit insurance and depositors were not compensated the last time a bank failed, (d) the income statement does not include accrued or unpaid interest or principal on nonperforming loans, (e) banks are required to produce consolidated financial statements, (f) bank directors are legally liable for erroneous information disclosed, (g) off-balance-sheet items are disclosed publicly, (h) banks disclose risk-management procedures, and (i) subordinated debt is part of capital.

some cases by government ownership. Thus, in Latin America, more than 80 percent of the market is controlled by the top five life insurance firms in four countries (Mexico, Peru, Trinidad and Tobago, and Uruguay), and more than 40 percent of the market is controlled by the top five life insurance firms in another five countries (Argentina, Brazil, Chile, Colombia, and the Dominican Republic).[39] The level of concentration usually is in excess of that for banks.

The Impact of Regulation on Governance

The fact that banks are key players in national payment and credit systems combined with fears of contagion means that virtually all governments energetically regulate and supervise banks.[40] To be sure, formal comparisons of the "degree of regulation" between banks and nonfinancial firms are not straightforward. It is true that some industries, such as nuclear power, also are heavily regulated, due to concerns about a different type of fallout. But even governments that intervene little in other sectors heavily regulate banking.[41] Moreover, the explosion of international standards in banking attests to the great degree of official involvement. The heavy hand of regulation not only results from banks being different—in many ways because of their opacity—but also results in making banks and their corporate governance different. In this section we review how regulation affects the different channels for corporate governance.

RESTRICTIONS ON SHAREHOLDERS. Although concentrated equity is a common mechanism for dealing with the inability of diffuse equity holders to exert effective corporate control, most governments restrict the concentration of bank ownership and the ability of outsiders to purchase a substantial percentage of bank stock without regulatory approval. These restrictions may arise from concerns about concentrations of power in the economy or about the type of people who control a bank.[42] These restrictions are put into effect usually by requirements that purchasers of bank stock have to alert government officials as their holdings increase above a

---

39. Data, from the World Bank, were not available for all Latin American countries.

40. This idea has been subject to much debate. See World Bank (2001, ch. 2) for a brief summary of some of these views. Whether legitimate or not, concerns about contagion have led to the rapid spread of deposit insurance schemes in recent years.

41. In the early 1990s it was said by the generally less interventionist U.S. authorities that twenty-three government supervisors reported daily to their work at Citibank.

42. As Louis Brandeis (1914) put it, "A license for banking is a license to steal."

certain level and may need regulatory approval above some proportion. Of the 107 countries in a recently compiled database of bank regulation and supervision, 41 limit the percentage of bank capital that a single entity can own to 50 percent or less, while another 38 put the limit at 25 percent or less.[43] Additionally, there may be constraints on who can own banks, such as the prohibition on ownership by nonbanks, or by securities firms or insurance companies (the United States recently lifted such a prohibition).

Government regulatory restrictions are often ineffective at limiting family dominance of banks, yet the regulatory restrictions on purchasing equity can actually protect these family-controlled banks from takeover and thereby hinder corporate control. Powerful families have used a plethora of channels to build up control in banks and nonbank firms, as in the case of East Asia.[44] The aforementioned restrictions then would not prevent concentrated family ownership, but rather would defend the existing owners. Where the restrictions are so effective that they thwart the emergence of controlling shareholders, they can give managers much greater power.

COMPLICATIONS FROM DEPOSIT INSURANCE. Deposit insurance, whether implicit or explicit, substantively changes the equity and debt channels of corporate governance. Deposit insurance reduces the incentives of depositors (and any other creditors who believe the government insures their claims) to monitor banks and thus directly hinders corporate governance. Furthermore, deposit insurance also induces banks to rely less on uninsured creditors with incentives to monitor and more on insured depositors with no incentives to exert corporate governance. Thus, deposit insurance indirectly reduces the percentage of financing raised from large creditors, who have the incentives and ability to monitor banks. Furthermore, deposit insurance has developed together with lower capital-to-asset ratios. As noted earlier, capital-to-asset ratios started declining before the advent of explicit deposit insurance. Nevertheless, the manifestation of a safety net for banking appears to be mainly responsible for the large subsequent drop. Moreover, the rise of central banks as lenders of last resort also reduced the need for capital in banking (compared with nonbanks). Thus deposit insurance tends to reduce the fraction of money raised through equity, and the smaller base of equity holders faces increased incentives to increase the risk of bank assets since they reap the benefits of success and share failure with debt holders.

43. Barth, Caprio, and Levine (2001b).
44. Claessens, Djankov, and Lang (1999).

LIMITS ON COMPETITION. Government interventions also limit competitive forces in banking. The direct and indirect restrictions on ownership reduce the role of market forces in the market for corporate control. Regulatory restrictions on banks' activities and even their pricing reduce competition in output markets. In addition to restrictions on banks' ability to underwrite equity, conduct real estate or insurance business, or take ownership in nonbank firms, banks in emerging markets are subject to a variety of other constraints.[45] Minimum branching requirements (often in rural areas), directed credit guidelines, portfolio restrictions (such as minimum percentages of deposits or assets invested in government securities) or liquidity requirements, and limits on interest rates and fees are among the restrictions that are more common in developing countries.

Governments also limit competition in other segments of the financial sector. Governments frequently manage pension funds directly or tightly limit competition by managers in an attempt to keep out possibly unqualified or unscrupulous managers. And for nonetheless sound reasons, choices for pension managers are quite constrained, and where the choice even exists, pension account owners often have restrictions on their ability to change their manager, a quite different situation from that under the Anglo-American regulatory framework. Thus in Argentina and Chile, banks outnumbered pension funds by as many as ten to one in the late 1990s, whereas in the United Kingdom and the United States, the number of banks was tiny relative to the number of pension funds. While the rationale for restrictions can be debated, the impact on competition seems unambiguous. In sum, as uncompetitive as emerging market banking appears to be, nonbank intermediation is even less competitive, so it is likely that this channel for governance is weaker still.

GOVERNING THE GOVERNORS. Owners and the markets, two key sources of governance over banks, are motivated to maximize or protect the value of their debt or equity claim. Governments' motives are quite different. Although governments at times behave like debt holders, enjoying all the downside but little of the upside from banking (although they should get higher tax revenue as banks profits grow), the government does not pay for the costs of bank failure but rather passes the bill to taxpayers. Government regulators and supervisors, without their own funds at risk, are insulated from market forces. Moreover, rather than serving as objective and independent monitors of banks, they are subject to a variety of political

45. Barth, Caprio, and Levine (2001a).

forces and even, as is the case in a number of emerging markets, are exposed to civil lawsuits, often for arbitrary reasons. Consequently, they may not enjoy much independence from the industry they regulate.[46] In contrast, such protection is more the rule in industrial economies.

Where democratic traditions are weak and where there is little oversight of supervisors through government checks and balances, the considerable scope these supervisors have to use their position to extract rents from the banks they regulate is perhaps of even more concern—particularly where supervisors are poorly paid. Barth, Caprio, and Levine in fact find a very strong positive relationship between corruption and countries with powerful supervisory agencies, tight restrictions on commercial bank activities, and entry barriers that limit competition.[47] They find a negative relationship between corruption and countries that promote private sector monitoring of banks (even when controlling for many other country characteristics). Although enhanced supervisory powers are associated with deeper financial systems in the presence of very strong political openness, greater supervisory power generally exerts a negative impact on bank development. In this context, the move to improve supervisory powers without political oversight can damage the corporate governance of banks in the sense of putting the supervisors directly at odds with the owners and markets.

Yet even in high-income countries, the task of supervision and its oversight is fraught with difficulty. For example, one "bonus" that supervisors face is the possibility of taking a job with the bank that they are supervising, a possibility that surely could lead to less vigorous supervision. This is not just a theoretical consideration: Horiuchi and Shimizu document that in the case of Japan, the regular "descent from heaven" (*amakudari*) of bank supervisors into senior positions with commercial banks led to less safe banking.[48] Banks with amakudari officials performed more poorly—that is, they had lower capital levels and higher numbers of nonperforming loans—than banks without them. Few countries in the world have any restriction on regulators' job choices or sources of compensation after their stint in government, and any restrictions likely would be difficult to enforce.[49] This suggests that without a revolution in the way regulators and

---

46. Boot and Thakor (1993). Interestingly, Barth, Caprio, and Levine (2001b) find that a composite indicator of supervisory independence from political interference and from civil lawsuits is associated with greater banking development.

47. Barth, Caprio, and Levine (2001b).

48. Horiuchi and Shimizu (2001).

49. Barth, Caprio, and Levine (2001a).

supervisors are compensated, expectations of their efficacy in monitoring banks, especially in emerging markets, should be modest.

Bankers as Bureaucrats

The ultimate way in which bureaucrats intervene with the operation of a bank is through outright government ownership. Although such ownership has been decreasing in recent decades, by the late 1990s, about 40 percent of the assets in the banking systems of emerging markets were in state-owned banks.[50] This figure is much higher in some of the more populous countries, such as Brazil, China, India, and since the 1997 crisis, Indonesia. The World Bank calculates that in the late 1990s more than 40 percent of the world's population lived in a country in which the majority of bank assets were in majority-owned government banks.[51]

When the government is both the owner and regulator, there is a conflict of interest between its two roles, and any hope of independent supervision would appear unrealistic. Indeed, in some countries, such as China, the government executives who run the state banks outrank the heads of any oversight agencies. More generally, as already noted above, bureaucrats might be expected to be less motivated by market forces and more responsive to political influence than are their counterparts in the private sector.[52]

Barth, Caprio, and Levine show that government ownership of banks is negatively associated with development of the banking sector and positively associated with measures of bank inefficiency, such as interest rate spreads and overhead costs.[53] They also find some link between government ownership and crises, although this link is less robust than that found by Caprio and Martinez.[54] There is no evidence, even in weak institutional

---

50. La Porta, Lopez-de-Silanes, and Shleifer (2002).

51. World Bank (2001).

52. Many would hope to come up with ways to improve bureaucratic performance, including by writing contracts to compensate bankers as in the private sector, or by delegating management or contracting out management of state-owned banks to private parties. However, the former appears difficult to do, and the latter is a dangerous path with little hope of success. As World Bank (1995) so carefully adumbrated, management contracting has worked only for businesses that are relatively simple and transparent, and in which reputation matters. So this strategy may work for hotels, where it is easy for one and all to see if service is up to standard and if the towels are clean. Banking is anything but transparent, and reputation, although it used to be important in some countries, does not matter here where government guarantees are present.

53. Barth, Caprio, and Levine (2001b).

54. Caprio and Martinez (2000).

settings, that government-owned banks overcome market failures and channel credit to productive ends.

The conflict of interest for the government as owner and regulator of banks likely becomes overwhelming when government owns a substantial stake in industry as well.[55] Thus if one set of bureaucrats—say, those overseeing a given firm—do their job poorly, they can try to hide the problems with a bank loan from a fellow bureaucrat. A similar tendency might operate between related parties controlling a bank and a firm, but at least then the markets and the government exist to provide some oversight, whereas with state banks, the government has been removed as an effective monitor. Last, although private sector participants, such as large creditors, have an incentive to monitor private banks, with state-owned banks there is no doubt that the government is providing a guarantee. Thus, private sector entities have no incentive to monitor state banks. In sum, neither the owners, the markets, nor the supervisors are likely to be providing effective corporate governance when banks are state owned.[56]

One potential check on government-run banks is competition in the output market, but here again these forces are muted. In particular, the banks that are most likely to be willing to compete against the state—foreign banks—usually are kept out of the market.[57] This lack of competition explains their aforementioned finding of higher interest costs and higher overheads. Government ownership also effectively stymies nonbank competition as well. The absence of standard corporate governance mechanisms does not necessarily mean that all state banks are bad. Rather, the results indicate that those countries with a greater share of state ownership in banking experience poor outcomes. Equally, considerations of corporate governance in emerging market banking without taking state ownership into account likely miss the major actor in the play.

55. Thus the success of Germany notwithstanding, the largest share among industrial countries of state ownership in banking may be partly due to the lack of state ownership in virtually any other sector. World Bank (2001, ch. 4) also notes that an impressive protection of creditor rights appears useful as well.

56. That explains why Barth, Caprio, and Levine (2001b) and La Porta, Lopez-de-Silanes, and Shleifer (2002) find uniformly negative results from state ownership in banking. Cornett and others (2002) also find that during the East Asian crisis, the performance of state banks deteriorated more markedly than that of privately owned banks, and this effect was greater the larger the overall presence of state banks. World Bank (2001) notes that the empirical evidence argues for a reduction in state ownership, especially where it is most widespread, but not necessarily a complete abandonment thereof. This last finding is consistent with this view, in that the costs of state ownership appear to grow as it increases.

57. Barth, Caprio, and Levine (2001b).

State ownership or control also features in pensions and insurance, much less so in other nonbank activities, such as investment banking. Countries, such as India, in which state ownership is important in banking (total assets in state banks totaled about 80 percent in the late 1990s) may have an even higher state presence in insurance (the top five state companies in India have 100 percent of the nonlife insurance market, the only one with data).

Implications for Policy and Future Research

To summarize then, the corporate governance problem in finance is pronounced. The severity of information problems in finance weakens all of the traditional corporate governance mechanisms—control by both diffuse and concentrated equity and debt holders, competitive forces in product markets and in the market for corporate control, regulation, and supervision. Significantly, the opacity of finance facilitates the ability of shareholders and senior managers to engage in risk shifting: shifting the assets and investments of the firm to riskier activities.

Governments intervene pervasively in the financial sector with adverse implications for the corporate governance of financial institutions. In banking, deposit insurance dampens the incentives of creditors to monitor banks, and regulatory restrictions often impose limits on competition and takeovers. Government ownership of banks removes the government as an independent monitor, greatly weakening incentives for the private sector to monitor and significantly weakening competition in banking. These government interventions together with an accommodating regulatory and legal environment can facilitate bankers' engaging in looting: profiting themselves while letting the bank go bankrupt.

Although the stated task of bank regulation and supervision is to enhance corporate governance, limit risk taking, and stop looting, the opacity of banking makes this difficult, and regulators and supervisors quickly can develop their own agendas that may have little to do with market-oriented corporate governance. Furthermore, the opacity of the supervisory process itself and the ability of private sector banks to pay highly attractive salaries relative to those in the public sector contribute to skills shortages in the supervisory agencies and heighten the risk of corrupt activities.

All these problems are more prevalent in emerging markets than in industrial countries. In emerging markets, information is scarce, and its quality is less reliable. Bank and nonbank finance concentration is usually high. The dominance of the economy by a relatively small number of families or conglomerates is pronounced, and competitive forces therefore muted. Regulation and supervision often are less developed, and state ownership is far more pronounced. As others have noted, the problem in emerging markets is not the separation of ownership and control. The problem is that ownership and control of significant parts of the economy, banking included, are so highly concentrated in the hands of politically powerful families that many of the mechanisms that serve as a check on insiders in high-income countries are not present or are distinctly weakened. Thus if banking is particularly fraught with corporate governance problems, banking in emerging markets experiences these difficulties even more so. This section briefly reviews policy recommendations to improve corporate governance in developing countries and also suggests future research efforts to support improvements in this area.

Strategy for Improving Governance

Existing research shows that countries enjoy better-developed financial systems with a lower likelihood of serious financial crisis when the government supports the ability of private sector entities to monitor banks, permits banks to engage in a wide range of activities, allows foreign entities, minimizes state ownership, and encourages diversification.[58] Stated differently, the government's job can be seen as fostering the ability and incentive of all the different potential monitors of banks to do their jobs well. This research does not imply that efforts to improve bank supervision are nugatory, but rather that they need to be focused on supporting the private sector, rather than on attempting to replace the responsibilities of private owners and market participants.

Existing research thus suggests a strategy for authorities seeking to improve governance in banking. As a first step, it is critical that governments recognize and curb any of their own behaviors that thwart the private sector's ability and incentive to monitor banks. Thus, for example, in countries in which government ownership is pronounced, private sector monitoring cannot be expected, and competitive forces clearly are blocked. In these cases, embarking on a program to reduce government ownership

---

58. Barth, Caprio, and Levine (2001b).

would seem to be essential; without this step it is difficult to conceive of the success of other efforts to ameliorate the governance problem. Private sector monitoring is virtually nonexistent in countries with blanket deposit insurance or extremely generous deposit insurance coverage (such as coverage in very low-income countries, where insurance levels are ten to fifteen times per capita gross domestic product). Reducing coverage to much lower levels is essential to enhance private sector monitoring.

A second step in improving governance in banking involves directly reducing the opacity of banks by improving the flow of information. Although transparency of banking information in emerging markets is receiving increased attention in the wake of the East Asian crisis (and perhaps more so in the aftermath of the Enron collapse), the likely reinforcement of opacity by existing ownership patterns in emerging markets suggests that this task is even more important and yet more difficult than has been recognized. In effect, authorities need to engage in the unpopular task of shaking up cozy relationships among powerful interest groups in their society. This task is not as simple as superficial adherence to international standards; rather, it is a process that requires sustained commitment over a period of time in order to effect. In addition to improvements in accounting and auditing, improvements to credit information will facilitate the expansion of banking by those interested in providing finance to groups that were previously excluded. Enhancing corporate finance reporting in the media and educating people about the importance of this issue in a wide swath of civil society will help make a lasting contribution to better corporate governance. This is not easy: the same family groups that control banks may also control the media, so broader antitrust activity may be necessary in order to make greater transparency effective. Moreover, it is worth stressing again that these changes will not happen to the extent that governments underwrite risk.[59]

Third, although better information may indirectly enhance the contestability of the banking market and invigorate the market for corporate control in banking, opening to foreign banks offers a direct mechanism for creating competitive pressures in banking. Barth, Caprio, and Levine

59. For example, it is no coincidence that before the existence of deposit insurance in the United States, the financial press included weekly and even daily "Bank Note Monitors," which reported on the health of banks issuing debt instruments that were actively traded. With the advent of deposit insurance, the market for this reporting disappeared.

found that it was not so much the presence of foreign banks as the contestability of markets (associated with relative openness to foreign entry) that contributed to the development and stability of emerging market banking.[60] Foreign banks, and indeed foreign entry in other markets, will serve to increase the competitiveness of the economy in general and lessen the reliance on family or conglomerates relationships. Clarke and others show that increased foreign presence in emerging market banking has the attractive benefit of improving access to credit, even by small and medium-size enterprises.[61] The resulting increase in competition in the economy can pay dividends in the long term to the corporate governance problems discussed here. Clearly the same should apply to foreign competition in insurance and pension management.

Fourth and most important, the potential monitors of banks—owners, markets (large creditors in particular) and supervisors—need clear and strong incentives to do their jobs well. As stressed above, the legal and bankruptcy systems do not operate well in many countries. Thus bank managers can control banks with little to fear from outsider investors or even from bankruptcy, as is clearly evident from Japan's ten-year banking crisis. Owners, particularly controlling shareholders, will have the incentive to monitor their banks well (meaning in accordance with society's goals) only to the extent that their own resources are really at risk and that there are healthy profits in return for safe and sound banking. Unfortunately, ensuring that capital is real and that weak lending practices have not eroded it is not simple in practice.

The incentives facing insider owners and managers can be enhanced in a number of ways. The ability of authorities to influence inside owners and managers is enhanced if regulators can impose penalties in cases of fraud or improper conduct. Similarly, the incentives of inside owners and managers are clearly enhanced if small shareholders and debtors can confidently use an efficient court system that supports their rights. More generally, regulation has not focused much attention on the compensation of senior managers. For example, an attempt to vary capital requirements in line with the extent to which banks' compensation policies encourage or discourage excessive risk taking is a promising area for new research.[62] The

60. Barth, Caprio, and Levine (2001b).
61. Clarke and others (2001).
62. John, Saunders, and Senbet (2000) show that adjusting management compensation to bring it in line with the risk premium on risk-based deposit insurance can reduce the risk-shifting behavior of

supervisory process in some countries is getting close to this issue when supervisors examine the systems that banks have in place for managing their risks. We suspect that as important as risk management is as a process, the incentives inside the individual banks for taking risk will determine the efficacy of any processes that are written down. Certainly, the threat of legal recourse for those who suffer losses when directors do not fulfill their fiduciary duties would improve the incentives for this group, and it might also encourage them to support reforms in compensation policies for senior bank officers. Compensation policies of directors themselves also demand greater attention to and further research on the extent to which bank and corporate performance is a function of differences in compensation.

To improve corporate governance of financial intermediaries, policy-makers must seek to enhance the ability and incentives of creditors and other market participants to monitor banks. Recently, subordinated debt proposals have received increased attention, although we fear that in the wake of the Argentine crisis, success in this area will be undervalued.[63] Unfortunately, in the discussion of revisions to the Basel capital accord, subordinated debt has not received much attention, and only the various shadow regulatory groups (in the United States, Europe, and Latin America) have seriously been promoting this idea. Although the ability of creditors to monitor banks will improve as the information environment develops, ensuring that market participants have incentives to do their job seems important as well. Just as strategic shareholders (large shareholders with significant exposure) are widely thought to be important in the governance process, large creditors, who did not benefit from upside risks, are a useful component of the oversight of the risk-taking behavior of banks.

Incentives for supervisors matter as well. In view of the slow progress in improving the incentives facing supervisors, it is not surprising that Barth, Caprio, and Levine find that enhanced supervisory powers had a generally *negative* payoff in terms of financial sector development and

---

bank managers. However, this presumes that the risk premium captures adequately the risks that are being borne by the bank, which in countries that have implemented this approach is unlikely in view of the slight difference in the premiums. In practice at the very least it is an untested system, but the central idea of the importance of linking compensation to risk taking is promising.

63. World Bank (2001). It should be recognized that the Argentine crisis resulted from inconsistency between fiscal policies and other macroeconomic factors and the exchange rate regime, not from the banking sector. In fact, two different administrations there were looking to the banks as a way to pay for the crisis, not as its source.

crisis prevention.[64] One explanation for their finding could be the presence of greater concentration of economic power and family control in emerging markets, which can easily weaken the de facto independence of bank supervision and make it easier to reward supervisors for weak supervision.[65] In this case, the adoption of international best practices in bank supervision is not likely to suffice. As in the case of customs collection, the outright hiring of foreign supervisors might be one way to achieve greater independence and lessen possible corruption. Although no country has yet formally chosen to hire a foreign supervisory agency to oversee its own banks, foreign entry into banking systems has in practice yielded the same result in countries such as New Zealand, where foreign banks compose virtually the entire banking sector. Improvements in the level and structure of compensation for bank supervisors also can contribute to better performance, and along with legal restrictions might reduce the migration of supervisors to the management teams of the banks that they supervise. Again, research here would be beneficial, but it will be problematic until better data are available on the extent of wage differentials between supervisory agencies and private sector banks.

The above arguments apply to nonbank financial intermediaries. Fortunately, pension funds and insurance companies are less subject to runs and generally have been smaller in developing countries. Until now, in emerging markets they generally have had far fewer assets under their control than banks, but this likely will change. Insurance products generally show a high-income elasticity of demand, and the lowering of population growth rates and flattening of demographic pyramids may heighten interest in funded pension systems, so attention to improving their governance is timely. Gathering more and better data on these branches of finance accordingly should be a priority, for if they follow the experience of high-income countries, their assets will soon dwarf those of banks.

The governance problem in finance is severe, but it is not hopeless. History shows that success is possible. Better-governed banks—banks that were able to contribute to development yet that could also withstand macroeconomic disturbances—used to be more common. Notwithstanding waves of failure by small U.S. banks in the nineteenth century, depositor losses in the now industrialized countries were minor and tax-

64. Barth, Caprio, and Levine (2001b); see also World Bank (2001).

6545. For example, if a family has extensive holdings, it can easily reward a bank supervisor with a sinecure well removed from banking activities.

payers' losses nil. This state of affairs resulted from clear incentives for the various actors reviewed here. Not the least of these incentives was the practice for bankers to post bonds and for supervisors even to receive deferred compensation. We can only hope that the scale of banking losses in emerging markets and the consequent increased attention to this topic will help promote reform efforts.

References

Akerlof, George, and Paul Romer. 1993. "Looting: The Economic Underworld of Bankruptcy for Profit." *Brookings Papers on Economic Activity* 2: 1–73.

Alchian, Armen. 1950. "Uncertainty, Evolution, and Economic Theory." *Journal of Political Economy* 58: 211–21.

Anderson, Christopher W., and Terry L. Campbell. 2000. "Corporate Governance of Japanese Banks." University of Missouri, University of Delaware.

Barth, James, Gerard Caprio, and Ross Levine. 2001a. "Bank Regulation and Supervision: A New Database." In Robert E. Litan and Richard Herring, eds., *Brookings-Wharton Papers on Financial Services*. Brookings.

———. 2001b. "Bank Regulation and Supervision: What Works Best." Policy Research Working Paper 2725. World Bank, Washington, D.C. (www.worldbank.org/research/interest/wrkpapers.htm).

Benston, George. 1999. *Regulating Financial Markets: A Critique and Some Proposals.* Washington: American Enterprise Institute.

Berger, Allen N., Rebecca S. Demsetz, and Philip E. Strahan. 2001. "The Consolidation of the Financial Services Industry: Causes, Consequences, and Implications for the Future." Board of Governors of the Federal Reserve System, Washington (papers.ssrn.com/sol3/papers.cfm?abstract_id=139456).

Berle, Adolf, and Gardiner Means. 1932. *The Modern Corporation and Private Property.* Harcourt Brace Jovanovich.

Boot, Arnoud W. A., and Anjan V. Thakor. 1993. "Self-Interested Bank Regulation." *American Economic Review* 83 (2): 206–12.

Boycko, Maxim, Andrei Shleifer, and Robert W. Vishny. 1995. *Privatizing Russia.* MIT Press.

Brandeis, Louis. 1914 (reprint, 1971). *Other People's Money and How the Bankers Use It.* New York: A. M. Kelley.

Calomiris, Charles, and Andrew Powell. 2000. "Can Emerging Market Bank Regulators Establish Credible Discipline? The Case of Argentina." World Bank, Development Research Group, Washington (www.worldbank.org/research/interest/intrstweb.htm).

Caprio, Gerard, Jr., and Maria Soledad Martinez-Peria. 2000. "Avoiding Disaster: Policies to Reduce the Risk of Banking Crises." World Bank, Washington, and Egyptian Center for Economic Studies Working Paper 47, Cairo.

Claessens, Stijn, Simeon Djankov, and Larry Lang. 1999. "Who Controls East Asian Corporations?" Policy Research Working Paper 2054. World Bank, Washington, D.C.

Clarke, George, and others. 2001. "Businesses in Latin America: Does Bank Origin Matter?" Policy Research Working Paper 2760. World Bank, Washington.

Cornett, Marcia, and others. 2002. "The Impact of Corporate Governance on Performance Differences in Privately Owned versus State-Owned Banks: An International Comparison." Southern Illinois University.

DeAngelo, Harry, and Linda DeAngelo. 1985. "Managerial Ownership of Voting Rights: A Study of Public Corporations with Dual Classes of Common Stock." *Journal of Financial Economics* 14: 33–69.

Flannery, Mark, S. Kwan, and M. Nimalendran. 1998. "Market Evidence on the Opaqueness of Banking." University of Florida, Department of Finance.

Gertner, Robert, David Scharfstein, and Jeremy Stein. 1994. "Internal versus External Capital Markets." *Quarterly Journal of Economics* 109: 1211–30.

Glaeser, Edward, and Andrei Shleifer. 2002. "The Rise of the Regulatory State." Discussion Paper 1934. Harvard University, Harvard Institute of Economic Research.

Grossman, Gene, and Alan Krueger. 1993. "Environmental Impact of a North-American Free Trade Agreement." In Peter Garber, ed., *The U.S.-Mexico Free Trade Agreement.* MIT Press.

Horiuchi, Akiyoshi, and Katsutoshi Shimizu. 2001. "Did *Amakudari* Undermine the Effectiveness of Regulator Monitoring in Japan?" *Journal of Banking and Finance* 25: 573–96.

Jensen, Michael. 1988. "Takeovers: Their Causes and Consequences." *Journal of Economic Perspectives* 2: 21–48.

———. 1993. "The Modern Industrial Revolution, Exit, and the Failure of Internal Control Systems." *Journal of Finance* 48: 831–80.

Jensen, Michael, and Kevin Murphy. 1990. "Performance, Pay, and Top Management Incentives." *Journal of Political Economy* 98: 225–63.

John, Kose, Anthony Saunders, and Lemma Senbet. 2000. "A Theory of Bank Regulation and Management Compensation." *Review of Financial Studies* 13 (Spring): 95–125.

Jorion, Philippe. 1995. *Big Bets Gone Bad: Derivatives and Bankruptcy in Orange County.* San Diego: Academic Press.

Laeven, Luc. 2001. "Insider Lending: The Case of Russia." *Journal of Comparative Economics* 29 (June): 207–29.

Laffont, Jean-Jacques, and Jean Tirole. 1993. *A Theory of Incentives in Regulation and Procurement.* MIT Press.

La Porta, Rafael, Florencio Lopez-de-Silanes, and Andrei Shleifer. 1999. "Corporate Ownership around the World." *Journal of Finance* 54: 471–517.

———. 2002. "Government Ownership of Commercial Banks." *Journal of Finance* 57 (February): 265–301.

La Porta, Rafael, Florencio Lopez-de-Silanes, and Guillermo Zamarripa. 2001. "Related Lending." Harvard University, Department of Economics.

Morgan, Donald. Forthcoming. "Judging the Risk of Banks: Why Can't Bond Raters Agree?" *American Economic Review.*

Myers, Stewart. 1977. "Determinants of Corporate Borrowing." *Journal of Financial Economics* 5: 147–75.

Myers, Stewart, and Raghuram Rajan. 1998. "The Paradox of Liquidity." *Quarterly Journal of Economics* 113 (3): 733–71.

Prowse, Stephen. 1997. "The Corporate Governance System in Banking: What Do We Know?" *Banca del Lavoro Quarterly Review* (March): 11–40.

Shleifer, Andrei, and Robert W. Vishny. 1994. "Politicians and Firms." *Quarterly Journal of Economics* 109: 995–1025.

———. 1997. "A Survey of Corporate Governance." *Journal of Finance* 52: 737–83.

Stigler, George 1958. "The Economies of Scale." *Journal of Law and Economics* 1: 54–71.

Tabalujan, Benny. 2001. "Corporate Governance of Indonesian Banks: The Legal and Business Contexts." Business Law Working Paper. Nanyang Business School, Singapore. April.

World Bank. 1995. *Bureaucrats in Business: The Economics and Politics of Government Ownership.* Oxford University Press.

World Bank (2001). *Finance for Growth: Policy Choices in a Volatile World.* New York: Oxford University Press.

Zingales, Luigi. 1994. "The Value of the Voting Right: A Study of the Milan Stock Exchange Experience." *Review of Financial Studies* 7: 125–48.

Valuing Governance: The "Corruption Premium" in Global Capital Flows

T HE ATTITUDE OF the developing world toward foreign capital flows has exhibited a sea change over the last five decades. Shortly after its independence in 1947, India began to nationalize many industries previously dominated by British and American firms. Throughout the next four decades, the business environment in India for foreign investment was intentionally suffocating. Then, in 1991, the government of India began a series of reforms and liberalizations designed partly to attract foreign investment. This turnaround of policies is not unique to India. Indeed, most developing countries have gone through this policy reversal at some point within the last five decades.

Once India decided to court foreign investment, it started to offer what appeared to be irresistible tax incentives. They included a 30 percent cut in corporate income taxes for ten years for new investment, plus a complete tax exemption for five years for investment in India's free trade zones. Again, with some difference in details, tax incentives to foreign investors

I thank Rupa Duttagupta, V. Sundararajan, and other participants of the conference for very useful comments and Yi Wu and Hayden Smith for efficient research assistance. The views in the paper are personal and may not be shared by any organization that I am or have been affiliated with. All errors are my responsibility.

are also a common feature of today's government policies throughout the developing world.

Such a change in attitude toward foreign direct investment reflects a new conviction that FDI is very important for economic growth. It provides not just the needed capital for the host country, but more important, the needed technology and managerial and marketing know-how.[1] Therefore, every unit of lost FDI is a lost opportunity for faster economic growth.

Most developing countries that have offered a generous tax giveaway actually do not see a significant volume of foreign investment rushing in to take advantage of this "gift" of reduced tax (or the cheap labor and other presumed benefits for foreign firms). The list of countries in this category includes India, Pakistan, and Kenya. One possible explanation is that tax giveaways and cheap labor are not the only things that motivate foreign investment. Other factors, especially bureaucratic corruption and red tape, can more than offset the advantages of low wages and tax rates. An apparent exception is China, which has reported a significant volume of foreign investment, especially in the last five years, despite its high level of corruption and red tape.

In this paper, I evaluate four hypotheses, drawing from recent empirical research that has systematically examined these issues:

—Governance is a quantitatively significant factor in the locational decision of foreign investment. Foreign firms generally would demand a "corruption premium," analogous to a risk premium, when investing in a country with a severe corruption problem.

—China is an apparent anomaly to the above proposition. However, upon closer scrutiny, it is in fact an exception that proves the rule.

—Corruption, or poor governance, not only reduces the volume of inward foreign investment; it also reduces the quality of foreign direct investment. For example, while transfer of technology by foreign firms is one principal source of benefits for the host countries, corrupt host countries would have a particularly hard time attracting firms that have a relatively high level of technological sophistication.

—The corruption–foreign direct investment connection should also be thought of in conjunction with a country's overall capital inflows (that is, together with borrowing from foreign banks or portfolio capital inflows). Through its impact on the composition of capital inflows, corruption

---

1. See, for example, the research paper by Borensztein, De Gregorio, and Lee (1996).

makes a country particularly vulnerable to a currency crisis like those that recently plagued Argentina, Asia, and Russia.

Throughout this paper, the term *corruption* is used to denote "poor public governance," which includes bureaucratic corruption, red tape, and deviations from the rule of law. While these dimensions of public governance could be differentiated in principle, they tend to go together in reality. For example, one would be hard-pressed to think of a country that has a high level of corruption but a minimum amount of red tape. In any case, a few risk assessment agencies attempted to measure these dimensions separately, but the available indexes on them are almost always highly correlated, making it difficult to identify their separate effects in a meaningful way. Hence, in this paper, I do not pretend to be able to separate these different dimensions of public governance.

The Corruption Premium

The objectives of this section are to demonstrate that a corruption premium exists and to provide a way to estimate the size of this premium as a function of the level of corruption. I proceed in two steps. First, using a data set on bilateral foreign direct investment from the world's fourteen major source countries to fifty-nine host countries, I employ a regression framework to examine whether and to what degree corruption in a host country discourages foreign direct investment (holding constant other determinants of FDI). Second, based on such a regression, I then infer the corruption premium in units of tax equivalent—the equivalent amount of increase in corporate tax that would discourage the same amount of inward FDI as the observed level of corruption.[2]

I start with an explanation of the regression specification. The specification can be motivated by a simple optimization problem solved by a multinational firm. Let $K(j)$ be the stock of investment the multinational firm intends to allocate to host country j. Let $t(j)$ be the rate of corporate income tax in host country j, $b(j)$ be the cost of corruption to the firm expressed in units of tax-equivalent, and r be the rental rate of capital. Let $f[K(j)]$ be the output of the firm in host country j. There are N possible

---

2. This empirical strategy was first developed in Wei (1997 and 2000a). The current paper updates the regression with the most recent data available on bilateral FDI, and for the first time adopts the term "corruption premium" to suggest an analogy with "risk premium."

host countries in which the firm can invest. The firm chooses the level of $K(j)$ for $j = 1, 2, \ldots, N$, in order to maximize its total after-tax and after-bribery profit:

$$\pi = \sum_{j=1}^{N} \{[1 - t(j) - b(j)]f[K(j)] - rK(j)\}.$$

Note that as a simple way to indicate that tax and corruption are distortionary, I let $[1 - t(j) - b(j)]$ premultiply output rather than profit. The optimal stock of FDI in country j, $K(j)$, would of course be related to the rates of tax and corruption in the host country: $K = K[t(j), b(j)]$, where $\partial K/\partial t < 0$ and $\partial K/\partial b < 0$.[3]

An important question to decide in the empirical work is whether one should look at the stocks or the flows of FDI. The above optimization problem suggests that the *stock of FDI* is the decision variable of the firms and should be the appropriate dependent variable. To put it differently, even though the observed stock of FDI in a given year contains investment flows made in the past, the current flow should be adjusted so that the current stock best reflects the current economic and policy fundamentals of the host countries. To minimize the influence of the year-to-year idiosyncratic fluctuations in bilateral investment, the average of FDI over the three most recent years (1996–98) is used.

Let $FDI(k,j)$ be the bilateral stock of foreign direct investment from source country k to host country j. The empirical work starts with the following benchmark specification:

$$\text{Log}[FDI(k,j)] = \Sigma_i \, \alpha(i)D(i) + \beta_1 \, tax(j) + \beta_2 \, corruption(j)$$
$$+ X(j)\partial + Z(k,j)\gamma + e(k,j),$$

where $D(i)$ is a source country dummy that takes the value of one if the source country is i (that is, if $k = i$), and zero otherwise; $X(j)$ is a vector of characteristics of host country j other than its tax and corruption levels; $Z(k,j)$ is a vector of characteristics specific to the source–host country pairs; $e(k,j)$ is an independently and identically distributed error that follows a normal distribution; and $\alpha(i)$, β_1, β_2, δ, and γ are parameters to be estimated.

This is a quasi-fixed-effects regression in that source country dummies are included. They are meant to capture all characteristics of the source

---

3. A more sophisticated generalization includes endogenizing the level of corruption (and tax) such as those in Shleifer and Vishny (1993) or Kaufmann and Wei (1999). These generalizations are outside the scope of the current paper.

countries that may affect the size of their outward FDI, including their size and level of development. In addition, these fixed effects control for possible differences in the source countries' definition of FDI under the assumption that the FDI values for a particular country pair under one definition is proportional to those under another except for an additive error that is not correlated with other regressors in the regression. Host country fixed effects are not imposed because doing so would eliminate the possibility of estimating all the interesting parameters including the effect of corruption.

Corruption Index

Perhaps the most crucial and the most difficult-to-measure variable in the empirical work is corruption.[4] Almost all of the various measures available are based on subjective perceptions by "experts" or by survey respondents. Generally speaking, measures that are based on surveys of firms are preferable to those based on the intuition of in-house experts. In this paper, I use as the basic measure of corruption a combination of the indexes from the surveys conducted for the *Global Competitiveness Report* and the *World Development Report*. Because of the high degree of correlation among the various measures of corruption, the results described in this paper are unlikely to change qualitatively when a different measure of corruption is used. Some of the references cited here indeed reported robustness tests when alternative measures of corruption were used.

To ensure that the regressors are predetermined relative to the dependent variable (FDI averaged over 1996–98), I use corruption indicators in 1996. The *GCR Index* is derived from the *Global Competitiveness Report 1997*, produced jointly by the Geneva-based World Economic Forum and the Harvard Institute for International Development. The survey for the report was conducted in late 1996 on 2,827 firms in fifty-eight countries. The GCR survey asked respondents (in Question 8.03) to rate the level of corruption in their country on a one-to-seven scale, based on the extent of "irregular, additional payments connected with imports and exports permits, business licenses, exchange controls, tax assessments, police protection or loan applications." The GCR index of corruption is based on the country average of the individual ratings.

---

4. Wei (2001) discussed various measures available.

The *WDR Index* is derived from a World Bank survey in 1996 of 3,866 firms in seventy-three countries, in preparation for its *World Development Report 1997*. Question 14 of that survey asks: "Is it common for firms in my line of business to have to pay some irregular, 'additional' payments to get things done?" The respondents were asked to rate the level of corruption on a one-to-six scale. The WDR index of corruption is based on the country average of the individual answers. For both corruption indexes, the original sources are such that a higher number implies lower corruption. To avoid awkwardness in interpretation, they are rescaled in this paper so that a high number now implies high corruption.

Each index covers a different subset of countries for which data on FDI or other forms of capital flows are available. It therefore may be desirable to form a composite corruption index that combines the two indexes. The two indexes are derived from surveys with similar methodologies and similar questions. The correlation between the two is 0.83. A simple three-step procedure is used to construct the composite index. First, the GCR is used as the benchmark; second, the average of the individual ratios of GCR to WDR is computed for all countries that are available in both GCR and the WDR; and third, for those countries that are covered by the WDR but not the GCR (which are relatively rare), the WDR rating is converted into the GCR scale by using the average ratio obtained in the second step.

The results of two regressions with this specification are reported in table 3-1. The first regression uses the list of regressors in Wei (2000a). The coefficients on both the GCR/WDR corruption index and the tax rate are negative and statistically significant at the 5 percent level. This implies that more corruption and higher tax would reduce inward foreign direct investment. Other regressors also have sensible signs. For example, larger host countries as measured by the log of GDP (gross domestic product) tend to receive more FDI. Two additional variables are used to capture possible special relations for certain pairs of source–host countries. Host countries tend to receive more FDI from a source country with which they share a common language (or a common historical colonial tie). Host countries also tend to receive more FDI from source countries that are closer geographically.

Correlation of Corruption and FDI Policies

Until very recently, the literature that examines the empirical determinants of FDI did not take into account the effects of the host government's poli-

Table 3-1. *Corruption and Foreign Direct Investment*

Independent variable	Dependent variable		
	(1)	(2)	(3)
GCR/WDR	−0.250**	−0.178**	−0.162**
	(0.076)	(0.074)	(0.079)
Tax rate	−0.015***	−0.017**	−0.015***
	(0.010)	(0.010)	(0.011)
FDI incentives	...	0.498*	0.486*
		(0.096)	(0.098)
FDI restrictions	...	−0.370*	−0.376*
		(0.060)	(0.061)
Log (GDP)	0.802*	0.761*	0.748*
	(0.054)	(0.055)	(0.059)
Log (per capita GDP)	0.015	0.041	0.068
	(0.090)	(0.093)	(0.103)
Log distance	−0.653*	−0.623*	−0.619*
	(0.066)	(0.062)	(0.063)
Linguistic tie	1.360*	1.246*	1.256*
	(0.213)	(0.201)	(0.202)
China dummy	...	...	0.285
			(0.481)
Adjusted R^2	0.66	0.70	0.70
Number	608	580	580

Source: Author's calculations.

Notes: Regression specification: log$FDI(j,k)$ = *source country dummies* + *b X(k,j)* + *e(k,j)*; where *FDI(k,j)* is FDI from source country *j* to host country *k*. Coefficients on the source country dummies are not reported to save space. Standard errors are in parentheses. To minimize year-to-year fluctuations, log(*FDI*), log(*GDP*) and log(per capita *GDP*) are averaged over 1996–98.

* Significant at the 5 percent level.
** Significant at the 10 percent level.
*** Significant at the 15 percent level.

cies toward FDI. That is because a systematic measure of the restrictions and the incentives related to foreign investment did not exist. This omission potentially could bias the estimated effect of corruption on foreign investment if corruption and government policies are correlated.

Many host countries have a variety of restrictions on the ability of foreign firms to operate in the country. For example, a country may forbid foreign firms from entering certain sectors, disallow foreign investors from having full control of the firms, or restrict foreign exchange transactions that could interfere with the ability of foreign firms to import intermediate inputs or repatriate profits out of the country. Of course, many countries also have special policies designed to attract foreign investment. These can range from tax concessions and subsidized loans to special incentives for export-related foreign investment. Notably absent from existing studies are empirical measures of restrictions (or incentives) in their relevant regressions. Their omission could potentially be significant. For example, if corruption and restrictions on FDI are positively correlated (that is, if corrupt countries are also more likely to impose restrictions on foreign investment), then the effect of corruption (*corruption*) on inward FDI as estimated in the previous studies could be exaggerated (because the negative effect of the FDI restrictions on inward FDI was not taken into account).

Logically, there are reasons to think that corruption and the FDI restrictions are indeed positively correlated. Shleifer and Vishny provided a conceptual framework in which bureaucratic hassle (such as license requirements) is endogenously determined to extract bribes.[5] In such a setting, bureaucratic hassle and bribes can be positively correlated. Using data on firm-level surveys, Kaufmann and Wei indeed found evidence that firms that pay more bribes also face more, not less, bureaucratic hassle in equilibrium.[6] (That is because both the level of corruption and the level of red tape are endogenously determined in response to characteristics of the sector or the firm in question.)

On the flip side, if the host governments systematically offer incentives to foreign investors to compensate for the corruption problem in the country, then previous estimates of the effect of the corruption could be downward biased if these incentives are not properly controlled for. This discussion suggests the possibility that the omission of host governments' policies toward FDI could have a big influence on the estimated effect of corruption on foreign investment.

Following earlier work I have done,[7] this paper employs a new cross-country measure of restrictions and incentives on inward foreign direct investment, based on a reading of the detailed descriptions compiled by PricewaterhouseCoopers (PwC) in a series of country reports written for multinational firms intending to do business in a particular country. They are collected in one CD-ROM titled "Doing Business and Investing Worldwide."[8] For each potential host country, the relevant PwC country report covers a variety of legal and regulatory issues of interest to foreign

5. Shleifer and Vishny (1993).
6. Kaufmann and Wei (1999).
7. Wei (2000b).
8. PwC (2000).

investors, including "Restrictions on foreign investment and investors" (typically chapter 5), "Investment incentives" (typically chapter 4), and "Taxation of foreign corporations" (typically chapter 16).

To convert textual information into numerical codes, I read through the relevant chapters for all countries that the PwC covers. For "restrictions on FDI," I created a variable taking a value from zero to four, based on the presence or absence of restrictions in the following four areas:

—Existence of foreign exchange control. (This may interfere with foreign firms' ability to import intermediate inputs or repatriate profits abroad).

—Exclusion of foreign firms from certain strategic sectors (particularly, national defense and mass media).

—Exclusion of foreign firms from additional sectors where foreign entry would be considered harmless in most industrial countries.

—Restrictions on foreign ownership (for example, forbidding them to have 100 percent ownership).

A dummy that takes the value one (in the presence of the specific restriction) or zero (in the absence of the restriction) can represent each of the four dimensions. We create an overall *FDI Restrictions* variable that is equal to the sum of these four dummies. The variable takes a value of zero if there is no restriction in any of the four categories, and four if there is restriction in each category.

Similarly, an *FDI incentives* index was created based on information in the following areas.

—Existence of special incentives to invest in certain industries or certain geographic areas.

—Tax concessions specific to foreign firms (including tax holidays and tax rebates, but excluding tax concessions specifically designed for export promotion, which is in a separate category).

—Cash grants, subsidized loans, reduced rent for land use, or other nontax concessions specific to foreign firms.

—Special promotion for exports (including existence of export processing zones, special economic zones, and the like).

An overall *FDI incentives* variable is created as the sum of the above four dummies. It takes a value of zero if there is no incentive in any of the four categories, and four if there are incentives in all of them.

In the second regression in table 3-1, these two new variables are included together with other regressors. As consistent with one's expectations, a country that offers more incentives to attract FDI receives more inward FDI on average. A country that places more restrictions on FDI receives less. Most important for the central task of this paper, the coefficient on the corruption variable is still negative and statistically significant at the 5 percent level.

I have experimented with including the squared terms of log(*GDP*), log(*per capita GDP*), and log(*distance*) as additional regressors. These changes do not affect the sign and the statistical significance of the coefficient on the corruption variable. They affect the size of the point estimate and goodness-of-fit (the adjusted R^2) only slightly.

Lost Foreign Direct Investment

To get an idea of the quantitative importance of corruption, the loss in FDI due to corruption can be calculated based on the coefficients in the second regression in table 3-1. First a "low corruption" benchmark is established using the marginal corruption score for the group of eighteen least corrupt countries in the sample, which include Chile, Singapore, the United Kingdom, and the United States. Second, a thought experiment is performed, asking how much increase in FDI each country in the sample would have received if it could reduce its corruption to the level prevailing in the average of the benchmark countries.

For an arbitrary host country k, use log*FDI*(k, *corruption* = k) and log*FDI*(k, *corruption* = *benchmark*) to denote the amount of FDI into country k, in logarithm, with the country's corruption at its actual level, and at the benchmark level, respectively. According to the regression specification, the change in log*FDI* into the host country k, due to a reduction in corruption to the benchmark level, is given by the following equation:

Log*FDI*(k, *corruption* = *benchmark*) − Log*FDI*(k, *corruption* = k)
$$= \beta_2 \, [corruption(benchmark) - corruption(k)].$$

The difference in log*FDI* on the left-hand side can be approximately interpreted as the percentage loss in FDI in country k because of its failure to reduce corruption to a level that prevails in the benchmark countries.

The point estimate on corruption in column 2 of table 3-1 is −0.178. With this methodology, Peru is estimated to have lost about 25 percent of FDI because of its higher level of corruption relative to the benchmark. Ukraine would have had 41 percent more FDI had its corruption been reduced to the level in the benchmark countries (table 3-2).

Table 3-2. *Examples of Estimated "Corruption Premium" and Lost FDI*

Country	Corruption (GCR/WDR)	Deterred FDI (percent)	Corruption premium in tax equivalent
Peru	3.4	24.9	15.0
Zambia	3.7	31.1	18.7
China	4.1	37.4	22.5
Brazil	4.2	39.1	23.6
Turkey	4.2	39.1	23.6
Nigeria	4.3	40.6	24.5
Ukraine	4.3	40.9	24.6
Mexico	4.4	42.7	25.7
Kenya	4.8	50.1	30.2
India	5.1	55.1	33.2
Russia	5.3	58.7	35.4
Benin	5.6	64.4	38.8
Kazakhstan	5.8	66.8	40.2
Azerbaijan	6.2	74.0	44.5

Source: Author's calculations, based on column 2 of table 3-1.

Needless to say, all estimates contain sampling errors. That is particularly true for the estimated effect of corruption on forgone FDI because the corruption level itself is not precisely measured. As a result, the estimated forgone FDI is only meant to illustrate the approximate magnitude of the problem and should not be taken too literally.

Estimating the Corruption Premium

To explore an analogy between the risk premium on an investment and the effect of corruption on FDI, it may be useful to convert the previous estimates of forgone FDI into something called a corruption premium. Indeed, the corruption premium should be conceptually considered as a component of the risk premium in global capital flows.

One way to make the conversion is to note that an increase in either corruption or the corporate tax rate would discourage inward FDI. Therefore, based on the regression estimates in table 3-1, the cost of corruption could be expressed in terms of an equivalent amount of increase in the (highest) marginal corporate income tax. To be more precise, for a particular host country k, the failure to reduce its corruption to the level in the benchmark countries is equivalent to raising the corporate income tax rate by X percentage points in terms of its negative effect on FDI. This value of X, or the tax-equivalent measure of the corruption cost, is the estimate of the corruption premium for the country in question.

From the regression specification, it can be seen that an increase of $1/\beta_1$ units in the corporate income tax rate and an increase of $1/\beta_2$ units in corruption have the identical effect on inward FDI. Therefore, the corruption premium for country k is the tax-equivalent measure of corruption for country k

$$= (\beta_2 / \beta_1) \, [corruption(k) - corruption(benchmark)].$$

As an illustration, the estimates of the corruption premium for a selected number of countries are reported in table 3-2. For example, the corruption premium in Peru is 15 percentage points. In other words, Peru would have to offer to cut taxes for foreign firms by 15 percentage points to offset its higher level of corruption relative to the benchmark countries in order for those firms to be as happy about investing in Peru as in the benchmark countries. Similarly, Russia's corruption premium is 35 percentage points. Therefore, to offset its relatively high level of corruption, Russia would have to offer expected returns *ex ante* that were 35 percentage points higher than the benchmark countries to induce the foreign investors to come. Again, these estimates are not to be taken too literally.

In passing, note a possible connection between the corruption premium for foreign investment and that for domestic investment. The corruption premium reported above is computed based on observations on foreign direct investment. On the surface, this estimate of corruption premium may appear not to be generalizable to domestic investment. In particular, one might think that domestic investment would be less sensitive than international investment to a given change in corruption and tax. For example, suppose that Russia has a higher degree of corruption than Poland. An American firm might find it easier than would a Russian firm to skip Russia and invest in Poland. However, with a relatively mild assumption, the tax-equivalent measure can be applied to domestic investment as well.

To see this, let e(*int-cap, tax*) and e(*dom-cap, tax*) be the elasticities of international and domestic capital with respect to the tax rate, respectively. Similarly, let e(*int-cap, corruption*) and e(*dom-cap, corruption*) be the elasticities of the two types of capital with respect to corruption.

It is possible to allow international investment to be more sensitive than domestic investment to both corruption and tax. That is, $e(int\text{-}cap, tax) > e(dom\text{-}cap, tax)$, and $e(int\text{-}cap, corruption) > e(dom\text{-}cap, corruption)$. As long as the ratios of the greater sensitivities by the international investment are proportional to each other, that is, $e(int\text{-}cap, tax)/e(dom\text{-}cap, tax) = e(int\text{-}cap, corruption)/e(dom\text{-}cap, corruption)$, then the tax-equivalent measure of the corruption cost backed out of a study of FDI would be the same as the tax-equivalent applicable to domestic investment.

Indeed, there are several reasons why the estimates from a study of FDI are more reliable than a study of cross-country data on domestic investment. First, for a given source country, the data on FDI to a set of host countries are based on the reporting by that single source country, which ensures a much better international comparability than a cross-section of national data on domestic investment. Second, the FDI data rely only on reporting by major industrialized countries whose statistics are more reliable than many developing countries in the sample.

How Exceptional Is China?

The central message of the previous section is that international investors demand a sizable corruption premium when investing in a host country with rampant corruption and poor quality of public governance. At this point, many people might ask: Isn't China a glaring exception to this proposition? By most accounts, bureaucratic corruption, heavy red tape, and arbitrary judicial judgments are common in the country. Yet, the volume of FDI into China has been on the order of $45 billion–$50 billion in recent years, making China far and away the largest developing country host of FDI. So the China case presents a serious challenge to my basic proposition that must be faced up front.

To understand the case of China better, let me note several things. First, you cannot always believe what you read. The figures on FDI into China that are commonly reported are based on China's own reporting (through its balance-of-payment statistics reported to the International Monetary Fund or other international organizations). There are two reasons to think that the reported FDI into China is upwardly biased. First, foreign investors have an incentive to exaggerate the amount of FDI they report to the Chinese government, partly to gain tax benefits later on. Second, local governments have an incentive to exaggerate the amount of FDI they report to the central government because the ability to attract FDI is one of the items high on the list that the central government uses to evaluate the performance of local officials.

One way to verify the existence of this upward bias is by comparing China-reported inward FDI with source-country-reported outward FDI. In 1997, for example, China reported that realized inward FDI from the United States reached $3.2 billion.[9] The U.S. companies, however, collectively told the U.S. Department of Commerce that they invested only $1.2 billion in China in that year, or less than half the amount China reported.[10] This pattern is broadly similar across different years. It is also broadly similar for other major source countries that report realized outward FDI by destination countries. For example, for 1997 China reported that it attracted $990 million (realized) in German investment. For the same year, German companies collectively told their government that they invested $680 million in China, which is about one-third less than the China-reported statistics.

Second, China's share of outward FDI from the world's major source countries is in fact not as big as popular phrases like "China fever"[11] or "the world's strongest magnet for overseas investment" imply. The world's major source countries for FDI are the United States, the United Kingdom, Japan, Germany, France, Canada, Italy, and other member countries of the Organization for Economic Cooperation and Development. Collectively, they accounted for more than three-fourths of all the international direct investment in the world. Yet, their investment in China as a whole has not been unusually big. For example, in 1997, the U.S. direct investment in fourteen other countries was greater than its investment in China, even though China is a large and fast-growing country with a huge reservoir of inexpensive labor. Even the Chinese official statistics on U.S. investment in China, which are likely to be biased upward by a big margin, show that nine other countries received more direct U.S. investment that year than China did.[12]

9. China Ministry of Foreign Economic Relations and Trade, *Almanac of China's Foreign Economic Relations and Trade*, 1999 (www.moftec.gov.cn/moftec_cn/tjsj/wztj/2000_9-22-16.html).

10. OECD (1999).

11. The phrase used to describe the international investors' interest in China in *Economist* (U.S. edition), March 1, 1997, p. 38.

12. For example, the U.S. investments in 1997 in Brazil, Mexico, and Ireland were $6.5 billion, $5.9 billion, and $4.5 billion, respectively—well ahead of China. Measured by the stock of U.S. FDI, rather than its annual flow, even more countries were ahead of China.

The third factor concerns the source of much of China's inward FDI. While Hong Kong would not rank in the top three on a list of the world's major source countries, its FDI accounts for roughly half of the FDI into China each year. Because Hong Kong does not collect or report bilateral outward FDI figures, it is not included in the statistical analysis as a source country. Therefore, strictly speaking, the statement on China's FDI potential does not apply to FDI from Hong Kong into China. However, several things are worth noting. One can legitimately ask whether investment from Hong Kong to the mainland should really be counted as "foreign" direct investment (much as whether New York's or Bombay's investment in the rest of the United States or India should be counted as foreign direct investment). Even if the Hong Kong–originated investment is considered foreign, no one knows how much of it is in fact mainland-originated money disguised as Hong Kong investment in order to take advantage of the preferential treatment that the Chinese government accords to foreign firms.

Moreover, Hong Kong's large investment in the mainland is not necessarily surprising. In an earlier study, I performed a hypothetical calculation of how much Hong Kong's investment in China would have been if it were an average source country from the OECD but happened to be next to China.[13] Given China's size, growth rate, and wage level, as well as the common language and cultural linkage between China and Hong Kong, Hong Kong's investment in China is neither unusually or surprisingly large.

Fourth, one should consider whether China is an exception to the general proposition in this article that corruption deters foreign direct investment. An analysis of this proposition can be performed within the regression framework reported in the last column of table 3-1. First, I create a China dummy that takes the value of one if the host country is China, and zero otherwise. This additional regressor is then included in the regression. If, for whatever reasons, corruption in China does not reduce FDI as much as corruption reduces FDI in other countries in the sample, the coefficient on the China dummy should be positive and statistically signficant. As column 3 of table 3-1 shows, the coefficient, while positive, is not statistically different from zero. In other words, there is no support for the notion that corruption does less damage in China than elsewhere or that China is a supermagnet attracting extraordinarily large amounts of FDI.

13. Wei (2000c).

China, of course, is the most populous country in the world. One might be concerned that the regression specification may not properly allow host countries with a large population to be somewhat different from those with a smaller population. To check this possibility, I have also implemented a new regression that adds the population squared as a regressor. In other words, I allow for the possibility that the potential FDI as a function of population is qualitatively different for very populous countries. The statistical result, however, does not support this exceptionist notion (not reported).[14] To sum up, the potential for China to attract more FDI from the major source countries can be fully tapped only if it can manage to tackle its corruption problem.

Hong Kong investment in China may possibly alleviate some of the damage that Chinese corruption has on inward FDI. In other words, U.S. companies may have reduced their direct investment into China because of corruption, but they could use their investment in Hong Kong as an imperfect stepping-stone to organize production in China. So maybe part of the U.S. investment in Hong Kong is really U.S. investment in China. This possibility cannot be investigated directly. But a superficial "feel" of the possibility can be obtained by seeing if the coefficient on the China dummy becomes statistically significant if one-third of the FDI investment in Hong Kong from the United States and other major source countries is considered actually to be investment from these countries into China. Although the positive coefficient becomes larger, it does not become significant. Of course, the one-third reassignment is completely arbitrary and likely represents an overadjustment as Hong Kong naturally should be an important host area on its own merit (much as Singapore is). Nonetheless, this experiment suggests that China may be lucky compared with other host countries in that the existence of Hong Kong may have mitigated the damage that corruption could inflict on China in terms of lost FDI. But the scope of this mitigation is still limited.

Corruption and Types of Foreign Direct Investment

The previous section illustrated how the existence of a corruption premium is manifested in a reduced volume of FDI into a corrupt host country. This

---

14. These results are consistent with the early findings reported in Wei (2000b, 2000c).

section examines another, somewhat subtle way, in which a corruption premium shows up: whether the quality of FDI may be affected by the extent of corruption for a given volume of FDI.[15]

Corruption makes dealing with government officials—for example, to obtain local licenses and permits—less transparent and more costly, particularly for foreign investors. In this case, having a local partner lowers the transaction cost (for example, the cost of securing local permits). At the same time, sharing ownership may lead to technology leakage. Both costs of local permits and losses from technology leakage are positively related to the extent of corruption in a host country. A simple model predicts that when the corruption level is sufficiently high, no investment will take place.[16] Holding the technological level constant, the more corrupt the host country, the more inclined a foreign investor is to have a local partner. However, a rise in corruption tends to discourage disproportionally more those investment projects that have a relatively high level of technological sophistication. In this sense, corruption reduces the quality of FDI as well.

These hypotheses are tested using a unique firm-level data set on FDI in twenty-five transition economies in Eastern Europe and the former Soviet republics. The data came from a survey of major multinational firms from Europe, North America, Asia, and elsewhere conducted by the European Bank for Reconstruction and Development. A unique feature of the data is that they disclose not only whether a firm has invested in a particular host country, but also whether the investment is a joint venture with a local partner or a foreign sole ownership. Because the identity of the parent company is known, the level of technological advancement of the FDI can be estimated by looking at the technological leadership position of the parent company in the respective industry as well as the technological leadership position of the industry relative to other industries.

A two-part system is estimated. The first part describes the investor's decision to enter a particular host country, k. The second part describes the decision on the choice between a wholly owned firm or a joint venture, conditional on FDI taking place. The results of the statistical work confirm the basic hypothesis.[17] That is, corruption in a host country has both a volume effect and a composition effect. The corruption premium not only manifests itself in a reduction in the volume of FDI, but also in a shift away

15. The discussion is based on Smarzynska and Wei (2000).
16. Smarzynska and Wei (2000).
17. Reported in Smarzynska and Wei (2000).

from technologically more advanced investment. In sum, corruption in a host country tends to reduce the quality as well as the quantity of foreign investment.

Corruption, Structure of Capital Inflows, and Currency Crisis

So far, I have discussed the corruption premium in terms of the negative effect of bad governance on foreign direct investment. In this section, I argue that another negative effect stems from the impact of bad governance on a country's vulnerability to currency and financial crisis. More precisely, a particular pattern of capital inflows—light in FDI but heavy in foreign bank borrowing, particularly short-term borrowing—makes a country susceptible to a sudden reversal of international capital flows, speculative attacks on currencies, and financial crisis. Unfortunately, countries with a severe corruption problem are likely to have this pattern of capital inflows.

In the context of a financial crisis in developing countries, one often hears the term *hot money*, or *fickle international capital*, referring to the fact that the international capital flows can be highly volatile. Capital flows to developing countries, in particular, are said to be subject to sentiment shifts by international investors, overreaction to minor changes in the fundamentals, momentum trading, herding, or contagion.[18] In other words, some types of capital flows are more volatile than others. For example, between 1980 and 1996, international bank loans were two to four times as volatile as international direct investment.[19]

That fickle international capital flows can trigger or contribute to a currency crisis has been well established both theoretically and empirically in the academic literature. The so-called "second-generation currency crisis models" emphasize multiple equilibria—the possibility that a massive change in international capital flows could precipitate a currency crisis in an emerging economy even where there was no or only a small change in the fundamentals.[20] Recognizing the difference in volatility among different types of capital flows, a large empirical literature on currency crises has

18. See Kim and Wei (2002) for a recent study of the possibility of momentum trading and herding by international investors in emerging markets.

19. The standard deviations of the external loan-to-GDP and FDI-to-GDP ratios, averaged over eighty-five emerging economies, were 0.046 and 0.012, respectively. The coefficients of variation for them were 2.19 and 1.27, respectively. See table 3-3 for more details.

20. See, for example, Obstfeld (1994).

confirmed that the composition of capital inflows is related to the likeli-hood that a country will run into a future currency crisis.[21] In particular, three types of composition measures have been highlighted in the literature as being particularly relevant: the lower the share of foreign direct invest-ment in total capital inflows, the higher the short-term-debt-to-reserves ratio, or the higher the share of foreign currency–denominated borrowing in a country's total borrowing, the more likely a currency crisis becomes.

By and large, domestic corruption and fickle international capital have been proposed as *rival* explanations of the crises in emerging economies. The aim of this section is to make a case that the two may be intimately connected: a country with a severe problem of crony capitalism is more likely to have a distorted structure of capital inflows that makes the coun-try vulnerable to a sudden reversal in international capital flows.[22]

Before examining this connection in more detail, let us first consider some counterarguments. As a start, not everyone agrees that FDI is less volatile than international bank loans. For example, Dooley, Claessens, and Warner, and more recently, Hausmann and Fernandez-Arias argue that FDI can be as volatile as or even more volatile than international bank loans (or portfolio flows).[23] This is a matter of observable patterns in the data. In an earlier study, I made a comparison of the volatility of the vari-ous types of capital flows (FDI, bank loans, and portfolio capital).[24] The calculations were based on data for all 103 countries for which reliable data could be collected from 1980 to 1996, as well as for a subset of 85 emerg-ing economies over the same period. The volatility is computed in two ways: as standard deviations of FDI-to-GDP, international bank loans-to-GDP, and portfolio capital inflow-to-GDP ratios, and as the coefficient of variation (standard deviations divided by the respective sample means) for the same three ratios. The evidence suggests that no matter which defini-tion of volatility one uses, by and large FDI is reliably less volatile than international bank loans (table 3-3).

The second possible counterargument is that corruption could tilt the composition of capital inflows in a direction other than what I have hypoth-esized here. Corruption is bad for both international direct investors and creditors. Corrupt borrowing countries are more likely to default on bank

21. See, for example, Frankel and Rose (1996); Radlet and Sachs (1998); and Rodrik and Velasco (1999).

22. The discussion is based on Wei (2001a) and Wei and Wu (2001).

23. Dooley, Claessens, and Warner (1995); Hausmann and Fernandez-Arias (2000).

24. Wei (2001).

Table 3-3. *Volatility of FDI/GDP, Bank Loan/GDP, and Portfolio Flow/GDP as Measured by Standard Deviation or Coefficient of Variation: 1980–96*

	FDI/GDP	Loan/GDP	Portfolio/GDP
Standard deviations			
Whole sample: 103 countries			
Mean	0.012	0.041	0.014
Median	0.008	0.033	0.009
Emerging markets: 85 countries			
Mean	0.012	0.046	0.012
Median	0.008	0.035	0.004
Coefficients of variation			
Whole sample: 103 countries			
Mean	1.176	1.567	2.764
Median	0.947	1.204	1.702
Emerging markets: 85 countries			
Mean	1.269	2.192	0.813
Median •	1.163	1.177	2.042

Source: Total inward FDI flows, total bank loans, and total inward portfolio investments are from IMF (various issues); GDP data are from the World Bank's *GDF & WDI Central Databases.*

Notes: Only countries that have at least eight nonmissing observations during 1980–96 for all three variables and whose populations were greater than or equal to 1 million in 1995 are kept in the sample. OECD countries (with membership up to 1980) include Australia, Austria, Canada, Denmark, Finland, France, Ireland, Italy, Japan, Netherlands, New Zealand, Norway, Portugal, Spain, Sweden, Switzerland, United Kingdom, United States. Emerging Markets refer to all countries not on the above list and with a GDP per capita in 1995 less than or equal to US$15,000 (in 1995 U.S. $).

loans or to nationalize (or otherwise diminish the value of) the assets of foreign direct investors. When that happens, there is a limit on how much international arbitration or court proceedings can help to recover the assets, just as there is a limit on how much collateral the foreign creditors or direct investors can seize as compensation.[25]

There are reasons to think that local corruption can hurt international banks more than it can hurt international direct investors. Explicit insurance against political risk is available for purchase by direct investors through the World Bank's Multilateral Investment Guarantee Agency

---

25. In the old days, major international creditors and direct investors might rely on their navies to invade a defaulting country to seize more collateral. Such is no longer a (ready) option today.

(MIGA). But such explicit insurance is not available for purchase by international banks. Indeed, the prolonged debt crisis in developing countries in the 1980s suggests that international creditors could lose a substantial amount of money. Furthermore, international direct investors may have an informational advantage over international portfolio investors (and presumably banks). International direct investors could obtain more information about the local market by having managers from the headquarters stationed in the country in which they invest. As a consequence, the existence of cross-border informational asymmetry may lead to a bias in favor of international direct investment.[26]

These counterarguments all seem reasonable. What are the reasons for arguing that corruption may tilt the composition of capital inflows to a higher bank-loan-to-FDI ratio? There are essentially two.

First, the need for international investors to pay bribes and deal with extortion by corrupt bureaucrats tends to increase with the frequency and the extent of their interactions with local bureaucrats. Given that international direct investors are more likely to have repeated interactions with local officials (for permits, taxes, health inspections, and so forth) than are international banks or portfolio investors, local corruption would be more detrimental to FDI than to other forms of capital flows. Along the same line, direct investment involves greater sunk cost than bank loans or portfolio investment. Once an investment is made, when corrupt local officials start to demand bribes (in exchange for not setting up obstacles), direct investors would be in a weaker bargaining position than international banks or portfolio investors. This ex post disadvantage of FDI would make international direct investors more cautious ex ante in a corrupt host country than international portfolio investors.[27]

In the modern theory of corporate finance, a body of literature argues that the risk of expropriation by the manager of a firm would induce the person who provides the external finance to the firm to prefer a debt contract over a direct equity participation.[28] This is so because a debt contract requires less costly verification of how the manager uses the funds. One can think of an analogy for international capital flows. Crony capitalism increases the possibility that the international capital may be expropriated in

26. This is the logic underlying Razin, Sadka, and Yuen's (1998) theory of "pecking order of international capital flows."

27. Tornell (1990) presented a model in which a combination of sunk cost in real investment and uncertainty leads to underinvestment in real projects even when the inflow of financial capital is abundant.

28. Townsend (1978); Gale and Hellwig (1985).

the capital-recipient country and raises the cost for international investors to inspect its actual use. As a consequence, international investors may favor a debt contract (including bank loans) rather than equity participation (including FDI).

There is a second reason why more international direct investment is deterred by local corruption than international bank credit or portfolio investment. The current international financial architecture is such that international creditors are more likely to be bailed out than international direct investors. For example, during the Mexican (and subsequent Tequila) crisis and the more recent Asian currency crisis, the International Monetary Fund, the World Bank, and the G7 countries mobilized a large amount of funds for these countries to minimize the potentially massive defaults on bank loans. So an international bailout of the bank loans in the event of a massive crisis has by now been firmly implanted in market expectations (even though a bailout may not be complete or certain). In addition, many developing country governments implicitly or explicitly guarantee the loans borrowed by the private sector in the country.[29] In comparison, there have been no comparable examples of international assistance packages for the recovery of nationalized or extorted assets of foreign direct investors. The insurance against political risk provided by the MIGA is insignificant in quantity and often expensive to acquire. This difference further tilts the composition of capital flows and makes banks more willing than direct investors to do business with corrupt countries.

Both reasons suggest the possibility that corruption may affect the composition of capital inflows in such a way that the country is more likely to experience a currency crisis. Ultimately, whether domestic corruption raises or lowers the ratio of external bank borrowing to FDI is an empirical question. For illustration, consider some concrete examples from New Zealand, Singapore, Thailand, and Uruguay. On the one hand, New Zealand and Singapore are two countries with low corruption. Their ratios of loans to FDI (0.11 and 0.44, respectively) and portfolio investment to FDI (0.07 and 0.09, respectively) are relatively low. On the other hand, Thailand and Uruguay are two countries with high corruption. They have much higher ratios of loans to FDI (5.77 and 1.77, respectively) and of portfolio investment to FDI (1.76 and 1.40, respectively). So these examples are consistent with the notion that local corruption is correlated with patterns of capital

---

29. McKinnon and Pill (1996, 1999) argue that the government guarantee generates "moral hazard," which in turn leads the developing countries to "overborrow" from the international credit market.

inflows. Of course, these four countries are just examples. As such, two questions need to be addressed more formally. First, does the association between corruption and composition of capital flows generalize beyond these four countries? Second, once a number of other characteristics that affect the composition of capital inflows are controlled for, would the positive association between corruption and the loan-to-FDI ratio remain?

The aim of the statistical work is to link a country's composition of capital inflows with a measure of its degree of crony capitalism. Because of a lack of variation in the degree of crony capitalism over time (say, over a few years) for most countries, I have to focus on a cross-section study. To obtain a meaningful number of observations to weed out noise in the data, I focus on a panel of bilateral bank lending and bilateral foreign direct investment. The data on bilateral bank lending, reported by the Bank for International Settlements, cover outstanding loans (that is, stocks) from thirteen lending countries to eighty-three borrowing countries. After excluding missing observations, there are altogether 793 country pairs. The data on bilateral direct investment, reported by the OECD, cover the end-of-year stock of foreign direct investment from eighteen source countries to fifty-nine host countries. Unfortunately, the two data sets have mismatched country pairs. When the ratio of bilateral bank loans to bilateral FDI is constructed, up to 225 country pairs are common to both data sets.

As far as I know, there are no comparable data sets on bilateral portfolio flows from the industrial countries to emerging markets. I have obtained bilateral portfolio flow data from the United States to a panel of foreign countries. The number of observations is small (thirty-nine). The statistical results on this data set will be noted briefly later.

Studying the effect of corruption on the composition of capital inflows is equivalent to asking whether corruption may have a differential impact on different forms of capital flows. To verify that this is indeed the case, I check directly the connection between the ratio of bank loans to FDI and host country corruption. A fixed-effects regression of the following sort is performed:

$$\text{Log}(Loan_{kj} / FDI_{kj}) = \textit{fixed effects} + \beta \ \textit{corruption}_j + X_{kj}\Gamma + e_{kj}.$$

source country

The regression result is reported in the first column in table 3-4. As expected, the coefficient on corruption is positive and statistically significant at the 5 percent level. Based on the point estimate, a one-standard-

Table 3-4. *Composition of Capital Flows*

Independent variable	Dependent variable and methodology					
	Fixed effects	Random effects	Fixed effects	Random effects	IV Fixed effects	
	GCR/WDR		TI		GCR/WDR	
Corruption	0.544* (0.126)	0.548* (0.221)	0.496* (0.167)	0.477 (0.278)	0.296** (0.181)	0.282*** (0.183)
Tax rate	0.013 (0.017)	0.015 (0.031)	0.010 (0.017)	0.011 (0.029)	...	...
FDI incentives	0.324* (0.151)	0.400*** (0.259)	0.152 (0.157)	0.224 (0.255)	0.111 (0.156)	0.114 (0.156)
FDI restrictions	0.374* (0.085)	0.342* (0.159)	0.382* (0.087)	0.337* (0.150)	0.336* (0.093)	0.311* (0.100)
Log (GDP)	−0.491* (0.107)	−0.529* (0.191)	−0.500* (0.111)	−0.522* (0.183)	−0.274* (0.115)	−0.236** (0.127)
Log (per capita GDP)	0.150*** (0.095)	0.184 (0.177)	0.190*** (0.119)	0.208 (0.204)	0.034 (0.103)	0.018 (0.105)
Log distance	0.355* (0.092)	0.530* (0.113)	0.355* (0.094)	0.514* (0.113)	0.123 (0.132)	0.157 (0.140)
Linguistic tie	−0.626* (0.295)	−0.653* (0.283)	−0.656* (0.304)	−0.674* (0.288)	−0.753* (0.289)	−0.769* (0.291)
Exchange rate volatility	4.293* (1.452)	5.086* (2.460)	4.638* (1.505)	5.319* (2.391)	...	−3.457 (4.800)
Over-identifying restriction (P-value of the test)	...	...	...	...	0.43	0.53
Adjusted R^2/Overall R^2	0.55	0.54	0.53	0.52	...	...
Number	225	225	225	225	180	180

Source: Author's calculations.

Notes: The dependent variable is log(*Loan*) − log(*FDI*), averaged over 1994–96. Standard errors are in parentheses.

* Significant at the 5 percent level.

** Significant at the 10 percent level.

*** Significant at the 15 percent level.

deviation increase in corruption is associated with roughly a 55 percent increase in the loan-to-FDI ratio (for example, from 100 percent to 155 percent).

Based on this regression, figure 3-1 presents a partial scatter plot of loan-to-FDI ratio against corruption, controlling for several characteristics of the host countries as described in the regression. A visual inspection of the plot suggests that the positive association between corruption and capital

Figure 3-1. *Composition of Capital Inflows and Corruption*

Ln(*Loan*) − Ln(*FDI*)

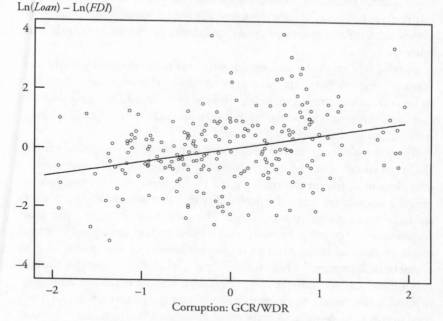

Corruption: GCR/WDR

Source: Author's calculations. (Partial correlation based on table 3-3, column 1.)

composition is unlikely to go away if any one or two observations are omitted. In other words, the positive association is not likely to be driven by outliers. Hence, the evidence suggests that a corrupt country tends to have a composition of capital inflows that is relatively light in FDI and relatively heavy in bank loans.

Also note that because FDI is more relationship-intensive (as proxied by physical and linguistic distances) than bank loans, the coefficients on geographic distance and the linguistic tie dummy are positive and negative, respectively.

Correlation in the residual due to other host-country-specific influences may be of concern. While this issue cannot be addressed completely by including host-country fixed effects, host-country random effects can be included in the regression. The result is reported in the second column of table 3-4. Although there are some changes in the size of the point estimates, the basic qualitative feature remains the same. Columns 3 and 4 of table 3-4 use a different measure of corruption—the Transparency International index. Again, there are some changes in the point estimates, but the central message stays the same: the level of corruption is positively associated with a country's relative dependence on the more volatile bank borrowing.

Finally, one might be concerned with possible endogeneity of the corruption measure. For example, survey respondents may perceive a country to be corrupt in part because they observe very little FDI going there. In this case, the positive association between the loan-to-FDI ratio and corruption can be due to reverse causality.

To deal with the potential endogeneity problem, instrumental variable (IV) regressions were performed on the key regressions. Mauro argued that ethnolinguistic fragmentation is a good IV for corruption.[30] His ethnolinguistic indicator measures the probability that two persons from a country are from two distinct ethnic groups. The greater the indicator, the more fragmented the country. In addition, La Porta and others argued that legal origin or colonial history has an important impact on the quality of government bureaucracy.[31] These variables are used as instruments for the corruption measure. A first-stage regression suggests that ethnically more fragmented countries are more corrupt. In addition, countries with a French legal origin (which includes colonies of Spain and Portugal) are more corrupt than former British colonies.

The IV regressions are reported in the last two columns of table 3-4. A test of over-identifying restrictions does not reject the null hypothesis that the instruments are uncorrelated with the error term. The results from these two IV regressions are still consistent with the notion that corruption deters FDI more than bank loans. Therefore, countries that are more corrupt tend to have a capital inflow structure that relies relatively more on bank borrowing than FDI.

While bilateral data on portfolio investment other than bank credits are not available for the whole set of capital-exporting countries, data on portfolio investment originating from the United States (to a set of developing countries) can be obtained. Unfortunately, the number of observations is small (between thirty-five and thirty-nine, depending on the regression specification). So the power of the statistical tests is likely to be low. Several fixed-effects regressions are performed in a way analogous to

---

30. Mauro (1995).
31. La Porta and others (1998).

table 3-4 (not reported). They show that, at least for this subsample, the portfolio-investment-to-FDI ratio is also positively related to the capital-importing country's corruption level. The more corrupt a country, the less FDI it receives (relative to portfolio capital). However, when the Transparency International corruption index is used, the coefficients on corruption are no longer statistically significant, although they are always positive. The insignificance can be consistent with a genuinely zero coefficient or can result from a low power of the test due to the small sample size.

Conclusion

The quality of public governance matters a great deal for the quantity and quality of capital inflows into a developing country. This is the central message of this paper. To be concrete, governance matters in at least three areas.

First, corruption, or bad governance, reduces the volume of foreign direct investment. The negative effect—the corruption premium—is quantitatively large.

Second, corruption reduces the quality of foreign direct investment. Foreign investment with a high potential of transferring technology to a developing country is more likely to be discouraged by poor governance.

Third, corruption alters the overall structure of a country's capital inflow (by raising the relative dependence on borrowing from foreign banks) in a way that increases the country's vulnerability to a currency attack or a financial crisis.

A corruption premium shows up in other ways as well. For example, corruption could also weaken domestic financial supervision and produce a deteriorated quality of banks' and firms' balance sheets. This would be an additional channel for corruption to raise the likelihood of a currency or financial crisis. The evidence on this awaits future research.

References

Borensztein, E., J. De Gregorio, and J-W Lee. 1995. "How Does Foreign Direct Investment Affect Economic Growth." NBER Working Paper 5057. National Bureau of Economic Research, Cambridge, Mass.

Dooley, M. P., Stijn Claessens, and A. Warner. 1995. "Portfolio Capital Flows: Hot or Cool?" *World Bank Economic Review* 9(1): 53–174.

Frankel, Jeffrey, and Andrew Rose. 1996. "Currency Crashes in Emerging Markets: An Empirical Treatment." *Journal of International Economics* 41 (November): 351–66.

Gale, D., and M. Hellwig. 1985. "Incentive-Compatible Debt Contracts: The One-Period Problem." *Review of Economic Studies* 52: 647–63.

Hausmann, Ricardo, and Eduardo Fernandez-Arias. 2000. "Foreign Direct Investment: Good Cholesterol?" Working Paper 417. Inter-American Development Bank, Washington.

International Monetary Fund. Various issues. *Balance of Payments Statistics.* Washington.

Kaufmann, Daniel, and Shang-Jin Wei. 1999. "Does 'Grease Payment' Speed Up the Wheels of Commerce?" NBER Working Paper 7093. National Bureau of Economic Research, Cambridge, Mass.

Kim, Woochan, and Shang-Jin Wei. 2002. "Foreign Portfolio Investors before and during a Crisis." *Journal of International Economics* 56: 77–96.

La Porta, Rafael, Florencio Lopez-de-Silanes, Andrei Shleifer, and Robert Vishny. 1998. "Law and Finance." *Journal of Political Economy* 106: 1113–55.

Mauro, Paolo. 1995. "Corruption and Growth." *Quarterly Journal of Economics* 110: 681–712.

McKinnon, Ronald, and Huw Pill. 1996. "Credible Liberalization and International Capital Flows: The Overborrowing Syndrome." In Takatoshi Ito and Anne O. Krueger, eds., *Financial Deregulation and Integration in East Asia*, pp. 7–45. University of Chicago Press.

————. 1999. "Exchange Rate Regimes for Emerging Markets: Moral Hazard and International Overborrowing." Stanford University and Harvard University. Forthcoming in *Oxford Review of Economic Policy.*

Obstfeld, Maurice. 1994. "The Logic of Currency Crises." *Cahiers de Economiques et Monetaires* (Banque de France) (43): 189–213.

OECD (Organization for Economic Cooperation and Development). 1999. *International Direct Investment Statistics Yearbook.* Paris. (An associated data diskette is also available.)

PricewaterhouseCoopers. 2000. "Doing Business and Investing Worldwide." (CD-ROM). New York.

Radelet, Steven, and Jeffrey Sachs. 1998. "The East Asian Financial Crisis: Diagnosis, Remedies, and Prospects. " *Brookings Papers on Economic Activity,* 1: 1–74.

Razin, Assaf, Efraim Sadka, and Chi-Wa Yuen. 1998. "A Pecking Order of Capital Inflows and International Tax Principles." *Journal of International Economics* 44: 45–68.

Rodrik, Dani, and Andres Velasco. 1999. "Short-Term Capital Flows." Paper prepared for the 1999 World Bank Annual Conference on Development Economics. Harvard University and New York University.

Shleifer, Andrei, and Robert Vishny. 1993. "Corruption." *Quarterly Journal of Economics* 108: 599–617.

Smarzynska, Beata, and Shang-Jin Wei. 2000. "Corruption and the Composition of Foreign Direct Investment: Firm-Level Evidence." NBER Working Paper 7969. National Bureau of Economic Research, Cambridge, Mass.

Tornell, Aaron. 1990. "Real vs. Financial Investment: Can Tobin Taxes Eliminate the Irreversibility Distortion?" *Journal of Development Economics* 32: 419–44.

Townsend, Robert. 1978. "Optimal Contracts and Competitive Markets with Costly State Verification." *Journal of Economic Theory* 21: 265–93.

UNCTAD (United Nations Conference on Trade and Development). 1998. *World Investment Report*. Geneva.

Wei, Shang-Jin. 1997. "Why Is Corruption So Much More Taxing than Taxes? Arbitrariness Kills." NBER Working Paper 6255. National Bureau of Economic Research, Cambridge, Mass.

———. 2000a. "How Taxing Is Corruption on International Investors?" *Review of Economics and Statistics* 82 (February): 1–11.

———. 2000b. "Why Does China Attract So Little Foreign Direct Investment?" In Takatoshi Ito and Anne O. Krueger, eds., *The Role of Foreign Direct Investment in East Asian Economic Development*, pp. 239–61. University of Chicago Press.

———. 2000c. "Local Corruption and Global Capital Flows." *Brookings Papers on Economic Activity* 2: 303–54.

———. 2001a. "Domestic Crony Capitalism and International Fickle Capital: Is There a Connection?" *International Finance* 4 (1): 15–45.

———. 2001b. "Corruption in Economic Development: Grease or Sand?" *Economic Survey of Europe* 2: 101–12.

Wei, Shang-Jin, and Yi Wu. 2001. "Negative Alchemy? Corruption, Composition of Capital Flows, and Currency Crises." NBER Working Paper 8187. National Bureau of Economic Research, Cambridge, Mass.

DANIEL KAUFMANN 4

Public and Private Misgovernance in Finance: Perverse Links, Capture, and Their Empirics

THANKS TO AN increasing body of empirical evidence, awareness is growing that public governance matters for economywide growth and development, although debate continues about the extent to which it matters and about what dimensions in particular matter most. The particular assessment of the links between public governance and financial sector development is a more recent undertaking, and open discussion and analysis about the importance of public governance in this area has consequently been scant at best.

Yet even if belated and modest so far, recognition is growing nowadays that public governance matters significantly for the health of the financial sector.[1] However, the complex corrupt mechanisms that undermine the

This paper complements the paper by Carmichael and Kaufmann (2001) and thus does not cover in detail several topics already presented in that work. Some sections of this paper draw on collaborative projects, notably with Aart Kraay, Joel Hellman, Jeff Carmichael, and Jaime Jaramillo. It has also benefited from the work on governance and anticorruption diagnostics with partner institutions in emerging economies. The very able research assistance of Massimo Mastruzzi is acknowledged, as is the assistance of Erin Farnand. The data used for the analysis in this paper originate from various surveys as well as outside expert rating agencies, and are subject to a margin of error. Views, errors, and omissions are the responsibility of the author, and may not necessarily reflect those of the institution or its executive directors. For further details on the materials presented here, contact the author (dkaufmann@worldbank.org) or visit (www.worldbank.org/wbi/governance).
    1. Carmichael and Kaufmann (2001).

financial sector are still underappreciated and understudied. Furthermore, the reverse link has not yet been addressed at all: how financial sector corporations use their powerful influence and strategies to shape or undermine public governance for finance.

This paper puts forth the following tenets, based on some empirical evidence:

—Public governance and corruption matter significantly for key dimensions of the development and stability of the financial sector.

—Corporate strategies of elite financial firms matter significantly in shaping public governance and often lead to de facto capture of the regulatory or state bureaucracy.

—Regulatory capture renders ineffective the conventional policy advice aimed at the public sector bureaucracy in many settings.

Recognition of this complex bidirectional interplay between the private and public sectors in shaping the governance environment for finance suggests the need for systemwide reforms focused on a strategy comprising transparency, incentives, and prevention (TIP) measures for improving governance and addressing corruption in this area. A TIP-based focus implies a move away from the excessive focus on narrow internal accountability rules within the executive branch and regulatory agencies, which do not account for the institutional realities in many emerging markets. The paper highlights the usefulness of particular new empirical diagnostic tools for improving transparency and for flagging vulnerabilities before a crisis occurs as well as for suggesting country-specific priorities for action.

The case made here for adopting a broader TIP-based systemic approach throughout the public sector and other institutions crucial to the health of the financial sector warrants a broader-than-usual approach to institutional reforms. Accordingly, this paper addresses broader issues of public governance reform, some of which would have an indirect, yet significant, impact on the financial sector. Given the scope of this paper, however, no exhaustive treatment of each reform area is given here.[2]

Definitions, Analysis, and General Findings

Worldwide evidence shows that a capable state with good and transparent government institutions produces income growth, national wealth, and

2. For details on some areas covered briefly, see Carmichael and Kaufmann (2001), and Vishwanath and Kaufmann (2001).

social achievements.[3] Higher incomes and investment growth, as well as longer life expectancy, are found in countries with effective, honest, and meritocratic government institutions with streamlined and clear regulations, where rule of law is enforced fairly and protects the citizenry and property, and where external accountability mechanisms involving civil society and the media are present. International and historical experience as well as ongoing research all show that capable and clean government does not first require a country to become fully modernized and wealthy. Rule of law, corruption control, or voice and external accountability mechanisms are not "luxury" goods that only rich countries can afford or for which wealth is needed to "acquire" them. The experience of emerging countries such as Botswana, Chile, Costa Rica, Estonia, Hungary, Poland, and Slovenia, as well as evidence over the past thirty years from countries like Spain, illustrates this lesson.

Defining Corruption and Governance

Corruption is commonly defined as the abuse of public office for private gain. Governance is defined as the exercise of authority through formal and informal traditions and institutions for the common good, thus encompassing the process of selecting, monitoring, and replacing governments; the capacity to formulate and implement sound policies and deliver public services; and the respect of citizens and the state for the institutions that govern economic and social interactions among them.

For purposes of measurement and analysis, this definition can be divided into three broad categories, each of which contains two components: first, *voice and external accountability*, which include the ability of the government to be externally accountable through citizen feedback, a competitive press, and the like, and *political stability and lack of violence*; second, *government effectiveness*, which includes the quality of policymaking and public service delivery, and *the lack of regulatory burden*; and third, *rule of law*, which includes protection of property rights and independence of the judiciary, and *control of corruption*.[4] Governance is thus a broader notion than corruption, the latter being one among a number of closely intertwined governance components.

---

3. World Bank (1997).
4. For details, see Kaufmann, Kraay, and Zoido-Lobatón (1999a, b; 2002).

Empirical Study and Measurement of Governance

Recent empirical studies confirm the importance of institutions and governance for development outcomes.[5] Applying the above definition of governance, Kaufmann and Kraay analyzed hundreds of cross-country indicators as proxies for various aspects of governance.[6] The data are mapped to the six subcomponents of governance and expressed in common units. The data are informative within measurable limits, but the imprecision in the estimates requires care in their use and presentation for policy advice. These six distinct aggregate governance indicators are then developed (according to the above classification), imposing structure on available variables and improving the reliability of analyses. For illustration, consider the measurement issues for one of the six composite governance components: control of corruption, using results of the updated worldwide composite measure, based on data from 2000–01. In figure 4-1, the vertical bars depict (the rather large) country-specific margins of error—or statistical confidence intervals—for the estimated levels (or point estimates) of this governance component. The interval reflects the disagreement among the original sources about the level of governance (control of corruption in this case). Similarly, composite indicators were also constructed for the five other components of governance, which are not shown here. This total of six indicators was first derived for 1997–98 and recently updated for 2000–01, thus permitting initial over-time comparisons.[7]

The differences among the overall sample are quite large for control of corruption as well as for the other five measures. Countries are ordered along the horizontal axis according to their rankings, while the vertical axis reports the estimates of governance for each country. The margins of error

---

5. One study (Knack and Keefer, 1997) performed cross-national tests of institutions using various indicators of institutional quality and found that the institutional environment for economic activity determines, in large part, the ability of emerging economies to catch up to industrialized country standards. See also Acemoglu, Johnson, and Robinson (2002); Engelman and Sokoloff (2002); and Kaufmann and Kraay (forthcoming).

6. These indicators came from a variety of organizations, including commercial risk rating agencies, multilateral organizations, think tanks, and other nongovernmental organizations (NGOs). They are based on surveys of experts, firms, and citizens and cover a wide range of topics: perceptions of political stability and the business climate, views on the efficacy of public service provision, opinions on respect for the rule of law, perceptions of the incidence of corruption. For detailed explanation on sources and access to the full governance indicators databank see www.worldbank.org/wbi/governance/govdata2001.htm.

7. Through a web-interactive tool adapted to the user's need, these governance research indicators are available online at (www.worldbank.org/wbi/governance/govdata2001.htm).

Figure 4-1. *A Governance Composite Indicator: Control of Corruption,* *2000–01*[a]

Normalized control of corruption index

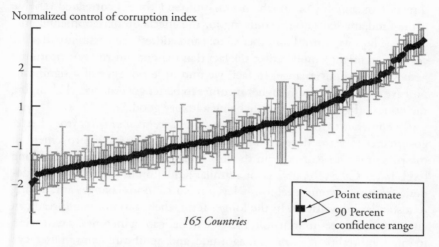

Point estimate
90 Percent
confidence range

165 Countries

Source: Kaufmann, Kraay, and Zoido-Lobatón (2002).
a. Point estimates and margins of error for 165 countries.

(at the 90 percent confidence level), depicted in figure 4-1 by the thin vertical line around each country estimate, permit some meaningful grouping comparisons. Yet, since the margins of error are not small, it is misleading to have countries "run" in seemingly precise worldwide "horse races" to ascertain their ranking on various governance indicators. Instead, an approach that groups countries into three or four broad categories for the various separate governance dimensions is more appropriate, and statistically consistent. Following such broad grouping classification, identification is possible of a group of thirty to forty countries where there is an urgent need to focus on better and cleaner government (those in the lower left-hand side, with poor control of corruption), which stand far apart from the top groupings (right-hand side), whose estimates indicate that they are performing well.

Causal Effects of Governance

The set of six governance indicators allows systematic assessment of the benefits of good governance in a large sample of countries. At the most basic level, the data reveal a very high correlation between good governance and key development outcomes across countries. Yet this is a "weak" finding in terms of policy application, since such correlations do not shed light on the direction of causality or on whether an omitted ("third") correlated variable is the fundamental cause accounting for the effects on developmental outcomes. Thus, we control for other factors and address the possibility that the correlation might simply reflect the fact that richer countries can afford the luxury of good governance. In fact, we find little evidence of a significant positive effect going from higher incomes to better governance, challenging the notion of governance simply being a luxury good.

By contrast, the analysis suggests a *large direct causal effect* from better governance to better development outcomes. Consider an improvement in the rule of law in Russia from the low levels it has today to the middling levels in the Czech Republic—or a similar reduction in corruption in Indonesia from its current level to the level in Korea (both changes amounting to a standard deviation). In the longer term, these actions would result in an estimated three- to four-fold increase in per capita incomes, a reduction in infant mortality of a similar magnitude, and significant gains in literacy.[8] These development impacts are illustrated in figure 4-2 for four development outcomes and four measures of governance. The heights of the vertical bars show the difference in development outcomes in countries with weak, average, and strong governance, illustrating the strong *correlation* between good outcomes and good governance. The solid lines illustrate the estimated *causal* impacts of governance on development outcomes— the "development dividend" of improved governance.

While composite indicators of governance have clear limits in their sole use for work on strategies within a particular country, they are powerful in flagging major vulnerabilities for particular countries, for drawing attention to governance issues focusing on country groupings and the various components of governance, and for monitoring broad trends over time (particularly now that there are measures for two points in time, 1998 and 2001). They are also indispensable for cross-country research into the causes and consequences of misgovernance.[9]

---

8. Note that the differences in governance for these two pairs of countries, at one standard deviation, are not very large. Much larger improvements in government effectiveness from the levels observed in Paraguay (well in the bottom quartile) to that in Chile (well in the top quartile) would nearly double the development impacts just mentioned.

9. Indeed, worldwide aggregate indicators are a blunt tool for informed action to improve governance within a given country. To move to a more concrete stage of specificity and usefulness within a country, and for useful action programming on the ground by a country intent on making inroads on

The empirical evidence from a number of scholars also points to the significant effects of public governance on other economic development variables, such as growth and investment rates (both domestic and foreign).[10] What has been less subject to systematic studies from an empirical standpoint is whether public governance matters for the development and soundness of the financial sector. In preliminary and exploratory fashion, we undertake this task below. Before presenting empirical results on this link, however, we first briefly define and discuss the key notion of transparency, the component of governance that has particular relevance to the field of finance.

Transparency: Key to Good Governance, Anticorruption, and Financial Stability

As with the concepts of corruption and governance, it is also important to define, unbundle, and operationalize the notion of *transparency*, and its intimately related key characteristics of an effective flow of information, namely: access, timeliness, relevance, and quality.[11]

Defining Transparency

Transparency refers to the flow of timely and reliable economic, social, and political information, which is accessible to all relevant stakeholders. It is thus about private investors' use of loans and the creditworthiness of borrowers; about properly audited accounts of key governmental, private, and multinational institutions; about the budgetary process and data from the government; about monetary and real economy statistics from the central bank and government service provision; about political and campaign finance disclosure and the voting records of parliamentarians, as well as about the activities of international institutions. Conversely, a lack of transparency occurs when an agent—whether a government minister, a public institution, a corporation, or a bank—deliberately withholds access to or

---

governance, in-depth country-specific diagnostic tools are required (see specific section on diagnostics below for details).

10. Mauro (1995, 1996); Wei (1999, 2000, 2002).

11. For further details on these definitional and related issues on transparency, see Vishwanath and Kaufmann (2001).

Figure 4-2. *The Development Dividend of Good Governance*

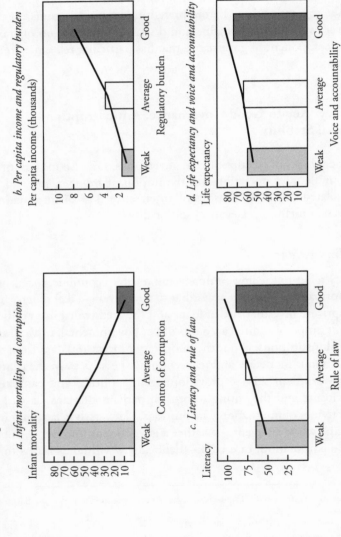

a. Infant mortality and corruption

Infant mortality

b. Per capita income and regulatory burden

Per capita income (thousands)

c. Literacy and rule of law

Literacy

d. Life expectancy and voice and accountability

Life expectancy

Source: Kaufmann, Kraay, and Zoido-Lobatón (1999b).
Note: The bars depict the simple correlation between good governance and development outcomes. The line depicts the predicted value when taking into account the causality effects ("Development Dividend") from improved governance to better development outcomes.

misrepresents information or fails to ensure that the information provided is timely, relevant, or of adequate quality.

Hence, a working understanding of transparency should encompass the following attributes of information: *access* (including timeliness and nondiscrimination), *comprehensiveness* (ensuring inclusion of key items, such as off-line financial and budgetary items), relevance (avoiding superfluous information overload), *quality,* and *reliability.* Together these attributes aid policymaking and provide market confidence to investors. Although transparency is desirable, markets on their own rarely induce socially desirable levels of transparency, partly because there can be payoffs from nondisclosure. Further, some key information related to transparency, such as economywide economic and financial statistics, can emanate only from government institutions. Consequently, government has a role in promoting a transparent flow of relevant information from its institutions.

Transparency and Financial Crisis: Short-Term Empirical Perspective

The Asian financial crisis, as well as similar crises in Argentina, Ecuador, Russia, and Turkey, has highlighted the nexus between misgovernance (including corruption) and lack of transparency on one hand, and financial sector fragility and a high likelihood of a crisis, on the other. Because these financial sector crises have had enormous welfare consequences, and because the evidence suggests a link between good (public) governance at the national level and a strong financial sector, understanding the nature of such linkages and key policy and institutional implications is critical to improving governance factors and thus the robustness of financial systems. In the recent financial crisis literature, several references are made to "lack of transparency" as one of the factors that either caused or contributed to the prolonged crises. Yet despite the importance of transparency for financial markets, little theoretical or empirical effort has been devoted to understanding the concept; often the notion of transparency is not defined.

However, evidence suggests a relationship between transparency and financial crises. Simple observation suggests, for instance, the deleterious effects of inadequate information on the firms' and banks' true balance sheets, compounded by the use of insider relations, masking poor investments. Once a downturn sets in, poor transparency makes it difficult for investors to distinguish between firms and banks that are healthy and those that are not. That in turn can force bank runs and destabilize economies.

Indeed, Mehrez and Kaufmann investigated the effect of financial liberalization, transparency, and control of corruption on the probability of a banking crisis.[12] The authors built and tested a model, finding that the risk of financial crisis can be particularly costly in economies with poor transparency and high levels of corruption. In the model, banks had imperfect information due to lack of transparency. Imperfect information generally leads banks to increase their credit exposure above optimal levels in the face of positive aggregate shocks or nontransparent policies. Once banks discover their large exposure, they are likely to roll over bad loans rather than declare their losses. That delays the crisis and increases its magnitude. Empirical investigation using data on fifty-six countries from 1977 to 1997 supports the model: the probability of a crisis is particularly high in the period following financial liberalization in settings with poor transparency and high corruption. It thus suggests the importance of paying attention to anticorruption and transparency-enhancing reforms and measures when financial liberalization takes place; neglecting these key governance components significantly raises the risk of financial crisis.

A Longer-Term Perspective

The public sector participates in the finance sector of most economies to an extent and in ways that are quite unlike its role in other sectors of the economy. The public sector may serve as the regulator of financial institutions, an owner of financial institutions, a market participant, and a fiduciary agent. It may perform some or all of these roles, and it may also intervene directly in the operations of the market.[13]

There is increasing recognition that corruption and misgovernance are no less prevalent in banking and finance than in other areas and sectors, such as energy, procurement, and taxation, that have been under scrutiny for many years on this front. In fact, at a simple level it is sobering to see the figures for even a narrowly confined form of misgovernance in finance, namely, bribes to obtain bank loans. Based on the Global Competitiveness Survey (GCS) of more than 6,000 enterprises in more than eighty countries, we find that in almost half of the countries, more than 25 percent of the firms rate bribery for obtaining loans from banks as a serious/very seri-

---

12. Mehrez and Kaufmann (1999).

13. See Carmichael and Kaufmann (2001) for further details on these differences of the financial sector.

ous problem. In more than one-third of these countries, enterprises report bribery for loans to be more common than bribery for alleviating tax payments, and in 60 percent of these countries bribery for loans is more prevalent than bribery to obtain connections for public utilities. These data support the notion that bribery and corruption are far from being exceptions in finance, either in absolute terms or in comparison with other sectors.

The existence of corruption and misgovernance in the financial sector (both from within and without) does not in itself mean that their presence significantly affects financial sector development. The next step, then, is a basic empirical exploration using microeconomic firm level data as well as the aggregate governance indicators to determine whether corruption and misgovernance matter. Specifically, we use two separate firm-based surveys: the *Global Competitiveness Report*, conducted by the World Economic Forum with Harvard University; and the World Business Environment Survey (WBES), conducted by the World Bank.[14] By empirically linking this survey data with the economywide composite governance indicators discussed earlier, we can test whether governance and various dimensions of financial sector development are related.

From the GCS dataset we obtained three relevant dependent variables reflecting the firms' rating on *quality of the financial markets, soundness of the banking system,* and *financial sector regulatory quality,* as shown in appendix tables 4-1, 4-2, and 4-3, respectively. We regressed these dependent variables against (the logarithm of) the country's income per capita (based on purchasing power parity) to control for the country's level of overall development and other possible institutional factors accounting for financial sector development, and we carried out the OLS econometric analysis with various overall economywide governance dimensions as independent variables.

Tellingly, the results suggest that not only is the composite governance variable *control of corruption* very significant across all financial sector development dimensions, but it also dominates other governance components. Indeed, its estimates exhibit much higher significance than the variables for overall regulatory quality economywide, the rule of law, and voice. The regression results suggest that controlling for the country's stage of development, a move from a high level of corruption to control of corruption can make the difference in whether a country moves from a low to a high quality of financial markets, to a sound banking system, and to a high level of financial sector regulatory quality (figures 4-3 and 4-4).

14. See Batra, Kaufmann, and Stone (2002).

Figure 4-3. *Soundness of Banks versus Control of Corruption*

Soundness of banks

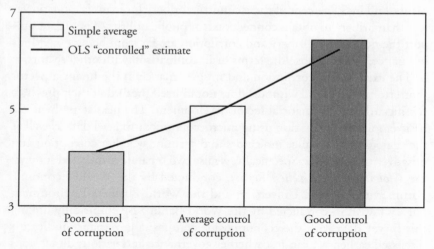

Source: Global Competitiveness Survey, 2001; Kaufmann, Kraay, and Zoido-Lobatón (2002).

Figure 4-4. *Quality of Financial Regulations versus Control of Corruption*

Quality of financial regulations

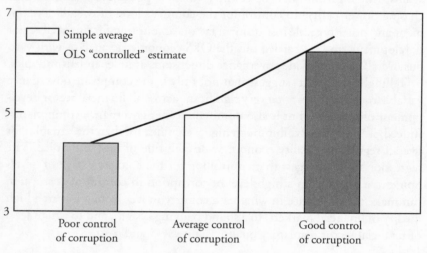

Source: Global Competitiveness Survey, 2001; Kaufmann, Kraay, and Zoido-Lobatón (2002).

We also tested whether bribery within the banking sector (as distinct from the economywide public corruption composite variable) matters for the soundness of the banking sector. As columns 7–10 of appendix table 4-2 show, the results are significant, suggesting that bribery within banking undermines the soundness of the sector. The significance of the economy-wide aggregate control of public corruption variable remains even after including the specific bribery-in-banking variable, suggesting that overall public corruption in the economy has an independently significant impact (even if indirect) on the financial sector over and above the effect of bribery within the sector itself. This finding buttresses the rationale for adopting a more comprehensive governance and transparency-enhancing strategy for financial sector development, which does not focus narrowly on misgovernance within the banking sector alone.

The other survey source, the WBES, provided one variable rated by the enterprises, namely, the extent to which finance is an obstacle to their business development (figure 4-5). As shown in appendix table 4-4, control of corruption matters significantly for ameliorating such obstacles (controlling for the country's level of development and other governance dimensions).

In sum, in this section I have presented preliminary empirical evidence indicating a significant link between overall misgovernance and corruption in the economy on the one hand, and impaired financial sector development and lack of soundness of the banking sector, on the other.

Analyzing the Crucial Reverse Link:
Corporate Strategies Affect Public Governance

The orthodox approach to viewing misgovernance and regulatory and policy obstacles is to focus on policymaking and governance inadequacies within the public sector and the effect such underperformance has on the private sector; from this perspective, the private sector is seen as being a business-climate "taker" at the mercy of such policymaking. This orthodox view is challenged, however, in settings where powerful forces outside of the public sector exert undue influence in shaping public policy. An extreme form of such undue influence is corporate capture of the state and regulatory apparatus.[15]

15. For seminal earlier work on regulatory capture, see Laffont and Tirole (1991).

Figure 4-5. *Financing Constraint versus Control of Corruption*

Financing constraint

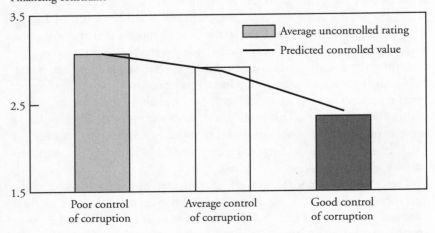

Source: World Business Environment Survey, 2000; Kaufmann, Kraay, and Zoido-Lobatón (2002).

The extent to which state and regulatory capture exists—a form of grand corruption—was measured and analyzed for twenty-two transition economies through an in-depth enterprise survey carried out in late 1999 and early 2000. State-regulatory capture is defined as the efforts of firms to shape the laws, policies, and regulations of the state to their own advantage by providing illicit private gains to public officials. In transition economies corruption has taken on a new image—one of so-called oligarchs or related elite enterprises manipulating policy formation and even shaping the emerging rules of the game to their own very substantial advantage. Although this form of grand corruption is increasingly being recognized as the most pernicious and intractable problem in the political economy of reform, few systematic efforts have been made to distinguish its causes and consequences from those of other forms of corruption. The enterprise survey permitted such empirical exploration.

By taking the average share of firms affected across the six dimensions of capture, namely the illicit purchase of influence through party financing, legislation, executive decrees, central bank policies, and criminal and civil court decisions, a state capture index for each country was developed. The index shows a very large gap between "high-capture" economies, where this form of corruption is seen as a serious problem, and "low-capture" economies, where it is a relatively modest problem. Among the low-capture economies are the most reform-minded, while the high-capture group includes countries regarded as partial reformers both politically and economically; indeed, their political regimes tend to be characterized by a greater concentration of power and limitations on political competition. State capture is negatively related to the level of civil liberties.

The survey also permitted the identification of firms that have paid bribes to influence the content of laws, rules, or regulations; these are called the *captor firms*. As seen in figure 4-6, captor firms in high-capture economies do derive private benefits from their strategy: they grow more than twice as fast as other (noncaptor) firms in these economies—in contrast with low-capture economies, where capture strategies are not privately beneficial on average. In the high-capture economies, however, while capture provides captor firms with substantial private gains, it is a large "tax" on noncaptor firms. The data also suggest that once a country has fallen into the trap of a capture economy, foreign direct investment can magnify the problem.[16]

These results do not, however, address the question whether the capture of the state and its regulatory apparatus is relevant for the institutions and corporations in the financial sector. To determine that, we unbundled the sample, distinguishing between firms in the financial sector of transition economies versus all others in the enterprise sector and found that the finance sector had a significantly higher percentage of captor firms than did the enterprise sector as a whole. Figure 4-7 shows that captor finance firms have a significant effect in influencing legislation and central bank regulations.

These results force a reassessment of the conventional premise that the financial corporate sector is merely a passive "taker" of the public governance and policies instituted by the public sector. In fact, many financial corporations appear to exert undue (and often illegal) influence in shaping regulations, laws, and policies affecting the overall financial sector. Our research also reveals significant evidence that foreign direct investors and multinationals also engage in these practices. The complexity of the policy-shaping process coupled with the empirical evidence indicating that overall public governance matters significantly for financial sector development and its soundness points to the need to consider a more comprehensive approach for improving governance and transparency—even where the main objective is to improve the workings of the financial sector.

16. Hellman, Jones, and Kaufmann (2001).

Figure 4-6. *Captors Benefit at Enormous Cost to Rest of Economy*

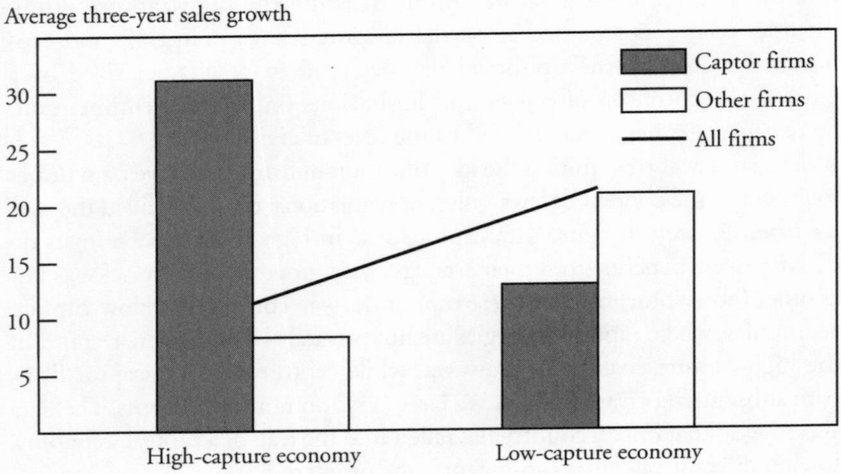

Average three-year sales growth

Source: Hellman and Kaufmann, September (2001).

A Multipronged Strategy for Improving Public and Financial Sector Governance

Given what is known about the main determinants of corruption, misgovernance, and lack of transparency systemwide, what kind of programs for promoting better governance may have an impact?[17]

The emerging lessons suggest that reducing corruption and improving public governance *systemwide* requires a system of checks and balances in society that restrains arbitrary action by politicians and bureaucrats and fosters the rule of law. Institutional arrangements that diffuse power and promote accountability and transparency are key to such a system. Furthermore, the recent work on state capture highlights the need to place checks and balances on the "elite" corporate sector (that is, the set of powerful influential firms) through promoting a competitive market economy. Another salient feature of a systemwide approach is a meritocratic and service-oriented public administration. This systemwide approach for improving the overall public governance climate, illustrated in figure 4-8, would positively affect financial sector development and the soundness of

17. This section draws on the author's chapter 6 in World Bank (2000).

Figure 4-7. *Extent of Regulatory-State Capture in Finance versus Enterprise Sectors in "Captured" Transition Economies*

Extent of capture, percent

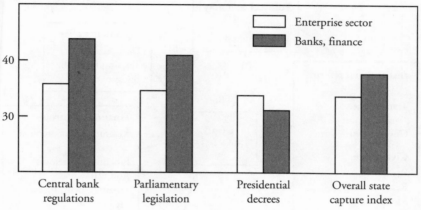

Source: Authors' calculations based on BEEPS Enterprise Survey.

the financial system, but a complementary strategy focused specifically on governance in finance is also required. This strategy would rely significantly (but not solely) on transparency-enhancing measures.

Promoting Competition and Entry

In many transition and developing countries, one source of grand corruption comes from the concentration of economic power in monopolies that then wield political influence on the government for private benefits. The problem is particularly acute in economies rich in natural resources, where monopolies in oil, gas, and aluminum, for instance, exert considerable economic and political power that leads to various forms of corruption, such as nonpayment of taxes, obscure offshore accounts, the purchase of licenses and permits, vote buying, and restrictions on entry and competition. Barriers to entry are a substantial challenge for the financial sector in many countries (as is exit, in that insolvent concerns are not allowed to liquidate or go bankrupt). Restrictions on the entry of foreign banks are still widespread, while barriers to exit placed on state-owned banks (many being artificially propped up) are a significant deterrent to the entry of private banks. The regulations governing the restrictions to entry and exit in banking and

Figure 4-8. *Multipronged Strategies for Improving Governance and Combating Corruption*

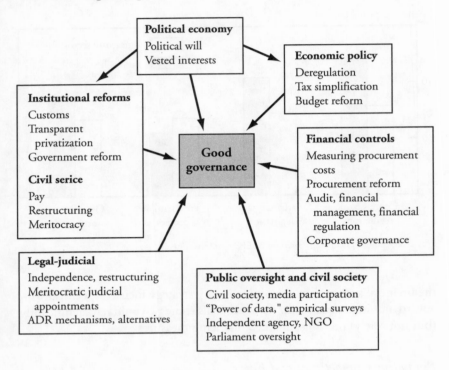

finance (associated with licenses with enormous potential rents), as well as the resulting monopolistic structure that emerges, are in turn associated with corruption and misgovernance in the sector.[18]

Civil Society Oversight and Participation in a Transparency-Enhancing Strategy

Civil society oversight and participation in the decisionmaking and functioning of the public sector have been a crucial counterweight for combat-

18. Correlation analysis based on the Global Competitiveness Survey data suggests a very significant relationship between restrictions to entry to foreign banks and corruption in banking in a country.

ing corruption and improving governance. Civil service oversight and transparency measures are also important tools in reducing the likelihood of state capture by corporations. That means making the state transparent to the public and empowering the citizenry to play an active role. Scandinavian countries have been in the forefront in implementing transparency reforms. But public sector culture in many transition and developing countries fosters secrecy of decisionmaking. Among members of the Commonwealth of Independent States, for example, parliamentary votes are not publicly disclosed (making it more likely that undue or illegal influence on lawmaking takes place), public access to government information is not assured, and judicial decisions are typically not available to the public. Moreover, despite a growing civil society, the government typically does not involve nongovernmental organizations (NGOs) in the monitoring of its decisionmaking process or performance. Concentrated media ownership and recent restrictions on reporting have weakened the ability of the media to ensure accountability of the public sector. Finally, in many countries the structure of business associations representing competitive segments of the private sector, such as exporter groups, small and medium-size enterprises, and trade associations, is underdeveloped. The empirical evidence from the research on state capture in transition economies suggests that the incidence of capture by the elite few is much higher in countries that lack business association activism.

Making such a culture more transparent involves a fundamental change in the way decisions in the public sector are made. The types of transparency reforms that have been demonstrated internationally to be effective include

—Public access to government information through initiatives such as Freedom of Information acts;

—Government meetings open to the public;

—Public hearings and referendums on drafts, decrees, regulations, and laws;

—Published judicial decisions;

—A strengthened system of administrative appeals, which provide the public with a process to challenge decisions of state;

—Promotion of freedom of the press by prohibiting censorship, discouraging use by public officials of libel and defamation laws as a means of intimidating journalists, and encouraging diversity of media ownership;

—Civil society oversight of public sector performance, especially the implementation of politically difficult reforms such as anticorruption measures, and public procurement.

Civil society's role ought to be seen as dynamic and supportive of political leaders committed to building the credibility of the state. For instance, in many countries where the World Bank is working in collaboration with donor agencies and local institutions, new activities involve supporting the collective action of civil society, the media, experts, the private sector, and reformists in the executive and legislative branches in formulating governance and anticorruption reform programs. Positive involvement by the key stakeholders in civil society creates a momentum toward ownership and sustainability of the reforms and builds credibility.

Accountability of the Political Leadership

In addition to participation by civil society, the political leadership needs to demonstrate its commitment to fighting corruption by disclosing publicly its own financing, income, and assets. Such disclosure is only one of several key initiatives promoting transparency and accountability that should reduce the incidence of state-regulatory capture. For example, in several advanced market economies, these checks and balances include

—Public disclosure of votes in parliament;

—Limits to prevent abuse of parliamentary immunity;

—Public disclosure of sources and amounts of political party finance;

—Public disclosure of incomes and assets of senior public officials and their key dependents;

—Measures to prevent conflicts of interest for public officials;

—"Whistle-blower" statutes that protect the personal and employment security of public officials who reveal abuse of public office by other officials in their organizations.

Building a Meritocratic and Service-Oriented Public Administration

Cross-country evidence conclusively shows that recruiting and promoting on merit (as opposed to political patronage or ideological affiliation) is positively associated with both government effectiveness and control of corruption. Although a merit system takes times to put in place, effective reforms in this area have included creating independent, professional institutions with checks and balances and introducing a comprehensive performance management system with pay and promotion linked to performance. In Malaysia and Thailand, this latter reform led to increased recruitment and retention of managerial and professional staff and to increased effectiveness in civil service performance. Pay levels for managerial and key professional staff need to be broadly competitive with the private sector, and often allowances and nonfinancial benefits need to be simplified, monetized, and made transparent.

Transparency and Accountability in Public Expenditure Management

Basic systems of accountability in the allocation and use of public expenditures constitute a fundamental pillar for a good and clean government. Accountability in public expenditure management requires a comprehensive budget and a consultative budget process, transparency in the use of public expenditures, competitive public procurement, and an independent external audit.

Many countries face problems of budgetary transparency, where a large proportion of expenditure remains off budget, major areas of budget expenditure do not pass through the treasury system, and there is substantial recourse to extrabudgetary (or off-budget) funds and a lack of any effective system of controlling expenditure commitments, leading to persistent accumulation of budget deficits. Several countries in transition, such as Hungary and Latvia, have made progress in addressing these problems with comprehensive treasury reform programs. Two conditions appear necessary for success: the budget must cover all of the government's activities; and disclosure matters. Many developed countries, for example, publish frameworks for public expenditure strategy.

TRANSPARENT AND COMPETITIVE PUBLIC PROCUREMENT. Corruption in public procurement is pervasive in transition and developing economies. Reducing corruption requires adhering to strict discipline in terms of transparent and competitive bidding for major contracts, maximizing the scope for public oversight and scrutiny. To make the process of government procurement more efficient and to curb corruption, three Latin American countries—Argentina, Chile, and Mexico—recently adopted electronic acquisition systems. All government procurement notices and their results are placed on a publicly available website. Other important innovations are also taking place. NGOs are increasingly playing a role in spearheading public audiences for setting out the rules of the game for large-scale procurement projects and throughout the transparent bidding process itself. The World Bank has also taken a very active role in aggressively pursuing firms engaged in misprocurement in connection with Bank projects. A list of firms that are ineligible for Bank projects because they engaged in corrupt procurement are available on the Bank's website.

ESTABLISHING INDEPENDENT EXTERNAL AUDITS. Several Eastern European countries have established Supreme Audit Institutions (SAIs) to perform external audits on the public budgetary process. These independent agencies have had a constructive impact on a number of public financial management systems. For instance, in the Czech Republic audit reports are not only published and presented to the legislature, but also discussed in the cabinet, along with a proposed plan for corrective actions, in the presence of the SAI and relevant ministers.

TRANSPARENCY IN FINANCE. The recent Enron debacle illustrates the need for sounder accounting and auditing practices, but it is not the only case where poor auditing standards have had costly ramifications. The strong case for strict accounting norms ought to note that disclosure alone is insufficient to implement transparency: information must be reliable and based on sound principles and standards that enable investors and lenders to make consistent assessments of firms' activities and risk profiles. Unfortunately, most developing countries have weak accounting systems, contributing to lack of transparency. Common problems include insufficiently rigorous accounting conventions, lack of uniform reporting requirements, poor information systems, and inadequate supervision and enforcement. Evidence from countries beset by recent financial crises suggests that accounting failures contributed to the crises. Specifically, the financial information that was disclosed did not show the underlying risks among firms and banks. Box 4-1 sets out some practical guideposts that central banks and banking sectors can take to improve accounting systems.

Freedom of Information Legislation

Institutional arrangements are necessary to help governments achieve transparency. Various media channels—television, newspapers, radio, and public notices—all facilitate transparency. Institutional channels are also needed for citizens to be able to voice concerns and provide feedback. Freedom of speech and a free press ensure that such channels remain open. To improve transparency, many governments have imposed disclosure requirements on government activities. For example, the Freedom of Information Act in the United States, passed in 1972, and similar legislation in other countries (recently in Malaysia, Mozambique, Namibia, and South Africa) require the government to make accessible to citizens an exhaustive array of records of government actions and debates. The International Monetary Fund has reviewed the many laws relating to fiscal transparency and disclosure and has developed a code of good practice on fiscal transparency (box 4-2).

Developing an Institutional Infrastructure for Transparency

To be effective, transparency and disclosure must be supported by an institutional infrastructure, one with high standards and accounting practices, incentives that promote disclosure, and mechanisms for balancing countervailing regulations to minimize perverse incentives generated by safety net arrangements such as deposit insurance.[19]

Practical means for improving disclosure should be part of all development agendas. Instituting sound accounting and auditing practices, streamlining reporting requirements, improving information technology (IT) systems, and bolstering institutional supervision are all key components of a good disclosure system. Experience suggests that given their limited resources, developing countries may best address these needs by taking advantage of private sector provision of information and accounting services, building regulatory structures to their best ability, and tailoring supervision and enforcement means to local capabilities and circumstances. This may militate against the institution of uniform international accounting standards—a subject of intense current debate. Such evidence as exists on means of mitigating incentive problems in financial markets illustrates the merit of using combinations of simple policies that are easily implemented.

Transparency in and of itself is not sufficient without accompanying enforcement mechanisms. Public institutions therefore need both to regulate disclosure and to enforce appropriate behavior. Indeed, as illustrated by the case of Indonesia, financial reform may be predicated on broader public sector reforms. Notably, the effectiveness of public institutions affects not only the performance of markets, including capital markets, but also the allocation of public goods and the distribution of risk and other implicit costs in an economy. Over and above the more specific recommendations on transparency in financial markets are broader imperatives to

19. An important suggestion is that because institutional development is gradual, relatively simple regulations, such as limits on credit expansion, may be best tailored to developing countries. Implicit in this section is the notion that there are absolute limits to transparency, in particular for lack of adequate enforcement.

Box 4-1. *Stopping Corruption and Promoting Good Governance in the Financial Sector: What a Central Bank Can Do*

A widely held orthodoxy in the anticorruption field is that specialized institutions, such as anticorruption commissions, are central to solving the problem.

Yet the evidence from many anticorruption commissions and ethics offices at high levels of government (or even from quasi independent commissions) has not supported the view that such institutions are highly effective overall. The challenge then is to induce existing institutions to address the problem of corruption in their area of responsibility in a more comprehensive and effective fashion. The central bank is the salient institution in the financial sector, although its potential has been underutilized.

Unbundling Corruption

Six classes of corruption are typically observed in banking. The first three listed below directly involve the central bank, while the remaining three affect the rest of the banking system.

1. Corruption in supervision. Banks evade prudential regulations by capturing the officials in charge of supervision. Long-term capture is common, usually with a "contract" securing a job in the capturing bank thereafter.

2. Corruption in the discount/developmental window—allocation of liquidity. This problem is also attributable to capture, typically through secured future job contracts for the captured officials. The risk, however, is different from that in corrupt supervision: bypassing prudential regulation affects the overall stability of the system, while corruption in resource and liquidity allocation affects competitiveness and efficiency.

3. Corruption in management of assets, reserves, and foreign exchange by the central bank. Diversion of resources or commissions in placement and investment result in losses in returns and efficiency.

4. Corruption in state-owned banking. Bribery in placing funds may lead to lax investments and the like, which can result in balance sheet crisis and ultimately liquidation or quasi fiscal problems.

5. Corruption associated with illegal bank operations, such as money laundering or bribing public officials to get deposits from public institutions. As public officials in charge of handling public resources tend to change with political rotation, their interest usually lies in receiving bribes, rather than in future employment opportunities.

6. Private sector bank fraud. Corruption and fraud in private banking are typically handled by the private institutions themselves, even though considerable externalities may arise in some cases, warranting supervisory intervention.

Practical Initiatives

The types of initiatives and actions that can be suitably adapted to meet specific country conditions include the following.

Supervision

—Stick to the essential prudential regulations and avoid unnecessary red tape.

—Set up the supervisory authority by functions and not by type of institutions.

—Establish a strict code of conduct for all supervisory personnel, penalizing conflicts of interest and barring employment in private finance or banking for at least a year after leaving a bank supervision position.

—Set up a toll-free line so that internal and external auditors can receive complaints and keep corruption in check, coupled with a system of incentives for informants, especially if these are financial institutions themselves.

—Carry out comparative analysis of compliance with prudential regulations across banks and whatever sanctions have taken place to detect atypical patterns.

—Conduct a life-style survey of supervisory personnel to detect odd patterns of behavior and income.

—Undertake regular surveys about the banks' and the public's perception of corruption in the central bank.

Discount/Developmental Window—Allocation of Liquidity

—Concentrate the discount/developmental operations in one single unit that can be easily supervised and controlled.

—Establish a strict code of conduct penalizing conflicts of interest.

—Perform comparative analysis of allocation of resources and liquidity across banks and beneficiaries to detect atypical patterns.

—Conduct a life-style survey of supervisory personnel to detect odd patterns of behavior and income.

—Undertake regular surveys of the banks' and the public's perception of corruption in the central bank.

—Undertake publicity campaigns to educate bankers and potential beneficiaries about their rights and how to exercise them.

Management of Assets, Reserves, and Foreign Exchange

—Establish internal control mechanisms, including an internal auditor, to follow these transactions.

—Establish external auditing by an independent auditor and follow the auditor's recommendations.

(continued)

Box 4-1. *Stopping Corruption and Promoting Good Governance in the Financial Sector: What a Central Bank Can Do (Continued)*

—Conduct a life-style survey of managerial personnel to detect odd patterns of behavior and income.

—Undertake regular surveys of the banks' and the public's perception of corruption in the central bank.

State-Owned Banking

—Carry out judicious supervision to ensure compliance with prudential regulations.

—Establish stern personal sanctions for managers, additional to those for state-owned banks, for violating the code of conduct or repeatedly breaking prudential regulations.

—Establish internal and external auditors in state banks.

—Publish regularly the main financial indicators of state-owned banks.

—Carry out comparative analysis of performance across state-owned banks to detect unusual patterns.

—Conduct a life-style survey of supervisory personnel to detect odd patterns of behavior and income.

—Undertake regular surveys about the banks' and the public's perception of corruption in the state-owned banks.

Illegal Bank Operations

—Establish stern personal sanctions for managers, in addition to those for the bank, for carrying out illegal bank operations. These sanctions should include banning violators from future work in the banking system.

—Carry out random supervisory visits to verify compliance with existing regulations for a given set of operations.

Note: Jaime Jaramillo-Vallejo was the main author of the material on which this box is based; his valuable input is appreciated. For specific recommendations on other institutional aspects of progovernance financial sector reforms, see Carmichael and Kaufmann (2001).

improve transparency in governance: implementing freedom of information legislation, instituting freedom of press laws, building legal enforcement mechanisms, and investing in information infrastructure to improve the gathering and sharing of information. Many governments are already doing this.

Box 4-2. *The IMF Code on Fiscal Transparency*

The IMF code on fiscal transparency has several sections that apply specifically to the public sector:

Clarity of Roles and Responsibilities. The government sector should be clearly distinguished from the rest of the economy, and policy and management roles within government should be well defined. Additionally, there should be a clear legal and administrative framework for fiscal management.

Public Availability of Information. The public should be provided with full information on the past, current, and projected fiscal activity of government.

Open Budget Preparation, Execution, and Reporting. Budget documentation should specify fiscal policy objectives, the macroeconomic framework, the policy basis for the budget, and identifiable major fiscal risks.

—Budget estimates should be classified and presented in a way that facilitates policy analysis and promotes accountability.

—Procedures for the execution and monitoring of approved expenditures should be clearly specified.

—Fiscal reporting should be timely, comprehensive, and reliable, and should identify deviations from the budget.

Independent Assurances of Integrity. The integrity of fiscal information should be subjected to public and independent scrutiny.

Source: IMF (1998).

Governance and Corruption Survey Diagnostic Tools Can Enhance Transparency Efforts

The collection, analysis, and dissemination of country-specific data on corruption are altering the policy dialogue on corruption and empowering civil society through collective action.

The first set of in-depth governance and corruption diagnostic surveys of public officials, firms, and citizens was carried out in Albania, Georgia, and Latvia. More recently, surveys have been conducted in other countries, and cross-country correlations of institutional and other variables have significantly expanded our understanding of corruption and its causes, particularly its institutional roots. These surveys, designed to complement other empirical approaches, ask various key stakeholders detailed questions about the costs and private returns of misgovernance and corruption.[20] The questionnaires survey *citizens* (service delivery users), *enterprises*, and, using a new instrument developed more recently, *public officials*. These studies demonstrate that respondents are willing to discuss agency-specific corruption with remarkable candor, and firms also volunteer detailed information about bribery and misgovernance that they and their peers are engaged in. Survey respondents report on embezzlement of public funds, theft of state property, bribery to shorten processing time, bribery to obtain monopoly power, and bribery in procurement, banking, and related activities. Detailed statistics collected on the frequency and cost of bribes paid by enterprises to regulators in different agencies can be used to sequence reforms. A significant share of petty bribes is paid to officials to avoid taxes, customs duties, and other liabilities to the state, resulting in lost revenues in many settings.[21]

A major virtue of these diagnostics is that they permit a systemwide, in-depth assessment of the governance and corruption vulnerabilities across major institutions in a country. The reform priorities identified after each survey is completed vary significantly from country to country, reinforcing the need to localize knowledge with the aid of these empirical tools. The multidimensional and complex nature of public governance and its public-financial sector links are such that a template of reforms applied uniformly to all countries is unlikely to bear fruit. A more effective strategy is to use common rigorous approaches and diagnostic tools to study the incentive structures and systems in each country and to then design reforms that address the specific circumstances. Furthermore, by diagnosing in depth with empirical tools the challenge within a country, this approach permits distancing from the common pitfall of individualizing the challenge of governance. Indeed most often misgovernance and corruption are too pervasive and systemic to disappear with the dismissal of a few individuals. To bear fruit, the strategy formulation approach needs to be more systemic,

---

20. This section on survey diagnostics is an abridged version of PREM Note 7, "New Frontiers for Diagnosing and Combating Corruption," October 1998. For additional results of these in-depth diagnostics, refer to the materials on the new governance diagnostic tools carried out by the World Bank Institute, at (www.worldbank.org/wbi/governance/tools.htm).

21. When the results from these diagnostics were presented in workshops to members of the business community and civil society, the policy debate abruptly changed from vague, unsubstantiated, and personal accusations to one focused on empirical evidence and systemic weaknesses.

focusing on transparency and incentive reforms to enhance prevention, rather than simply enforcing rules, passing laws, or getting rid of a few individuals.

Another challenge is to sustain the reform effort with broad-based participation involving all government branches, civil society, financial sector institutions, and the business community. Data collection needs to be institutionalized, so that statistics on agency-specific corruption can be tabulated annually. Broad dissemination of the statistics can further empower stakeholders to use this information to continue the reform. The next frontier is to deepen the design of agency-specific surveys and other empirical tools to complement existing methods, and to institutionalize these diagnostic mechanisms into periodic monitoring tools useful for quick response and policymaking by governments.

The use of enterprise surveys for specific areas of assessing financial sector development can also have payoffs. Kaufmann, Mehrez, and Schmukler investigate whether resident enterprise managers have an informational advantage about the countries they work on.[22] Methodologies to extract enterprise survey–based information available to resident managers (but unknown to investors and forecasters) are presented. The hypothesis that enterprise managers have an informational advantage is then tested by means of the Global Competitiveness Survey, a firm-based, cross-country data set. The findings suggest that local managers do have valuable private information about the country in which they reside that is often not captured by investors or analysts. Information provided by local managers' survey responses improves conventional estimates of future financial volatility and changes in the exchange rate. Such conventional estimates are typically based on economic fundamentals, interest rate differentials and rating decisions, and assessments by credit rating agency analysts, which often are found to be incomplete. Thus, using information gathered through surveys of multiple resident enterprises can be a transparency-enhancing measure that would improve information flows to the markets. Such survey information could complement the conventionally available information, given that local enterprise managers can also have incomplete information for predicting financial or exchange rate developments.

22. Kaufmann, Mehrez, and Schmukler (2002).

Transparency and External Accountability through Voice and Participation

Misgovernance and corruption can yield to knowledge and an informed citizenry and economic agents—investors, bankers, firms, and consumers. Indeed, a key pillar of good governance is empowering civil society and economic agents by providing more rigorous and reliable information. Transparency is important in this context. Research shows that the greater the participation of private agents in ownership and management, the better the service performance. Empirical research with the thousands of projects financed by the World Bank also shows that participation and civil liberties are vital for improved performance of government projects in emerging markets. The obvious challenge is finding the means of doing so. Numerous experiences have demonstrated that listening to the voice of stakeholders can be a significant factor in meeting this challenge. For example, in Mendoza, Argentina, citizens have participated in drafting transparent rules governing public procurement, and more recently similar reforms have been taking place in Buenos Aires. A number of localities throughout the world, notably the city of Porto Alegre, Brazil, have embraced a similar participatory approach to drafting the public budget. As part of its pioneering system of participatory budgeting, Porto Alegre holds assemblies where expenditure priorities are discussed for education, health, transport development, taxation, city organization, and urban development.

Conclusions

The recognition that public governance matters significantly for the health of the financial sector is gradually becoming more accepted—even if the corrupt mechanisms by which the financial sector is undermined are still underappreciated. Yet to be addressed, however, is the reverse link: how financial sector corporations use their powerful influence and strategies to shape or undermine public governance for finance.

The recognition of the complex two-way interplay between the private and public sector in shaping the governance environment for finance points to the importance of systemwide reforms focused on a strategy that uses transparency, incentives, and prevention to improve governance and reduce corruption in this field. This approach is likely to be far more effective in dealing with the institutional realities that exist in many emerging countries than is the excessive focus on narrow internal guidelines and regulation by fiat that so often prevails. The paper highlights the usefulness of new empirical diagnostic tools for improving transparency, flagging vulnerabilities before a crisis, and guiding priorities for action.

Governance needs to take center stage in institution-building strategies, and the particular vested interests held by influential groups, particularly the financial sector, must also be recognized. In this approach, transparency-related mechanisms and a proper set of institutional incentives are the key to preventing corruption. Indeed, prevention mechanisms ought to play at least as important a role as traditional legal or individualized enforcement initiatives. The latter, in the absence of a comprehensive system of prevention, can be extremely costly and often ineffective, particularly in settings with low levels of institutional sophistication or political will.

Experience and analysis begins to show the necessary components of an effective transparency, incentives, and prevention (TIP) strategy for improving governance. These are:

—*Transparent information and knowledge,* including rigorous data, diagnostic and empirical analysis and monitoring, and improved disclosure and access standards for financial, budgetary, and related data;

—A proper set of institutional *incentives for prevention,* including a meritocracy within institutions, transparent monitoring and disclosure mechanisms, civil service reforms, and enhanced external accountability mechanisms;

—Strengthened *leadership through mechanisms designed to instill and reward integrity;* and

—*Collective action* through a systematic participatory and consensus-building approach, with key stakeholders in society benefiting from the new information and transparency tools, enhancing external accountability, and thus assisting in prevention.

Beyond the natural role that governments need to play to improve governance, the roles and responsibilities of the financial and corporate sector are also important, both in their domestic and international dimensions. As recent survey results indicated, corporate responsibility (or lack thereof) can have an important impact on the strategies the corporate sector (including foreign direct investors and multinationals) opts to carry out, which may either improve or undermine governance. The corporate sector, abroad and domestically, has an active role to play in improving overall governance.

Participation and voice are vital in increasing transparency, providing for the necessary external accountability mechanisms and thus for the checks and balances that even the best internal accountability rules and systems within government cannot fulfill completely. Transparency-enhancing mechanisms involving a multitude of stakeholders throughout society can be thought as creating millions of "auditors." Indeed, such external accountability mechanisms, which often also include very activist media involvement, can be powerful factors supporting a change in the incentive structure of institutions that are monitored. For the enterprise sector, the public is increasingly applying pro-transparency pressure on publicly listed firms, demanding better information on the true state of the financial accounts of enterprises in the wake of costly financial scandals in the United States. Shareholders are quickly divesting from institutions with uncertain or nontransparent accounts, increasingly applying market pressures. Finally, the media, shareholders, and the public are also beginning to question the influence-peddling links between certain influential segments of the corporate sector and the political-legislative arena, probing further than in the past into the way corporations may have adversely influenced the legal and regulatory regimes affecting them. Institutionalizing the gathering and dissemination of information fully exposing these links between the private sector and public policy will be a major step toward providing the transparency needed for good governance anywhere.

Appendix Table 4-1. *Determinants of Quality of Financial Markets as Rated by Firms*

	Dependent variable: Quality of financial market					
Independent variables	*1*	*2*	*3*	*4*	*5*	*6*
Constant	3.76 (38.58***)	−0.61 (−0.66)	−0.67 (−0.71)	−0.72 (−0.76)	−1.10 (−1.07)	−1.12 (−1.08)
Overall control of corruption	0.99 (11.01***)	0.32 1.94*	0.34 (1.94*)	0.38 (2.02**)	0.50 (2.15**)	0.53 (2.20**)
Overall regulatory quality (economy-wide)			−0.06 (−0.36)	−0.04 (−0.21)	−0.03 (−0.17)	−0.01 (−0.06)
Overall rule of law					−0.28 (−1.05)	−0.27 (−0.98)
Voice and accountability				−0.10 (−0.62)		−0.09 (−0.51)
GDP per capita (log)		0.55 (4.77***)	0.56 (4.69***)	0.57 (4.71***)	0.62 (4.71***)	0.62 (4.71***)
Number of observations	81	81	81	81	81	81
Adjusted R^2	0.61	0.69	0.68	0.68	0.68	0.68

Source: Global Competitiveness Survey (2001).

Note: GDP (gross domestic product) per capita (expressed in purchasing power parity terms) is computed in logarithms; all other control variables are aggregate, economywide measures. All dependent variables reflect the view of the enterprise sector. Figures in parentheses are *t* statistics.

*** Indicates significance at 99 percent confidence interval.

** Indicates significance at 95 percent confidence interval.

* Indicates significance at 90 percent confidence interval.

Appendix Table 4-2. *Determinants of Soundness of Banks as Rated by Firms*

Independent variable	\multicolumn{10}{c}{Dependent variable: Soundness of banks}									
	1	2	3	4	5	6	7	8	9	10
Constant	4.70 (41.87***)	3.58 (2.99***)	3.25 (2.68***)	3.23 (2.64***)	3.74 (2.83***)	3.73 (2.80***)	−0.49 (−0.49)	2.08 (1.64*)	2.40 (1.90*)	2.45 (1.96**)
Overall control of public corruption	0.99 (9.48***)	0.81 (3.83***)	0.92 (4.12***)	0.94 (3.85***)	0.74 (2.48**)	0.76 (2.46**)		0.75 (3.00***)	0.67 (2.74***)	0.63 (2.86***)
Bribery in banking loans							0.71 (3.42***)	0.52 (−2.48**)	0.51 (2.41**)	0.51 (2.44**)
Overall regulatory quality			−0.34 (−1.45)	−0.33 (−1.37)	−0.38 (−1.59)	−0.37 (−1.49)	−0.20 (−0.85)	−0.35 (−1.49)		
Rule of law					0.33 (0.95)	0.34 (0.97)				
Voice and accountability				−0.04 (−0.18)		−0.06 (−0.29)	0.22 (1.08)	−0.02 (−0.09)	−0.09 (−0.42)	
GDP per capita		0.14 (0.94)	0.19 (1.27)	0.20 (1.27)	0.13 (0.77)	0.13 (0.78)	0.23 (1.41)	0.03 (0.18)	−0.01 (−0.09)	−0.03 (−0.16)
Number of observations	81	81	81	81	81	81	81	81	81	81
Adjusted R^2	0.53	0.53	0.53	0.53	0.53	0.53	0.51	0.56	0.55	0.55

Source: Global Competitiveness Survey (2001).

Note: GDP (gross domestic product) per capita (expressed in purchasing power parity terms) is computed in logarithms; all other control variables are aggregate, economywide measures. All dependent variables reflect the view of the enterprise sector. Figures in parentheses are *t* statistics.

*** Indicates significance at 99 percent confidence interval.

** Indicates significance at 95 percent confidence interval.

* Indicates significance at 90 percent confidence interval.

Appendix Table 4-3. *Determinants of Financial Regulatory Quality as Rated by Firms*

Determinants	Dependent variable: Financial regulatory quality				
	1	2	3	4	5
Constant	4.45 (51.76***)	2.22 (2.50**)	2.29 (2.52**)	2.20 (2.42**)	2.66 (2.70***)
Control of corruption	0.86 (10.84***)	0.52 (3.29***)	0.49 (2.94***)	0.58 (3.19***)	0.41 (1.81*)
Overall regulatory quality			0.07 (0.40)	0.12 (0.66)	0.09 (0.48)
Rule of law					0.31 (1.20)
Voice and accountability				−0.20 (−1.22)	−0.22 (−1.36)
GDP per capita		0.28 (2.53**)	0.27 (2.34**)	0.29 (2.48**)	0.23 (1.80*)
Number of observations	81	81	81	81	81
Adjusted R^2	0.59	0.62	0.61	0.62	0.62

Source: Global Competitiveness Survey (2001).

Note: GDP (gross domestic product) per capita (expressed in purchasing power parity terms) is computed in logarithms; all other control variables are aggregate, economywide measures. All dependent variables reflect the view of the enterprise sector. Figures in parentheses are t statistics.

*** Indicates significance at 99 percent confidence interval.

** Indicates significance at 95 percent confidence interval.

* Indicates significance at 90 percent confidence interval.

Appendix Table 4-4. *Determinants of Finance as an Obstacle to Firms as Rated by Firms*

Independent variables	Dependent Variable: Finance as obstacle to firms					
	1	2	3	4	5	6
Constant	2.77 (80.46***)	2.66 (8.69***)	2.61 (8.34***)	2.69 (8.19***)	2.57 (8.36***)	2.68 (8.22***)
Control of corruption	−0.35 (−9.16***)	−0.37 (−5.90***)	−0.38 (−4.03***)	−0.38 (−3.98***)	−0.33 (−4.99***)	−0.35 (−5.09***)
Regulatory quality			−0.11 (−1.75*)	−0.12 (−1.87*)	−0.10 (−1.60)	−0.11 (−1.82*)
Rule of law			0.08 (0.71)	0.05 (0.48)		
Voice and accountability				0.06 (0.81)		0.07 (0.97)
GDP per capita		0.01 (0.37)	0.02 (0.58)	0.01 (0.28)	0.03 (0.70)	0.01 (0.31)
Number of observations	81	81	81	81	81	81
Adjusted R^2	0.51	0.50	0.51	0.51	0.51	0.51

Source: World Business Environment Survey (2000) (info.worldbank.org/governance/beeps/).

Note: GDP (gross domestic product) per capita (expressed in purchasing power parity terms) is computed in logarithms; all other control variables are aggregate, economywide measures. The dependent variable reflects the view of the enterprise sector. Figures in parentheses are t statistics.

*** Indicates significance at 99 percent confidence interval.

* Indicates significance at 90 percent confidence interval.

Glossary of Variables in Appendix Tables 4-1–4-4

Dependent Variables

"Quality of Financial Markets": The level of sophistication of financial markets is [1: lower - . . . - 7 higher than international standards].

"Soundness of Banks": Banks in your country are: [1: insolvent - . . . - 7: healthy].

"Quality of Financial Regulations": Regulations and supervision of financial institutions are: [1: inadequate - . . . - 7: among the world's most stringent].

"Financing as Obstacle": "Can you tell me how problematic is 'financing' for the operation and growth of your business?" [1: No Obstacle - . . . - 4: Major Obstacle].

Independent Variables

"Control of Corruption," "Regulatory Quality," "Rule of Law," and "Voice and Accountability" are aggregate, economywide indicators drawn from Kaufmann, Kraay, and Zoido-Lobatón (info.worldbank.org/governance/kkz/).

"Bribery in Loans": "How commonly do firms in your industry give irregular extra payments or bribes connected with loan applications?" [1: common - . . . .- 7: never].

"GDP per capita" is expressed in Purchasing Power Parity terms and was introduced in regressions in logs. Source: Summers and Heston Penn World Table, available at http://pwt.econ.upenn.edu (Center for International Comparisons, University of Pennsylvania, Philadelphia).

References

Acemoglu, Daron, Simon Johnson, and James A. Robinson. 2001. "The Colonial Origins of Comparative Development: An Empirical Investigation." *American Economic Review* 91 (5): 1369–1401.

Batra, Geeta, Daniel Kaufmann, and Andrew H. W. Stone. 2002. "Voices of the Firms 2000: Investment Climate and Governance Findings of the World Business Environment Survey (WBES)." (www.worldbank.org/wbi/governance/pubs/voicesfirms.htm).

Carmichael, Jeffrey, and Daniel Kaufmann. 2001. "Public Sector Governance and the Finance Sector." Paper prepared for the World Bank-International Monetary Fund-Federal Reserve Board Conference on Policy Challenges for the Financial Sector in the Context of Globalization. Washington.

Hellman, Joel, Geraint Jones, and Daniel Kaufmann. 2001. "Seize the State, Seize the Day: State Capture, Corruption and Influence in Transition." Policy Research Working Paper 2444, World Bank, Washington; forthcoming in *Journal of Comparative Economics* (2002) (www.worldbank.org/wbi/governance/pubs/seizestate.htm).

International Monetary Fund. 2002. *Manual on Fiscal Transparency*. Washington.

Kaufmann, Daniel, Aart Kraay, and Pablo Zoido-Lobatón. 1999a. "Aggregating Governance Indicators." Policy Research Department Working Paper 2195. World Bank, Washington (www.worldbank.org/wbi/governance/pubs/aggindicators.htm).

———. 1999b. "Governance Matters." Policy Research Department Working Paper 2196. World Bank, Washington (www.worldbank.org/wbi/governance/pubs/govmatters.htm).

———. 2002. "Governance Matters II—Updated Indicators for 2000/01." Policy Research Department Working Paper 2772. World Bank, Washington (www.worldbank.org/wbi/governance/pubs/govmatters2001.htm).

Kaufmann, Daniel, and Aart Kraay. 2002. "Growth without Governance." *Economía* 3(1).

Kaufmann, Daniel, Gil Mehrez, and Sergio Schmukler. 2000. "Predicting Currency Crises: Do Resident Firms Have an Informational Advantage?" Policy Research Working Paper 2259. World Bank, Washington, D.C. (www.worldbank.org/wbi/governance/pubs/currencyflux.htm).

Knack, Stephen, and Philip Keefer. 1997. "Does Social Capital Have an Economic Payoff? A Cross-Country Investigation." *Quarterly Journal of Economics* 112 (4): 1251–88.

Laffont, Jean-Jacques, and Jean Tirole. 1991. "The Politics of Government Decision Making: A Theory of Regulatory Capture." *Quarterly Journal of Economics* 106: 1089–127.

Mauro, Paulo. 1995. "Corruption and Growth." *Quarterly Journal of Economics* 110 (3): 681–713.

———. 1996. "The Effects of Corruption on Growth, Investment, and Government Expenditure." Working Paper WP/96/98. International Monetary Fund, Washington.

Mehrez, Gil, and Daniel Kaufmann. 1999. "Transparency, Liberalization and Financial Crises." Policy Research Working Paper 2286. World Bank, Washington. (www. worldbank.org/wbi/governance/pubs/translib.htm).

Vishwanath, Tara, and Daniel Kaufmann. 2001. "Toward Transparency: New Approaches and Their Application to Financial Markets." *World Bank Research Observer* 16:41–57.

Wei, Shang-Jin. 2000. "How Taxing Is Corruption on International Investors?" *Review of Economics and Statistics* 82 (1): 1–11.

World Bank. 1997. *World Development Report: The State in the Changing World.* Oxford University Press.

———. 2000. *The Quality of Growth.* Oxford University Press.

World Economic Forum and Harvard University. 2001. *The Global Competitiveness Report 2001.* Oxford University Press.

PART II

Financial Sector Governance and the Role of the Public Sector

JEFFREY CARMICHAEL 5

Public Sector
Governance and the
Finance Sector

IN THE WAKE of the drive toward privatization of state-owned assets in central Europe and financial disruptions in other emerging market countries, a growing focus of financial sector reform programs sponsored by international organizations has been the need to improve corporate governance not only within the financial sector, but throughout the economy. This recognition of the importance of corporate governance has also extended to industrial countries, as reflected in the adoption by the OECD (Organization for Economic Cooperation and Development) in 1999 of its Principles of Corporate Governance.

This paper focuses on the less popular and considerably more sensitive parallel need for international improvements in public sector governance. Until very recently public sector governance has been regarded as off limits for international organizations; advising governments how their private sectors should behave in business is one thing, but advising them how they should conduct the business of government has been viewed as an unacceptable transgression of national sovereignty. Since the Asian financial crisis, however, the International Monetary Fund has begun to include transparency and anticorruption measures as part of its loan conditionality. Not

I would like to thank Michael Pomerleano and Dani Kaufmann of the World Bank and V. Sundararajan of the IMF for helpful comments on an earlier draft of this work.

unexpectedly, this testing of the boundaries of sovereignty has attracted considerable criticism, with governments charging that the IMF is overstepping its mandate and possibly even compounding the problems of the recipient countries.

This paper explores the ways in which the public sector participates in and affects behavior in the finance sector. It also explores the implications of poor public sector governance for the performance of the finance sector. The work draws on and extends a small but growing and innovative literature that has been emerging in the past few years, mostly from the World Bank and the Brookings Institution, on public sector governance. This paper is narrower than its predecessors in that it focuses largely on issues related to the finance sector.

Some Definitions

According to the OECD, corporate governance is "the system by which business corporations are directed and controlled."[1] It involves the "set of relationships between a company's management, its board, its shareholders and other stakeholders. Corporate governance also provides the structure through which the objectives of the company are set, and the means of attaining those objectives and monitoring performance are determined."[2] In essence, corporate governance is about the way in which a company proposes to reconcile the conflicting interests of its various stakeholders and the structures it puts in place to ensure that these objectives are met; that is, it encompasses both policy and practice.

While the concept of corporate governance is reasonably precise, in practice it covers a very wide range of issues from the way in which a company distributes rights and responsibilities among different participants (board, management, and so forth) to the way in which a company's culture is established and maintained.[3]

No such generally agreed definition exists for the concept of public sector governance. Wei provides a good starting point when he defines public

1. OECD (2001, p. 1).
2. OECD (1999, p. 2).
3. This breadth of coverage is reflected in the fact that at the recent OECD regional roundtable discussions of corporate governance, the Russian roundtable focused on issues related to minority shareholders, while the Asian roundtable focused on disclosure. See Nestor (2001, p. 12).

governance as "the set of institutions and structures that define how public goods (or public "bads") are created and delivered to citizens and the private sector and how public policies are made."[4] For the purposes of this paper, however, I prefer the more cumbersome, but also more general definition of Kaufmann, Kraay, and Zoido-Lobaton, namely:

> the traditions and institutions that determine how authority is exercised in a particular country. This includes (1) the process by which governments are selected, held accountable, monitored, and replaced; (2) the capacity of governments to manage resources efficiently and to formulate, implement, and enforce sound policies and regulations; and (3) the respect of citizens and the state for the institutions that govern economic and social interactions among them.[5]

An important aspect of both definitions, which is retained in this paper, is their implicit extension of the public sector to cover not only the government, but also its appointed bureaucracy and agents, including regulators.

The Case for Good Governance: The Corporate Parallel

The need for good public sector governance parallels very closely the case for good corporate governance. The parallel is worth developing.

Source of the Corporate Governance Problem

The need for good corporate governance arises from three sources. The first is widely known as the principal-agent problem.[6] Drawing on the concepts in the principal-agent literature, I label the second source the principal-principal problem and the third the principal-stakeholder problem.

The essence of the principal-agent problem is the inherent conflict that arises whenever the owners of a business (the principals) are separate from the managers (the agents). The agents, as the primary decisionmakers, have an incentive to manage the business to maximize their own personal welfare

---

4. Wei (2001b, p. 1).
5. Kaufmann, Kraay, and Zoido-Lobatón (2000, p. 10).
6. See Jensen and Meckling (1976).

rather than that of the principals by whom they are employed. This conflict was evident in the corporate excesses of the international financial markets in the late 1980s and early 1990s, which saw many corporate executives live the life-styles of feudal barons, while the companies they ran suffered losses.

The principal-principal problem arises from the conflicting interests that can arise among different groups of principals. The best understood of these is the conflict between majority and minority shareholders. This problem has been common among central European countries following the rush to privatize and list previously publicly owned companies. Romania, for example, is currently facing a principal-principal problem associated with an attempt by some majority shareholders to control strategic industries for their own benefit by delisting and thereby disenfranchising minority shareholders. Other aspects of the principal-principal problem relate to the rights of shareholders in voting, in receiving information, and in liquidation.

The principal-stakeholder problem arises from the conflicting interests of the owners and other participants in the system. The traditional narrow concept of corporate governance usually limits outside stakeholders to creditors and employees. However, to the extent that a firm's behavior can affect the community much more widely through its impact on other firms, on the environment, and on society generally through the ethics of its business practices, a broader definition of stakeholders would include all those affected by a firm's behavior. The two most common forms of principal-stakeholder conflict that arise in this respect are anticompetitive behavior and market misconduct. It is an unfortunate (though undeniable) characteristic of human nature that left to their own devices, many individuals and firms will collude, exploit market power, misrepresent the products and services they sell, conceal information, and even defraud in their business transactions. These are all forms of market failure and underline the fact that the capitalist system, based on the primacy of market forces, provides efficient outcomes only when markets are not subject to market failure.

Whereas the principal-agent and principal-principal problems involve resolving conflicting interests within the firm, the principal-stakeholder problem is essentially about resolving conflicts between the interests of the firm and those of external parties. Since corporate governance is largely about the way in which firms deal with these conflicts, I refer to these as internal governance problems and external governance problems, respectively.

The Cost of Poor Corporate Governance

OECD's adoption of principles of good governance reflects, among other things, the perception that good corporate governance (both internal and external) has some public good characteristics.

Resolution of the principal-agent problem encourages firms to use resources more efficiently in the pursuit of profit maximization. Without such resolution, management can be tempted to squander corporate resources in the pursuit of its own interests. The result is not only inefficiency but also a misallocation of capital.

Resolution of the principal-principal problem is even more important. As noted by the preamble to the OECD principles, "the degree to which corporations observe basic principles of good corporate governance is an increasingly important factor for investment decisions. . . . If countries are to reap the full benefits of the global capital market, and if they are to attract long-term 'patient' capital, corporate governance arrangements must be credible and well understood across borders."[7]

The importance of good corporate governance has been highlighted by the Asian crisis. The inability of banks to perfect collateral and to pursue insolvent firms in courts of law has been a major hurdle in restoring health to the troubled banking systems in a number of Asian countries. The opacity of Korean corporations such as Daewoo, for example, denied lending institutions as well as investors the opportunity to make informed financial decisions. Corporate governance within financial institutions has also been recognized as a major hurdle in the attempts to restructure banks.

Resolution of the principal-stakeholder problem is also important, especially with respect to anticompetitive behavior and market misconduct. Abuse of monopoly power leads to overpricing and underprovision of goods and services and is antithetical to efficiency and innovation. Market misconduct is equally destructive. A basic tenet of efficient markets requires that participants have confidence in the ability of the market to price efficiently and to deliver fair value.

Ultimately, good corporate governance is a prerequisite for the establishment of deep, efficient markets for goods, services, and capital, and for the long-run efficient allocation of capital.

7. OECD (1999, p. 3).

Addressing Corporate Governance Problems

The main response to the principal-agent problem has been to strengthen internal corporate governance through better incentive structures, improved disclosure, and greater accountability. As noted by the OECD, "good corporate governance should provide proper incentives for the board and management to pursue objectives that are in the interests of the company and shareholders."[8] The essence of "proper incentives" is the establishment of incentive-compatible contracts, designed to better align the interests of the two parties. The widespread adoption during the 1990s of the practice of remunerating management with stock options, for example, was one way of more closely aligning the performance rewards received by agents with the rewards received by shareholders.

The second aspect of internal corporate governance directed at the principal-agent problem has been greater accountability and disclosure. Disclosure is fundamental to good governance. The more transparent the actions and decisions of management are, the greater the opportunity for shareholders to assess the motives behind those actions and the more difficult it becomes for management to pursue its own interests in secret. Accountability is the other side of the coin. Whereas transparency provides shareholders with the information needed to assess the actions of management, accountability ensures that managers are responsible for their actions.

Although the principal-principal problem is essentially a problem internal to the corporation, it is less easily resolved internally than the principal-agent problem. Weaker groups of principals have no leverage over stronger groups of principals to exert their rights. The importance of this problem is reflected in the fact that it is the primary focus of the OECD principles. The first principle, for example, deals with the rights of shareholders, while the second deals with their equitable treatment. The fifth principle deals with the responsibilities of the board (a special subgroup of the principals) to shareholders. The fact that the problem is not easily resolved internally means that external intervention is required, through regulation, to establish governance rules and to enforce them.

Regulations are simply rules of behavior. In the same way that societies establish rules of social behaviour to reconcile the conflicting rights and interests of individuals in their social interactions, societies also establish rules of business behavior to reconcile the conflicting rights and interests of

8. OECD (1999, p. 2).

individuals and corporations in their business interactions. Regulations that address the principal-principal problem include stock exchange rules on the rights of minority shareholders and the general infrastructure of corporate regulations and courts dealing with shareholder rights and responsibilities.

The main response to the principal-stakeholder problem has also been through regulation. As was the case with weaker groups of principals, outside stakeholders have no leverage over the firm to resolve their conflicts. Consequently, the authority of an external party is required to correct the market failure that might otherwise occur. Competition regulation, for example, involves the design of rules to limit market abuse through collusion or exploitation of monopoly power. Market conduct regulation involves the design of rules to reduce the likelihood of insider trading, market manipulation, misrepresentation, and fraud. As with most forms of regulation, competition and market conduct regulation are implemented primarily through laws enacted by the public sector that make the undesirable activities illegal, backed up by a regulator with the power to prosecute those who break the laws.

While a superficial consideration of the theory might suggest that the resolution of internal conflicts should be left largely to the firm itself, with external conflicts left to a regulator, the demarcation in practice between self-regulation and official regulation is much less clear cut and has shifted significantly in recent years. While it should be in the interests of both principals and agents to develop a good system of internal governance to resolve internal conflicts of interest, too few firms have achieved this without external pressure. Public disclosure, in particular, is an area where regulatory intervention is needed, if only for consistency. The formation of the OECD task force on corporate governance, and the subsequent adoption of the principles, was implicit acknowledgment of the failure of many firms to develop good corporate governance on their own. The net effect of these developments has been to shift the primary responsibility for imposing good corporate governance (both internal and external) away from the domain of the individual firm and into the bailiwick of regulators.

The Source of the Public Sector Governance Problem

Following the corporate sector analogy (at least for a multiparty democracy), the principals in the public sector are the supporters of the political party in power, while the external stakeholders are the supporters of the opposition parties. The principals elect the government of the day as their board to represent their interests, and the government appoints a bureaucracy as its agent to manage the day-to-day operations of the public sector.

In an almost exact parallel of the corporate situation, the public sector involves a principal-agent problem, a principal-principal problem, and a principal-stakeholder problem. The problems, however, are more complex and more difficult to resolve, and the costs of poor public sector governance are potentially much greater than those of poor corporate governance.

The first level of complexity relates to the difficulty of measuring and therefore monitoring the principal-agent problem. The extent of the principal-agent problem in the corporate context is measurable, at least to a first approximation. Corporate profitability and its scaling to a rate of return on capital invested provides a metric against which the performance of management can be measured, if not perfectly, at least with a reasonable degree of consistency across firms and across time. The impact of resources wasted by management in pursuing its own interests should be reflected in this measure. The greater the transparency, the more readily shareholders will be able to detect mismanagement. No such single metric exists for the public sector.

The output of the public sector is multifaceted and includes economic growth, income distribution, poverty and literacy levels, and inflation. In many areas of the bureaucracy, output consists largely of noncompetitive services. The absence of a usable metric for the bureaucracy is reflected in the fact that most measures of its contribution to national product are based on the cost of services provided.

The true cost of the public sector, however, lies in its opportunity cost, rather than its input cost or any measure that might be devised of its output. For example, the cost (in terms of forgone production and human suffering) of poor advice from a department of finance that leads to recession bears no relationship to the cost of employing the bureaucrats in the department; the cost of an inadequately staffed and funded regulatory agency that fails to prevent an impending financial crisis imposes costs on the system far in excess of the agency's budget; the cost of a poorly conceived guarantee of deposits or insurance policies creates a contingent liability that is rarely reflected fully in the government's budget.

To add to the problem, the outputs of the public sector are mostly macroeconomic in nature, so that it is unusual for any one part of the bureaucracy to be identified with a single output. To use the corporate analogy, the various parts of the bureaucracy are like departments of a single firm, but without any simple way of disentangling their individual contributions to the multiplicity of outcomes.

The second level of complexity relates to the absence of a "market" for principals who wish to reduce or end their exposure. The principal-principal problem involves periodic disenfranchisement. Members of the majority party vote only periodically. Once elected, the government and its agents are largely unaccountable to the other principals until the next election. Unlike shareholders, citizens cannot "sell" their vote other than at election time. Like minority shareholders, they have little leverage, other than at election time, to force the government to alter its behavior. It is true that dissatisfied principals and other stakeholders can force political change without an election by taking to the streets, as was the case in the Philippines recently. The potential costs of such political upheavals, however, are great enough to limit their use to extreme circumstances.

Measurement of the government's performance is a little easier than that of the bureaucracy since, as the primary decisionmaker, the government is ultimately responsible for overall economic performance, although, again, opportunity cost is much more relevant than actual performance.

The principal-stakeholder problem is also more difficult to resolve in the case of the public sector. While governments are technically responsible for all members of the community, their first allegiance is to the supporters who elected them. Consequently, it is not uncommon for new governments to reverse the redistributive policies of their predecessors and for the community to view such maneuvers as an acceptable part of the political process.

In addition to these corporate sector parallels, the public sector governance problem is overlaid with additional problems that do not have immediate counterparts in corporate sector behavior. Arguably the most important of these is that governments and their bureaucracies possess temporary monopoly power. The department responsible for issuing importing licenses, for example, does not do so in competition with other departments; the department or agency responsible for managing the public pension scheme is unlikely to have to compete for funds; the immigration clerk issuing entry visas or work permits has an unequal bargaining position relative to the applicants.

The main effect of this temporary monopoly power is the opportunity it creates for corruption. Given the potentially significant economic impact of corruption, it is understandable that the literature on public sector governance has focused almost exclusively on corruption. Indeed, Wei, for example, equates poor public sector governance directly with corruption of public officials.[9]

While corruption is arguably the main manifestation of poor public sector governance, it is by no means the only one. Indeed, the definition of public sector governance suggested by Kaufmann, Kraay, and Zoido-Lobaton implies manifestations beyond corruption. The importance of this distinction is more apparent in the finance sector than in other sectors of the economy because of the pervasiveness of the public sector in finance.

Special Characteristics of the Finance Sector

The public sector participates in the finance sector of most economies to an extent and in ways that are quite unlike its role in other sectors of the economy. This participation typically includes some or all of the following:
   —as the regulator of financial institutions,
   —as an owner of financial institutions,
   —as a market participant,
   —as a fiduciary agent, and
   —through direct intervention in the operations of the market.

The Public Sector as a Financial Regulator

As noted earlier, the external governance of corporations has traditionally been assigned to regulators, and increasingly, so too are the responsibilities for internal corporate governance. The regulatory responsibilities associated with competition, market conduct, and internal corporate governance are, however, quite different in concept from those associated with many of the other regulators that are often found throughout the economy. Whereas most nongovernance regulators are associated with the implementation of social policies (immigration, business licensing, traffic control, and the like), the governance regulators derive their rationale for existence from the correction of market failure. Where the finance sector is most strongly differentiated from other sectors is in the nature and potential importance of the market failures involved.

9. Wei (2001b).

The least differentiated source of market failure is competition. As with all other markets, competition is critical for efficiency in the finance sector. Since the need for competition in financial markets is not unique, it is normal for countries to include regulation of competition in financial markets within a broader framework for competition regulation.

Regulation of market conduct, however, takes a much higher profile in financial markets than elsewhere. Market conduct regulation attempts to promote confidence in the efficiency and fairness of markets by ensuring that they are sound, orderly, and transparent. The fact that financial contracts are complex and involve time (financial claims are essentially promises to make specified payments at future dates under specified circumstances) means that the level of integrity and confidence required is considerably higher than is required, for example, in the markets for computer equipment or furniture. As a result, market integrity regulation in the finance sector goes well beyond that in other sectors and is typically delegated to a specialized regulatory agency (such as a securities and exchange commission).

But the sources of market failure in financial markets also go beyond anticompetitive behavior and market misconduct. In the finance sector information asymmetry and systemic contagion also cause market failure. Information asymmetry occurs where products or services are sufficiently complex that disclosure by itself is insufficient to enable consumers to make informed choices. Asymmetries arise where the knowledge of buyers and sellers of particular products or services can never be equally balanced regardless of how much information is disclosed. While this source of market failure is not unique to financial products (for example, it is also present in aviation and pharmaceuticals), the complexity of financial products and the often lengthy time horizons involved make this source of market failure much more common in financial markets than elsewhere.

The fourth main source of market failure in the finance sector is systemic contagion. It is a fundamental characteristic of parts of the financial system that they operate efficiently only to the extent that market participants have confidence in their ability to perform the roles for which they were designed. The more sophisticated the economy, the greater its dependence on financial promises and the greater its vulnerability to failure of the financial system to deliver against its promises. Systemic contagion arises where failure of one institution to honor its promises leads to a general panic, as individuals fear that similar promises made by other institutions may also be dishonored. A crisis occurs when contagion of this type leads to the distress or failure of otherwise sound institutions. Again, contagion is not unique to the finance sector, although its high leverage and heavy reliance on confidence make it by far the most vulnerable sector of the economy. The importance of finance to economic growth and the potential for financial failure to lead to systemic contagion introduces an "overarching externality" that warrants regulatory attention.

In summary, therefore, the finance sector is normally subject to much more intense and intrusive regulation than other sectors of the economy— for perfectly valid reasons. The problem posed by this need for extensive regulation is that it creates conflicts of interest for the public sector because the public sector has responsibility for setting the rules of behavior at the same time that it is a major participant in the system.

Public Sector Ownership of Financial Institutions

Historically governments have played a major role in financial markets as providers of financial services. It is quite common for governments to own banks and insurance companies, and in some cases ownership has extended to other financial institutions. In some instances governments have deliberately decided to participate in the financial system as a provider. In others, such as following financial crises, governments have become unintended owners as a consequence of public sector rescues of failed private sector financial institutions. The motives for deliberate ownership range from a lack of confidence in the security of private sector institutions to the use of public sector institutions for pursuing social policy objectives (such as providing housing for the underprivileged or business finance to certain geographical areas or demographic groups).

Whatever the motives, the presence of publicly owned financial institutions creates significant imbalances in the financial system. To the extent that government institutions carry a guarantee that is not extended, either implicitly or explicitly, to private sector institutions, the government institutions have a distinct competitive advantage over their private sector counterparts. That advantage may be compounded if the public sector institutions are not required to meet the same prudential requirements as their competitors.

The conflict of interest, however, extends beyond the guarantee. Governments are often privy to inside information about policy changes, including changes in strategic economic variables such as interest rates and exchange rates. Access to such information can create a major conflict of interest for governments that own financial institutions with exposures to that information.

Finally, public ownership of financial institutions increases the scope for corruption. Ministers and bureaucrats with significant private interests face great temptation to channel funds from public sector financial institutions to their private interests at preferential rates and without appropriate prudential screening. This temptation is increased greatly when their private interests are facing financial stress.

The Public Sector as a Market Participant

As financial markets grow in sophistication and depth, it is natural for governments to utilize the liquidity of these markets by issuing their own marketable securities. Not only is this natural in terms of diversifying their sources of funding, it is widely regarded as responsible to the extent that it provides an alternative to monetizing budget deficits. Even further, the existence of a deep and liquid market for government securities is often regarded as a prerequisite for the establishment of a corporate debt market.

Again, however, the public sector's role as an issuer and trader in its own securities brings it into potential conflict with its role as a regulator of market conduct. This conflict is diminished to an extent where the various roles are shared among different government agencies. However, in many countries, the central bank plays all the key roles as issuer, trader, and regulator of the government securities market. The potential for conflicts in these cases is significant.

The Public Sector as a Fiduciary Agent

As international enthusiasm grows for pension reform, governments are increasingly finding themselves acting as fiduciary agents for their citizens. This role carries with it an implied responsibility for the public sector manager to select an investment strategy that balances risk and return appropriately for the citizens on whose behalf he or she is investing. It also carries an implied responsibility to administer the funds with appropriate safeguards against operational risk, including fraud.

However, where the public sector retains direct control of the funds, there is a temptation to use those funds for political and even personal purposes. The temptation is increased by the fact that the timing of the payoff

to members of the funds is usually far removed in time, whereas the benefits from exploiting the available resources are usually available immediately.

Public Sector Intervention in Financial Markets

The most pervasive role that the public sector plays in the financial sector
of many countries is through direct intervention. At the broadest level,
governments are called on from time to time (usually in times of crisis) to
provide public guarantees to back the liabilities of privately owned financial institutions, such as banks and insurance companies. Alternatively,
they may be called on to provide liquidity support directly to troubled
institutions.

Less motivated by the need to restore confidence and stability, governments intervene in financial markets to the extent that they explicitly or
implicitly endorse certain financial institutions, products, or markets.
Many governments also intervene in the normal business of private sector
financial institutions to direct the flow of finance to particular groups or
sectors. This intervention ranges from the imposition of minimum financing entitlements for certain activities (such as housing finance or venture
capital finance) to requests by individual ministers for funds to be made
available to businesses owned or operated by their families or associates.

Implications of Public Sector Involvement in the Financial Sector

The roles that most governments and their agents play in financial markets
are far-reaching and, in some cases, reasonably justifiable. These roles
extend well beyond the roles that can be justified in other sectors of the
economy.

One significant problem is that by increasing the dependence of private
sector efficiency on its interaction with the public sector, each of these roles
increases the scope for corruption. Indeed, the potential for corruption is
probably higher in the finance sector than it is in any other sector of the
economy. Dealing with this incentive for corruption is a major challenge
for public sector governance.

The problems, however, extend beyond corruption because many of the
public sector involvements with the finance sector are legitimate and occur
even in countries with advanced financial systems and low levels of corruption. The ultimate challenge therefore is to define a set of manageable

public sector governance practices that constrain the role of the public sector to its legitimate roles, and that do so in a way that mitigates the inefficiencies and conflicts that might still arise, while minimizing the temptation for corruption.

The Cost of Poor Public Sector Governance

The cost of poor public sector governance is significant. As noted above, contributions to the literature on this topic to date have focused on the effects of poor governance on corruption and, through a series of creative studies, have established an empirical link between corruption and economic performance that is remarkably robust. In the finance sector, however, poor public sector governance can also introduce significant costs through its impact on public sector liabilities, inefficiencies, and resource misallocation.

The Cost of Corruption

The available measures of corruption are based largely on survey information. Although these surveys are subjective, and ordinal rather than cardinal, the picture they produce is remarkably consistent across the different measures and sources. Several innovative studies have used these various data series to test for the impact of corruption on various economic and social outcomes.[10] The main conclusions of this research are surprisingly robust.

—Corruption reduces domestic investment. For example, a ceteris paribus reduction from the high levels of corruption perceived in the Philippines and China to the low levels perceived in Hong Kong and Singapore would increase the ratio of investment to gross domestic product (GDP) by more than 6 percentage points.

—Corruption reduces foreign direct investment. Again, the high levels of corruption perceived in the Philippines and China are equivalent to a marginal tax increase of more than 20 percentage points compared with the low levels of corruption perceived in Hong Kong and Singapore.

10. See, for example, Fisman (1998); Gray and Kaufmann (1998); Johnson, Kaufmann, and Shleifer (1997); Kaufmann, Kraay, and Zoido-Lobatón (1999); Kaufmann and Wei (1999); Mauro (1997); Tanzi and Davoodi (1997); and Wei (2000, 2001a).

—Corruption reduces economic growth. A ceteris paribus reduction from the Philippines-China level to that of Hong Kong-Singapore would increase average annual growth of GDP by around 1.5 percentage points.

—Corruption reduces government revenue, increases the size of government expenditure, and tends to bias it away from operations, maintenance, and social infrastructure such as health and education, in favor of new equipment and physical infrastructure.

—Corruption reduces the effectiveness of financial regulation and leaves the system more vulnerable to currency crises.

—Corruption tends to increase the size of the underground economy.[11]

The most striking features of this growing research are the sizes of the estimated impacts of corruption and the extent to which they carry social as well as economic implications. For example, if corruption biases government spending away from health and education (because these areas of spending are less open to manipulation), then corruption indirectly affects birthrates, mortality rates, and literacy levels.

The Cost of Other Areas of Poor Governance in the Finance Sector

As noted earlier, the many areas of the financial sector in which the public sector may become involved all add to the scope for corruption. Even without the explicit motive of personal gain, however, government involvement, without adequate rules to govern that involvement, can impose substantial costs on the community. Some of the more important of these follow.

—Poorly designed financial regulation can expose the financial system to crisis and collapse.

—Where publicly owned financial institutions are not subject to the same prudential and conduct regulation as private sector firms, competition can be distorted, innovation can be retarded, and signs of financial distress in the public institutions are likely to be disguised until the problem becomes a crisis.

—Attempts to reform regulation and governance among private sector financial institutions are likely to fail unless publicly owned or managed financial institutions are subject to rules of behavior at least as stringent as those imposed on private firms.

11. The estimates of impact in each of the cases below are based on the numbers presented in the survey by Wei (2001a).

—A lack of transparency in public sector fiduciary relationships can be a source of long-term financial hardship and disappointed expectations.

—Since the attitude of the public sector with respect to its own market conduct conveys an important signal to private sector market participants, the way in which it handles conflicts of interest, privileged information, and disclosure has an important bearing on the integrity of private sector financial markets.

—Government intervention in financial markets carries a significant element of moral hazard.

The following discussion addresses just a few of these issues.

THE COST OF INADEQUATE FINANCIAL SECTOR TRANSPARENCY. Inadequate transparency has been suggested as one of the factors that contributed to the Asian financial crises. The lack of transparency clouded decisionmaking during the years preceding the crisis. Limited information about mutual guarantees and the true value of firms and banks and extensive reliance on related-party transactions masked poor investments. Many investors believed that governments would stand behind firms related to powerful families and politicians and relied on this implicit guarantee as a substitute for due diligence. Once the crisis began, poor transparency made it difficult for investors to distinguish between firms and banks that were healthy and those that were not. Consequently, many investors abandoned all institutions, thereby precipitating bank runs and destabilizing the economies.

The limited empirical research available from this period suggests that when financial liberalization takes place in an environment where transparency is absent, a financial crisis is more likely.[12]

In an interesting line of research, Caprio and others devised a scoring system to evaluate the role of information and incentives in financial crises.[13] They developed a ranking system for the regulatory systems of a dozen East Asian and Latin American countries. Their ranking of transparency is based on a composite measure of whether bank ratings are required, the number of top ten banks with ratings from international rating firms, and an index of corruption. Their transparency rankings are broadly consistent with the overall ranking of regulatory environments. Not surprisingly, they find that the crisis-hit Asian economies have the

12. See Mehrez and Kaufmann (1999).
13. Caprio and Kligebiel (1996).

lowest overall scores. Singapore, the highest-scoring country in the sample, overall and in terms of transparency, was the least affected by the crisis.

Further evidence on the possible impact of poor transparency on the Asian crisis is provided by a 1998 United Nations Conference on Trade and Development study, which reviewed the accounting practices of financial institutions in five East Asian countries (Indonesia, Korea, Malaysia, Philippines, and Thailand).[14] The study assessed the extent to which actual accounting practices deviated from international accounting practices in areas including related-party-transactions, foreign currency debt, derivative instruments, and contingent liabilities. The findings suggested that the five countries did not follow International Accounting Standards (IAS) in the mentioned categories and that this failure may have helped trigger the financial crisis to the extent that users of the accounting information were misled and unable to take precautionary action in a timely fashion.

The study included the following telling findings.

—Only a third of the total number of companies sampled disclosed information about related-party borrowing and lending.

—Although 60 percent of the sample revealed foreign currency debt in local currency, only 19 percent disclosed foreign currency translation gains and losses, according to IAS.

—Levels of loan loss provisions were inappropriate to the risks involved.

—More than 80 percent of those companies that reported the use of derivative instruments did not disclose either the amount of interest and losses relating to derivatives or the terms, conditions, and policies regarding these instruments.

—Fewer than half the surveyed firms recognized contingent liabilities, and even fewer disclosed the amount of such liabilities.

While the evidence to hand is not definitive, it is consistent with empirical work in developed countries that finds a share price premium for private sector corporations that list in jurisdictions that impose rigorous standards of transparency and governance. In short, good governance appears to add value.

THE COST OF INADEQUATE PRUDENTIAL REGULATION. The cost of poor regulation in the financial sector has been highlighted by the Asian crisis. Although few would argue that poor regulation caused the crisis, there is little argument that poor regulation deepened the impact of the cri-

14. UNCTAD (1998).

sis and prolonged the recovery of many of the economies in the region. Indonesia, one of the hardest hit of the Asian economies, illustrates the costs that can be imposed by inadequate regulation.

The impact of the 1997 crisis fell mostly on the banking sector, and its results were devastating. Nonperforming loans in the Indonesian banking sector have been estimated to have peaked at somewhere between 65 and 75 percent of total loans. The cost of recapitalizing the banking system has been estimated at as high as $87 billion, which is more than 80 percent of Indonesian GDP.[15] Significant funds have already been injected into the financial and corporate sectors, but much of Indonesia's financial and corporate sector institutions remain vulnerable to insolvency. Ongoing restructuring and further injections of funds are likely to be required for some time before the system will again begin to function normally.

While by no means unique to Indonesia, several regulatory weaknesses were particularly evident there, including inadequate corporate and financial regulation; a financial system that was excessively dependent on banks; imprudent lending practices; a pervasive influence of families and relationship-based conglomerates incorporating both financial and commercial enterprises and a consequent problem with connected lending; and weak corporate governance, including poor compliance with accounting, audit, and disclosure standards. There is now a general recognition, supported by a number of recent studies, that governance and enforcement in Indonesia have been inadequate at all levels, including at the regulatory, institutional, and conglomerate levels.[16]

Concentrated ownership was a primary cause of weak corporate governance in Indonesia. There, as in other parts of Asia, the commercial sector has been dominated by conglomerate groups of companies controlled by a small number of shareholders, often from the same family. Only a small proportion of Indonesia's companies are listed on the exchanges, and a significant number of these are only partially listed because of a dominant owner. With concentrated ownership, outside shareholders have virtually no input into the corporate decisionmaking process. This problem in Indonesia (and elsewhere in Asia) was exacerbated in the lead-up to the crisis by the close relationships that had evolved between commercial and

15. Standard and Poor's, *Credit Week,* June 23, 1999. This estimate is considerably higher than the Indonesian government's official estimate of $70 billion. All dollar amounts are U.S. dollars unless otherwise noted.

16. See, for example, Australian Department of Foreign Affairs and Trade (1999); Harwood, Litan, and Pomerleano (1999); and Capulong and others (2000).

financial enterprises. In these circumstances, corporate finance was largely provided from in-house, relationship-based sources including banks and nonbank financial institutions. Without the need to go to the market for fund-raising, financial decisions were not subjected to the discipline of markets, the scope for manipulation of markets was increased, and transparency was absent.

THE DEMONSTRATION EFFECT. One of the potential opportunity costs of public sector involvement in the financial sector is that the public sector's behavior will be taken as a role model by the private sector. If government-owned financial institutions (and the government's agents, including policy departments and regulatory agencies) do not meet the same standards of disclosure, accountability, and conduct expected of the private sector, attempts to reform poor private sector practices are likely to fail. In a nutshell, good public sector governance and good corporate governance are complementary social goods.

The same argument applies to attempts to fight corruption. For a corrupt public sector to profit from its actions, the payments must be provided by the private sector. It stretches credibility to imagine that the corporate sector could behave corruptly in its dealings with the public sector, while remaining incorruptible in its dealings within the private sector. The mere existence of tough corporate governance laws is unlikely to deter firms that are used to "purchasing" legal outcomes from a corrupt system of courts. The same line of thinking suggests that it would be illogical for corruption to be rampant in the nonfinance sector, while leaving the finance sector untainted.

Another aspect of the complementary relationship between the public and private sectors in financial markets, where they often operate side by side, relates to the way in which private sector firms may attempt to capture the regulatory process. In a recent study, Hellman, Jones, and Kaufmann analyzed the relationship between firms and governments in transition economies.[17] They argue that there is a need to move beyond the traditional one-dimensional view of corruption in which the returns to corruption are monopolized by public officials. They suggest an alternative form in which firms seek to "capture" the officials and share the returns from colluding with them. They distinguish three types of corrupt relationships between firms and government: first, "state capture," in which the firm controls legal and regulatory reforms to its own benefit through

17. Hellman, Jones, and Kaufmann (2000).

illicit payments to government; second, "influence," where the firm achieves the same outcomes without the need for illicit payments, simply because of its size or special relationship with government (such as ownership or repeated business); and third, "administrative corruption," in which the firm makes illicit payments to public officials to distort the intended outcome of public rules and policies.

The authors find that influential and captor firms grow at a "substantially faster rate than other firms."[18] However, they also find that the returns to these forms of corrupt behavior are significant only in highly corrupt countries. In other words, where governments have a low level of corruption, the return to corrupt behavior by firms is, on average, zero or negative.

The implications of this work are threefold. First, corruption is a two-way process requiring complicity on the part of both the public and private sectors. Second, the gains for the firms involved in corrupt behavior are greatest where there are a high level of public sector corruption and significant potential benefits from controlling the formation of regulations or their implementation. That suggests that the financial sector is highly unlikely to be free from corruption in countries where public sector corruption is high. Third, improving public sector governance is a critical foundation stone if there is to be any hope of implementing a strong corporate governance system.

PUBLIC SECTOR INTERVENTION. There are many illustrations of the potential cost of government intervention in financial markets. Two recent examples highlight the dangers of such intervention.

First, during the Asian crisis, the Indonesian government in January 1998 announced a blanket guarantee of all deposits and other nonsubordinated liabilities of domestic banks. At the time, such a wide-ranging guarantee was considered necessary to stop the run on banks and to restore sufficient confidence in the banking system for it to continue operating.

Several years later, and despite passing two deadlines for the expiration of the guarantee, the government's commitment is still in place, and the implicit liability is growing.[19] A major contributor to the problem (both to the government's liability and to its inability to remove the guarantee) was the moral hazard associated with the guarantee. As noted above, banking

---

18. Hellman, Jones, and Kaufmann (2000, p. 4).

19. The Asian Development Bank is currently working with the Indonesian government to establish a deposit insurance scheme that should provide the necessary foundations for removing the guarantee.

supervision standards in Indonesia were, and still are, below required international standards.[20] Indonesian banks continue to have ownership conflicts, with close ties to tightly held commercial enterprises. Without strong prudential and governance standards, a government guarantee affords these institutions the capacity to raise cheap finance for related enterprises.

The extent of the risk created by this intervention was reflected in the assessment by the Indonesian Supreme Audit Agency during 2000 that a large part of the $17 billion of liquidity support extended by Bank Indonesia to private banks was lost in currency speculation and in bailing out affiliated companies.

The second example is the role apparently played by the Albanian government in the 1997 pyramid investment schemes. The temptations of promised returns ranging from 5 percent to 20 percent a month proved too attractive for many Albanians struggling to build a market economy following years of communist orthodoxy. The schemes attracted almost one in three Albanians as investors, some of whom sold their houses and other assets to chase the fictitious returns. At their height the schemes had liabilities close to half the country's GDP. When the schemes collapsed in 1997, investors were left with missing funds of around $1 billion. The subsequent riots claimed more than 2,000 lives.

Rather than moving quickly to shut down the schemes, the Albanian government at the time appeared to have close links with some of the major scheme operators, thereby providing them with tacit endorsement. There have even been suggestions that vans owned by a state-controlled bank were used to transport cash from one of the larger schemes across the border for deposit into Greek banks.[21]

Addressing Public Sector Governance in the Financial Sector

I do not pretend to have a fully worked-out solution at this stage for improving public sector governance problems. The following are some sug-

20. While there is still much work to be done, the Indonesian authorities have been working with the IMF to implement a *Master Plan for Strengthening Banking Supervision System for 2000–2002* and an action plan for banks to comply with international regulatory standards. Under this plan, Bank Indonesia is taking steps to strengthen its capabilities in: special surveillance; problem bank management; on- and off-site supervision; and research and training.

21. J. Mason and K. Hope, "Albanian Pyramid Savings Gone," *Financial Times*, August 16, 2000.

gestions about several key components policymakers should consider as part of a larger solution.

—Agree on a framework for assessing the appropriate role of the public sector in the financial system.

—Where public sector participation extends beyond appropriate roles, devise a process for winding back that involvement.

—Establish a set of public sector governance principles to apply to the legitimate, ongoing participation of the public sector in the financial system.

—Where the gap between the ultimate objective and the starting point is significant, identify some practical steps to begin the process.

In discussing these steps, I draw heavily on the excellent work that has already been done by the OECD, IMF, World Bank, and Brookings Institution.

Appropriate Public Sector Role in the Finance Sector

There is no single agreed model for the appropriate level of participation of the public sector in the finance sector. The level of participation at any given point in time depends on the stage of financial development, the quality of the regulatory structure, and cultural heritage. This overall proposition notwithstanding, a few general principles can be applied in most situations.

First, the public sector of every country has a legitimate role in setting and enforcing financial regulations. For this involvement to have minimal interference with the efficient working of the financial system and to minimize the opportunity for corruption, the regulatory structure should be efficiently designed and clearly focused on the correction of market failure. The effectiveness of the regulatory system is critical and remains a major challenge to all countries (as discussed later).

Second, while public ownership of financial institutions may be justified in some situations, there is a powerful case for public ownership to be replaced by private ownership as quickly as can be sustained by the market. The main case for public ownership arises where there is a shortage of private sector capital for the establishment of domestic financial institutions of efficient scale. In such a situation, the government may provide capital on behalf of the population at large. This case also exists where private capital is available but is owned too closely to satisfy the requirements for independence from the commercial sector with which the financial institutions will do business. Public ownership can involve significant costs, however. Publicly owned enterprises are inefficient in many cases. Without pressure from shareholders, publicly owned enterprises often fail to develop the skills or performance efficiencies of privately owned enterprises. More important, public ownership confers an implicit public guarantee over the products that it provides. In the case of financial services, this implied guarantee not only destroys the natural spectrum of risk among financial products, it confers an unfair advantage on publicly supplied financial services that can inhibit the development of viable private sector alternatives. Not only can public ownership inhibit market development, there is no compelling evidence that it enhances market stability. On the contrary, high levels of state ownership and control of financial institutions have been found to be strongly correlated with banking crises in both developed and emerging markets.[22] For these reasons, public ownership of financial institutions has, at best, a limited role to play in the development of the financial sector.

Third, government has a legitimate role to participate in the financial system as an issuer of its own debt. Further, the public sector has a legitimate role as a trader in government debt for monetary policy purposes.

Fourth, since governments have no obvious comparative advantage as fiduciary agents nor as asset managers (unless they trade on inside information, which is contrary to good governance), there is little justification for the government to act as a fiduciary agent or asset manager for its citizens. Subject to satisfactory safeguards against operational risk and fraud, these roles should be outsourced to the private sector wherever possible.

Fifth, the most dangerous area of participation by the public sector in financial markets is through direct intervention. This danger results both from the moral hazards that can arise from public sector guarantees and endorsements and from the opportunities individual intervention can create for corruption. Where such intervention can be anticipated, it should be circumscribed by legislation that expressly limits the extent of the government's commitment (for example, limited deposit insurance) and accompanied by measures to counter the moral hazard problem (for example, an effective regulatory framework, co-insurance, risk-based premiums, and the like). Where unplanned intervention occurs in a crisis situation, it should be as transparent as possible and limited both in coverage and time horizon.

22. Garcia (1996).

Winding Back Redundant Participation

While identifying the ideal level of public sector participation in the finance sector may be relatively easy, getting there may be an arduous process of privatizing, strengthening regulations, and designing support schemes. As with any reforms, sequencing is important.

Large-scale privatization of public sector financial enterprises should logically follow strengthening of the regulatory system. The dangers of reversing this order have been illustrated in several central European countries in recent years. As a step toward privatization, however, a number of countries have implemented "corporatization," a process that may have merit in many situations. Corporatization involves establishing an independent board and private sector–style corporate governance structures for public enterprises before their privatization. This intermediate step can help distance the public sector from the conflicts of interest that arise from public ownership while the long process of regulatory development takes place.

Possibly the most critical element of developing the regulatory framework is for the government to eschew direct intervention in the financial system while the requisite regulatory skills and practices are being established.

Some Principles of Public Sector Governance

One of the most effective sources of pressure for reform in any area comes from international trading partners and "clubs" such as the OECD, the Basel Committee, the International Organization of Securities Commissions (IOSCO), and the International Association of Insurance Supervisors (IAIS). In this respect, a strong case can be made for developing a set of principles of public sector governance to parallel the OECD Principles of Corporate Governance, coupled with international pressure to encourage their widespread adoption. Important components of this set of principles are already contained in the IMF Code of Good Practices on Transparency in Fiscal Transparency and the Code of Practices on Transparency in Monetary and Financial Policies.

Developing such a set of principles for the public sector as a whole would be an ambitious project and would need to go beyond issues of transparency and accountability to cover internal governance arrangements for the public sector and its agencies, decisionmaking processes, and so forth. In this respect it is important to draw the distinction between good transparency and good policies and good policymaking processes. Good policies and governance provide the essential platform for good transparency. While the following discussion refers to the broad concept of the public sector, it would be sensible to start with a set of principles for regulatory agencies and then to consider extending them to other public sector agencies and operations. Consistent with this suggestion, the main focus of the discussion below is on regulatory agencies.

A set of principles for public sector governance should recognize the separate roles played by the three main areas of the public sector: the government and its policy bureaucracy, government-owned enterprises (government-owned financial enterprises in particular), and government-appointed regulatory agencies. The lines of demarcation between these three are often blurred, but the fact that each has some unique governance challenges suggests that, to the greatest extent possible, they should be institutionally and functionally separate.

As a starting point for discussion, the principles might cover the following areas:

—transparency and accountability of the public sector,

—independence and accountability of financial regulatory agencies,

—other factors affecting the effectiveness of financial regulatory agencies, and

—anticorruption measures.

TRANSPARENCY AND ACCOUNTABILITY OF THE PUBLIC SECTOR. The IMF good practice codes for fiscal, monetary, and financial policies provide an excellent guide for public sector transparency and accountability.[23] The key elements can be summarized as follows:

—*Clarity of roles, objectives, and responsibilities is fundamental to transparency and accountability.* The public sector agencies responsible for formulating and implementing these policies should be clearly distinguished from other sectors of the economy. Their objectives should be clearly defined in law, regulations, or memoranda of understanding with the government. The relationships between the agencies should be transparent, and the terms of appointment and procedures for appointing and dismissing the governing bodies should be publicly disclosed.

---

23. These practices are set out in much greater detail in the Code of Good Practices on Fiscal Transparency and Code of Good Practices on Transparency in Monetary and Financial Policies. Both are available on the IMF's website (www.imf.org-external-standards-index.htm).

—*Information about monetary, fiscal, and financial policies should be available publicly.* Information should be made available on a regular timetable; it should be timely and should meet the IMF's data dissemination standards. Budgetary information should include the extrabudgetary activities and consolidated position of the government. Information should include assets and liabilities of the government and its agencies.

—*The processes for formulating, executing, and reporting on policies should be open and transparent.* The policy framework, instruments, and actions should be disclosed and explained. Substantive changes in regulatory policy should be carried out in consultation with stakeholders.

—*Policymakers should be accountable, and the agencies responsible for formulating policies should be subject to independent assessment of their integrity.* Officials of government agencies should be available to appear before designated public authorities to report on and account for their actions. Where fiscal information is provided, an independent audit of the quality of the data and projections should be provided. The agencies themselves should provide audited statements of their operations. Internal governance procedures should ensure the integrity of operations and prevent conflicts of interest. These procedures, any legal protections for staff and officials, and ethical standards for public servants should be publicly disclosed.

These practices are an excellent starting point for a comprehensive set of principles of public sector governance. Based on the earlier discussion, however, their application to general public sector involvement in the financial sector might be usefully expanded in two areas: government-owned financial institutions, and liabilities created by government intervention in the finance sector.

The only place in which government-owned financial (and other) institutions are mentioned in the existing IMF code is in the first practice on clarity under fiscal transparency. In the details of that principle, the IMF suggests that "government involvement in the private sector (e.g., through regulation and equity ownership) should be conducted in an open and public manner, and on the basis of clear rules and procedures that are applied in a nondiscriminatory way."[24]

In view of the potential costs of government involvement in the financial system through the ownership of financial institutions, there is a need

24. IMF (2001, p.1, subsection 1.1.5).

to go beyond this cursory treatment and to establish an explicit code for these institutions. This code should be at least as comprehensive as that for the three groups of agencies currently covered, and even stronger in some areas. Namely, government-owned financial institutions should meet the full range of regulatory requirements to which their private sector competitors are subjected, including capital adequacy, disclosure, accounting and actuarial standards, and governance requirements. Government-owned financial institutions also should be established in a way that demonstrably quarantines them from access to sensitive policy information. For example, they should be accountable to an independent board, rather than to a minister, and board members should not include officials of the central bank or fiscal agency.

The IMF code's treatment of liabilities off the balance sheet is also a little cursory. The code on fiscal transparency suggests that "statements describing the nature and fiscal significance of central government contingent liabilities and tax expenditures, and of quasi-fiscal activities, should be part of the budget documentation."[25] While this statement could be interpreted as encompassing government guarantees in the finance sector, the sheer potential size of these commitments needs explicit treatment. Government intervention in the form of guarantees of deposits can run to several years of budgetary expenditure. Even more significant in many countries is the potential liability under pension schemes. The most obvious of these are commitments under "Pillar 1" pay-as-you-go schemes. However, significant liabilities can also be incurred under "Pillar 2" plans. For example, several central European countries have introduced mandatory pillar 2 defined-contribution pension schemes. It is not uncommon, however, for these schemes to include minimum return provisions; some of these are a direct liability of the government, while others are passed to the pension managers (although the government remains implicitly liable if the manager fails). The net effect in either case is to turn a defined-contribution scheme into a hybrid defined-benefit scheme with the government as the guarantor. The cost can be significant.

The code could be extended to include a special section on the accounting for and disclosure of implicit liabilities arising from government intervention in the finance sector. These contingent liabilities should be separately valued by an independent agency. It is also important that ac-

25. IMF (2001, p. 2. subsection 2.1.3).

countability for these often open-ended promises is attached to the minister or department that has made them.

INDEPENDENCE AND ACCOUNTABILITY OF REGULATORY AGENCIES. Independence is a concept that has different meanings in different countries and cultures. It has been both used and abused in different contexts for achieving particular outcomes. Policymakers should recognize from the outset that independence is a means to an end, not an end within itself. Accountability refers to the ways in which the entity reports its decisions and is held responsible for its actions. Importantly, independence and accountability must be considered together, because one without the other is at best meaningless and at worst dangerous.

The sole motivation for granting a degree of independence to a regulatory agency is to enhance its effectiveness by ensuring that it is able to pursue and achieve its legislated objectives. Good regulation is primarily about making decisions that are based on objective criteria directed toward the achievement of the objectives specified in the law and free from extraneous considerations and influences. Independence is about removing those extraneous influences to the greatest extent possible. Accountability is about ensuring that they are replaced by the legislated objectives. As a general rule, the greater the level of independence, the greater also should be the level of accountability.

In the context of a financial regulator, independence means that the regulator should have the capacity to develop, implement, and enforce regulatory policy without inappropriate interference from the national legislature, government, or industry.

Several key issues in the institutional design of a regulatory agency determine its overall independence and accountability. These include

—the legal nature of the agency and how it relates to the government and the legislature;

—the structure of the agency's governing board;

—the mechanisms for appointing and dismissing board members;

—legal indemnities for staff who act in good faith;

—accountability mechanisms to the government, the legislature, and other stakeholders;

—internal governance arrangements;

—mechanisms for dealing with appeals and disputes; and

—the conditions under which the government may overrule the agency on matters of policy or implementation.

Legal Nature of the Agency. The legal nature of a regulatory agency is a critical factor in its effectiveness. The two main alternatives in this respect are for the agency to be established as a government department or as an independent statutory authority.[26]

There is no common legal model for the establishment of regulatory agencies around the world. Structures vary according to constitutional and cultural inheritances, but agreement is widespread among regulatory agencies that independence is enhanced greatly under the statutory authority model, relative to the departmental model. The reasons are relatively straightforward. A government department is, by definition, subject to direction by the responsible minister, and a government department is, by definition, subject to the financing constraints imposed by the government's budget. Even where a government department is supported by an external board, the board is usually limited to an advisory role (to have greater responsibilities than advice creates an automatic conflict with the ministerial line of responsibility). Thus the independence added by the board is largely illusory. Finally, employees of a government department are usually civil servants, a fact that limits the ability of the agency to create a non–civil service culture and to pay market-related remuneration packages to attract high-quality staff.

It is possible to structure certain mechanisms into the departmental model to enhance the independence of the agency. For example, funding can be isolated to some extent from the budgetary process by imposing levies on the industry and hypothecating the funds directly to the regulator. Similarly, some of the more constraining aspects of civil service employment (particularly in the area of remuneration) can be overcome by statute. These mechanisms notwithstanding, the greatest shortcoming of the departmental model is that a government department cannot effectively be removed from the direction of the minister, since this aspect is fundamental to being a government department.

The challenge of providing independence in a departmental framework has been highlighted in recent times in central Europe where regulatory reforms have been handicapped by legal heritages that do not contemplate the transfer of powers from the government to statutory authorities other than the central bank. A number of countries have looked for innovative ways of meeting this challenge. In Estonia, for example, the transfer of

---

26. The essence of a statutory authority is that, while it is still technically a part of the executive structure, it draws its powers from the laws that establish it.

independence and powers was recently achieved by establishing a financial regulatory agency as a subsidiary of the central bank; in Latvia, the constitution was rewritten to enable the establishment of a separate independent statutory authority to undertake financial regulation.

The Structure of the Agency's Governing Board. Boards of directors or commissioners play two main roles in statutory authorities involved with financial regulation: they enhance independence and accountability.

Boards enhance independence by vesting responsibility for high-level decisions in a group of board members rather than in a single chief executive officer or departmental head. The existence of the board should reduce the likelihood of inappropriate interference in regulatory policies and decisions. To the extent that the staff of the agency is accountable to the board, it also provides a measure of protection for staff against pressure that might otherwise be brought to bear on them as individuals. Additionally, the involvement of a group of experts in the high-level decisionmaking process should provide a measure of reassurance for the government and other stakeholders that decisions will be made in a manner consistent with the legislated objectives of the agency.

Boards also provide an important accountability mechanism for the staff of the agency. Since the CEO and senior staff of the regulatory agency make decisions with the express delegation of powers from the board, they must be accountable to the board for those decisions.

To meet these objectives of enhancing both independence and accountability, the board of a regulatory agency should ideally have a majority of nonexecutive members. Where interagency coordination is necessary, it is appropriate to include heads of other agencies as ex officio board members. Without competent, independent nonexecutive board members, however, the gains in independence and accountability are unlikely to be realized.

Mechanisms for Appointing and Dismissing Board Members. A major factor in the legislated independence for a regulatory agency is the process by which board members are appointed and dismissed. The greater the protection afforded against capricious dismissal, the greater the likelihood that individual board members and executives will act in accordance with the requirements of the legislation, free from coercive pressure from outsiders. At the same time, board members and senior executives should not be so confident of their tenure that they regard themselves as unaccountable for their performance and for the performance of their agency. There is clearly a balance to be struck. The balance is most likely to be achieved where the appointment of board members is seen to be open and accountable; for example, where the responsible minister or head of state nominates candidates who are then subject to approval by the legislature.

The dismissal process should also be transparent to avoid unfair dismissal or dismissal for political or personal reasons. Board members are best protected from capricious dismissal by including a statutory list of conditions for dismissal in the law establishing the agency. The most common grounds for dismissal are bankruptcy, criminal conviction, and mental incapacity. The more difficult grounds to identify and handle relate to misconduct and incompetence. It is possibly going too far in the direction of protection to rule out dismissal on these grounds; at the same time, it is very difficult to establish in the legislation precisely what is meant by misconduct and incompetence.

Legal Indemnities. One design aspect that has diminished regulatory independence in a number of countries has been the absence of legal indemnities for staff members who have acted in good faith. It is a fact of life that regulatory decisions affect the capacity of firms and individuals to earn income. Most regulatory decisions favor the rights of one group at the expense of others. It is implicit in the objectives of any regulatory agency that it will be required from time to time to uphold the rights of individual deposit holders, policyholders, and investors relative to those of financial institutions and licensed individuals. It is an inevitable consequence of this requirement that aggrieved parties may seek legal redress where they believe the decisions of the agency have unjustly deprived them of their rights.

To act in the national interest in carrying out their regulatory responsibilities, regulators must have legal protection against damages generated by their actions, provided those actions are taken in good faith and in pursuit of the objectives set out in the legislation. Without such protection it is difficult for regulators to make decisions; it can also be difficult to recruit good quality staff, given the knowledge that they are taking on substantial personal risks through their work. Many countries have such legal protections in their legislation.

The potential for capricious legal action in some countries has also led to the extension of the indemnity to the agency itself, provided that its office bearers act in good faith and within the legal powers provided by the law.

Accountability to the Government, to Parliament, and to Other Stakeholders. The first line of accountability of any regulatory agency should be to the government, and through the government to the legislature. The primary mechanism for acquitting that accountability is through statutory reporting requirements. Full accountability requires the highest levels of transparency and disclosure in these reports. Ideally, the principles, auditing requirements, and minimum content of these reports should be spelled out in the law. For example, the agency might be required to outline its policies and operations as well as matters affecting the achievement of its statutory objectives. Beyond the reporting requirements to government, other reporting responsibilities of the agency might usefully be included in the law:

—The responsibility to report to the relevant minister as requested by the minister;

—The responsibility to appear before legislative committees, as requested, to provide information and explanations concerning its policies and operations, subject to appropriate safeguards to avoid infringing the rights of persons under investigation or prejudicing ongoing operations;

—The responsibility to keep the relevant minister regularly apprised of any licensed financial institution that the agency has reason to believe is experiencing financial difficulty and is at risk of failing; and

—The requirement to submit all routine reports to the legislature and to publish them.

An important part of accountability is the need to ensure that policy changes are carefully considered and understood by all stakeholders. Policies that are introduced without adequate consultation are likely to contain unintended consequences. With respect to the formulation of regulatory policy, the law should require the agency to consult with the government, industry, any other affected agencies, and the public before introducing major policy changes.

Regulatory agencies must also be accountable to the industries that they regulate and to the public at large. Some of this accountability is provided for in the annual reporting process and also through the consultation provisions mentioned above. There is a strong case, however, for accountability to industry to go beyond these basic disclosure and consultation processes. At a minimum, industry advisory panels should be established to ensure that the agency has the benefit of industry expertise in its formulation of policy.

Internal Governance Mechanisms. Good governance imposes certain additional requirements on the internal structure of a regulatory agency to ensure that the necessary checks and balances are in place and that governance policies are adhered to. At a minimum the agency should have an internal risk management and audit subcommittee of its board. Good practice requires that the chief executive officer and the board chairman should not be formal members of this subcommittee, although they may be required to attend if needed. Depending on the size and scope of the agency, a human resources subcommittee would normally also be considered good practice.

Every financial regulatory agency should have a code of conduct for staff. Such a code should deal with conflicts of interest, improper behavior by staff, and general issues of how staff members are expected to conduct themselves. The requirement for such a code should ideally be included in the law, although the detail (other than on the broadest issues) should be a matter for the board to determine from time to time.

Mechanisms for Dealing with Appeals and Disputes. As suggested earlier, regulatory agencies and their staff should be protected against legal action for decisions made in good faith in carrying out their duties under the law. Such an indemnity, however, should be balanced by adequate provisions to protect industry participants against capricious decisions by the agency. Natural justice requires both that the agency's decisions and the basis of those decisions be available to affected parties and that there be adequate processes for appealing decisions. Ideally, these processes should allow for internal review as well as appeal to an external tribunal or court.

Checks and Balances: The Government's Right to Overrule. While the ideal legal structure of a regulatory agency is an independent statutory authority with the power to formulate, implement, and enforce regulations and regulatory policy, it is impossible to rule out the prospect that circumstances may arise in which the national interest may dominate the legislated objectives of the agency. In such circumstances, the government should have the right to overrule the agency, but subject to this being done in an open and transparent manner.

One way in which this provision can be implemented with suitable safeguards would be to include a provision in the agency's law along the following general lines.

—Ministerial directions may be made to the agency after consultation with the agency and where they are in the national interest.

—These directions should be on broad policy matters only, in writing, and submitted to the legislature.

—The legislature should be able to disallow a ministerial direction to the agency in the event that it is not made in accordance with the provisions or in the spirit of the law (this power is more debatable and should be considered in the legal and cultural heritage of the country involved).

OTHER FACTORS AFFECTING THE EFFECTIVENESS OF REGULATORY AGENCIES. Effectiveness of financial regulatory agencies is a worldwide problem. Effectiveness relies on a combination of the independence and accountability factors described in the section above, the actual policies formulated by the agency, and the way in which it implements them. Excellent guidance on the policy elements is provided by the Core Principles issued by the Basel Committee, IOSCO, and the IAIS. These are principles to which every regulatory agency should aspire. The problem, however, is that having world best practice prudential and market conduct standards is of limited value unless the agencies involved are capable of implementing them. A common message being returned from the Financial Sector Assessment Programs carried out by the World Bank and the IMF is that where regulation is failing, it is failing because of a failure of implementation. This raises issues of culture, funding, and quality of staff.

Culture. An effective regulatory culture is one built on independence. The three preconditions for genuine independence of a regulatory agency are legislated indepdendence, financial independence, and attitudinal independence.

Legislated independence refers to the legal provisions that both require the regulator to act independently and provide legal support for regulators who exercise that independence (as discussed earlier). A legally independent regulator can form regulatory judgments and decisions without fear of retribution from individuals or groups within the industry or government. Financial independence refers to the extent to which the resources available to the regulator are free from influence by individuals or groups within the industry or government. A financially independent regulator can form regulatory judgments and decisions without fear that its resources will be reduced in retaliation. Attitudinal independence refers to the willingness of regulatory staff to act independently in practice.

It is often argued, correctly, that independence is largely a state of mind. There are examples around the world of regulatory agencies that have high levels of legislated or financial independence that still succumb to interference from various sources. There are also examples (albeit much rarer) of regulators that are structurally very close to government yet, for all practical purposes, act with almost total independence in their formulation and implementation of regulatory policy; the Monetary Authority of Singapore is a good example of this latter case.

Perhaps the strongest message from these examples is that independence ultimately relies most heavily on attitudinal independence; that is, it requires a culture of strong-mindedness and a willingness to assert independence. Put differently, legislating strong independence provisions does not guarantee that the agency will embrace those provisions in practice; development of an independence-oriented culture is critical, and that comes down largely to individuals.

This does not suggest that legislated independence and financial independence have no roles to play. Indeed, all three aspects of independence are complementary. It is much easier to develop a culture of independence if the agency involved is supported by strong legislation and financial independence. Individuals are more likely to take a firm stance against inappropriate directions from outside parties if they know that they are not likely to be subject to arbitrary dismissal for their actions. Similarly, they are more likely to take firm enforcement actions where they know that they are not exposing their livelihoods or the resources of the agency to financial ruin by doing so. There is nonetheless a human element that requires effective leadership. Unfortunately, this critical element cannot be legislated.

Funding. It is essential for regulatory agencies to be properly funded if they are to be effective. Adequate funding enables the agency to pay for better-quality staff. The question of whether funding should come from the government's budget or from the industry is specific to the circumstances. In general, however, industry funding has the advantage that the agency is not required to bid for funds at every budget round, in competition with social policies and other, politically driven considerations.

Staff Skills and Motivation. A common problem among many regulatory agencies is demoralized and unmotivated staff. In part, these problems arise because of conflicting responsibility and accountability structures (as noted above). Staff members are unlikely to be willing to pursue difficult action against a financial transgressor if the legal basis of the enforcement is in question, if they are not adequately protected against prosecution for carrying out their duties, or if they lack the expertise to carry the action through. Some practical steps toward improving staffing deficiencies include:

—Payment of adequate salary levels. Not only do inadequate salaries militate against being able to secure adequately skilled staff, they provide a justification in many minds for corruption as a means of supplementing unsustainable incomes.

—Reward structures based on outputs rather than inputs or seniority (to encourage initiative).

—Adequate protection from legal action and dismissal, consistent with the need to carry out regulatory duties.

—Clear lines of authority and decisionmaking within the agency.

—Adequate funding for professional training and staff development.

—An even greater focus by the World Bank and regulatory agencies in the developed world on providing practical training and assistance in the implementation of regulatory practices (rather than on the reform of regulatory policies).

—Mentoring by regulatory agencies in more developed jurisdictions.

ANTICORRUPTION MEASURES AND FINANCIAL SECTOR INTEGRITY. The principles outlined above for good public sector governance are important not only for their potential impact on public sector performance, but also because they provide essential deterrents against corruption. Corruption thrives on secrecy. Therefore, any measures that improve disclosure and accountability are natural opponents of corruption. So too are measures that provide regulators with legal protections against capricious removal from office and against prosecution for doing their jobs in good faith.

Additional measures can be implemented to further reduce the ease with which corrupt practices can otherwise take hold. One such measure is general anticorruption legislation. A second involves targeting specific aspects of the financial system that facilitate corruption, such as the relationship between electronic funds transfer and money laundering. Together with strong internal governance of public sector agencies, these provide a sound foundation for financial sector integrity.

General Anticorruption Measures. Anticorruption legislation comes in various guises. The first is an explicit identification of corrupt payments to government officials and agents as criminal activities and the institution of severe penalties for those caught doing so.

The second involves legislation prohibiting domestic firms from making corrupt payments to foreign governments. Such legislation has its origins in the twenty-year-old Foreign Corrupt Practices Act of the United States, which makes it a criminal offense for American companies to bribe foreign officials. In 1998 all twenty-nine members of the OECD, plus five nonmembers, signed a "bribery convention" based on the U.S. concept. The most innovative feature of the OECD convention is that countries are required to cooperate with each other in prosecuting cases. There are encouraging signs that this convention is having some effect; the *Economist,* for example, cites Shell and Unilever as examples of non-American firms that responded quickly and positively to the convention.[27]

The third type of anticorruption measure involves including explicit anticorruption provisions into legislation governing regulatory and other government agencies. For example, Article 9 of the Bank Indonesia Act 1999 requires that other parties shall not intervene with the bank in discharging its duties and that the bank shall refuse or disregard any form of intervention conducted by other parties.[28] Article 42 requires the governor, senior deputy governor, and deputy governors to swear an oath not to receive any promise or gift in any form related to the conduct of their duties. Other provisions spell out prohibitions on other conflicts of interest and a general code of conduct. To be effective, measures such as these must be supported by broader public sector governance conditions covering disclosure and accountability and also by a system of independent courts and judiciary.

Anti-Money-Laundering Agreements. One consequence of globalization and technical advances in the international electronic transfer of funds over the past decade has been the emergence of international money laundering as a major "growth area" of crime. IMF estimates put the volume of money being "cleaned" through the world's financial system at between $500 billion and $1.5 trillion a year (equivalent to more than 1 percent of world GDP).

The Financial Action Task Force (FATF), created by the G7 countries in 1989 to coordinate action against money laundering, has begun in recent years to take a stronger stance against countries and banks that fail to meet international standards of integrity in this area. The dilemma facing banks has been that customers, particularly private banking customers, demand secrecy with respect to their transactions. A bank that asks too many questions risks losing its customer base.[29] To some extent, this aspect is being addressed by the public embarrassment being caused to major international banks in the United Kingdom and the United States by official reports that have named institutions whose customers have been involved with money laundering. Given the nature of the conflict for individual banks, it has been essential for the problem to be addressed at the national

27. "Stop the Rot," *Economist,* January 16, 1999.

28. Republic of Indonesia (1999).

29. This same dilemma faces auditors and actuaries and is a major problem for financial regulators worldwide.

and international levels. Public disclosure and embarrassment for otherwise prestigious institutions is a start, but stronger and more coordinated efforts are also required. The issue is as much one of public sector governance as it is of corporate governance.

During 2000 the FATF published a list of "noncooperating" jurisdictions, including such countries as Israel, Lebanon, the Philippines, Russia, and most of the well-known tax-haven countries such as the Cayman and Cook Islands, Liechtenstein, and Panama. These countries face the threat of (as yet unspecified) international sanctions if they remained on the list after mid-2001. Far from being seen as victimizing or persecuting these jurisdictions, the message should be that reducing financial crime, and improving public sector governance, are socially and economically desirable both within countries and globally.

Some Practical Steps for Addressing the Impossible

Wei notes that many political leaders are unwilling to undertake bold reforms because of the political risks.[30] Not only do reforms risk alienating the supporters who elected them (even if they are the major beneficiaries of inefficiencies or corruption), rapid change is always disruptive, even in the unlikely event that everyone agrees that the end objective is worthwhile. For this reason, recommendations about how countries (particularly emerging nation countries) might address the problem of public sector governance must provide practical solutions and measures that can be taken as steps toward more comprehensive reforms.[31] Many of the suggestions covered above can be implemented in stages.

The most immediate returns with the lowest risk are likely to be gained from the following measures:
—Increasing the independence of financial regulatory agencies;
—Increasing the salaries of regulators;
—Increasing the legal protections available to regulators;

---

30. Wei (2001b).

31. In the context of practical steps, Wei (2001b) makes the novel suggestion that leaders willing to start the fight against corruption could consider the establishment of "special governance zones"— regions in which bold and comprehensive reforms can be implemented. While this novel idea may have some potential with respect to the fight against corruption, the interlinked nature of the financial sector would make such an experiment difficult for a broader test of public sector governance in the financial sector.

—Increasing the resources available to regulators, particularly in the area of training;

—Corporatizing public sector financial enterprises (with appropriate corporate governance rules);

—Taking any measures that increase transparency of the public sector; and

—Applying coordinated international pressure to meet agreed standards of public sector governance through the publication of lists of noncomplying jurisdictions.

Conclusion

The evidence suggests that far from being off limits to international institutions assisting with the reform process in emerging markets (and even some developed markets), public sector governance is quite possibly the central issue. Without good public sector governance, financial markets are unlikely to operate efficiently or effectively, corruption is likely to retard economic growth and welfare, and efforts to reform private sector performance—through regulatory reform, corporate governance reform, and anticorruption measures—are largely doomed to failure. The stakes are significant.

This paper does not present definitive answers. Rather, it represents a preliminary exploration of public sector governance issues in the context of the finance sector. The main conclusions follow.

—The finance sector is sufficiently different from other sectors to warrant separate consideration. This difference arises from the legitimate roles that the public sector should play in the financial system (in addition to the many and varied roles that governments often choose to play).

—The cost of poor public sector governance in the finance sector is potentially substantial. Not only does poor governance lead to significant opportunities for corruption, it carries significant costs in its own right.

—The case for good public sector governance is even more compelling than that for good corporate governance, although the two are largely complementary public goods.

—Importantly, efforts to improve corporate governance are likely to fail unless they are accompanied by measures to improve public sector governance.

References

Australian Department of Foreign Affairs and Trade. 1999. *Asia's Financial Markets: Capitalizing on Reform*. Canberra.

Caprio, Gerald, and D. Kligebiel. 1996. "Bank Insolvencies, Cross Country Experience." Policy and Research Working Paper 1620. World Bank, Washington, D.C.

Capulong, V., D. Edwards, D. Webb, and J. Zhuang. 2000. *Corporate Governance and Finance in East Asia: A Study of Indonesia, Republic of Korea, Malaysia, Philippines, and Thailand*, vol. 1. Asian Development Bank, Manila.

Fisman, R. 1998 "It's Not What You Know . . . Estimating the Value of Political Connections." Unpublished manuscript. Columbia University, New York.

Garcia. 1996.

Gray, C. W., and Daniel Kaufmann. 1998. "Corruption and Development." *Finance and Development* 35 (March): 7–10.

Harwood, A., Robert E. Litan, and Michael Pomerleano, eds. 1999. *Financial Markets and Development: The Crisis in Emerging Markets*. Brookings.

Hellman, J. S., G. Jones, and Daniel Kaufmann. 2000. "Seize the State, Seize the Day: State Capture, Corruption, and Influence in Transition." Policy and Research Working Paper 2444. World Bank, Washington, D.C.

International Monetary Fund. 2001. Code of Good Practices on Transparency. See www. imf.org/external/np/fad/trans/index.htm.

Jensen, Michael C., and William H. Meckling. 1976 "Theory of the Firm: Managerial Behavior, Agency Costs and Ownership Structure." *Journal of Financial Economics* 3 (October): 305–60.

Johnson, Simon, Daniel Kaufmann, and Andrei Shleifer. 1997, "The Unofficial Economy in Transition." *Brookings Papers on Economic Activity* 2: 159–239.

Kaufmann, Daniel, Aart Kraay, and Pablo Zoido-Lobatón. 1999. "Aggregating Governance Indicators." Working Paper 2195. World Bank, Washington, D.C.

———. 2000. "Taking the Offensive against Corruption." *Finance and Development* (June). International Monetary Fund, Washington, D.C.

Kaufmann, Daniel, and Shang-Jin Wei. 1999. "Does 'Grease Payment' Speed up the Wheels of Commerce?" NBER Working Paper 7093 (April). National Bureau of Economic Research, Cambridge, Mass.

Mauro, P. 1997. "The Effects of Corruption on Growth, Investment and Government Expenditure: A Cross-Country Analysis." In K. A. Elliott, ed., *Corruption and the Global Economy*. Washington, D.C.: Institute for International Economics.

Mehretz, G., and Daniel Kaufmann. "Transparency, Liberalization, and Banking Crises." Working Paper 2286. World Bank, Washington, D.C.

Nestor, S. 2001. "Building Global Corporate Governance." *Company Director* (February).

OECD. 1999. *OECD Principles of Corporate Governance*. Ad Hoc Task Force on Corporate Governance, Paris.

———. 2001. "OECD Principles of Corporate Governance, Questions and Answers" (www.oecd.org/daf/governance).

Republic of Indonesia. 1999. "Act of the Republic of Indonesia, Number 23 of 1999 Concerning Bank Indonesia." Eng. trans. Bank Indonesia, Jakarta.

Tanzi, V., and H. Davoodi. 1997. "Corruption, Public Investment and Growth." Working Paper 97/139. International Monetary Fund, Washington, D.C.

UNCTAD (United Nations Conference on Trade and Development). 1998. *World Investment Report*. Geneva.

Wei, Shang-Jin. 2000. "How Taxing Is Corruption on International Investors?" *Review of Economics and Statistics* 82 (1): 1–11.

———. 2001a. "Bribery in the Economies: Grease or Sand?" In United Nations, *Economic Survey of Europe*, No. 2, pp. 101–12. New York.

———. 2001b. "Corruption and Poor Public Governance, Project Overview." Brookings (www.brookings.edu/views/papers/wei/20000115.htm).

UDAIBIR S. DAS
MARC QUINTYN

6

Financial Crisis Prevention and Management: The Role of Regulatory Governance

A FINANCIAL SYSTEM IS only as strong as its governing practices, the financial soundness of its institutions, and the efficiency of its market infrastructure. Instilling and using sound governance practices are a shared responsibility of regulatory agencies and market participants. This responsibility has three components. First, market participants bear the ultimate responsibility for establishing good governance practices in their institutions in order to gain and keep the confidence of their clients, counterparties, and the markets. Second, regulatory agencies play a key role in instilling and overseeing implementation of the use of such good practices. The third layer, the main theme of this paper, is that *regulatory agencies themselves need to establish and operate sound governance practices.* By failing to apply good governance principles in their own operations, regulatory agencies lose the credibility and moral authority necessary to promulgate good practices in the institutions under their oversight. That could lead to a moral hazard problem, contribute to unsound practices in the markets, and ultimately exacerbate crises in the financial system.

The authors would like to thank V. Sundararajan, Michael Pomerleano, Pat Brenner, Michael Andrews, Dong He, and Steven Seelig (all of the International Monetary Fund), and Edward Kane and participants at an IMF seminar for valuable input. Vania Etropolska and Plamen Yossifov provided excellent research assistance.

Indeed, recent experiences with systemic or significant financial sector crises have strongly underlined the importance of good governance on the part of regulatory agencies. In nearly all financial crises of the past decade—Ecuador, East Asia, Mexico, Russia, Turkey, Venezuela—political interference in the regulatory and supervisory process, forbearance, and weak regulations and supervision have all been mentioned as contributing factors to the depth and size of the systemic crises. Each of these phenomena is a symptom of weak regulatory governance, while some are at the same time manifestations of the lack of public sector accountability and transparency.

The need for good regulatory governance in the context of financial sector policymaking and crisis prevention has recently begun to receive attention. However, more work is needed to enhance good regulatory governance as a key element of a well-functioning financial system. Partly as a result of the experiences in recent financial crises, a wide range of initiatives has been taken aimed, directly or indirectly, at enhancing good governance in regulatory agencies.

In cooperation with the international standard-setting bodies, several financial sector standards—some sector-specific, others across sectors—have also been promulgated in recent years to establish international practices and standards.[1] Since 1999 the main vehicle through which the financial sector surveillance work and strengthening of financial systems have been brought together is the Financial Sector Assessment Program (FSAP), conducted jointly by the International Monetary Fund and the World Bank. While the FSAP's main focus is on analyzing strengths and vulnerabilities of the financial system and on assessing financial sector standards, it has become a key instrument for assessing and, where necessary, assisting in improving good governance of regulatory agencies in IMF-World Bank member countries.

This paper analyzes the early outcome of the FSAP evaluation of good governance practices in regulatory agencies and draws some preliminary lessons. Since the domain under analysis is relatively new and uncharted, we first define the concept of regulatory governance and its four main components—independence, accountability, transparency, and integrity. The analysis of the FSAP assessments finds that overall the various regulatory

---

1. International standard-setting bodies include the Basel Committee for Banking Supervision, the International Organization of Securities Commissions (IOSCO), the International Association of Insurance Supervisors (IAIS), and the Committee on Payment and Settlement Systems (CPSS).

standards do not provide a complete (and consistent) framework for regulatory governance and that there are many gaps in implementing the good governance practices based on the four identified components. Finally, the paper suggests additional governance practices that can help in managing a systemic financial crisis.

Regulatory Governance—Conceptual Framework

Adhering to good governance practices themselves is a precondition for regulatory agencies that want to instill good governance practices in the supervised sectors. The channel by which regulatory governance leads to good governance by the firms and the markets runs through credibility. Good and consistently applied governance practices help build an agency's credibility, and credible regulating agencies are able to enforce their actions or sanctions, and promote good governance practices in the supervised sectors.

For the purposes of this paper, regulatory governance applies to those institutions that possess legal powers to regulate, supervise, or intervene in the financial sector.[2] Regulatory governance can therefore be seen as a somewhat narrower, more specific concept than public sector governance.[3] While the principles of good regulatory governance apply obviously to all public institutions, the (regulatory) scope of their actions may differ vastly, depending on legal, institutional, and political traditions. At one end of the spectrum, for example, a deposit insurance agency may have a fairly narrow mandate (pay out depositors in case of a bank failure); although good governance practices are important in such an institution, there are few critical issues involved. At the other end of the spectrum, bank supervisors typically have "the coercive power of the state against private citizens" when they are involved in revoking bank licenses.[4] This is a far-reaching power not shared by any other financial agency, including central banks, and its responsible exercise requires high governance standards.

Kaufmann, Kraay, and Zoido-Lobaton define public sector governance as: the traditions and institutions that determine how authority is exercised

---

2. Thus, the term *regulatory agency* is used here to refer to all institutions involved in financial sector regulation and oversight. These include the central bank, sectoral regulators and supervisors, deposit insurance agencies, and, in systemic crisis situations, restructuring agencies and asset management companies.

3. See the paper by Carmichael in this volume.

4. Lastra and Wood (1999).

in a particular country. This framework includes (1) the process by which governments are selected, held accountable, monitored, and replaced; (2) the capacity of governments to manage resources efficiently and to formulate, implement, and enforce sound policies and regulations; and (3) the respect of citizens and the state for the institutions that govern economic and social interactions among them.[5] This definition is, by extension, also applicable to appointed bureaucracies and official agents, such as financial sector regulators.

Using that definition as a foundation, one might refine the definition of regulatory governance as

—the capacity to manage resources efficiently and to formulate, implement, and enforce sound policies and regulations—to be seen as the duty to meet the delegated objectives;

—the respect of citizens and the state for the institutions that govern economic and social interactions (in other words, protection of the agency from industry capture and political interference); complemented by an important element of the principal-agency theory of regulation:

—the respect of the agency for the broader goals and policies of the (elected) legislature.

The principal-agent theory assumes that information is asymmetrically distributed, with agents typically having more information than their principals. A related problem could be that the agent may have a different objective function than the principal. Thus, to prevent (independent) regulatory agencies from becoming a "fourth branch of the government" outside the normal channels of political control, it is important as a principle of good governance that they "stay in touch" with the political realities while pursuing their mandate.

Evidence suggests that independent regulatory agencies do not behave as an irresponsible or headless fourth branch. One of the currently prevailing theoretical models on the interaction between political authorities and independent agencies is the "dialogue model"—largely inspired by the agency theory and the new institutionalism—which supports the view that statutory independent agencies in fact do their best to be informed about the intentions, wishes, and opinions of the political leadership and to anticipate their reactions to new policy proposals.[6] In other words, the model indicates that independent regulatory agencies are subject to some form of political control—almost self-imposed censorship.

5. Kaufmann, Kraay, and Zoido-Lobaton (2000, p. 10).
6. Majone (1993).

Reassuring though this view of good governance is, many authors are of the view that it is too informal and needs to be supplemented with more formal arrangements. Such formal arrangements bring us to the components of good governance.

Components of Good Regulatory Governance

How can the quality of regulatory governance be analyzed with a view to improving it? [7] To answer this question, we need to define the four components that bring together most of the elements that can ensure good regulatory governance. These are independence, accountability, transparency, and integrity.

Independence

Agency independence has been practiced, discussed, and accepted for a much longer time in the United States than in Europe or any other part of the world. A consensus is growing worldwide that good regulatory governance can best be achieved by giving the agency a fair degree of independence from both the political sphere and the supervised entities. [8] In the specific area of financial sector oversight, central bank independence is now much more widely accepted than is independence of other agencies. [9]

Two main arguments have been offered in favor of delegating to independent agencies—as opposed to a government agency, a specific ministry, or a local body—the tasks related to economic and social regulation: the advantage of resorting to and relying on expertise, particularly in complex

7. This paper takes the need for regulation and supervision of the financial system for granted. For arguments in favor of regulation and supervision, see, for example, Goodhart and others (1998), and Quintyn and Taylor (2002).

8. Independent regulatory agencies have existed in the United States since the 1890s (the first one was the Interstate Commerce Commission, which became the model for other similar bodies, including the Securities and Exchange Commission), even though their actual degree of independence has varied over time, in line with political moods. In other industrial countries, such bodies have been established in more recent years, fueled by factors such as privatization of utilities, reform in Europe inspired by the drive for a common market, World Trade Organization agreements, and policy advice from the international financial institutions.

9. Central bank independence has been discussed widely. Independence of regulatory and supervisory agencies has not been discussed widely until recently. See Quintyn and Taylor (2002) for arguments. In his paper in this volume, Carmichael also provides arguments for regulatory and supervisory independence.

situations; and the advantage of potentially shielding market intervention from political interference, thus improving transparency and stability of the output. As such, agency independence increases the possibility of making credible policy commitments.

The issue of credible policy commitments needs to be taken a little further. The time-inconsistency literature points out that political executives find it very difficult to commit themselves credibly to long-term strategies and solutions. Politicians live with the short-term cycles of elections, and their horizons usually do not go beyond the next election. In addition, politicians face another commitment problem in that they cannot bind a subsequent legislature and government, making public policies vulnerable to reneging and therefore a lack of credibility.[10] Hence, referring back to Kaufmann, Kraay, and Zoido-Lobaton's principle regarding sound policy-making, delegating the authority of regulation to an independent agency not only resolves the government's credibility problem, but it would be proof of good governance by the politicians—and would address one of their key governance problems.

Accountability

Theory increasingly recognizes that independence goes hand in hand with accountability. One of the underlying premises of this paper is that there is no trade-off between independence and accountability, but rather that the two are complementary. Independence cannot be achieved without accountability.

Accountability is essential for an agency to justify its actions against the background of the mandate given to it. Agencies should give the reasons for their decisions. Independent agents should be accountable not only to those who delegate the responsibility—the government or the legislature—but also to those who fall under their jurisdiction, and to the public at large.

While the principle of accountability has been generally accepted—both as a complement of independence and as a component of good governance—implementing it in practice has met with difficulties. In general, proper accountability requires a complex combination of approaches. Majone argues that "a highly complex and specialized activity like regulation can be monitored and kept politically accountable only by a combination of control instruments: legislative and executive oversight, strict

10. Majone (1997).

procedural requirements, public participation, and, most importantly, substantive judicial review."[11] In many countries, this mix has not yet been achieved. Moreover, the ultimate objective of the agency also matters. Accountability is easier to implement when the agency has a clearly defined and measurable objective. Central banks pursuing an inflation target can be held accountable for reaching this target. In contrast, supervisors typically have broader and less defined objectives, such as preserving financial stability or consumer protection. Holding them accountable for achieving such objectives is much trickier than in the case of a central bank's monetary policy mandate.[12]

Transparency

Making the structure and the actions of the regulatory agency transparent is the third component of good governance. Transparency in monetary and financial policies refers to an environment in which objectives, frameworks, decisions and their rationale, data and other information, as well as terms of accountability are provided to the public in a comprehensive, accessible, and timely manner.[13]

Transparency has increasingly been recognized as a "good" in itself, but it also serves other purposes related to the other components of governance. Policymakers are recognizing that globalization in general and the integration of financial markets and products in particular require a greater degree of transparency in monetary and financial policies, and in regulatory regimes and processes, as a means of containing market uncertainty. In addition, transparency has become a powerful vehicle for countering poor operating policies and practices. Indeed, it is one thing to be transparent *in* the policies, but it is another thing to be transparent *about* bad policies. As such, efforts to enhance transparency—mainly driven by the International Monetary Fund's Code of Good Practices on Transparency in Monetary and Financial Policies (MFP Code)—are helping to focus on the need for enhanced disclosure of monetary and financial policies and their operating framework.[14]

11. Majone (1993).
12. See Goodhart (2001) on this topic.
13. IMF (2000).
14. IMF. "Code of Good Practices on Transparency in Monetary and Financial Policies" (www.imf.org/external/np/mae/mft/code/index.htm).

Increased transparency also supports the achievement of other components of regulatory governance and thus contributes to credibility. First, it directly supports accountability by making the actions of the agency clear to governments, markets, and the public. Second, it protects the independence of the agency by demonstrating when and under which form interference is taking place. Supervision, for instance, is a highly invisible function, which makes it vulnerable to interference—by both politicians and the supervised entities—and such interference can be very subtle. Thus, transparency—balanced by the legitimate need for commercial confidentiality—may discourage politicians and the supervised from interfering in the process.[15] Furthermore, transparency may limit self-interest on the part of the supervisors. Finally, transparency in regulation and supervision may also be instrumental in increasing the commitment of bank managers, directors, and owners to prudent behavior and risk control of the financial business.[16]

Integrity

This final component of regulatory governance reflects the mechanisms for ensuring that staff of the regulatory agencies can pursue institutional goals of good regulatory governance without compromising them due to their own behavior or self-interest. Integrity affects regulatory agency staff at various levels. First, procedures for appointment of heads, their terms of office, and criteria for removal should safeguard the integrity of the agency's policymaking officials. Second, the integrity of the agency's day-to-day operations also needs to be ensured. Effective internal governance implies that internal audit arrangements are in place to ensure that the agency's objectives are clearly set and observed, decisions are made and implemented, and accountability is maintained. Thus, ensuring the quality of the agency's operations will maintain the integrity of the institution and strengthen its credibility with the outside world. Third, integrity implies the presence of standards for the conduct of personal affairs of management and staff to

---

15. Quintyn and Taylor (2002).

16. See also Halme (2000) who also discusses the need for, and difference between, ex ante and ex post disclosure practices. She notes that supervisory agencies with well-established disclosure procedures (such as the Financial Services Authority in the United Kingdom) typically have ex post disclosure requirements. Ex ante disclosure requirements are recognized to be more problematic as they can create more ambiguity.

prevent exploitation of conflicts of interest. A fourth element of integrity is legal protection for the regulatory staff for actions taken while discharging their official duties. Without such legal protection, objectivity of staff is prone to challenge—and staff to bribery or threat—and the overall effectiveness and credibility of the institution can suffer greatly.

These four components of good regulatory governance—independence, accountability, transparency and integrity—interact and reinforce each other. Independence and accountability represent two sides of the same coin. Transparency is a vehicle for safeguarding independence; it is also a key instrument to make accountability work. Transparency also helps to establish and safeguard integrity in that published arrangements provide even better protection for staff of the regulatory agencies. It can also be argued that independence and integrity reinforce each other. For instance, legal protection of agency staff, as well as clear rules for appointment and removal of agency heads support both their independence and their integrity. Finally, accountability and integrity are also mutually reinforcing. Accountability requirements give agency heads and staff additional reasons to maintain their integrity. The preconditions for meeting these four components are discussed in the next section, as part of the discussion of the various standards used to evaluate regulatory governance.

Regulatory Governance and Crisis Prevention

Promoting good governance has become an area of key importance for the International Monetary Fund (IMF) and international financial institutions in general (box 6-1). The IMF limits itself to the economic aspects of governance and promotes good regulatory governance through the use of several instruments. These include advice and technical assistance to strengthen policymaking institutions (central banks and regulatory agencies) and actions aimed at strengthening integrity and transparency in financial transactions. Prominent in this second category are

—safeguards assessments[17]
—implementation of good policy transparency practices

17. The safeguards assessments fulfill an "assurance role" by identifying vulnerabilities in a central bank's control, reporting, auditing systems, and legal structure that may impair the bank's integrity and affect its operations.

Box 6-1. *The IMF and Promotion of Good Governance*

The IMF is concerned about poor governance as an obstacle to growth and a threat to economic stability. During its review of governance in February 2001, the IMF Executive Board welcomed the proactive role of the Fund in this area, and reaffirmed that this role emanates from the Fund's mandate to promote macroeconomic stability and sustained noninflationary growth among its members.

The Fund contributes to good governance through its policy advice, technical assistance, and program conditionality. It does so within its areas of expertise, which cover the effective and transparent management of public resources and the maintenance of a stable, economic, regulatory, and legal environment.

In the interest of safeguarding Fund resources, the Fund has a policy for strengthening the accounting and auditing of central banks of program countries. The Fund's *Code of Good Practices on Transparency in Monetary and Financial Policies* also constitutes an important governance initiative. The Fund's *Code of Good Practices on Fiscal Transparency* is also an important governance-related initiative. The code emphasizes the need for clarity of roles and responsibilities of the government; public availability of information; open budget preparation, execution, and reporting; and assurances of integrity.

The IMF's approach rests heavily on initiatives across the membership, especially the codification of best practices in policy transparency and accountability. However, the Fund also addresses individual instances of poor governance or corruption—in advice or conditionality—when they are of macroeconomic importance. The Fund's executive board has been highlighting governance as an issue of concern in roughly one-third of its country discussions, as reflected in the public information notices issued afterward.

—evaluation of anti–money laundering supervisory regimes

—steps put in place to combat financing of terrorist activities by financial intermediaries.[18]

The main vehicle for evaluating regulatory governance practices in the overall context of macroeconomic stability is the joint IMF-World Bank Financial Sector Assessment Program, which is aimed at identifying the

---

18. Money laundering and the financing of terrorism have been recognized as global problems that not only affect security, but also harm the transparency, efficiency, and overall stability of financial systems. In evaluating the framework for combating money laundering operations and terrorist financing, an assessment is also made of the organizational and administrative arrangements of relevant agencies.

risks, vulnerabilities, and development needs in the financial system.[19] One of the main principles underlying the FSAP is the view that shortcomings in the regulatory governance framework are a source of risk, particularly in a period of a financial crisis. The FSAP thus integrates regulatory institutions into its analysis, based on the premise that they are fundamental to the structure of financial systems and that the manner in which regulatory functions are conducted influences the performance characteristics of the financial system.[20]

The FSAP analyzes the financial sector of a country and evaluates the likely impact of macroeconomic and structural factors on its performance and stability. In this context, the assessment of regulatory governance issues supports a more complete evaluation of the financial system, allowing an examination of the relative importance of various types of financial institutions in the overall policy, regulatory, and institutional context (box 6-2). Drawing upon the expertise of the IMF-World Bank staff, and a broad range of experts, the FSAP provides an assessment framework that offers "peer review" of national financial systems, and a common platform for policy advice and technical assistance from the IMF and the World Bank.[21]

The main instrument the FSAP uses to assess regulatory governance practices is the key international financial sector standards.[22] Since the inception of the FSAP in 1999, regulatory governance issues have been assessed in more than 45 countries, through more than 200 standards assessments. The standards routinely assessed under the FSAP covering regulatory governance issues are

—The IMF Code of Good Practices on Transparency in Monetary and Financial Policies (MFP Code)

19. For a more detailed description of the FSAP, along with a review of experience with the program, see IMF-World Bank, "Financial Sector Assessment Program (FSAP), A Review: Lessons from the Pilot and Issues Going Forward" (www.imf.org/external/np/fsap/2001/review.htm), together with the associated public information notice (www.imf.org/external/np/sec/pn/2001/pn0111.htm).

20. The regulatory governance assessments under the FSAP do not go into aspects such as control of corruption in the financial system, unrest in the financial system, and rule of law.

21. The experts come from the fifty Cooperating Official Institutions under the FSAP, consisting of central banks, regulatory and supervisory agencies, standard setting bodies and multilateral development banks.

22. Standards assessments under the FSAP are used to support the broader assessment of the macroeconomic and structural risks affecting domestic financial systems. They help to identify shortcomings in financial sector regulation, supervision, and market infrastructure, thus providing input into the determination of priorities for financial system reform and development. The assessment findings also help countries evaluate their systems against international benchmarks.

Box 6-2. *How Does the FSAP Help to Assess Regulatory Governance?*

Good governance within a financial system is predicated on good regulatory governance. The evaluations made under the FSAP thus help to:

—understand how the regulatory authority is exercised in a country, including the processes through which regulators are selected, held accountable, monitored, and whether shortcomings with respect to these are leading to vulnerabilities in the domestic financial system;

—assess the level of observance of good governance practices required under the various financial sector standards;

—determine whether or not the regulatory resources are being properly managed so as to ensure the pursuit of consistent and effective regulatory and supervisory policies;

—assess whether the governance framework is conducive for preserving policy continuity, which is a necessary condition for policy credibility;

—determine the extent to which regulatory governance is risk-oriented (operational risk) and whether adequate systems are in place to identify, disclose, and manage the risks;

—ascertain the credibility and integrity of the regulatory body as a policymaking and enforcment body; and

—prioritize financial sector reform to enhance the governance framework and provide support through technical assistance.

—Basel Core Principles for Effective Banking Supervision (BCP)

—Committee on Payments and Settlement Systems Core Principles for Systemically Important Payment Systems (CPSIPS)

—International Organization of Securities Commissions Objectives and Principles of Securities Regulation (IOSCO Principles)

—International Association of Insurance Supervisors Insurance Core Principles (ICP).[23]

While the MFP Code applies to transparency practices in all financial regulatory agencies, the other four regulatory standards are intended for use specifically in their individual sectors. These focus almost exclusively on the independence of the regulatory agency as a starting point and then shift their focus to how regulatory agencies instill good governance prac-

---

23. The Principles of Corporate Governance issued by the Organization for Economic Cooperation and Development are also being assessed on a selective basis under the FSAP. They are used as a diagnostic tool for assessing the strengths and weaknesses of the corporate governance framework.

tices in the regulated entities. This approach, while useful, seems to be based on the straightforward "agency" perspective, requiring a separation of ownership (by the government or legislature) and control. The regulatory standards, therefore, do not provide a comprehensive overview of regulatory governance and its four components: independence, accountability, transparency, and integrity. The MFP Code, in contrast, focuses more directly on transparency arrangements, mainly as a prerequisite for the practice of good governance. Thus, the four components of regulatory governance cannot be meaningfully analyzed directly. The analysis of the assessment findings of governance practices requires that the different governance-related elements from the regulatory standards and the MFP Code be brought together in an attempt to distill an overview.

Although the evaluation of financial sector governance issues under the FSAP is based primarily on qualitative measures, steps are under way to integrate governance issues into the FSAP's quantitative framework. As this work progresses, the FSAP findings should help shed more light on issues such as the extent to which good regulatory governance is correlated to financial stability or improved performance of the banking system, or in finding causal relationships between good regulatory governance and growth and development of financial systems.

Regulatory Standards and Regulatory Governance

Regulatory standards are premised on the view that effective regulation and supervision of the financial system depends on several factors that lie outside the regulatory and supervisory framework. These standards emphasize the importance of a proper governance structure within which the regulatory bodies operate. This is regarded as an important prerequisite given the regulatory objectives, such as the preservation of systemic stability, or ensuring that the regulated markets operate on a fair and efficient basis. Based on a comparative analysis of the regulatory standards undertaken by the Joint Forum (comprising the Basel Committee, IAIS, and IOSCO), the following governance-related components can be identified:[24]

—All regulatory standards require that the regulators have *operational independence* and that the rules and regulations are applied in a consistent manner to all regulated entities. This is essential to ensure that the regulatory objectives are pursued without interference from either the political

24. Joint Forum (2001).

and the executive apparatus or the regulated entities. While independence is considered essential for operational objectivity and efficiency, good regulatory governance practice also requires that the regulators maintain open communication with the regulated entities and markets and consult with them in the formulation of regulations and oversight mechanisms.

—Another regulatory requirement relates to adequacy of minimum staff resources, legal protection for the regulatory staff, and expectations that the staff will maintain the highest professional standards. These hint at the integrity aspects of regulatory governance. In turn, the regulatory agencies should be accountable for their actions, through mechanisms such as reports to the legislature, annual reports, and audited financial accounts.

—Effectiveness of the governance framework is integrally connected with the enforcement powers and capabilities of the regulator. The internal and external governance structure should allow regulators to take remedial action on a timely basis to deal with impending and actual problems. While all banking, insurance, and securities regulators should have the authority to investigate possible violations and take legal action against regulated institutions and associated individuals, securities regulators should have wider authority to take action against nonsupervised entities and individuals for violations of securities laws.

—The regulatory standards call for clarity and transparency of the regulatory process as another element of good governance. Regulators should adopt clear policymaking processes, and the practices must be transparent and comprehensible to the interested institutions and individuals. Such clarity allows regulated entities to be certain of the rules to which they must adhere when undertaking their business activities. It also facilitates regulatory accountability to the public.

Transparency Code and Regulatory Governance

The MFP Code emphasizes a set of transparency procedures the IMF believes is desirable. Transparency, in itself, is not the end. However, through public accountability mechanisms, disclosing and explaining the governance structure, and clarifying the decisionmaking process, the regulatory agency gains market credibility, which in turn, should contribute to policy effectiveness. The release of adequate information to the public on the activities and financial operations of financial agencies provides an additional mechanism for enhancing the credibility of agency actions. Public accountability of decisions by financial agencies may also reduce the potential for moral hazard in some cases. Financial market participants are better able to assess the actions of the regulator and the context of financial policies. The element of uncertainty is considerably reduced, thus helping promote financial system stability.

The MFP Code addresses governance-related aspects of transparency as follows:

—*Accountability of the regulator.* Financial agency officials should be available to explain the agency's objectives and performance to the public; the agencies should issue periodic public reports on the policies used in the pursuit of their overall objectives and the developments in the financial sectors under their jurisdiction; and the agencies should disclose their audited financial statements and their underlying accounting policies, aggregate market transactions, and operating revenues and expenses.

—*Integrity of the regulator.* There should be public disclosure of procedures for appointment, terms of office, and dismissal of financial agency officials; of codes of conduct regulating staff's personal financial affairs and conflicts of interest; and of any legal protections for officials and staff of financial agencies.

—*Transparency of regulatory policy.* Public disclosure and explanation of the financial agencies' regulatory framework and operating procedures, of significant changes in financial policies, and public consultations whenever substantive changes in financial regulations are proposed;

—*Oversight of consumer protection and client asset protection schemes,* specifically requiring public disclosure of the nature, form, source of financing, and performance of client asset protection schemes, and of information on any consumer protection arrangements operated by financial agencies.

—*Transparency of regulatory operations.* In addition to recommending that agencies disclose their objectives, their institutional framework, and their procedures for appointing and dismissing officials, public disclosure of the relationship between various financial agencies, including formal procedures for information sharing and consultation, between financial agencies, and self-regulatory organizations under their oversight.

Prerequisites for the Conduct of Good Regulatory Governance

The regulatory standards describe several prerequisites that are essential for the conduct of good regulatory governance. The first requirement is the existence of sound and sustainable macroeconomic policies that are conducive to intermediation of household savings and investment. Volatile conditions in the money market, or the foreign exchange markets, and uncertain inflationary tendencies create conditions under which regulatory principles cannot always be applied consistently, thus undermining regulatory objectives.

Creation of an effective market infrastructure is also important for a well-governed regulatory agency. Elements of a market infrastructure include a fair and effective legal and judicial system and a tax and accounting framework.[25] These are regarded as essential for the regulatory body to be able to perform its functions in a coherent, credible, and consistent fashion. In the absence of these prerequisites, "regulatory forbearance" becomes relatively easy to conceal or disguise. The objectivity and credibility of the regulatory agency can also be concealed (couched under the pretext of "confidentiality considerations" or "systemic concerns")—especially when the regulator and the regulated entity believe that hiding the regulatory actions is in their mutual interest.

The above approach adopted by the regulatory standards and the MFP Code toward regulatory governance can be summarized in ten main elements. Most of the elements, in turn, can be related to the four components of good governance—independence, accountability, transparency, and integrity (box 6-3).

Relationship between Regulatory and Financial Sector Corporate Governance

All the regulatory standards require that the regulators encourage sound corporate governance within the supervised entities. Wherever legally permissible, the regulators are required to regulate the corporate governance requirements. The regulatory standards thus provide a balance between the governance requirements for the regulator and for the regulated entities. Corporate governance mechanisms vary across the financial sectors, and among economies. There is growing awareness that good corporate gover-

---

25. The importance of preconditions for effective governance are increasingly being emphasized. Kane (2001) for example, in an analysis of financial safety nets, emphasizes that the implementation of international best practices does not necessarily lead to the desired policy effectiveness and that more attention needs to be given to existing preconditions, which he summarizes under three headings: the existing degree of transparency, deterrence, and accountability in the society.

nance practices are important both to the firm itself and the economy as a whole. The respective roles and responsibilities of the board, management, auditors, and actuaries (in insurance) in the risk management process are of particular interest.

The primary responsibility for the conduct of business of the entity lies with the board and management of the firm. In particular, their responsibilities include establishing and maintaining policies and procedures regarding risk management and internal controls and to ensure the firm complies with the statutory and supervisory obligations imposed on it. Supervisors in all three sectors devote a great deal of time and attention to these areas.

Persons filling key roles should have the necessary skills and experience to carry out their tasks appropriately, and the regulator has a role in assessing the qualifications and integrity of these key personnel. The participation of board members who can exercise objectivity, independent of management, is recognized good practice. Internal audit, external audit, and the oversight function of the board in the financial area (directly or through a committee such as the audit committee) support the effective operation of supervised firms.

Although regulatory goals in this area may be approximately the same, regulators often use different methods to encourage good corporate governance. For example, several countries issue guidance to their firms, while others use a common supervisory program to be applied during on-site inspections. Other methods include setting out detailed mandatory statutory requirements, publishing a reference document for supervisors, or drawing up tripartite contracts among the regulator , the external auditors, and the company. There is a clear trend toward both greater emphasis on corporate governance issues and on increasing the transparency of the supervisors' and other standard setters' expectations regarding what constitutes a good or appropriate corporate governance framework at a supervised firm.

Regulatory Governance in Practice: Main Findings from Country Assessments

In this section, we present the main findings relating to observance of good regulatory governance practices by regulatory bodies in banking, insurance, securities, and payment systems oversight. The assessment findings

> Box 6-3. *Regulatory Governance Framework Based on the Financial Sector Standards*
>
> Ten core elements, derived from international financial sector standards, should be part of any good regulatory governance framework.
>
> *Independence*
>
> 1. Regulatory bodies should have a well-founded and modern legal and institutional structure for licensing, regulating, and overseeing financial intermediaries and financial markets.
>
> 2. Regulatory bodies should be empowered to enforce legal and regulatory provisions relating to corporate governance among the regulated financial firms.
>
> 3. Regulatory bodies should be free from politically motivated interference and be ensured independence in decisionmaking.
>
> 4. Regulatory agencies should have adequate staff skills and resources, with competitive pay scales to allow professional conduct of regulatory functions.
>
> *Accountability*
>
> 5. Formal mechanisms should exist for collaborative partnerships and interagency coordination among regulatory bodies. In areas of overlap, accountability in decisionmaking should be clearly established.
>
> 6. The accountability framework (of the board and the regulatory staff) should be clearly defined and cover reporting relationships, powers to appoint and remove regulators, liability, independence, and business ethics.

are helping national authorities to focus on issues of accountability, independence, and integrity within a transparent framework, thus enhancing the regulatory governance framework.

These assessments are limited, however, because the regulatory standards are couched in general terms, thus leaving the assessments of governance practices open to considerable scope for interpretation. Moreover, several assessments have been carried out in the absence of a fully developed assessment methodology, which so far has constrained the evaluation of the implementation issues.[26] Consequently, valid and statistically well-founded conclusions are difficult. Nonetheless, the findings

---

26. Assessment methodologies are being developed for the assessment of securities regulation and monetary and financial policy transparency.

Integrity

7. Regulatory bodies should have formal systems to ensure integrity, including codes of conduct for regulators and members of the regulatory board.

8. Consultative processes should be established through which the regulated firms and users of financial services participate in the formulation of rules, regulations, and legal reform.

9. Mechanisms should be established for regulated firms and consumers to seek redress when they believe their rights have been violated.

Transparency

10. Each regulatory body should adequately disclose information on its governance structure, policies, performance, regulatory objectives, and internal polices relating to internal audit and control, and the mechanisms through which it avoids fraud and conflicts of interest.

Crisis Management

Two additional principles are central to good governance in managing systemic financial crisis:

Exceptional measures should be formulated and implemented in a transparent manner and the authorities should adhere to high accountability standards.

The four components of regulatory governance should underpin all exceptional institutional arrangements.

provide several useful insights and indications of the overall trends in regulatory governance.

Before looking at individual financial sectors, there are several general observations to be made:

—Many regulatory bodies promote good governance across a full range of internationally accepted principles and practices, while others are more selective. Some regulatory agencies appear to be operating in an environment that has a tradition and culture for more openness than others do.

—The governance framework is influenced by institutional factors, the underlying legal framework, and country-specific circumstances. Some regulatory agencies are "composite," that is, they are responsible for more than one financial sector; some are independent agencies, while others are part of a larger government unit. These differences explain the divergent approaches toward regulatory governance. The creation of composite financial regulatory agencies in a number of countries has enhanced the focus on the role and form of governance arrangements, although the governance practices that have been adopted are relatively recent, experimental, and not yet fully tested.

—In several countries, the governance framework applies to all units of government and to all or identified public servants. Regulatory agencies are typically subject to these governmentwide provisions and must follow the same practices as other units of government. In some cases, however, regulatory agencies reconfirm or supplement the governmentwide governance practices in their publicly available bylaws or similar document.

—Substantial effort is needed to build public understanding of the need for and objectives of good regulatory governance. In many cases the rationale for an independent and accountable regulator is not always clear, hence undermining efforts to instill good governance practices.

—Differences also exist in the governance framework within which enforcement of regulations takes place. In the banking sector, supervisory remedial actions of a prudential nature are not always publicly announced for fear of compounding financial problems even though public attention increases the chance of the action being effective. Similar considerations apply to prudential issues in the insurance sector, although insurance supervisors in some jurisdictions favor disclosure of remedial actions involving conduct of business. Securities investigations are not public, but enforcement proceedings generally are. Securities supervisors typically publish the results of proceedings and sanctions imposed to warn customers of particular entities or schemes.

—The transparency aspects relating to regulatory governance are mostly weak and require considerable strengthening. This shortcoming is made worse through technical or complex legislative or regulatory requirements and poor public accessibility of texts of laws and regulations. Accountability documents such as memoranda of understanding among the regulatory bodies are often treated as sensitive internal documents. Similarly, delays in publishing documents such as annual reports, which provide a good basis to report on the practice of governance, serve better as a document of record than as a timely source of information.

—The content of governance-related disclosure also varies. In many instances, the information being provided is not particularly relevant to the issue at hand. Regulatory agencies often explain their performance in very general and often contradictory terms. Similarly, in some cases the governance framework is not applied consistently (for example, an agency many reverse a previously applied practice in the face of unfavorable developments).

—Recommendations arising out of the assessments of regulatory governance carried out in the context of the broader macroeconomic and prudential considerations are helping the regulatory bodies to focus on governance-related issues and are strengthening the institutional arrangements in the overall context of risk and control environment.

—Finally, the approach to good regulatory governance appears to be evolving, reflecting changes in the international environment. Policymakers everywhere are considering the benefits and costs of good governance, whom it protects, and how it can improve financial system stability. The notion of improved regulatory governance is gaining greater public attention, alongside the emphasis being given to enhanced corporate governance on the part of the regulated entities.

Regulatory Governance across Financial Sectors

Governance frameworks differ across financial sectors based on the primary objectives of regulation. Securities regulatory agencies primarily emphasize market efficiency, for example, while banking regulators and payment system oversight agencies focus on market and systemic stability. Insurance regulators focus principally on policyholder protection.

Each of the regulatory governance principles was assessed on the grading scale suggested by the individual standard setter. The assessment for each principle or practice was then aggregated across the assessed countries. The main observation to emerge from this comparison is that securities regulators have a better governance structure than the other sectoral regulators, while insurance regulators need to carry out more work to strengthen their governance framework.[27]

BANKING REGULATOR. The assessments show that in many countries, banking regulatory agencies lacked an explicit framework to promote good

27. These have been presented according to the country classifications (advanced, developing, transitional) used by the IMF's World Economic Outlook (WEO) in order to show differences across various groups of countries. However, given the limitations of the assessment sample, less than comprehensive treatment of regulatory governance by the respective standards, and some of the assessment methodological problems, any inference about which group of countries has a high or low degree of regulatory governance needs to be approached with caution. Both weak and strong regulatory governance practices are present within all the WEO-based groupings.

regulatory governance. The assessments indicate several instances where regulators encountered political interference, including interference in the decisionmaking and budgetary process and arbitrary removal of the senior personnel. Apart from political interference, there are shortcomings relating to operational independence and overlapping regulatory responsibilities.[28] The lack of clear separation of functions (or of mechanisms for regulatory coordination) is among the main reasons for a lack of authority highlighted by the assessments.

The governance framework for banking regulators is also impaired in many cases by the lack of trained agency supervisors who are able to enforce consistent and transparent application of rules and regulations. Assessments reveal that where legal protection for supervisors does not exist, legal actions against them, or the threat of such actions, have interfered with consistent application of supervisory measures. Legal protections for supervisors vary greatly, ranging from explicit provisions in the banking law to administrative provisions, to no protections at all.

Effective governance is also undercut by inadequate enforcement powers given to the banking supervisors. This inadequacy often undermines the credibility and integrity of the banking supervisor in trying to enforce prudential regulations or other regulatory directives, with institutions typically found to be noncompliant with the prudential regulations. A related problem is weak enforcement (delays or other shortcomings in the judicial system, political interference, lack of decisionmaking, or low staff morale). In addition, the assessments are revealing shortcomings in the macroeconomic framework or market infrastructure, which are beyond the direct purview of the regulators and require time and political will to be corrected.

Priority recommendations for addressing these shortcomings include improving the functioning and independence of the banking supervisor, addressing the organizational weaknesses, and strengthening the legal framework and supervisory powers to take prompt corrective action in a transparent and accountable manner. Other recommendations call for legal protection for the regulators and strengthening of the formal mechanisms for the exchange of supervisory information.

---

28. Also see IMF review of the "Experience with the Assessment of Basel Core Principles" (www.imf.org/external/np/mae/bcore/exp.htm), and IMF-World Bank (forthcoming.)

INSURANCE REGULATORS. Assessments reveal several shortcomings in the overall governance of the insurance sector.[29] The main problems are weak institutional capacity of insurance supervisors, characterized by inadequate supervisory skills and staff; lack of financial resources and operational independence; and a nontransparent accountability framework.

Governance arrangements that can ensure integrity of the insurance supervisor are deficient. Among other common problems: internal governance procedures are not documented; cooperative and information-sharing agreements with other supervisory agencies are not in place; financial statements of the insurance supervisor are not audited on a preannounced schedule; and some of the procedures for appointment, terms of office, and removal of insurance supervisory officials are not clearly defined.

In several cases, the legal powers for carrying out insurance regulation were inadequate. Relevant legislation and regulations failed to set out the role and responsibilities of the board of directors of insurance companies, and supervisors did not have the authority to define the role of directors. Similarly, powers relating to enforcement and taking prompt action against problem insurers or for ensuring an orderly wind-up of insolvent insurers were missing.

The preconditions for effective insurance supervision varied from country to country. In some, good laws were either in the process of being adopted or were recently passed but not yet tested in practice. In some countries, familiarity with the laws was weak, while in others, assessors concluded that the judiciary system was weak, laws were outdated, and there were few qualified actuaries, accountants, auditors, and financial analysts. In a few cases where the laws were outdated, the judiciary system was found to be satisfactory and some qualified professionals were present.

The main recommendations for strengthening the governance arrangements include: increasing the number of professional staff in the supervisory agency; providing budgetary independence to safeguard the agency's independence and effectiveness; improving the supervisory framework; enhancing the independence of the supervisor; and strengthening indemnity of the supervisory staff. Governance-related prerequisites such as the legal infrastructure, accounting, and disclosure practices were also recommended for strengthening.

29. Also see IMF-World Bank, "Experience with the Insurance Core Principles Assessments under the Financial Sector Assessment Program" (www.imf.org/external/np/mae/ins/2001/eng/).

SECURITIES REGULATORS. The assessments reveal that governance-related practices are well in place in securities regulatory agencies but that weaknesses exist in some of the key elements.[30] In particular, operational independence and accountability are impaired by inadequate financial and staff resources. Similarly, the objectives of the securities regulator in terms of the scope of responsibility and independence were weak.

Several securities regulators, particularly in developing markets, were assessed as having resources that were inadequate for discharging the functional responsibilities assigned to the agency. The assessments also revealed the spread of regulatory responsibilities across several agencies or a lack of clarity of roles (particularly between self-regulatory organizations and the regulator). These shortcomings tend to dilute the overall effectiveness of the regulatory regime and often result in the use of informal administrative arrangements to ensure that appropriate oversight is maintained.

Operational independence was potentially compromised in some jurisdictions where the Ministry of Finance or other governmental body retained administrative control of the regulator's budget. The manner in which the head of agency was appointed was also seen as having the potential to lead to unnecessary political intervention in the operations of the regulator.

Inadequate enforcement power was also a problem for securities regulators. While comprehensive powers of inspection, investigation, and surveillance exist, several shortcomings were found with regard to enforcing compliance and prompt corrective action. In some cases, the effectiveness of oversight is constrained by limited availability of sanction powers or by an inefficient judicial system through which sanctions have to be applied.

Recommendations therefore call for strengthening the independence of the regulator and assigning adequate budgetary and staff resources, expanding inspection programs and market surveillance operations, providing greater enforcement and sanction powers, and establishing mechanisms for enhancing cooperation and information sharing among domestic regulators. In cases where securities regulatory reforms were under way, governance-related aspects were integrated in the planned reform.

PAYMENT SYSTEMS OVERSIGHT. The assessments reveal significant deficiencies in the effectiveness of the governance structure relating to pay-

---

30. Also see IMF-World Bank, "Experience with the Assessments of the IOSCO Objectives and Principles of Securities Regulation under the Financial Sector Assessment Program" (www.imf.org/external/np/mae/IOSCO/2002/eng/041802.htm).

ment systems. More than half of the systemically important payment systems operated by central banks are not subject to adequate oversight. Nor do central banks fully cooperate with other relevant authorities, domestic or foreign. In some countries the central bank lacks the statutory authority to oversee those payment systems that it does not itself operate. Independence and functional clarity relating to the central banks' oversight objectives are also weak.

Considerable divergence in governance practices has emerged among different groups of countries. The assessments suggest that in a significant majority of developing countries governance of the payment system is weak. Although transition economies appear, in general, to be markedly less vulnerable than developing countries to systemic shocks arising from their payment systems, weaknesses remain with in the governance and oversight of those payment systems, including those operated by the central banks themselves. The governance structures for payment systems in advanced countries appear generally well established.

Most of the governance-related recommendations on payment systems have related to central bank oversight. Recommendations include strengthening the oversight power of the central bank and providing it with a statutory base; improving the resources and expertise of the oversight staff; separating the oversight function from other central bank tasks, including banking and payment system operations and, where applicable, banking supervision; clarifying the respective roles and responsibilities of the central bank and the banking supervisors regarding the payment system and its participants; and developing a cooperative arrangement with the banking supervisor, including a formal protocol or memorandum of understanding.

Transparency of the Governance Framework

The assessment of how well regulatory agencies meet the MFP Codes transparency practices reveal that transparency of the governance framework is strongest among security markets regulators, followed closely by their counterparts in banking and payment systems. Among all regulatory bodies, governance-related transparency practices on disclosure of the regulatory and policy framework are well established, followed by transparency related to general accountability and disclosure of objectives, institutional framework, and responsibilities.

GENERAL OBSERVATIONS. In most countries the broad governance framework of the financial agencies is specified in legislation or regulations.

In some countries, however, this is not the case for one or more of the following: procedures for appointment, terms of office, and criteria for removal of members of the governing body of the regulatory agency.

Transparency is markedly inadequate in the area of public disclosure of relationships between financial agencies and of formal procedures for information sharing and consultation between agencies.[31] Transparency is lacking in financial accountability, particularly of insurance supervisors, and disclosure of integrity safeguards.

Whereas almost all independent financial agencies publish audited financial statements, deficiencies in financial accountability of regulatory agencies that are either entirely or partly funded by the state budget were frequently noted. In these cases either the transparency of the budgetary process was deemed inferior to direct disclosure of financial statements, or audits were performed internally and not by an independent audit agency.

Significant shortcomings in the public disclosure of internal governance procedures for ensuring integrity of operations including internal audit arrangements were found in all four sectors but were most pronounced among insurance and securities regulatory agencies. In many of these cases, internal governance arrangements were not disclosed at all, or existing codes of conduct were only available upon request.

FINDINGS ACROSS COUNTRIES. The assessments show that developing countries significantly lag behind advanced countries, especially in the areas of published and financial accountability and in the public disclosure of the relationship between financial agencies. This latter aspect of transparency is also weak in transitional countries, where transparency practices are otherwise on a par with advanced countries. Public disclosure of broad objectives, institutional framework, and responsibilities is stronger among banking and payment systems supervisors in transition countries than in any other financial sector or country grouping. The fact that these countries' legal systems are new and may have benefited from the collective experience of other countries may account for this strength. The relatively high average degree of observance of governance-related transparency practices by supervisory agencies masks an underlying deep transparency divide

---

31. Assessments have noted that while procedures for information sharing and cooperative agreements exist, they are not publicly disclosed; only the partial text of the memoranda of understanding between agencies is published; the relationship between financial agencies remains informal and confidential; the law does not clearly delineate the roles and responsibilities of agencies.

between advanced and transition economies on the one hand and developing counties on the other.

TRANSPARENCY IN BANKING SUPERVISION. With some exceptions, the good relative standing of banking supervisors on transparency issues is attributable in part to the fact that in many countries this function is carried out by the central bank, which tends to be stronger institutionally and better funded. Banking regulators demonstrate a strong ability to disclose publicly their supervisory objectives and responsibilities, their regulatory framework and operating procedures, and financial reporting requirements on which regulatory oversight and surveillance is conducted, and to consult with market constituents on changes in the regulatory or the operational framework.

In contrast, accountability and integrity of banking supervisors are weak and need strengthening. The assessments also reveal several shortcomings in the content and scope of information disclosed on annual operating expenses and revenues related to banking supervision. For instance, the operating costs and expenses relating to banking regulation may be consolidated with the overall accounts of the central bank, or information on total revenue and expenses may be available only through the annual report, but with no further details available. Common weaknesses in published accountability are the lack of any periodic public report on major developments in the sector and the long and variable delays in its publication.

Another element relates to the institutional and accountability arrangements among the different financial agencies. Assessments reveal that the rules governing the exchange of information and the relationship between financial agencies remain informal and confidential. Accountability as it relates to the activities of these agencies in the areas of overlap is also weak. In almost all countries, procedures for information sharing exist, but they are not publicly disclosed. Most developing and transition economies are still working out the details regarding the information-sharing arrangement with the various domestic and international supervisory bodies.

Recommendations on enhancing transparency have emphasized increased and timely disclosure of statistical data for the banking sector, including emergency financial support, publication of formal information-sharing agreements between financial agencies, annual disclosure of the results of banking sector operations, and public dissemination of regulatory guidelines and rules.

TRANSPARENCY IN INSURANCE SUPERVISION. Insurance supervisors' transparency practices are strongest in the public disclosure and explanation of the regulatory framework and operating procedures governing their activities, and in involving market participants in the making of policy changes. As in the case of banking supervisors, considerable weaknesses remain with respect to accountability and assurances of integrity of insurance supervisors.

The assessments find that insurance law does not prescribe any formal accountability mechanism; that accountability is hindered by legislative provisions that make one part of the government responsible for appointing the head of the agency, while supervision is conducted by another agency; that dissemination of information on regulatory activities is limited, sometimes going only to other government agencies; that agency officials are not required by law to appear before a public authority; that existing internal governance procedures are not disclosed to market participants; and that one or more elements of the procedures for appointment, terms of office, and removal of officials are not specified in legislation.

Similarly, practices relating to public disclosure of formal procedures for information sharing and consultation with market participants are weak. In several instances, only the partial text of the memoranda of understanding between agencies is published; in other cases the cooperation agreements are not publicly disclosed at all. Public availability of audited financial statements is irregular, making it impossible for the market to know when it can expect such information.

Recommendations have focused on implementing transparency practices in formulating and reporting insurance regulatory policies. In particular, recommendations have sought improvements in transparency about the relationships between the insurance, banking, and securities regulatory agencies and of the formal information-sharing arrangements with other insurance regulators.

TRANSPARENCY IN SECURITIES REGULATION. The strength of securities regulators' governance-related transparency practices is based on their success relative to other financial agencies in the public disclosure and explanation of their regulatory framework and operating procedures, in involving market participants in determining future courses of action, and in disseminating information on consumer protection and client asset protection schemes.

But there were also several weaknesses in the transparency of the securities regulatory governance framework. Because governance arrangements were inadequate in areas of overlapping responsibilities among banking, insurance, and securities regulators, public disclosure of formal procedures for information sharing and consultation between regulatory agencies was insufficient. In most cases, agencies shared information but the cooperative agreements were not made sufficiently clear to the public or in some cases not publicly disclosed at all. Procedures for appointment, terms of office, and removal of officials, and internal governance procedures and audit arrangements were also not often publicly disclosed.

There were deficiencies in the accountability framework as well. For example, periodic reports on the activities of securities regulators were either not produced or were submitted only to the legislature or another oversight body. When such reports were released, they were lacking in quality and coverage—omitting the activities of the stock exchange, for example. Other shortcomings include a lack of explicit procedures for holding the organs of the stock exchange accountable and an absence of law or tradition requiring regulators to testify on agency activities in public.

The main recommendations for improving transparency in this area have focused on formulating and reporting regulatory policies, accountability, and assurances of integrity of the securities regulators. Other recommendations have called for improving the transparency of the relationship between regulatory authorities and among national and lower-level securities agencies and for clear and transparent rules on appointment, term, and removal of chief regulators.

TRANSPARENCY IN PAYMENT SYSTEMS OVERSIGHT. Because payment systems oversight is the responsibility of the central bank in many countries, officials are generally available to explain their institution's objectives and performance to the public. At the same time, however, these agencies (mostly being central banks) report on overall financial issues, with relatively little reporting on the actual operations, risks, and how they are being managed in the payment systems. Other disclosure deficiencies relate to availability of information on operating expenses and revenue. Often these details are not available separately from the overall accounts of the central bank; existing data are dated and published irregularly if at all, and reporting on developments in the payment system is often ad hoc.

Furthermore, the disclosure of general policy principles for agencies overseeing the payment system is often incomplete, especially those related to risk management policies, which are either nonexistent or not disclosed. Another important governance issue is the relationship and accountability between payment system oversight and the banking supervisor. In most cases the relationship was not clearly defined despite the existence of a potential conflict of interest; where a relationship was claimed to exist, it either lacked a legal or a regulatory basis or was not disclosed.

Recommendations on payment systems have focused on public availability of information on policies and clarity of roles, responsibilities, and objectives of the oversight agency. They emphasize the need for better communication of general principles of payment systems policy to the public (including risk management policies), clarity in the law separating the roles and responsibilities of the central bank and other agencies as they relate to payment systems, and clarifying the role of the clearinghouse, the central bank, and clearinghouse member banks.

Regulatory Agencies versus Central Banks

The larger part of this paper on regulatory governance has been devoted to regulators and supervisors, even though at the beginning of the paper central banks were included as a key agency for financial sector oversight. The main reason for this omission is because central bank governance, independence, and accountability are fairly well documented, whereas very little has been written about regulators and supervisors. To provide a full perspective on regulatory governance issues in the context of financial stability, however, it is useful to compare regulatory agencies with the central banks.

There is no internationally recognized standard for central banks' monetary policy operations, equivalent to, for instance, the Basel Core Principles for Effective Banking Supervision (though the IMF has issued guidance on good governance relating to various aspects of central banking, including organization and accounting practices). The discussion below is based on the IMF's MFP Code to the extent that it covers accountability and integrity aspects of the central bank governance framework.

Sundararajan, Das, and Yossifov define a policy transparency index in which they compare all agencies, including central banks.[32] They conclude

---

32. Sundararajan, Das, and Yossifov (forthcoming). The index measures the degree of observance of the MFP Code by IMF member countries in the areas of monetary policy, and financial sector polices. The value of the index for each sector of the financial system in a given country is computed as unweighted averages of the overall scores assigned to the country's implementation of four dimensions of transparency: (1) means of disclosure, (2) timeliness of disclosure, (3) periodicity of disclosure, and (4) observance of requirements related to the form and content of disclosure set forth in the MFP Code. The data used in the construction of the transparency index are derived from a 1999 survey on

Figure 6-1. *Financial Regulators: Average Degree of Transparency Observed Based on the Transparency Index*

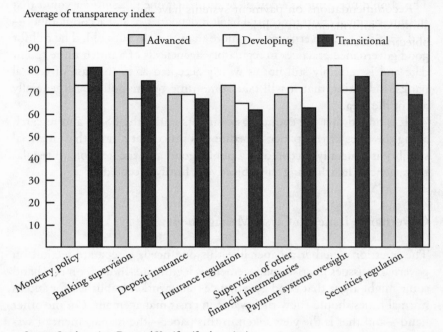

Source: Sundararajan, Das, and Yossifov (forthcoming).

that the average degree of observance of the MFP Code is the highest for monetary policy. The index reaches 90 percent for advanced countries, 81 percent for transition countries, and 73 percent for developing countries. These percentages are significantly higher in each country grouping than the indexes for most other agencies; only the transition economies come close to matching the central bank index in some of the other financial regulatory areas.

These findings, in conjunction with the well-documented fact that central banks across the world have also reached a higher degree of independence

the implementation of the MFP Code by IMF member countries. The survey asked IMF member countries to describe the modalities of implementation of the MFP Code, not to grade their observance. The values of the index are derived based on detailed analysis of countries' responses.

from the political sphere, *indicate that central bank governance practices are better established than good governance practices of other regulatory agencies.* This should not come as a complete surprise if one takes into account that the international effort for central bank independence and accountability—and with it good governance—is more than two decades old. The call for good governance practices in regulatory agencies is of a much more recent date and is certainly still not as widely accepted as in the case of central banks, indicating that it will take some time before politicians generally accept the idea.

It is hoped that the country assessments under the FSAP, and research along the lines of this paper, expedite this process at a time that financial stability is generally accepted as a public good and the key role of regulatory agencies in achieving this objective is firmly accepted.

Governance Issues in Crisis Management

The question whether a paper like this one needs a separate section on governance issues in crisis management is legitimate. Indeed, on one hand some might argue that good governance frameworks established for and in normal times should show their value in crisis management. On the other hand—and that is the view taken in this paper—the management of systemic banking crises raises a set of specific or exceptional governance issues that government agencies might be unfamiliar with. This section highlights those exceptional circumstances. It should nevertheless be borne in mind that crisis governance is predicated on governance practices in normal times.

In a crisis where a systemically important part of the financial sector is affected to such an extent that the operation of the payments system, and therefore of the economy, is at best threatened, or at worst stalls, government intervention is inevitable, because financial stability itself is at stake. Such government intervention typically has two key elements: setting up the appropriate institutional structure; and taking exceptional measures.

The Institutional Structure

Intervention during a systemic banking crisis goes beyond the more common intervention that regulatory agencies engage in when banks are failing or have failed. In a systemic crisis, the government steps in to develop and implement a broad strategic plan to address the crisis. Broader government intervention, better defined as *political leadership*, is justified for several reasons: budgetary resources will be called upon in the restructuring of financial institutions—a responsibility that goes beyond those of the traditional regulatory agencies; the strategic plan has to be shepherded through the legislative body, for which strong political support is needed; a systemic banking crisis involves burden sharing and redistribution of wealth among people at all layers of society, all of whom are voters in democratic societies; and resolution of a systemic crisis typically also involves breaking vested interests, a task that also needs political leadership. So governments are confronted with taking a host of highly technical decisions and measures, but these measures all have a highly politically sensitive content.

To achieve those objectives in a crisis, the authorities need to set up an institutional framework that cuts across the traditional division of responsibilities among regulatory agencies. Setting up such a crisis management framework involves revisiting some of the mechanisms underlying the components of good governance in the individual agencies (independence, accountability, transparency, and integrity); and redefining the contents of these same components for the (temporary) crisis management structure.

Exceptional Measures

This temporary institutional structure will be called upon to take exceptional measures—measures that often need to be very innovative and creative but that are therefore, by definition, also unfamiliar to the authorities. Such measures may have outcomes that are unknown or unpredictable and may not necessarily be completely market-oriented. One of the greatest challenges in crisis intervention is to avoid moral hazard. Appropriate governance mechanisms should prevent this outcome from happening.

Applied to a crisis situation, good governance practices are needed to get out of the crisis as quickly as possible, that is, to shorten the "policy lag"; to achieve an equitable burden sharing; and to ensure proper coordination between government agencies. *The leading principle should be that adequate accountability, transparency, and disclosure is needed for each and every step in order to build up or maintain the authorities' credibility.*[33]

33. See also Sundararjan and Das (2002), who make this point in the broader context of financial sector reform.

Key Governance Issues in Crisis Management

This section goes through the different stages of an unfolding systemic crisis.[34] Starting from the stylized facts about the unfolding and resolution of a systemic banking crisis, we move to the key governance issues regarding the role of the lender of last resort, the resort to a blanket guarantee for depositors and some creditors, the use of deposit freezes, the role and establishment of a restructuring agency and of asset management companies (AMC), and issues pertaining to bank restructuring techniques. Some of these issues are discussed at more length in other papers in this volume and are therefore only briefly discussed here.

A Systemic Banking Crisis: Stylized Facts

As experienced during the 1990s around the world, banking distress typically turns into a banking crisis when triggered by some exogenous shock. Such an event can be closely related to the state of the banking system, or it can be more remote, like a political statement that drains the confidence in the (political and) financial system. The beginning of the crisis is then characterized by deposit runs. The problem becomes systemic when the continued smooth operation of the payments system is threatened.

The first task of the authorities in such a situation is to try contain the bank run by restoring some degree of confidence with the public at large. During this initial period, the central bank could be asked to provide emergency liquidity support to all financial institutions that are still viable. It might also be useful, depending on the circumstance, to announce a blanket guarantee for some creditors and depositors. Other measures could include the immediate closure of nonviable or fraudulent banks and the imposition of capital controls. Some countries have also experimented with deposit freezes to (re)gain control over the situation.

Once this package of measures has succeeded in stopping the run on banks, the crisis enters the restructuring stage. This is the time for the authorities to take stock of the situation and put in place an organizational structure that can begin the restructuring quickly. Immediate actions in this stage include valuation of the banks; triage of viable and nonviable entities; and development of strategies to deal with the nonviable ones, to

---

34. References to and discussions of the sequencing of systemic banking crises are based on Lindgren and others (1999), and Scott (2001).

recapitalize and reorganize the viable ones, to deal with the impaired assets; and to begin any necessary corporate sector restructuring.

The final phase concerns the exit strategy. Issues to be dealt with at this point include the exit from the blanket guarantee if there was one and from other measures such as capital controls; the reprivatization of financial institutions that were deemed to be only temporarily under government control; and the design of an efficient safety net, including a limited deposit insurance scheme. These exit strategies are beyond the scope of this paper.

Governance Issues in Crisis Containment

A key issue that could be labeled a governance problem is the *recognition* that a crisis is unfolding. In several recent crises governments and regulatory agencies were in denial, thereby allowing the crisis to widen and deepen. Often the recognition problem comes from politicians who neglect or overrule alarms from supervisors because of vested interests.[35] On other occasions, supervisors themselves do not take the necessary steps. With established arrangements for accountability, transparency, and integrity, regulators and politicians could not ignore the signs of a crisis for very long.

Once it is clear that a crisis is systemic in nature, the first priority for the authorities is to stop the deposit run, stabilize the financial institutions' liabilities, and keep the payments system running. Typically at this stage, coordination among government agencies is not yet established and the main responsibility, almost by default, lies with the central bank. Its key objective must be to keep the payments system running through some form of liquidity support.

EMERGENCY LIQUIDITY SUPPORT. The central bank's role in reestablishing confidence in the financial system is crucial at this stage. Although some have argued that substantial liquidity support may delay crisis recognition and increase the macroeconomic costs, failure to provide the necessary liquidity will result in a collapse in the payments system and, therefore, in economic activity.[36] So, central banks have to walk a very fine line.

Good governance under such circumstances should focus on transparency and accountability. Under the circumstances, central banks may

35. Lindgren and others (1999).
36. See, for example, Klingebiel and Laeven (2002).

have to deviate temporarily from their main policy objective (such as maintaining price stability) to "stop the bleeding" and preserve the operation of the payments system. Clear principles should be established regarding the amounts, forms, and circumstances under which emergency support can be provided. Established accountability channels, in combination with full transparency in its operations should be used to explain and justify the central bank's actions and to preserve its credibility—or even enhance it.[37]

Transparency would also require the government to compensate the central bank for its losses if liquidity loans cannot be repaid by the borrowing institutions. So clear budgeting arrangements between the government and the central bank are needed from the first hours onward.

BLANKET GUARANTEES. A blanket guarantee is an announcement by the government that it will ensure that a well-defined set of the banks' or financial institutions' liabilities will be honored. While such a commitment can improve confidence in the financial system, stabilize the banks' funding, and preserve the operation of the payment system, it is a far-reaching measure which, if not announced and implemented properly, may create moral hazard.

The key issue is that a successful guarantee requires the government's promise to be credible. That implies that the government has the financial capacity to honor the guarantee, an issue that is directly related to the country's fiscal and public debt situation. However, credibility also depends on how the measure is "governed." Disclosure and transparency are the key requirements here: the announcement must be clearly spelled out (parties covered, payment modalities, measures taken to contain moral hazard, the way the exit from the guarantee will be announced).[38] In addition, the announcement must be perceived as having the full support of institutions within the government and from all political parties. Any signs of dis-

---

37. A general principle is that central bank liquidity support should go to illiquid but solvent banks. However, the situation faced by the authorities might be so confused and uncertain—and hard data so lacking—that some liquidity support in the end may turn out to be solvency support. For such cases transparency is needed because the central bank may later have to explain on which grounds it decided to provide support. Deviation from other stipulations in the central bank law may also be necessary and should be disclosed. For instance, it might be necessary to broaden the definition of acceptable collateral to accommodate all institutions that are still deemed viable and therefore eligible for emergency support.

38. The exit from the blanket guarantee is a very sensitive issue, as the experiences of several countries has shown.

agreement or dispute will undermine the credibility. So, this is a matter of public sector governance.

CLOSURES OF NONVIABLE INSTITUTIONS. It would be proof of sound governance practices if the regulatory agencies—in cooperation with the government—seize the opportunity at the outbreak of the crisis to close institutions that are clearly insolvent (and often fraudulent) and seen by the markets as nonviable. This way, the authorities clearly demonstrate to the markets that poor governance practices in the sector are penalized by imposing losses on uninsured depositors, creditors, and shareholders. Such action gives the authorities some "early wins" that underpin their credibility in containing the crisis, and, ultimately will also reduce the resolution costs.

Accountability, transparency, and integrity once again surface as the three key elements to the success of such intervention. If banks are to be closed, the closures must be based on transparent, uniform, simple, and defensible criteria, and these criteria should be communicated and explained to the banks and the public. There should be no exceptions to the specified rule, since the credibility of the entire operation is only as strong as its weakest link.

DEPOSIT FREEZES. Deposit freezes, because of the host of negative effects they bring along, should only be used as a last resort, when all else fails. While deposit freezes allow the government time to elaborate a strategy, the loss of output and the loss of confidence in the government and the financial system that they create are difficult to restore. Moreover, exit from a freeze has proven to be highly problematic. Of the measures discussed here, freezes are the least market-oriented measure as they actually interrupt the functioning of the markets.

If imposing a freeze is the only way out for the authorities, the measure should be transparent: its rules should be clearly announced, the measure should be fair and equitable, exceptions should be spelled out but at the same time be limited to avoid circumvention and undermining, the period of the freeze should be as short as possible, and the unfreezing should be prepared carefully and its stages announced in detail.

Governance Issues in Bank Restructuring

Once the acute crisis is contained, the situation is still likely to be confused and uncertain. Authorities will need to take coordinated, credible, and rapid action to move into the restructuring phase. Key areas where the authorities should demonstrate good governance practices include the establishment of a single accountable authority to coordinate and implement the restructuring plan; a sound legal framework that supports good governance practices; and restructuring and asset management practices that provide the right incentives. All of these actions need to be clearly communicated to the public at large. These are the areas where weaknesses in governance have contributed to the slowdown of the restructuring process in some recent crises.

COORDINATION BETWEEN AGENCIES. The establishment of a single and accountable authority responsible for coordinating and implementing the bank restructuring plan is of prime importance for any resolution strategy to gain credibility. The establishment of such an agency is a clear signal from the political leadership that it stands behind the restructuring.

A restructuring agency is needed because restructuring policies exceed the mandate and capacity of the regulatory agencies. An umbrella structure can coordinate the work of these agencies and also counter the perception that they are operating at cross purposes or that "turf battles" are taking place.

The restructuring agency will most likely be established by emergency legislation or decree. It should have a clear (and preferably single) mandate and be awarded a sufficient degree of political autonomy in its day-to-day operations to accomplish its goals; accountability measures should be established; and the agency's actions should be clearly transparent to everyone. Communication with the markets and the public at large is critical for the success of the undertaking.

At the same time, the establishment of a restructuring agency with far-reaching powers may imply that the autonomy and powers of some other institutions be curbed for a limited period of time.[39] Given their mandate, this applies in particular to regulatory authorities. For example, the decision to close an institution or intervene (that is, provide government financial support) should be taken in coordination with all the other agencies involved and against the background of the overarching strategy. Other agencies may also have to accept limitations on their original mandate. Whatever the limitations, decisions by the restructuring agency should be taken after due consultation with the "specialized" agencies.

There is also a theoretical argument for limiting agency autonomy in times of systemic banking crisis. As Majone explains, the model of dele-

---

39. Laws in several countries stipulate this possibility explicitly.

gating to autonomous agencies is suitable for areas of economic and social regulation for efficiency reasons.[40] However, it is not suitable for redistributive policies or policies with significant redistributive effects. Such policies should remain directly under the control of the elected political executives. Systemic crisis management has wealth distribution effects and therefore should be closely controlled by the political authorities. Of course this does not mean that day-to-day management of the restructuring agencies should be politically controlled, but regular briefings and debriefings are a necessity—in other words, a less than arm's-length relationship should be developed between the politicians and the restructuring authority.

The example of the Indonesian Bank Restructuring Agency (IBRA) is unfortunately one of the best examples of poor (public sector) governance in a restructuring effort. During the Habibie presidency, the Financial Sector Action Committee (FSAC), comprising a number of economics ministers, intervened several times in IBRA's operations. The FSAC, for example, intervened to reject shareholder settlements that had been negotiated by IBRA management and to demand that the bank recapitalization scheme favor the indigenous business community over "Chinese" banks. These political interventions undermined the credibility of the bank restructuring effort, particularly the requirement of uniformity of treatment. Meanwhile, IBRA has already had eight chairpersons, another sign of political interference in this key institution. Just like day-to-day supervision, the credibility of bank restructuring is significantly enhanced if it is under the direction of an agency with a strong and independent board and a clear mandate.

A LEGAL FRAMEWORK. Ideally, this topic should not be an issue. A proper legal framework supporting good governance practices in the financial sector should be in place at all times. Country experience however indicates that specific provisions or articles that have been on the laws for years come into play only in highly exceptional situations such as banking crises, and then, they prove to be inadequate, either hindering a smooth restructuring process or providing the wrong incentives.

Crucial provisions in legal frameworks in providing the right incentives include the power to write down shareholders and to remove management.[41] Legal authority is also needed to permit efficient exit policies for

40. Majone (1997).

41. Proper incentives should also be present in other pieces of legislation, such as the bankruptcy law, contract laws, and laws on collateral and foreclosure. Even the quality of the judiciary becomes a governance issue in crisis management.

banks. In many countries exit policies are never brought to a test. In some recent crises, governments have been unable to intervene effectively in insolvent banks and shareholders have retained sufficient power to impede loss recognition and restructuring, thus stalling or even reversing the restructuring process. An important element of the legal framework in this regard as that the integrity of the supervisors and restructurers be protected. They should be immune from lawsuits as a consequence of discharging their official functions. Without such immunity the entire restructuring process might stall.

TRANSPARENCY AND ACCOUNTABILITY IN RESTRUCTURING. As events in several recent financial crises have shown, governments sometimes become owners-of-last-resort, a situation that poses another set of governance problems.[42] Transparency and accountability are key factors in this situation. By being transparent in its actions, the government can ease concerns of foreign or domestic (strategic) investors about participating in the restructuring effort and help maintain or rebuild depositors' confidence in the banking system. Following are some of the steps where transparency and accountability play a crucial role:[43]

—The triage process of separating viable from nonviable banks, following a thorough valuation of the banks, should be based on clear and transparent criteria, and these should be communicated to the markets.

—Transparency and good communications are required when the government decides to close a bank, because closures can cause uncertainty and concern about the fate of remaining institutions. The authorities should also provide clear statements about the reasons for closure to avoid giving inappropriate incentives to other banks in the system.

—Recapitalization schemes involving incentives for the markets should be clearly communicated to the markets.

—If the government decides to participate in the recapitalization, proper incentives should be communicated to the private sector to "bail in." The impact of recapitalization on public finances should also be spelled out clearly.

—If the government decides to take over a bank, shareholders of the banks must be the first to lose their investments. If the shareholders are to

---

42. Many of these are set out in Carmichael's paper in this volume and are not discussed here.

43. In some cases ex ante transparency is desirable or needed. In other cases, ex post transparency might be more desirable because of confidentiality issues.

retain some equity position in their banks, they must contribute to the recapitalization. Uniform treatment of all institutions in the same situation and clear communication with the public can assist in this process.

—Speed of the recapitalization should be treated transparently to allow the markets to make a sound judgment of the health of the banks.

ASSET MANAGEMENT COMPANIES. A last but highly important and complex area of bank restructuring is the way the authorities deal with impaired assets. Good governance is essential to maximize the value of the impaired assets, minimize the fiscal costs, and stop a deterioration of credit discipline. However, an AMC is not a company like any other. AMCs are typically meant to be temporary institutions; by achieving their goal, they make themselves redundant. This specific aspect of the AMC business requires a solid governance structure. AMC managers should be provided with the right set of incentives to achieve the company's objective(s).

A separate paper by Cooke has been prepared for this volume dealing with governance issues in asset management companies, so we limit ourselves to highlighting the main governance issues to be taken into account when establishing the infrastructure for dealing with impaired assets. First, the governance infrastructure for managing problem assets (centralized versus decentralized; public versus private) should correspond as closely as possible to the conditions in and structure of the market (size of the banking problem; dominant type of impaired assets; structure of the financial system—public versus private).

When the choice is for a public AMC, good governance principles are similar in many ways to those discussed for other agencies: AMCs should have a clearly defined goal and a governance structure that is supportive of this goal.[44] Many AMCs have indeed run into problems because their mandate was not clearly spelled out or because they had to pursue multiple— often conflicting—objectives. It is important that they be independent from day-to-day political interference (and enjoy budgetary independence) in the disposition and restructuring of assets and have the proper incentive structure to achieve their goals. At the same time they should be accountable to their (many and diverse) stakeholders for their actions and performance. To ensure transparency, AMCs should be required to publish regular reports describing their performance in pursuing their goals. In addition to making detailed financial information public, AMCs should be

44. See Klingebiel (2000) for a listing of objectives for AMCs in different countries.

audited regularly to ensure that their financial statements are accurate, that representations as to the value of assets are reasonable, and that the AMC has proper internal controls in place to safeguard the assets under its management. Independent auditors chosen by the government should undertake such audits.

Public AMCs should be given the proper legal powers to expedite loan recovery and bank restructuring and they should provide the right incentives to the financial institutions, attaching conditions to purchases of non-performing loans and using their leverage over debtors. To facilitate the phase-out of AMCs as they complete their job, stakeholders should give incentives, such as providing employee outplacement assistance and compensation incentive programs for rewarding timely and final resolution of assets.

Conclusions

Good regulatory governance in the financial system is increasingly being recognized as a key component to achieve and preserve financial stability. All of the recent systemic crises list weaknesses in the regulatory governance—or poor public sector governance more generally—among the contributing factors to the crisis.

Good regulatory governance is essential for the credibility of regulatory agencies in the discharge of their regulation and oversight functions. As various standard-setting bodies have recognized, good regulatory governance is a necessity for instilling good governance practices in the financial sector. Despite this linkage, research on issues of regulatory governance in the financial system has thus far not been very systematic or deep. Sugestions for strengthening regulatory governance have also been very tentative. This paper has therefore tried to contribute to the debate on regulatory governance issues in the context of financial stability and development.

Four components have been identified as being key to good regulatory governance: independence of the agency from political and industry interference, accountability, transparency, and integrity. These components interact and reinforce each other in ways that, taken together, lay the foundations for the practice of good regulatory governance.

The FSAP effort is the first, and so far most comprehensive, effort to analyze regulatory governance issues. However, more work is needed before a systematic approach can be presented. The assessments of regulatory standards, as part of the FSAPs, provide valuable insights for analyzing regulatory governance issues through the four key components of regulatory governance.

This paper has attempted to provide an (early) overview of the "state of the art" of regulatory governance with special reference to banking, insurance, securities, and payments system oversight areas. The following conclusions can be drawn from it:

—Bank regulators seem to have more independence than regulators in the other financial sectors. To some extent, that might be because many bank supervisors operate from within the central bank and can "piggy-back" on the central bank's independence in the conduct of monetary policy.

—Securities supervisors score better than the others in making transparent their objectives, operations, accountability, and integrity. One is tempted to say that securities regulators need a high degree of transparency to be credible in securities market where transparency and disclosure are key to the functioning of safe and efficient markets.

—Insurance supervisors score the worst on all counts. For a long time, the insurance sectors in most countries have not received adequate policy and institutional attention. They have mostly grown as an agency or department within the government.

—Comparing these results with some of the results from other work on central banks leads to a straightforward conclusion: in general central banks are much more advanced in terms of governance issues. The reason for this better performance is that the quest for central bank transparency, independence, accountability, and integrity started approximately two decades before the emphasis on regulatory governance. In other words, regulators and supervisors still have a long way to go.

—Good governance practices established and applied in normal times should help significantly in times of crisis. The exceptional circumstances, however, require exceptional measures and an appropriate institutional setup to take such measures and implement them. Key conditions here are appropriate accountability arrangements for those in charge of the measures and a high degree of transparency of the restructuring strategy to ensure that all parties involved—and in times of a systemic crisis, that is basically the entire society—are well-informed about the authorities' intentions. Transparency will expedite the process and ensure that the outcome is what the authorities expect.

However, experience from recent crisis episodes around the world seems to indicate that the statement above—that having good governance practices in normal times helps to adhere to good practices in crisis times—is still theory. The reality is more often that we learn from crisis experiences and, therefore, that the seeds of good governance practices are planted in crisis times.

This finding, then, closes the circle and brings us back to crisis prevention. In this light, the findings of this paper also provide a work agenda for the future in terms of assessment, analysis, and recommendations:

—Governance practices in central banks as they relate to monetary policy should serve as the leading example for establishing good governance in regulatory agencies. The twelve main elements of regulatory governance identified here can be used to strengthen regulatory governance standards.

—The trend toward large financial groups and conglomerates necessitates a further harmonization of regulatory and supervisory approaches toward good governance. Unification of supervisory agencies and enhanced emphasis on exchange of information among the regulators are providing an opportunity to improve the regulatory governance practices.

—The FSAP offer the first vehicle to assess regulatory governance practices. The assessment findings need to be further analyzed. It would be useful to build upon the FSAP framework to come to a more comprehensive assessment of governance practices. As this develops, the FSAP findings could help in shedding more light on issues, such as the extent to which good regulatory governance is correlated with financial stability or improved performance of the banking system, or in finding causal relationships between good regulatory governance and growth and development of financial systems.

—With more assessments in the pipeline, it will be useful to undertake more cross-sectional analyses; to analyze in more depth the linkages between good regulatory governance and good corporate governance practices—one of the premises of this paper; and to analyze the linkages between good regulatory governance practices and (measures of) financial stability.

—Finally, good regulatory governance can only be effective if it is complemented by good public sector governance. As long as the cost of interference in the regulatory process is low for politicians, interference will continue to occur. This nexus needs to be further explored through a closer analysis of the preconditions for good regulatory governance.

References

Enoch, Charles, and others. 2001. "Indonesia: Anatomy of a Banking Crisis. Two Years of Living Dangerously 1997–99." Working Paper WP/01/52. International Monetary Fund, Washington.

Goodhart, Charles. 2001. "Regulating the Regulators—Accountability and Control." In E. Ferran and C. A. E. Goodhart, eds., *Regulating Financial Services and Markets in the 21st Century,* pp. 151–64. Oxford, UK: Hart Publishing.

———, and others. 1998. *Financial Regulation. Why, How and Where Now?* London: Routledge.

Halme, Liisa. 2000. "Bank Corporate Governance and Financial Stability." In Liisa Halme and others, eds., *Financial Stability and Central Bank: Selected Issues for Financial Safety Nets and Market Discipline.* London: Bank of England, Centre for Central Banking Studies.

International Monetary Fund. 2000. "Supporting Document to the Code of Good Practices on Transparency in Monetary and Financial Policies" (www.imf.org).

IMF-World Bank. Forthcoming. "Implementation of the Basel Core Principles for Effective Banking Supervision, Experiences, Influences, and Perspectives."

Joint Forum. 2001. "Risk Management Practices and Regulatory Capital: Cross Sectoral Comparisons" (www.bis.org/publ/joint03.htm). November.

Kane, Edward. 2001. "Financial Safety Nets: Reconstructing and Modelling a Policymaking Metaphor." Paper presented at the Economics Public Lecture Series, Deakin University, Melbourne, Australia.

Kaufmann, Daniel, Aart Kraay, and Pablo Zoido-Lobatón. 2000. "Taking the Offensive against Corruption," *Finance and Development.* Washington: International Monetary Fund.

Klingebiel, Daniela. 2000. "The Use of Asset Management Companies in the Resolution of Banking Crises—Cross-Country Experience." Policy Research Paper 2284. World Bank, Washington.

Klingebiel, Daniela, and Luc Laeven, eds. 2002. "Managing the Real and Fiscal Effects of Banking Crises." World Bank Discussion Paper 428. World Bank, Washington.

Lastra, Rosa Maria, and Geoffrey Wood. 1999. "Constitutional Approach to Central Bank Independence." *Central Banking* 10 (3): 34–39.

Lindgren, Carl-Johan, and others. 1999. "Financial Sector Crisis and Restructuring. Lessons from Asia." IMF Occasional Paper 188. International Monetary Fund, Washington.

Majone, Giandomenico. 1993. "Controlling Regulatory Bureaucracies: Lessons from the American Experience." Working Paper SPS 93/3. European University Institute, Florence, Italy.

———. 1997. "From the Positive to the Regulatory State: Causes and Consequences of Changes in the Mode of Governance." *Journal of Public Policy* 17 (2): 139–67.

Quintyn, Marc, and Michael W. Taylor. 2002. "Regulatory and Supervisory Independence and Financial Stability." Working Paper WP/02/46. International Monetary Fund, Washington.

Scott, David. 2001. "A Practical Guide to Managing Systemic Financial Crises: A Review of Approaches Taken in Indonesia, Korea, and Thailand." World Bank, Washington.

Sundararajan, V., and Udaibir S. Das. 2002. "Transparency in Monetary and Financial Polices and Its Role in Financial Sector Reform." In Montek Singh Ahluwalia, Y. V. Reddy, and S. S. Tarapore, eds., *Macroeconomics and Monetary Policy: Issues for a Reforming Economy.* New Delhi: Oxford University Press.

Sundararajan, V., Udaibir S. Das, and Plamen K. Yossifov. Forthcoming. "Transparency of Monetary and Financial Policies: Some Issues Relating to Measuring Transparency and Its Relevance." Working Paper. International Monetary Fund, Washington.

DAVID C. COOKE

The Governance of
Asset Management Companies:
Selected Observations

MUCH ATTENTION HAS been given to the topic of corporate governance over the last ten years and its importance in the development
of capital markets that attract both domestic and foreign investors.
Corporate governance refers to the framework and relationships used by an
organization to establish and achieve its objectives. A number of notable
international institutions have proposed guidelines to achieve good corporate governance with the primary focus on publicly traded companies. The
benefit of applying good corporate governance principles to state-owned
enterprises, particularly those that may someday be privatized, also has
been recognized, and guidelines have been issued.

Relatively little has been written, however, about governance principles as they relate to asset management companies (AMCs). AMCs are
entities established by governments to help solve serious problems in the
financial sector. The manner in which an AMC is governed can have a significant impact on the pace of problem resolution and economic recovery
as well as on a country's fiscal budget. In part, the lack of attention in this
area may reflect the limited scope and functional life of AMC operations.

The author is grateful for the valuable contributions of Norman Baxter, a senior manager with the
Barents Group of KPMG Consulting. Dr. Baxter is an expert in corporate governance issues. A special
thanks also goes to Jason M. Foley, a manager with the Barents Group of KPMG Consulting.

As problems in the financial sector are resolved, an AMC becomes less important. Nonetheless, governments should strive to ensure that AMCs have developed and are implementing good governance practices.

While the role of the AMC is unique, many of the published corporate governance principles and guidelines are relevant to AMC operations. Providing a comprehensive set of governance guidelines is beyond the scope of this paper, but the paper does offer some specific suggestions for AMCs to consider when reviewing their governance framework.

The Growing Interest in Corporate Governance

In their seminal work, *Corporate Governance,* Robert Monks and Nell Minow define corporate governance as "the relationship among various participants in determining the direction and performance of corporations."[1] Monks and Minow identify the shareholders, board of directors, and managers (led by the chief executive officer) as the primary participants, with employees, customers, suppliers, creditors, and the community classified as other participants. Over the last decade, these "other participants," now referred to as "stakeholders," have been prominently featured in the codes of corporate governance issued throughout the world.

Before the 1980s, corporate governance received little attention other than in seldom-read academic tomes. Since the 1980s—the decade of hostile takeovers, mergers, and leveraged buyouts—increasing attention has been paid to the relationship among those who determine "the direction and performance of corporations." Institutional investors, individual shareholders, interested observers, and academics began to question who was benefiting most from the direction and performance of corporations, the shareholders or management. Shareholders, especially in the United States, became much more active and vocal as they began to focus on the role, independence, and performance of the board of directors and how it protected the interests of shareholders.

Subsequently, because of the increased emphasis on corporate governance, Canada, the United Kingdom, and the United States set a trend in the 1990s of developing corporate governance guidelines and codes that has since spread throughout the world. Moreover, shareholder activism that started in the United States spread to western Europe, where, for example,

1. Monks and Minow (1995, p. 1).

previously docile investors have now publicly confronted corporate boards and management in Germany and France.

On the international scene, the World Bank, the International Monetary Fund, and international organizations have stressed the importance of good governance. The Organization for Economic Cooperation and Development (OECD), the Commonwealth Association for Corporate Governance (CACG), and the Basel Committee on Bank Supervision have each published principles and guidelines for strengthening corporate governance.[2] While the focus may vary somewhat, all of these codes emphasize the importance of sound and proper leadership and the obligation of boards and senior managers to their company and its owners and stakeholders.

The OECD principles are an attempt to codify corporate governance principles that all countries can accept as a framework for implementing good corporate governance practices. These guidelines focus on shareholder rights, the role of stakeholders in corporate governance, disclosure and transparency, and board responsibilities. The OECD stated that the standards and guidelines were intended to help governments "evaluate and improve the legal, institutional, and regulatory framework for corporate governance in their countries, and to provide guidance and suggestions for stock exchanges, investors, corporations, and other parties that have a role in the process of developing good corporate governance." The CACG expanded that focus to include state-owned enterprises; while the Basel Committee issued papers to support and amplify the OECD corporate governance principles for banking organizations. Additionally, numerous individual countries throughout the world have developed and issued their own reports and codes. The Cadbury Code in England, the Ney Report in Canada, and the King Report in South Africa are a few examples.[3]

Initially, the increased emphasis on the need for improving governance was focused on publicly traded corporations, primarily in the more

---

2. *The OECD Principles of Corporate Governance*, adopted by the OECD Ministers in May 1999, are available on the Internet at (www.oecd.org); *Principles for Corporate Governance in the Commonwealth*, the Commonwealth Association for Corporate Governance (CACG), November 1999, may be purchased through the Commonwealth Business Council (CBC) (www.cbc.to); *Enhancing Corporate Governance for Banking Organizations*, Basel Committee on Banking Supervision, September 1999, is available through (www.bis.org). The Basel Committee was established by the Central Bank Group of Ten countries to formulate broad "best practice" supervisory standards and guidelines.

3. The European Corporate Governance Institute web site (www.ecgi.org) is excellent for identifying and obtaining codes and principles of corporate governance from around the world.

advanced economies. Now, however, with the worldwide trends of privatization in emerging and transition economies and global capital flows that affect virtually every country in the world, the issue of corporate governance in general, not only in publicly traded corporations, has gained worldwide prominence.

In the old command economies (such as the Russian Federation and the other former Soviet republics, China, and Vietnam), corporate governance is a new concept because the government/party bureaucrats were long accustomed to making economic decisions while seldom being held accountable to anyone. There were no shareholders, and the concept of "stakeholders" was unknown. Today in these economies, newly privatized and partially privatized companies and their shareholders, majority and minority, government and private, have entered an entirely new world. Foreign and local investors now demand information, transparency, and accountability, all of which were almost entirely absent before the 1990s. Now, both local and foreign investors, governments, and private shareholders are paying attention to corporate governance issues and practices. The new emphasis on good corporate governance practices is also having a spillover influence on state-owned enterprises, which are under increasing pressure to make available more reliable financial information.

In the market-driven economies of Southeast Asia that grew so rapidly in the early 1990s, the cozy relationship between local business and political elites was shattered by the financial crisis of 1997–98, when foreign investors who had so eagerly, but almost passively, provided financing to fuel economic growth during the boom years abruptly withdrew their investments. Before the crisis these investors had paid relatively little attention to issues of information, transparency, and accountability. The spectacular economic growth of the 1980s and 1990s overshadowed everything else, causing investors to ignore corporate governance practices for the most part. After the Asian financial crisis struck, many foreign investors rapidly withdrew from Asia as they saw the region's impressive records of earnings and value growth evaporate. Now the "rules of the game" have changed, and investors have become much more rigorous in evaluating their investment decisions. Investors are demanding better information about the business practices and finances of the companies in which they are being asked to invest. They are demanding more transparency and accountability in operations and want a legal framework that recognizes and supports both the businesses they invest in and their position as shareholders. All of these requirements are integral components necessary for good corporate governance, and the good news is that governance in Asian countries is improving.

The pressure to implement good corporate governance practices is not limited to Asia. Governments increasingly recognize that as investors scour the globe for potentially lucrative investments, they rely on transparency and disclosure of financial information and that a nation lacking good corporate governance practices is less likely to attract foreign investment. Nor is the pressure coming only from investors; the World Bank and the IMF are actively encouraging countries to implement a legal framework that supports good corporate governance practices of transparency and accountability. In 2001 the IMF updated its *Code of Good Practices on Fiscal Transparency—Declaration of Principles*, originally issued in 1998, to provide guidance for its member countries on increasing fiscal transparency.[4] The World Bank has also developed a structured approach for evaluating a country's corporate governance framework. Clearly, all stakeholders are paying closer attention to issues of governance.

The Role of the Board and Senior Management

Creating a supportive corporate governance framework should benefit all of an organization's stakeholders, but a management that is either unwilling or unable to achieve objectives of transparency and fairness can easily undermine such efforts. The importance of a strong commitment from executive management to such principles cannot be overstated. One has only to look at the Enron scandal in the United States. Before the giant energy trader went bankrupt amid allegations that it had deliberately inflated its earnings, most Americans took great pride and comfort in their corporate governance framework, which includes experienced securities regulators, internationally recognized rating agencies, investment bankers, stock market analysts, and independent outside auditors. They felt even greater confidence when a company's board of directors included reputable and experienced independent members. Now, American and other investors are not as confident. Despite all its checks and balances, the United States still experienced the biggest bankruptcy in its history. Countless numbers of stakeholders from investors to employees lost their

---

4. *Code of Good Practices on Fiscal Transparency—Declaration of Principles*. International Monetary Fund (IMF), adopted by the Interim Committee in September 1999, available at (www.imf.org).

stake in the energy company when it declared bankruptcy in December 2001. The system of corporate governance designed to protect shareholder interests did not work.

Investigations are under way, but early reports indicate that neither Enron's board nor its management supported or practiced many of the principles of good governance and that none of the other checks and balances worked in time. The United States has one of the most reliable capital markets in the world, and the Enron debacle will certainly lead to further improvements to protect investors. However, as Enron demonstrates, practicing good governance requires the unwavering commitment of governing boards. As Ira Millstein has noted, "the board is the focal point of the governance process; it is the fulcrum of accountability in the system."[5] Simply put, corporate governance cannot succeed without a structure that allows the active support of an informed governing board. The board has the responsibility of setting organization objectives and priorities within the law and of directing and monitoring the progress in achieving them. This responsibility cannot be relegated to a single board member or an organization's senior managers. Board members, particularly independent, nonexecutive members, cannot be expected to understand, let alone participate in, all of an organization's activities. However, board members must view their participation on an organization's board not simply as an honor or reward, but as a responsibility. Should an organization fail because of poor management, ignorance should not be a valid excuse for board members who did not make the effort to understand how the organization operates and the checks and balances in place to achieve its objectives.

Governance Guidelines for Asset Management Companies

The guidelines put forth thus far primarily address the governance of private sector businesses and, to a lesser extent, state-owned enterprises, although not AMCs. Although they have different goals than either publicly traded or state-owned enterprises, AMCs still can have a major impact on a country's economic development and fiscal budget. AMCs are limited-purpose government agencies established to help maintain or restore the health of the banking sector. This function usually involves

5. Quoted in Monks and Minow (1995, p. 451).

taking over and resolving the burden of nonperforming loans (NPLs) as expeditiously and economically as possible. The very nature of this mission makes an AMC's operations much more susceptible than other entities to criticism by opposing politicians, unhappy bankers, debtors, and a public that does not understand its mission, strategy, or operations. AMCs also have a limited functional life cycle in that their primary business shrinks as financial sector problems are solved. This itself raises unique governance issues for AMCs.[6]

AMCs are not in business to generate earnings or maximize company or shareholder value. They are created for the specific public objective of resolving financial sector problems and minimizing taxpayer losses. Their primary activity is acquiring problem loans from ailing financial institutions and then resolving these loans in the best way possible. How best to resolve problem loans is not always clear, and the bigger the problems, the less clear the solution becomes. The relative success of the various approaches is usually debatable and difficult to measure—even for the AMCs' governing bodies, let alone other stakeholders. This makes it all the more important that governments put in place an AMC governance structure with a capable governing body that can objectively and effectively measure and guide operations.

Many of the guidelines already promulgated by the OECD and others provide an excellent starting point for establishing an AMC governance structure that best serves the public interest. The fundamental governance principles—setting clear objectives and understanding who is accountable for what and who the stakeholders are—apply to all organizations. Governments and AMC boards are encouraged to review the applicability of these principles and guidelines and apply them where appropriate. In the sections below, recent AMC experience is reviewed and some suggestions are offered for strengthening the governance of AMCs. The focus is on Asia, where the largest AMCs are located.

Government Objectives for AMCs

As previously noted, the reason governments establish AMCs is to help maintain or restore the health of the banking sector by taking over the

---

6. In an increasing number of countries, the residual AMC function is being absorbed into permanent deposit insurance agencies.

burden of nonperforming loans (NPLs) and maximizing the recoveries on such assets as expeditiously as possible. However, some AMCs such as Indonesia's IBRA also are directly charged with rehabilitating the banks that created the NPLs. In most Asian countries, the larger ailing banks tend to be state-owned or private banks acquired by the government in return for capital injections or the removal of NPLs, or both. Most governments indicate plans to privatize these banks to recoup capital invested and reduce ongoing risk exposure as well as to provide a "level playing field" for competing private banks.

Although this paper focuses primarily on the AMC's responsibility to resolve NPLs, it is important to recognize that assigning an AMC responsibility for both minimizing NPL resolution costs as well as rehabilitating and privatizing banks will lead to internal conflicts, particularly over the price at which assets are transferred to the AMCs. The higher the price paid, the better for the AMC division charged with rehabilitating the bank, but the worse for the division charged with minimizing NPL losses. Resolving such conflicts requires clear guidance and leadership by governing boards.

Evaluating AMC Governance

For AMCs the ultimate governance test is how well they accomplish their mission. Measuring success is far from an exact science and is influenced by the relative size and complexity of loan problems, the AMC's operational independence, and the legal infrastructure within which it operates. These variables also influence the strategies and action plans used by an AMC, which in turn affect both the rate of success and how it is measured. For most AMCs, success in resolving NPLs is usually measured by how much is recovered after expenses and how long recovery takes. Similarly, for resolving troubled banks, the quantifiable measures are the length of time to privatization and the net costs involved. However, qualitative measures of success must also be considered. These include factors such as stakeholder and public perceptions of transparency, fairness, and the degree of economic disruption involved.[7]

AMCs use different strategies and techniques to minimize losses, ranging from promptly selling such loans as is for the best cash price possible to

---

7. Economic disruption may involve unexpected shocks to employment levels in the enterprise sector or create market or competitive imbalances in the financial sector.

investing time and money to enhance recovery values through financial and operational restructuring of borrowing entities. In general, the larger and more complex the relative size of NPL problems, the less likely a country is to use a rapid disposition strategy. As a result, measuring success is more difficult, because it is relatively easy to measure net recoveries for all cash sales, but much more difficult to measure the success of intermediate strategies that require making value judgments regarding noncash proceeds and contingent liabilities.

As mentioned earlier, differences in approach and success are influenced not only by the magnitude and complexity of NPL problems, but also by the framework within which they must be resolved. The AMCs established in countries with transitional economies must begin their work without the legal framework and market infrastructure enjoyed by AMCs in more developed economies such as those in the United States and Sweden. Nonetheless, results also are influenced by an AMC's approach to governance. Also, the larger the problem, the greater the risk of political interference in AMCs' operations—and this risk is likely greater in transitional economies than in more developed economies and established democracies.

Recent AMC Experience

Over the past fifteen years, more than two dozen countries have established AMCs, and a review of admittedly limited data indicates their levels of success have varied considerably. The United States created the Resolution Trust Corporation (RTC) in 1989 to resolve failing thrift institutions.[8] In 1991 Sweden established two AMCs, Securum and Retriva, to manage NPLs of large commercial banks.[9] Both Sweden and the United States are widely recognized as having successfully accomplished their objectives. The health of the banking sectors was improved, and the AMCs were closed after having disposed of most of their holdings of NPLs and other assets.

8. The RTC managed the liquidation of 747 financial institutions with assets totaling more than $400 billion, most of which were illiquid or nonperforming. When the RTC was closed in 1995, approximately 98 percent of its assets were resolved at an average recovery rate of 87 percent of book value, although the recovery rate on NPLs was much lower. Remaining assets were transferred to the Federal Deposit Insurance Corporation for resolution.

9. Sweden's AMCs managed the disposition of more than $10 billion in NPLs. The disposition strategy was to create multiple subsidiaries based on the type and location of assets that would eventually be privatized. Remaining Securum assets were transferred to a state asset agency in 1997.

Table 1. *Nonperforming Loan Volumes of Selected Asian Countries*

	China	Indonesia	Malaysia	South Korea	Thailand
NPLs as percent of total loans at peak	40	70	30	35	50
NPLs as percent of GDP at peak	55	50	40	35	70
Current NPLs as percent of total loans	40	59	23	18	27
Current NPLs as percent of total loans except AMCs	10	24	15	12	18
Assets transferred to AMCs as percent of GDP	17	30	12	11	45
Assets disposed as percent of those transferred	<1	7	61	48	25

Source: World Bank.
Note: See table 2 for full names of AMCs in these countries.

Mexico established Fobaproa in 1994 to resolve its banking crisis when an estimated 50 percent of bank loans were NPLs. Ownership of many of these NPLs was transferred to Fobaproa, which was closed six years later with the remaining work transferred to IPAB, the country's new deposit insurance agency.[10]

More recently, large AMCs were established in Asia as a result of that region's financial crises. Indonesia, Malaysia, South Korea, and Thailand established AMCs in 1998, followed by China in 1999. Each of Asia's AMCs is still in operation. Table 1 compares the estimated peak magnitude of NPLs in each of these Asian countries against recent World Bank estimates of NPLs, including those transferred to AMCs.

As the table indicates, the level of NPLs held by banks in these countries declined dramatically following transfers to AMCs. After about four years, Korea and Malaysia appear to have made the most progress in restoring the health of their financial sector. The percentage of nonperforming loans held by financial institutions dropped from 35 percent to 12 percent in South Korea. Almost one third of this decline appears attributable to trans-

---

10. The government strategy for reducing these levels included buying the loans and allowing the selling banks to service them. The level of nonperforming loans was drastically reduced, but the recovery rate and collection experience on these loans is believed to have been poor.

fers to KAMCO and KDIC, nearly half of which the AMCs report as having resolved. In Malaysia, NPLs held by banks dropped from an estimated peak of 30 percent to 15 percent after 40 percent of the NPLs were transferred to Danaharta, of which more than 60 percent are reported as resolved.

The level of NPLs held by banks also declined significantly in Thailand, from 50 percent to 18 percent, and in Indonesia, from 70 percent to 24 percent. However, the AMCs in these countries appear to have resolved a much smaller portion of the NPLs they acquired than has either South Korea or Malaysia. Indonesia's IBRA appears to have made the least progress, with only 7 percent of its loans resolved. However, it is important to recognize that both Indonesia's and Thailand's NPL problems were substantially worse than those of Korea and Malaysia, and this almost certainly influences the manner and pace with which they can be resolved. The bigger a problem becomes, the more difficult it is to solve and the fewer the options available.

Recovery Strategies

Another consideration when evaluating AMCs is the type of NPL recovery transaction employed. Some transactions take much longer to implement and evaluate than others. One approach is simply to sell the NPLs to investors for the best cash price possible. Net recoveries are relatively easy to quantify on cash sales, except perhaps for allocating an AMC's operating costs to the sale.[11] Several years may elapse before the final results of other disposition transactions are known. For example, many of the sales by South Korea's KAMCO involve retaining an equity interest in joint ventures with third parties or providing loss guarantees to buyers, both of which are difficult to evaluate. In Malaysia the primary resolution strategy has been to restructure loans, but the extent to which this process resulted in cash recoveries is not clear. Reportedly, a number of restructured loans are in default, and it is not known what, if any, impact such defaults would have on Danaharta. Recovery transactions involving loss guarantees, joint venture arrangements, loan restructuring, or debt equity swaps may be perfectly sound, but they also involve making subjective value judgments. Such

---

11. Allocation of an AMC's expenses to sales transactions is likely to become much more noticeable as asset inventories shrink.

transactions make it even more important for governing boards to have the proper information and checks and balances in place so that they can objectively assess the values and risks involved.

Selling assets rapidly involves much less subjectivity, but this approach is not practical for many countries. In the United States, the RTC restructured some loans and maintained an equity interest in some loan portfolio sales, but its primary strategy became to offer large asset portfolios for sale to the highest bidder. However, the United States was in a better position than most Asian countries to pursue such a strategy. NPL problems were smaller, and the market for sales was bigger. NPL problems represented less than 5 percent of gross domestic product and less than 10 percent of the loans held by financial institutions. Also, problem loans were largely concentrated in the real estate sector and did not seriously threaten either the viability of financial markets or large-scale unemployment. Finally, the legal infrastructure as well as the financial and capital markets were well developed, and the RTC was given special legal powers to overcome shortcomings where necessary. In other words, the NPL problem was big but not so big that the United States could not solve it rapidly—and even then the process took several years. In Asia the size of NPL problems relative to both the financial sector and the economy is much larger and more complex. The potential impact on fiscal budgets and the economy is much more extensive, a fact that makes rapid sales strategies far less appealing from both a fiscal and political perspective. At the same time, governing boards must be able to make an objective comparison of disposition alternatives for individual transactions.

AMC Mission and Objectives

The mission and strategy of AMCs are not always clear or well understood by the public or even many stakeholders. In large part the confusion stems from inherent conflicts in their mission. AMCs often are under pressure by bankers and government officials to buy loans at high prices to help rehabilitate ailing banks, but they also face considerable pressure from potential investors wanting them to sell their assets at market prices.

In theory, the price paid for NPLs should be close to or below the value the AMC can achieve through better management and marketing. The overriding government objective, however, is to rehabilitate the banking sector, not to make a profit on NPLs. Moreover, the market for NPLs is very small and unstructured with little in the way of pricing benchmarks. Sophisticated investors tend to offer very low prices to achieve the high rates of return they demand for the substantial risks involved. Moreover, investors tend to demand large portfolios to justify the investments in systems and processes they will have to make to collect on these loans. In practice, therefore, NPL prices are driven much more by what a selling bank can afford to lose than what the loans are worth to investors.

An AMC that pays banks above market prices for their loans must usually pursue strategies such as loan restructuring and debt-for-equity swaps to increase recovery value and avoid, or at least defer, recording a loss. These strategies take time and are not without costs and risks. As indicated earlier, the final resolution cost will not be known until the restructured loan or equity interest is sold. Perhaps more important, such strategies are very likely to draw criticism from investors and the public at large. This can have a significant adverse impact on the leadership and operation of an AMC. Malaysia's Danaharta appeared to apply pricing models that were more consistent with market prices. After its initial wave of NPL acquisitions, South Korea's KAMCO also began to use more conservative pricing models.

It takes time to restructure and season a loan before it can be sold at higher prices. Although restructuring the debt of a viable business can enhance value, the process also can lead to increased loan losses and undermine efforts to improve an economy's credit culture. Additionally, loan restructuring requires making many judgments regarding the viability of borrowers and the extent of any loan concessions negotiated, these judgments expose the government to charges of political favoritism. In summary, AMCs face conflicting views from various stakeholders who will seek to see strategies change to best suit their interests.

AMC Governance Structure and Stakeholders

The governance structure and lines of authority for most AMCs can also be confusing and more complicated than those of other state-owned businesses. Table 2 provides an overview of the mission and governance structure of the Asian AMCs. Governments in each of the five countries in the table established their AMCs as separate entities. All of the AMCs were given the mission and authority to acquire and resolve NPLs in a way that

Table 2. *Mission and Governance of AMCs in Selected East Asian Countries*

Country	Asset management company (AMC)	Mission and approach	Governance and management
China (1999 to present)	Four separate AMC subsidiaries for each of the four large state-owned banks: CINDA, Orient, Great Wall, Haurong	Purchase and manage NPLs transferred from bank. Most NPLs are to state-owned enterprises. Broad range of asset authority including liquidation and sales. Restructures debts and enterprises; arranges debt-equity swaps. Funding provided by banks and refinancing from People's Bank of China.	Ministry of Finance supervises financial activities of AMCs. State Council appoints supervisory board that oversees management. Board members include representatives from State Audit Bureau, People's Bank of China, State Securities Supervision Committee. Ministry of Finance appoints chairman; PBoC appoints vice chairman. Board also includes AMC employee representative and independent expert who can be removed by chairman. Board responsibilities include reviewing strategic decisions and management policies, developing operations plan, and supervising compliance with laws. AMC president and vice president are recommended by Board of Supervisors, qualified by the People's Bank of China, and appointed by the State Council.
Indonesia (1997 to present)	Indonesian Bank Restructuring Agency (IBRA)	Rehabilitate troubled banks, and minimize fiscal cost. Acquire NPLs in return for bank rehabilitation. Restructure largest NPLs and manage collections or sales of other assets.	Overseen by Oversight Committee (OC), composed of public and private officials, and the Financial Sector Policy Committee, composed of government officials. OC includes Ombudsman and Audit Committee (to which IBRA's internal audit division reports). Reports to Ministry of State-Owned Enterprises. Managed by a chairman, approved by president of Indonesia, and four deputy chairmen.

Malaysia (1998 to present)	Danaharta	Acquires, manages, and disposes of banking system's NPLs. Restructures loans and companies.	Nine-member board of directors (mix of government and private sector) approves all policies and supervises all activities. Board committees include Executive, Audit, and Remuneration. Executive Committee formulates policies and strategies, appoints key management team, assesses financial and operational performances, and ensures appropriate information is made available. Oversight Committee appointed by Ministry of Finance consists of representatives from Ministry of Finance, Securities Commission, and Bank Negara Malaysia. Responsibility limited to special administration powers.
South Korea (1997 to present)	Korean Asset Management Corporation (KAMCO)	Acquires and resolves NPLs to rehabilitate financial sector. Also manages NPLs transferred by KDIC. Originally paid above market prices for NPLs and later lowered pricing. Restructure, equity swaps for largest NPLs; joint ventures, securitization, sales for others.	Overseen by Financial Supervisory Commission. Managed by board of directors of public and private sector officials; president and management oversee daily operations.

(continued)

Table 2. *Mission and Governance of AMCs in Selected East Asian Countries (Continued)*

Country	Asset management company (AMC)	Mission and approach	Governance and management
	Korean Deposit Insurance Corporation (KDIC)	Manages Deposit Insurance Fund; resolves failed financial institutions; develops effective funds recovery methodology; determines failure culpability; and manages analysis of insured institutions. Assigns NPLs to subsidiary and KAMCO for resolution.	Overseen by a policy committee composed of fourteen individuals from Ministry of Finance, Budget Office, Financial Supervisory Commission, Bank of Korea, National Bankers Association, and private sector. Policy committee responsibilities include establishing key operating principles; reviewing management plans; and funding support for financial resolution institutions. Chairman appointed by Ministry of Finance. Board of directors composed of chairman and operating directors.
Thailand (1997 to present)	Financial Sector Restructuring Authority (FRA)	Evaluates finance companies' rehabilitation plans. Rapid liquidation of nonviable companies and sale of assets.	A board of directors oversees operations and approves all sales transactions. The board consists of three individuals with private sector experience appointed as directors by the Minister of Finance, one of which serves as chairman; one representative each from the Bank of Thailand, the Minister of Finance, and the Secretary General of the FRA.

Asset Management Corporation (AMC)	Serves as bidder of last resort for FRA's "bad" assets to avoid fire-sale pricing. Manages, rather then sells, acquired assets.	Board is chaired by an official from the Ministry of Finance and is composed of six additional members appointed by the Ministry of Finance from government and private sector.
Bank-based Asset Management Companies (BBAMCs)	Manage recovery of state owned banks. Restructure and collect work to transfer to TAMC.	Managed as separate bank subsidiary.
Thai Asset Management Company (TAMC)	Manages NPLs from state-owned banks and selective NPLs from commercial banks and BBAMCs. Maximizes recoveries through corporate restructuring, not sales.	Overseen by a Supervisory Committee (SC), comprising a chairman and members from the government and private sector. The SC sets policy guidelines and approves major restructuring cases. An Executive Committee and a chief executive officer carry out the policies of the SC. Operational committees oversee debt restructuring undertaken by asset managers.

minimizes costs. These NPLs were acquired as part of a rehabilitation plan at prices based on net carrying value or discretionary pricing models. Except for the FRA established to resolve finance companies in Thailand, the primary NPL recovery strategy emphasized maximizing recovery value, rather than the pace of recovery. Generally, the NPLs were paid for with bonds issued or backed by the governments, which also significantly improved the risk-based capital position of the selling banks.

With regard to an AMC's governance structure, the allocation of responsibilities is not always clear. The governance structures of the AMCs in the five Asian countries generally appear to separate policymaking functions from AMC operations. Most AMCs report to oversight committees consisting of representatives from the ministry of finance, the central bank, and other government departments. These oversight entities also may include nonexecutive members with government or private sector experience. For example, Indonesia's IBRA reports to an oversight committee headed by the minister of finance, while its operations are managed by an operating board headed by a chairman who serves as the chief executive officer.[12] The extent of involvement of these oversight groups in AMC operations is not known, but presumably their role is limited to making policy and reviewing AMC performance.

Part of the rationale for separating policy from operations is to insulate government leadership from a job that is very likely to be unpopular and time consuming. This allows the AMCs to operate more independently and also helps to insulate government officials from undue influence. The structure makes it easier for elected officials to resist constituent pressures to influence AMC operations. This in turn allows the AMCs to make operating decisions based on economic merit rather than political considerations. Separating oversight from operations also allows oversight committees to exercise greater objectivity when reviewing the operations of the AMCs. At the same time, separating policy from operations can confuse the public and other stakeholders and even operating management, as it is not always clear where policy stops and operations begin. Many transaction

---

12. Recently the government changed the role of IBRA's Oversight Committee to overseeing IBRA's audit and ombudsman functions and put IBRA under the Ministry of State-Owned Enterprises. Recent changes also stressed the obligations of IBRA's deputy chairmen to support the efforts of the chairman. Previously the chairman had only limited authority over the deputy chairmen, who were independently appointed and who managed each of IBRA's key activities.

decisions have policy implications, so there needs to be clarity over who makes decisions and how they will be made.[13]

Another issue to consider is the degree to which an oversight committee can effectively oversee and monitor an AMC's operations. Separating oversight from management increases objectivity, but it also decreases familiarity and understanding of the issues and risks involved in operations. To effectively monitor performance, oversight committees should have access to and even authority over internal and external auditors. This reporting arrangement helps ensure the independence of the audit function.

AMC operations are usually vested in an operating board that includes a chairman or chief executive officer and members of executive management. Senior executives typically include heads of major operating divisions. Some AMCs include the head of the internal auditing function as a member of senior management. Some boards also include nonexecutive members. For the most part, operating board members tend to have extensive experience in the public sector but limited private sector experience.

In a number of AMCs, the auditor is on or reports to the operating board. Ideally, the auditor function should be independent of operations. The integrity and thoroughness of the audit function is likely to be hampered in AMCs where operating boards are dominated by executive managers. It is also noteworthy that most of the Asian AMCs do not include a chief financial officer (CFO) as part of senior management. An experienced CFO can be invaluable in overseeing the myriad of financial issues and risks involved in AMC operations.

Not all AMCs have oversight committees. For example, Danaharta in Malaysia does not have an oversight or policy committee but is governed by a board consisting of government officials and private sector individuals empowered to set policy as well as manage operations. This arrangement should result in greater operational efficiency, although it also increases the risk of undue political influence and public criticism and reduces the likelihood of an independent evaluation of operations.

Governance structures should be designed to achieve public policy objectives and maintain operational efficiency and independence. Consideration should be given to strengthening the expertise and objectivity of

---

13. Examples include decisions involving the provision of representation and warranties, the qualifications of investors, and the weight to give variables such as employment impact in loan restructuring transactions.

governing boards as much as possible. Both oversight and operating boards should include a significant representation of well-informed, nonexecutive board members who have access to key staff and auditors. All board members should receive training regarding their respective responsibilities with outside members receiving additional education to understand the AMC's operations.

AMC Stakeholders

Defining and understanding the stakeholders in an AMC's operations is very important when reviewing the governance structure. As noted earlier, good governance requires managing a myriad of dispersed stakeholder interests to achieve desired objectives. Certainly, all branches of central government as well as many provincial governments are stakeholders. Usually, a government ministry or central bank has oversight responsibility for the AMC and needs to be kept well informed about operations. A country's legislature also must be considered, given the politically sensitive nature of AMCs' operations and the budget implications involved. Members of the legislature are likely to become involved in specific AMC transactions that involve their constituents. Managing relationships with members of the legislature requires keeping them well informed and addressing any concerns they may raise but not allowing them to unduly influence operations. This balancing operation requires establishing mechanisms to communicate and educate the members of the legislature regarding the AMC's goals, objectives, and progress. Organization charts do not always clearly show how AMCs are managing legislative relationships, but all AMCs should consider enhancing communications by establishing an office dedicated to recording and responding to specific issues.

In addition to the executive and legislative branches of government, AMCs must also manage relationships with the judicial branch. AMC activities involve a wide range of legal issues, and the court system may not be supportive of AMCs' objectives, particularly in cases involving the enforcement of claims against influential debtors. To some extent, problems can be overcome by enacting laws to provide special powers to AMCs that allow them to avoid going through the normal bankruptcy process. (It should be noted, however, that AMCs are not always willing to use these powers.) Nonetheless, the courts will be involved in many transactions, and establishing a unit to educate judges and others in the judicial branch regarding the objectives of an AMC can be very helpful.

AMCs also must deal with many powerful and influential stakeholders with a direct interest in AMC activities. These stakeholders include financial institutions seeking to sell their NPLs on favorable terms, debtors attempting to avoid their NPL obligations, investors looking to buy AMC assets at attractive prices, and any number of investment bankers and consultants trying to sell their services to the AMC or its clients, or sometimes both. Managing these relationships requires clearly communicating what the AMC's policies are regarding buying or selling assets or services, how decisions are to be made, and who has authority to make them. It is also very important for operational units to establish clear points of contact for interested parties. Additionally, AMCs should consider establishing and tracking performance benchmarks for responding to inquiries to help ensure the responsiveness of operating units. An AMC might also establish a separate ombudsman office to address complaints regarding the responsiveness of units with primary functional responsibility.

Another very important stakeholder group includes the employees and management of an AMC. At some point, the government and the AMC supervisory boards must focus on achieving the unpleasant and very difficult task of downsizing staff or closing altogether. As noted earlier, the workload already appears to be declining at some AMCs, and staffing reductions may have already begun. This process can be an emotionally wrenching experience that governing bodies everywhere tend to defer as long as possible. It should come as no surprise that most AMC employees really do not look forward to the day their job is finished and they might become unemployed. One approach to reduce this challenge is to outsource as much work as possible to contractors and keep core staffing levels as small as possible. It also may be possible to arrange for the transfer of some staff to other government agencies such as a deposit insurance agency. Still, the unpleasant reality is that many people in an AMC will be working themselves out of a job, and the better they work, the faster they lose it. Oversight groups should closely monitor staffing levels relative to workload and review staffing plans. Governing boards of AMCs must develop mechanisms to maintain employee morale and encourage good performance throughout this process. Incentives might involve paying higher salaries than other government employees receive or providing bonuses or other compensation incentives based on performance. Providing employees with advance notice and outplacement employment services also can help. Most employees recognize the implications of declining workloads, and managing their concerns and expectations requires good communications. One approach would be to establish a special executive committee to deal with sensitive personnel issues and to allow employee representatives to interact with such committees.

In summary, AMCs face conflicting views from various stakeholders who all seek change that best suits their interests. Each stakeholder has an agenda that may not match that of the government when it created the AMC.

Suggestions and Recommendations

As previously stated, strengthening an AMC's governance requires a comprehensive review of its mission, its procedures and processes, and its relationships with its stakeholders and their interests. There is no "one size fits all" governance structure. The structure will vary depending upon the country and tasks assigned. Based on a review of the existing AMCs, however, the following suggestions are offered for consideration.

Mission and Objectives

—Avoid conflicting objectives as much as possible, but when necessary indicate priorities that will be followed.

—Establish a realistic action plan with defined performance benchmarks including target recovery rates and timetables.

—Provide for regular monitoring of performance.

Governance Structure

Provide for an independent and informed oversight committee to establish policy objectives and review an AMC's performance in achieving those goals:

—Prohibit direct involvement in the AMC's operations and transactions.

—Authorize approval authority over the AMC's proposed business strategy, plans, risk policy, and budgets; and over the AMC's proposed performance targets and objectives.

—Provide specialized training to enhance understanding of the AMC's operations.

—Provide access to financial and operational reports.

—Provide authority to meet with internal and external auditors, review their findings, and order special audits.

Provide an independent operating board with authority to manage the AMC's activities:

—Directors should be appointed by president or ministry of finance and serve for a specified term.

—Prohibit conflicts or self-serving practices.

—Provide personal liability protection against lawsuits.

—Authorize the board to fulfill certain key functions, including selecting, compensating, monitoring key executives; ensuring the integrity of accounting and financial reporting systems, including the independent audit and risk monitoring systems; overseeing the process of disclosure and communications to stakeholders, and overseeing and supporting the preparation of meaningful information regarding the performance and risk of the AMC's operations. This information should include audited financial statements including balance sheet, earnings, cash flow statements, and accompanying notes; estimated valuation of NPLs and other assets owned including methodology used; information regarding the expenses incurred to recover assets or enhance values; and information regarding any guarantees provided to enhance asset sales including estimated cost and methodology used.

—Include sufficient independent representation on the board to ensure knowledgeable judgment on business matters independent from management. The board should include independent members on financial reporting and audit committees and involve independent members in the process of transparent disclosure and communications. The board should also provide independent members access to key managers and auditors.

—Provide board members training to ensure understanding of responsibilities.

—Require operating board members to disclose any personal interests in the AMC's transactions and refrain from voting on such matters.

—Provide authorization to establish operating policies not already addressed or inconsistent with oversight policies.

—Establish delegations of authorities and require approvals for certain transaction levels such that the majority of transactions can be approved by management. Medium and large transactions can be approved by the management committee, and only the largest deals should require board approval.

—Establish a strong chief financial officer position with reporting lines direct to the chief executive officer and overall responsibility for asset pricing and financial operations.

—Establish a strong internal auditor position with reporting lines to the chief executive officer and the oversight committee.

Relationships with Stakeholders

—Encourage stakeholder participation in corporate governance by periodically opening oversight meetings on policy issues to the public and by establishing a process to collect public comment on key policy decisions.

—Minimize eventual downsizing issues by relying on contracting work as much as practical; establishing employee outplacement assistance programs; and establishing compensation incentive programs that reward employees for timely and final resolution of assets.

—Establish offices and points of contact. These offices should include sales offices for investors interested in buying assets, a public relations office for media and other interested parties, and an ombudsman office to register complaints and seek redress.

—Use communication channels such as the Internet to facilitate timely and cost-efficient access to meaningful and timely information on asset inventory and aging; sales and other disposition transactions; descriptions of policies; and governance structures, especially the division of authority between management and board members.

Conclusion

Good governance is important to all organizations including government-owned asset management corporations. Establishing a workable governance framework for an AMC is likely to be more challenging than that needed by most business organizations. AMCs face conflicting objectives and a diverse array of stakeholders with opposing and even adversarial interests. Nonetheless, the way an AMC is governed can have a dramatic impact on the economy and perceptions of government fairness and integrity. An AMC's governance requires identifying the many stakeholders and their interests and establishing mechanisms to communicate and manage relationships to achieve company objectives. This paper has offered suggestions on how governance might be achieved. However, as recent experience in the United States has demonstrated, governance design will not work without the unwavering commitment of executive management to the principles of good governance.

References

Asian Development Bank. 1999. *Rising to the Challenge in Asia: A Study of Financial Markets.* Special Issue, vol. 2. Manila.
Monks, Robert A. G., and Nell Minow. 1995. *Corporate Governance.* Malden, Mass.: Blackwell Publishers.

Asset Management Companies Referenced
China Asset Management Corporation (CINDA) (www.cindamc.com.cn)
China Great Wall Asset Management Corporation (GWAMC) (www.gwamcc.com.cn)
China Huarong Asset Management Corporation (CHAMC) (www.chamc.com.cn)
China Orient Asset Management Corporation (COAMC) (www.coamc.com.cn)
Danaharta: Malaysia's National Asset Management Company (www.danaharta.com.m)
Indonesian Bank Restructuring Agency (IBRA) (www.bppn.go.id)
Korean Asset Management Company (KAMCO) (www.kamco.or.kr)
Korean Deposit Insurance Corporation (KDIC) (www.kdic.or.kr)
Thailand Financial Sector Restructuring Agency (FRA) (www.fra.or.th)

Public Sector Banks
and the Governance Challenge:
The Indian Experience

THIS PAPER DETAILS the Indian experience in meeting the governance challenge regarding public sector banks (PSBs), or state-owned banks, as they are described in some countries. After reviewing the historical context of the Indian experience and the governance reforms that have been put in place, the paper highlights tentative issues and lessons that are emerging and offers some random thoughts intended to provoke analysis and debate on enhancing corporate governance in public sector banks.

Historical Context

India had a fairly well-developed commercial banking system in existence at the time of independence in 1947. The Reserve Bank of India (RBI) was established in 1935. While the RBI became a state-owned institution after January 1, 1949, the Banking Regulation Act, enacted in 1949, provided a framework for regulation and supervision of commercial banking activity. The first step toward the nationalization of commercial banks was the result of a report written in 1951 by the Committee of Direction of All India Rural Credit Survey (under the aegis of the RBI); the report is still the classic work on the subject. The committee recommended one strong, integrated commercial banking institution, to be partnered by the state, to stimulate the development of banking in general and rural credit in particular. Thus, the Imperial Bank was taken over by the government and renamed the State Bank of India (SBI) on July 1, 1955, with the RBI acquiring an overriding majority of shares. A number of erstwhile banks owned by princely states were made subsidiaries of the SBI in 1959. Thus, the beginning of the planned economy era in India, more commonly known as the Plan Era, also saw the emergence of public ownership of one of the most prominent of the commercial banks.

By the mid-1960s, the Indian banking system had made considerable progress, but there was a widespread belief that the close links between commercial banks and big industry had crowded agriculture and small business out of the credit market. To meet these concerns, the government in 1967 introduced the concept of *social control* in the banking industry, which was intended to bring some changes in the management and distribution of credit by the commercial banks. The close link between big business houses and big banks was to be snapped, or at least made ineffective, by reconstituting boards of directors of the banks so that 51 percent of the directors would have to have special knowledge or practical experience. Appointment of a full-time chairman of the board with special knowledge and practical experience of working in commercial banks or in financial, economic, or business administration was intended to professionalize the top management. Restrictions on loans granted to businesses in which the directors had interests were another step toward breaking the close link between the banks and big businesses. The scheme also provided for the takeover of banks under certain circumstances.

Political pressure, attributed in part to inadequacies of the social control plan, led the government of India in 1969 to nationalize fourteen major scheduled commercial banks that had deposits above a specific size. The objective was to better serve development needs of the economy in conformity with national priorities and objectives. Eleven years after this first nationalization, the government announced the nationalization of six more scheduled commercial banks that had assets above the cutoff size. The second round of nationalization gave the impression that a private bank that grew to the cutoff size would be under the threat of nationalization.

Beginning in the 1950s, a number of exclusively state-owned development financial institutions (DFIs) were also set up both at the national and state level. The lone exception was the Industrial Credit and Investment Corporation, which had a minority private share holding. Mutual fund activity was also a virtual monopoly of a government-owned institution, namely, the Unit Trust of India. State-owned refinance institutions in agriculture and industry sectors were also developed, similar in nature to the DFIs. Insurance, both life and general, also became state monopolies.

The Situation before Reform

The regulatory framework for the banking industry under the Banking Regulation Act was circumscribed by the special provisions of the Bank Nationalization Act, enacted in 1970, which also had elements of corporate governance regarding composition of boards of directors. While the Bank Nationalization Act technically provided for competition between banks and nonbanks and among banks, competition in practice was conditioned by policy as well as by the regulatory environment, common ownership by the government, and agreements between the government of India as an owner and unionized bank employees. Hesitancy in permitting industrial houses to engage in banking business as well as to allow foreign-owned banks should be viewed in this historical context.

Before the reform almost all financial intermediation was through the public sector, with PSBs being the most important source of mobilization of financial savings. Resources for DFIs were also made available either by banks or through encouraging contributions from commercial banks, privileged funding by central banks, and concessions from government. The major thrust was an expansion of branch banks, provision of banking services, and mobilization of deposits. Interest rates were fixed on deposits and loans. At the same time, there was a large preemption of banks' resources under the cash reserve ratio (the RBI's prescription of cash balances that banks had to maintain with the RBI) or in the form of a statutory liquidity ratio (RBI's prescription for maintaining a portion of liabilities in specified securities). The delivery of credit was also by and large directed through an allocative mechanism or as an adjunct to the licensing regime. In the process, private sector banks tended to be confined to local areas and were unable to expand in such an environment. Banks, mainly public sector banks, dominated financial intermediation in the country. To a large extent, entry was restricted, exit was impossible, and there was little or no scope for functions of risk assessment and pricing of risks. In short, the government combined in itself the roles of owner, regulator, and sovereign.

The legal as well as the policy framework emphasized coordination in the interest of national development as per Plan priorities with the result that issues of corporate governance became subsumed in the overall development framework. To the extent that each bank, even after nationalization, maintained its distinct identity, governance structure as incorporated in the concerned legislation set out a formal relationship between the RBI, the government, the board of directors, and management. As a regulator, the RBI acted essentially as an extended arm of the government so far as highest priority was accorded to ensuring coordinated actions in banking activities, particularly activities of the PSBs. The SBI, which was owned by the RBI, was in substance no different from the other banks owned by the government in terms of board composition, and appointment procedures of executive management and nonexecutive members of the board. Both the government and the RBI were represented on the boards of the PSBs. Significant cross-representation occurred between banks and all other major financial entities. In other words, cross-holdings and interrelationships were more a rule than an exception in the financial sector, since the basic objective was coordination for ensuring planned development. As a result, checks and balances and other governance safeguards against conflicts of interest among the players were subordinated to the social goals of the *joint family* headed by the government.

Reform Measures

The major challenge of the reform, which commenced in 1992, has been to introduce elements of market incentive as a dominant factor, gradually replacing the administratively coordinated planned actions for development. Such a paradigm shift has several dimensions, with corporate governance being one of the important elements. The evolution of corporate governance in banks, particularly in PSBs, reflects changes in monetary policy, regulatory environment, banking structure, and to some extent the character of the self-regulatory organizations functioning in the financial sector.

Policy Environment

During the reform period, the policy environment enhanced competition and provided greater opportunity for exercise of what may be called a genuine corporate element in each bank, replacing the elements of coordinated actions that characterized the joint family under the previous regime. The measures taken so far can be summarized as follows:

First, greater competition has been infused into the banking system by permitting entry of private sector banks (nine licenses since 1993), and liberal licensing of more branches by foreign banks and the entry of new foreign banks. With the development of a multi-institutional structure in the financial sector, emphasis is on efficiency through competition irrespective of ownership. Since nonbank intermediation has increased, banks have had to improve efficiency to ensure survival.

Second, the reforms accorded greater flexibility to the banking system to manage both the pricing and quantity of resources. Statutory preemptions have been reduced to less than a third of commercial banks' resources. The mandatory component of market financing of government borrowing has decreased. Although directed credit continues, it is now on near-commercial terms. Valuation of banks' investments is also attuned to international best practices so as to appropriately capture market risks.

Third, the RBI has moved away from microregulation to macromanagement. The RBI has replaced detailed guidelines for individual banks with general guidelines and now leaves it to individual bank boards to set their guidelines on credit decisions. A regulation review authority was established in the RBI, whereby any bank could challenge the need for any regulation or guideline issued by the RBI, and the department had to justify the need and usefulness for the guideline relative to costs of regulation and compliance.

Fourth, to strengthen the banking system as it copes with the changing environment, prudential standards have been imposed in a progressive manner. Thus, while banks have greater freedom to make credit decisions, prudential norms setting out capital adequacy norms, asset classification, income recognition and provisioning rules, exposure norms, and asset liability management systems have helped to identify and contain risks, thereby contributing to greater financial stability.

Fifth, an appropriate legal, institutional, technological, and regulatory framework has been put in place for the development of financial markets. Volumes and transparency have increased in primary and secondary market operations. Development of the government securities, money, and foreign exchange markets has improved the transmission mechanism of monetary policy, facilitated the development of a yield curve, and enabled greater integration of markets. The interest rate channel of monetary policy transmission is acquiring greater importance compared with the credit channel.

Regulatory Environment

Prudential regulation and supervision have formed a critical component of the financial sector reform program since its inception, and India has endeavored to attain international prudential norms and practices. These norms have been progressively tightened over the years, particularly against the backdrop of the Asian crisis. Bank exposures to sensitive sectors such as equity and real estate have been curtailed. The Banking Regulation Act of 1949 prevents connected lending (that is, lending by banks to directors or companies in which bank directors are interested).

Periodic inspection of banks has been the main instrument of supervision, although recently there has been a move toward supplementary "on-site inspections" with "off-site surveillance." An annual financial inspection was introduced in 1992, replacing an earlier system. The inspection objectives and procedures have been redefined to evaluate the bank's safety and soundness, to appraise the quality of the board and management, to ensure compliance with banking laws and regulation, to provide an appraisal of the soundness of the bank's assets, to analyze the financial factors that determine the bank's solvency, and to identify areas where corrective action is needed to strengthen the institution and improve its performance. Inspections based upon the new guidelines began in 1997.

A high-powered Board for Financial Supervision (BFS), comprising the governor of the RBI as chairman, one of the deputy governors as vice chairman, and four directors of the Central Board of the RBI as members, was set up in 1994 and charged with supervising and inspecting banking companies, financial institutions, and all nonbanking financial companies. A supervisory strategy has been implemented, consisting of on-site inspection, off-site monitoring, and control systems internal to the banks, based on the CAMELS (capital adequacy, asset quality, management, earnings, liquidity, and systems and controls) methodology for banks. The RBI has instituted a mechanism that allows banks to make a critical analysis of their own balance sheet and to present that analysis to their boards as an internal assessment of the health of the bank. The analysis, which is also made available to the RBI, forms a supplement to the system of off-site monitoring of banks.

Keeping in line with the merging regulatory and supervisory standards at the international level, the RBI has initiated certain macroeconomic-level monitoring techniques to assess the true health of the supervised institutions. The format of balance sheets of commercial banks has now been prescribed by the RBI with disclosure standards on vital performance and growth indicators, provisions, net nonperforming assets (NPAs), staff productivity, and the like, appended as "Notes of Accounts." To bring about greater transparency in banks' published accounts, the RBI has also directed the banks to disclose data on movement and provisions of NPAs as well as on lending to sensitive sectors. These proposed additional disclosure norms would bring the disclosure standards almost up to par with international best practices.

Structural Environment of Banking

Under an amendment to the Banking Companies (Acquisition & Transfer of Undertakings) Act in 1994, the nationalized banks are permitted to dilute their equity in Government of India, bringing down the minimum government shareholdings in PSBs to 51 percent. The RBI's shareholding in SBI is subject to a minimum of 55 percent. Ten banks have already raised capital from the market. The government proposed, in the Union Budget for the financial year 2000–01, to reduce its holding in nationalized banks to a minimum of 33 percent, while maintaining the public sector character of these banks. Diversification of ownership of PSBs has made a qualitative difference to their functioning because private shareholding has been accompanied by attendant issues of shareholders' value, representation of private shareholders on boards of directors, and airing of interests of minority shareholders.

The governance of banks rests with boards of directors. In the light of deregulation in interest rates and the greater autonomy given to banks in their operations, the role of the board has become more significant. Boards have been required to lay down policies in critical areas such as investments, loans, asset-liability management, and management and recovery of NPAs. As a part of this process, banks are required to appoint several board-level committees, including a management committee.

In 1995, the RBI directed banks to set up an audit committee of the board, with the responsibility of ensuring efficacy of the internal control and audit functions in the bank besides compliance with the inspection report of the RBI, internal, and concurrent auditors. To ensure both professionalism and independence, banks are required to have chartered accountants on their boards, but the chairman may not serve on the audit

committee. Banks are also required to set up risk management and asset liability management committees and are free to establish any other committees they feel are necessary.

The government introduced a bill in parliament to omit the mandatory
provisions regarding appointment of RBI nominees on the boards of public sector banks and instead to empower the RBI to appoint a nominee to
the boards of public sector banks if the RBI is of the opinion that doing so
is in the interest of banking policy, the public, or the bank or it depositors.
Since December 1997, the RBI has been appointing additional directors
only to those boards of private banks that are considered weak as demonstrated by losses for more than one year, a capital-to-risk-weighted-assets
ratio below 8 percent, NPAs exceeding 20 percent of advances, or a management dispute.

The government appoints the chairmen, managing directors, and executive directors of all PSBs. The Narasimham Committee II had recommended that bank boards be allowed to appoint the chairman and managing director and that the boards themselves be elected by shareholders. The
government rejected this recommendation and instead, a board chaired by
the governor of the Reserve Bank of India has been made responsible to
advise on these appointments. More recently, the government has formed
a search committee with two outside experts to nominate the chief executive officer of those PSBs identified as weak.

Appointment or removal of PSB auditors requires prior approval of the
RBI. There is an elaborate procedure by which banks select auditors from
an approved panel of names circulated by the RBI. Statutory auditors for
private sector banks are appointed at the annual general meeting with the
prior approval of the RBI.

Self-Regulatory Organizations

India has had the distinction of experimenting with self-regulatory organizations in the financial system since before independence. Currently the
financial system has four self-regulatory organizations: Indian Banks Association (IBA); Foreign Exchange Dealers Association of India (FEDAI);
Primary Dealers Association of India (PDAI); and Fixed Income Money
Market Dealers Association of India (FIMMDAI).

The IBA, established in 1946 as a voluntary association of banks, strove
toward strengthening the banking industry through consensus and coordination. Since nationalization of banks, PSBs have tended to dominate the

IBA, which has developed close links with the government and the RBI. Often, the reactive and consensus approach of the IBA bordered on cartelization. To illustrate, the IBA had worked out a schedule of benchmark charges for the services rendered by member banks, which were not mandatory in nature, but were being adopted by all banks. The practice of fixing rates for services of banks was consistent with a regime of administered interest rates but not with the principle of competition. As a result, the RBI directed the IBA to stop issuing benchmark service charges. Responding to the imperatives caused by the changing scenario in the reform era, the IBA has over the years refocused its vision, redefined its role, and modified its operational modalities.

The FEDAI was established in 1958 to prescribe terms and conditions that banks must follow for transacting foreign exchange business. In light of the reforms, the FEDAI has refocused its role. It no longer fixes exchange rates, but instead concentrates on training bank personnel in foreign exchange transactions, establishing accounting standards for such transactions, evolving risk measurement models like the VaR, and accrediting foreign exchange brokers.

The two self-regulatory organizations active in the financial markets—the PDAI and the FIMMDAI—are of recent origin (1996 and 1997, respectively). They are proactive and closely involved in contemporary issues relating to development of money and government securities markets. The representatives of the PDAI and the FIMMDAI are members of important committees of the RBI, both on policy and operational issues, including technological infrastructure. To illustrate, the chairmen of the PDAI and the FIMMDAI are members of the Technical Advisory Group on Money and Government Securities Market of the RBI. The FIMMDAI has now taken on the responsibility of publishing the yield curve in the debt markets. Currently, the organization is working toward development of uniform documentation and accounting principles in the repossession market.

Advisory Group Recommendations on Corporate Governance in PSBs

A standing committee on International Financial Standards and Codes was constituted by the RBI to, inter alia, assess the status of governance standards and codes in India relative to the best global practices. An Advisory

Box 1. *Recommendations of the Advisory Group on Corporate Governance*

Following is a summary of the major conclusions reached by the Advisory Group on Corporate Governance of the Reserve Bank of India (RBI). Its report was filed in March 2001.

All banks, public and private, should be brought under a single law so that the corporate governance regimes do not differ just because the entities are covered under different legislation or because their ownership is in the private or public sector.

The chairmen, executive directors, and nonexecutive directors on the boards of the PSBs (including the State Bank of India and its subsidiaries) need to be appointed on the advice of an expert body set up on the lines of the Union Public Service Commission with similar status and independence. Such a body may be set up jointly by the RBI and the Ministry of Finance. There is no need to have directors that represent narrow sectional and economic interests. All the objectives that the banks are supposed to achieve should become an integral part of the corporate mission statements of these institutions.

Because it acts as a regulator, the RBI should not have representation on any bank board, given the fact that it leads to conflicts of interest with its regulatory functions. This should apply even in the case of the SBI where the RBI is the major shareholder. Further, any policy measures that protect banks that are less careful in their lending policies at the expense of taxpayers should be amended to discourage profligate lending by banks.

Current regulatory provisions do not permit a bank to lend money to a company if any of its board members also serve on the board of the company. As a result of the rule, banks have been unable to get good professionals for their boards. This archaic rule should be modified immediately so that it applies only to those bank directors who are have a stake in the company beyond being merely a director. In the interest of good governance, government directors should not participate in the discussion or vote on matters affecting companies on whose boards they serve.

Source: The full Report of the Advisory Group on Corporate Governance may be found at (www.rbi.org.in).

Group on Corporate Governance, headed by Dr. R. H. Patil, made a detailed assessment and offered recommendations, including many related to the PSBs. This report provides the most comprehensive set of recommendations on the subject (box 1). The report of the Advisory Group on Banking Supervision, chaired by M. S. Verma, has also made some recommendations on corporate governance. These are summarized in box 2.

Box 2. *Recommendations of the Advisory Group on Banking Supervision*

Following are the key recommendations made in May 2001 by the Advisory Group on Bank Supervision of the Reserve Bank of India (RBI).

The quality of corporate governance should be the same in all banking organizations irrespective of their ownership. Banks need to develop mechanisms to help them infuse their strategic objectives and corporate values throughout the organization. Boards need to set and enforce clear lines of responsibility and accountability for themselves as well as the senior management and personnel throughout the organization. Compensation committees should be set up to establish links between contribution and remuneration or reward.

Nomination committees should be established to assess the effectiveness of the board and to direct the process of appointing board members. Disclosures about the committees of the board, the qualifications of the directors, the board's incentive structure, and the nature and extent of board members' transactions with affiliated and related parties need to be encouraged. Finally, large shareholders should be prohibited from accepting loans and advances from their banks, just as bank directors and their related parties are under Section 20 of the Banking Regulation Act of 1949.

Source: The full Report of the Advisory Group on Banking Supervision may be found at (www.rbi.org.in).

These two reports contain far-reaching proposals to improve corporate governance, and many, if not all, must be approved in parliament before they can take effect. That is a time-consuming process, and so these recommendations are likely to be realizable only in the medium term. While proceeding with analysis and possible legislative actions, it may also be necessary to consider and adopt changes that could be implemented within the existing legislative framework.

To this end, the governor of the Reserve Bank of India established a consultative group of directors of banks and financial institutions in October 2001 to review the supervisory role of boards of banks and financial institutions, to obtain feedback on the functioning of the boards regarding such matters as regulatory compliance, transparency, disclosures, and audit committees, and to recommend ways to make boards of directors more effective. The group made its recommendations very recently after a comprehensive review of the existing framework as well as of current practices and benchmarked its recommendations with international best practices as enunciated by the Basel Committee on Banking Supervision, as well as of other committees and advisory bodies, to the extent applicable in the Indian environment. The report has been put in the public domain for a wider debate; its major recommendations are summarized in box 3.

Tentative Issues and Lessons

The Indian experience shows recognition of
—the importance of corporate governance and the challenges in redefining institutional relations in the financial sector regarding PSBs;
—the need for a broader view on enhancing corporate governance to take account of law and policy as well as the operating and institutional environment; and
—the desirable changes in the composition and functioning of boards of directors.
The processes by which some progress has been made so far and actions contemplated are also instructive. Needless to say, these issues and lessons have to be viewed as tentative and of course contextual.

Corporate governance in PSBs is important, not only because PSBs dominate the banking industry, but also because they are unlikely to exit from the banking business even though the government is likely to reduce its holdings in these banks. To the extent PSBs remain publicly owned, the multiple objectives of the government as owner and the complex principal-agent relationships that ownership entails cannot be wished away. PSBs cannot be expected to blindly mimic private banks in governance even though general principles of governance are valid for both state-owned and private banks. Complications arise when public ownership is treated as a transitional phenomenon, and uncertainties about ownership are widespread. The anticipation or threat of change in ownership also has some impact on governance, since the expectation is not merely a change in ownership, but a change in the very nature of the owner. Mixed ownership where government has a controlling interest is an institutional structure that poses potential conflicts between one set of owners who look for commercial return and another who seek something more and different to justify ownership. Furthermore, the expectations, the reputational risks, and the implied, even if not exercised, authority associated with a government owner affect the governance of such PSBs and should be recognized.

In brief, the issue of corporate governance in PSBs is important and also complex.

The most important challenge in enhancing corporate governance relates to redefining the interrelationships among the institutions within the broadly defined public sector, that is, the government, the RBI, and the PSBs, as the government moves away from the original joint family approach. So far there has been partial but significant success on this front. As part of reform, the government had to differentiate, conceptually and at the policy level, its role as sovereign, owner of banks, and overarching supervisor of regulators including the RBI. The central bank also had to move away from microregulation of developmental schemes to a more even handed treatment of all banks as regulator and supervisor. Furthermore, the bureaucracy of the RBI has been made accountable to an independent Board for Financial Supervision. The large publicly owned development financial institutions had to recognize the need to raise and deploy funds on competitive terms. Similarly, the PSBs had to reorient their approach to each other as they sought to intensify their competitiveness while guarding against excessive risk taking under guidelines issued by a supervisor seeking to meet international standards.

Another noteworthy aspect of enhancing corporate governance is the narrowing of the gap between PSBs and other banks in terms of policy, regulatory, and operating environments. The PSBs, wholly owned by the government with no share value quoted in stock exchanges, accounted for more than three-fourths of India's banking business in the early 1990s; by 2002 they accounted for less than a quarter.

A third area where improvements in the quality of governance have been made or are contemplated relates to selection of chief executives and the composition and functioning of boards of directors. In this regard, it is noteworthy that recently, the functioning of bank boards in the private sector seems to have attracted significant adverse notice, both from the market and the supervisor. That RBI representation on the boards of the private banks is not desirable has been conceded even as the RBI has expressed interest in divesting all its ownership functions.

The processes by which these changes have been and are being brought about may also be of some interest. First, the RBI has taken the initiative in bringing about changes rather than keeping aloof from the regulated entities as pure theory may suggest. The RBI's role of promoting and funding institutions and channeling development credit to schemes under

Box 3. *Recommendations of the Consultative Group of Directors of Banks/Financial Institutions*

Following are the key recommendations made by the Consultative Group of Directors of Banks/Financial Institutions in April 2002:

Before a director of any bank, public or private, is appointed his or her qualifications and technical expertise should be reviewed. Boards should consider setting up a nomination committee to direct the process. The government should consider adopting the criteria suggested by the Bank for International Settlements for ensuring that nominees to the boards of PSBs meet "fit and proper" norms. Bank boards should actively search for directors who have the technical or specialized expertise to guide the bank through the complex challenges it faces. Nomination of independent, nonexecutive directors to boards of banks in both the public and private sectors should be from a list of professional and talented people prepared and maintained by the RBI. Banks should deviate from this procedure only with the prior approval of the RBI.

Independent, nonexecutive directors should provide the checks and balances ensuring that the bank does not build up exposures to entities connected with the promoters or their associates. The independent, nonexecutive directors should provide effective checks and balances particularly in widely held and closely controlled banking organizations.

All directors should formally state that they have read through the guidelines defining the role and responsibilities of directors, understand what is expected of them, and promise to discharge their responsibilities to the best of their abilities, individually and collectively.

To attract quality professionals, the level of remuneration payable to the directors should be commensurate with the time required to be devoted to the bank's work as well as with the quality of inputs expected from a member. The statutory prohibition on lending to companies in which a director is interested severely constricts the availability of quality professional directors on bank boards; consideration should be given to amending this prohibition. The positions of chairman and managing director of large public sector banks should not reside in the same person. The directors could be made more responsible to their organization by requiring them to attend briefings or workshops to acquaint them with emerging developments and challenges facing the banking sector. The RBI could take the initiative in organizing such seminars. The RBI might also update its guidelines on the role expected of and the responsibilities of the individual directors. Full-time directors should have sufficiently long tenure to enable them to leave a mark of their leadership and business acumen on the bank's performance. All banks should consider appointing a qualified person as the secretary to the board and a compliance officer (reporting to the secretary) to monitor and report on directors' compliance with various regulatory and accounting requirements.

Information furnished to the board should be comprehensive and enable the board to make meaningful decisions. The board's focus should not be on day-to-day operations, but rather on strategy issues, risk profiles, internal control systems, and overall performance.

Information on the bank's exposure to stockbrokers and sensitive sectors such as real estate should be reported to the board regularly. The bank should submit progress reports on implementing a progressive risk management system, the risk management policy strategy followed by the bank, exposures to related entities, the asset classification of such lendings or investments, and conformity with corporate governance standards, to the board of directors at regular intervals as prescribed.

Boards of directors should have a supervisory committee charged with monitoring the bank's credit and investment exposures, the adequacy of the risk management process and any necessary upgrading, internal control systems, and regulatory compliance.

Ideally, the board's audit committee should be made up of independent directors, and the executive director should only serve ex officio. Audit committees of public sector banks, however, can continue to include the executive director and nominee directors of the government and the RBI. Members of audit committees need not be professional accountants, but they should have knowledge about finance and banking.

Boards should have a nomination committee for appointing independent, nonexecutive directors of banks. The nomination committee of the board of a public sector bank that issues capital to the public should nominate directors representing shareholders.

The formation of risk management committees should be speeded up in pursuance of the guidelines issued by the RBI, and their role further strengthened. To build credibility among investors, boards should set up a committee to investigate investor and shareholder grievances; grievances should be submitted to the company secretary.

Finally, the banks should be asked to come up with a strategy for implementing the governance standards and should submit progress reports after the first twelve months, and then every six months or year, as deemed appropriate.

Source: The full Report of the Consultative Group of Directors of Banks/Financial Institutions can be found at www.rbi.org.in.

government approved plans has changed to that of developing a more robust financial system, especially the country's banking structure and system. Sometimes, closer involvement of the RBI in some transitional arrangements, such as in advising the government on appointment of chief executives of PSBs, was needed to bring about changes. The RBI's advisory and consultative groups helped ensure that the inputs were professional and that the recommendations followed good governance practices.

Second, as RBI Governor Bimal Jalan articulated early in 2002, "markets are more free and more complex now; what happens in banks is a concern for all because we live in a more volatile and interlinked world where economic effects, including those of contagion, occur nearly instantaneously."[1] Hence, in the process of freeing up markets as part of the reform, the RBI has had to equip the participants, especially the dominant PSBs, with the tools and capabilities necessary to manage these complexities.

Third, the path of reform, of which corporate governance is one element, had to be considered carefully and evolved through a consultation and participation process at every step. Thus, the basic framework was provided by the two Narasimham Committees, in which all stakeholders were represented, followed by a series of committees and consultation papers to refine, redefine, and apply the basic framework.[2] A collaborative and consensual approach to reform was adopted, although participants did not deviate greatly from the original goals of the reform. The most recent example of this approach has been described in the Report of the Advisory Groups on various international standards and codes.

Fourth, reformers needed to resist the temptation to demoralize the PSBs on their presumed inefficiency and instead make every effort to enable and empower them to meet the new challenges. There has been clear recognition that governance is not merely one of structures, but also one of culture. A variety of mechanisms and forums have been set up to nurture the new culture. One salient example occurred when the RBI governor, who also chaired the National Institute of Bank Management, yielded the chairmanship of the institute to a former chairman of a public sector bank, and the RBI distanced itself from the day-to-day running of the institute without withdrawing its interest and support.

Fifth, the importance of self-regulating organizations in bringing about change has been recognized, and the orientation of existing institutions, in

1. Jalan (2002).
2. Reserve Bank of India (1991, 1997).

particular the Indian Banks' Association, has changed to meet new challenges. Various mechanisms have been found to ensure an environment supportive of sound corporate governance by not only pursuing legal and policy changes with the government, but also by interacting closely with auditors and banking industry associations.[3]

Random Thoughts

The Indian experience provokes some thoughts on a few fundamental issues regarding PSBs and corporate governance. First, is public ownership compatible with sound corporate governance as generally understood? Since various corporate governance structures exist in different countries, there are no universally correct parameters of sound corporate governance. Government ownership of a bank, unless government happens to have such a stake purely as a financial investment for return, necessarily has to have the effect of altering the strategies and objectives as well as the structure of governance. Government as an owner is accountable to political institutions whose goals may not necessarily be compatible with purely economic incentives. Mixed ownership brings into sharper focus the divergent objectives of shareholding and the issues of reconciling them, especially when one of the owners is government. In such a situation, one can argue that as long as the private shareholders are aware of the special nature of shareholding, there should be no conflict. In other words, the idea of maintaining the public sector character of a bank while government holds a minority shareholding is an intensified and modified version of the "golden share" experiment of the United Kingdom. The question remains whether such a mixed ownership is the most efficient form of organization, particularly for banks, which are in any case generally under intense regulation and supervision.

Second, is corporate governance generally better in the private sector, in particular, in private sector banks? Almost all of the Indian private sector banks that were established before the reforms continue to be closely held, and many of them resist broadening their shareholder base and thus avoid deepening of corporate structures. More often than not, takeover bids have been by equally closely held groups. The promoters of new private sector

3. A framework for this sort of close cooperation was set out by the Basel Committee on Banking Supervision (1999).

banks, which were licensed after close scrutiny in the reform period, were expected to dilute their stakes to below 40 percent within three years. That has not happened in two cases, and in most of the others, the banks are still effectively controlled by their promoter institutions. Governor Jalan made an interesting observation on this in a recent lecture, noting that the old private banks had poor accounting and auditing systems, while the new banks were generally good on accounting, but poor on accountability. One feature both old and new banks had in common, he continued, was a highly centralized corporate governance structure that imposed "very little real check on the CEO, who is generally also closely linked to the largest owner groups."[4]

Third, what are the differences between public and private banks in the way the dynamics of insider and outsider models work in terms of separation between ownership and management? One view is that there is not much difference between public and private sectors in India. According to the chairman of the National Institute of Bank Management,

> The literature on governance deals mostly with the financial disclosures and restrictions on the managements that remain within the corporation and the influence that the external stakeholder or shareholders can hold. But in developing countries, the problem is slightly the other way round. In developing countries and more particularly in India, the major corporate issue is not how outside financiers can control the actions of the managers but how outside stakeholders including the minority shareholders can exert control over the big inside shareholders; and this does not apply only to the public sector, but it applies equally strongly or probably more strongly to the private sector as well.[5]

Others disagree with this perception however. Governor Jalan believes that the private sector has greater elements of the insider model. The dominant view, backed by more recent research, is that the issue in India often relates to minority shareholders. "Rather than conflict between owners and managers of firms, it is the conflict between the interests of minority shareholders and promoters (say, business groups) that is more relevant for India and that needs to be addressed," according to the National Stock Ex-

---

4. Jalan (2002).
5. Bhide (2002).

change.[6] In other words, if the governance structures are weak, the risks of private ownership of banks need to be assessed before embarking on large-scale privatizations.

Fourth, is the performance of PSBs demonstrably better than that of the private sector banks? The evidence here is not conclusive, because comparison is beset with several difficulties. Clearly, old private sector banks as a group do not perform well, while new private sector banks as a group outperform the PSBs as a group. Given the size and variety of PSBs, it is possible to find banks that could equal the good private sector banks in performance. In addition, PSBs have to reckon with the "legacy" problems, such as the nonperforming assets that they are saddled with. Some PSBs operate in relatively backward areas with limited discretion for management to pull out of the area. The question still remains: Is it better to enable PSBs to improve their performance while promoting private sector banks or to transfer ownership and control from the public banks to the private sector? Will greater scope for mergers and acquisitions within and between the public and private sector add to greater efficiency than keeping the two sectors separate from each other?

Finally, what should be the most operationally relevant approach for enhancing governance in PSBs, recognizing that the extent of public ownership is determined predominantly by considerations of political economy while the functioning of institutions could possibly be influenced by technoeconomic factors. The Indian experience so far, including the identified agenda for debate, seems to indicate that clear-cut demarcation of responsibilities of various institutions and participants is critical because the joint family approach needs to be ended with the friendly and amicable "partition" of assets, liabilities, and activities. This partition needs to be accompanied by transparency in dealing with each other and proper managerial reporting and financial accounting of transactions. Simultaneously, checks and balances should be consciously put in place to replace the tradition of all-pervading bureaucratic coordination.

In brief, the central bank has a developmental role even in the period of reform, but that role is not to develop finance directly, but to help develop systems, institutions, and procedures to enable a paradigm shift in public policy. In the process corporate governance, particularly in the PSBs, will be enhanced. While legislative changes are necessary for an enduring improvement in corporate governance, and such legislative changes are not

6. Kakani, Biswatosh, and Reddy (2001).

easy to effect in a democratic multiparty parliamentary system, it is reassuring to observe that significant improvements in corporate governance in the Indian financial sector are being implemented even within the existing legislative framework.

References

Basel Committee on Banking Supervision. 1999. *Enhancing Corporate Governance for Banking Organisations.* Basel: Bank for International Settlements.

Bhide, M. G. 2002. "Corporate Governance in Banks and Financial Institutions." Speech delivered at the National Institute of Bank Management, January 6, in Pune.

Jalan, Bimal. 2002. "Corporate Governance in Banks and Financial Institutions." Speech at the National Institute of Bank Management Annual Day, January 6, in Pune.

Kakani, Ram Kumar, Biswatosh Saha, and V. N. Reddy. 2001. "Determinants of Financial Performance of India Corporate Sector in the Post-Liberalization Era: An Exploratory Study." NSE Research Initiative Paper 5. National Stock Exchange, Mumbai.

Reserve Bank of India. 1991. *Report of the Committee on the Financial System* (Chairman Shri M. Narasimham). Mumbai.

———. 1997. *Report of the Committee on Banking Sector Reform* (Chairman Shri M. Narasimham). Mumbai.

PART **III**

Governance Issues and Banks

RYSZARD KOKOSZCZYŃSKI 7

How Can Banks Exert Better Governance on Corporations? The Polish Experience

IN RECENT YEARS corporate governance in Poland has been improving, in large part because banks, in seeking to improve the behavior of their corporate clients, have improved their own corporate governance. Under the socialist regime banks already had some experience in using their expertise and knowledge to control the behavior of enterprises. Reforms in the late 1980s gave banks some responsibilities for controlling the wage discipline and efficiency of investment projects and their implementation. That was part of the more general effort directed toward using financing as a controlling device in the so-called reformed socialist economies. Under the reform two kinds of state economic plans existed side by side. One was the typical plan, defined in physical categories (such as producing so many tons of steel a year), designed and implemented by the state administration system. The second was a credit plan (such as planned loans to households and enterprises from all existing banks and their refinancing by the central bank), designed and implemented by the central bank, which at that time was treated as a separate agency within the government and independent

I would like to thank Jan Krzysztof Solarz and Wojciech Rogowski for discussions I had with them. Comments by V. Sundararajan are gratefully acknowledged. The views expressed here are my own and do not necessarily reflect the official position of the National Bank of Poland.

from other ministries. The process of plan preparation did not guarantee consistency of the physical and credit plans.

Polish experience suggested that this two-part institutional setup was difficult to understand even for the parliament of that time, although the major reason may be the lack of earlier cases of public discussions within the government rather than the substance of the discussion itself. It is impossible to assess the sustainability of that system in Central and Eastern Europe now. Its effective functioning would have required major changes in the relations between the state institutions and the Communist Party.[1]

The end of the socialist period and the beginning of the next stage of development involved the introduction of a two-tiered structure into the Polish banking system. This introduction should be thought of as a process rather than an event. When it became clear that the first economic reforms of the 1980s had done little to improve microeconomic efficiency, the National Bank of Poland initiated the so-called second stage of reform in 1987, which culminated in a new legal framework for the country's banking system in January 1989. The institutions set up by the new banking law and the law on the central bank looked quite similar to their counterparts in a market economy. But these changes were not unambiguously positive. On one hand, from today's perspective they seem to form the initial part of a systemic transformation. On the other hand, these reforms did not make any effort to change the economic regime, especially the ownership structure of the economy. Nevertheless, these changes meant that before the systemic transformation began, Polish banks were already learning how to actively monitor their customers.

The Polish Enterprise and Bank Restructuring Program

In the beginning of the transformation, banks seemed unlikely to play much of a role in promoting improved corporate governance. The most important sector of the economy was to be the private sector. However, the newly established private banks had few funds, and the state-owned banks were not perceived as eager promoters of private enterprises. (Indeed, some administrative measures were applied to push the state-owned banks to

1. The description of that period in Poland from an economic perspective can be found in Wyczański and Golajewska (1995); Polański (1995); and Kokoszczyński and Kondratowicz (1994). Staniszkis (2001) discusses these issues for other countries and in a more general framework of political and social change.

lend funds to new private enterprises.)[2] It is very difficult to apply strict governance standards in an economy where structural changes are so widespread. However, the bad-loan problem of the early 1990s and Poland's solution to it were major steps in this direction.

The focus on Poland's solution to the bad-loan problem in the context of corporate governance requires some explanation. The orthodox Anglo-Saxon approach to corporate governance tends to concentrate on minority shareholder protection and similar issues. The major assumptions here are that share ownership is widely dispersed and that corporate control mechanisms are predicated on a liquid capital market with a sophisticated infrastructure.[3] Comparative corporate governance studies seem to suggest that this approach is quite adequate for the United Kingdom and the United States, but banks play a much greater role in corporate control in continental Europe and in Japan.[4] This bank influence comes not primarily from the shares they own in companies, but from the external financing they supply corporations in the form of debt.[5] Debt as a controlling device was a major factor in banks' role as an active force in corporate governance in Poland in the early 1990s, and it still plays a dominant role today. This paper does not elaborate on the more traditional approach to the corporate governance issue, that is, banks' role as shareholders, because in Poland that role is negligible. The recent data (for the end of the third quarter of 2001) show that stocks are 0.4 percent of banks' net assets.[6]

The first major experience Poland's banks had in exerting control on corporations came after adoption of the Enterprise and Bank Restructuring Program (EBRP) in 1993. The need for the program was the result of three different, though closely interrelated, processes. First, the transformation of the economic system in 1989–90, initial tight macroeconomic policies, and some major shocks of the early 1990s (including the breakdown of Comecon (Council of Mutual Economic Assistance), the Persian Gulf conflict, and a longer-than-expected period of high inflation and high interest rates) put a great number of enterprises into distress. There was strong

2. Banks were obliged to maintain some share of the new loans directed to those enterprises; at the same time, the central bank extended guarantees for some part of that portfolio.

3. Allen and Gale (2000, ch. 4); Bergloef and von Thadden (1999).

4. Allen and Gale (2000); Dittus (1994).

5. The influence of banks as shareholders in corporations seemed to be overrated, even in Germany, in the earlier literature; see Edwards and Fischer (1994).

6. Banking statistics compiled and published regularly by the National Bank of Poland (www.nbp.pl). Tamowicz and Dzierżanowski (2001, p. 16) also conclude that banks do not play any important role among enterprises' shareholders.

political pressure for solving the debt problem in some unorthodox way, which for most parties lobbying on their behalf meant finding a way for the corporations not to pay back loans extended to them by banks. Second, one of the major assumptions of the Balcerowicz plan of 1990 was that macro-economic policy would press private enterprises into positive structural adjustment.[7] That could be brought about only if a hard budget constraint applied to all enterprises. However, a substantial number of banks supplied liquidity even to those enterprises that were obviously insolvent. That kind of behavior was definitely a major obstacle for successful restructuring of the manufacturing sector. Third, state-owned banks required restructuring themselves if they were to become effective financial intermediaries.[8] The EBRP was meant to solve all three issues together, and that is why its design was rather complicated and required enactment of a special law.[9]

The EBRP was a comprehensive program addressing many objectives simultaneously. Corporate restructuring was to be led by banks, which were given some new tools for a fixed period of time. The most important among them, in my opinion, was the bank conciliation (workout) proce-dure (similar to chapter 11 of U.S. bankruptcy law) as an alternative to tra-ditional bankruptcy, court-supervised conciliation, or state enterprise liq-uidation. Bank restructuring was also a part of the EBRP; most of the bank restructuring was designed to give banks incentives that were compatible with the bank-led enterprise restructuring (conditional recapitalization plus active monitoring by the owner). Many other details of the program have been described in the literature, so let me concentrate only on those program features pertinent to the subject of this paper.[10]

First, some important preliminary steps were undertaken as early as 1991, when the magnitude of the bad-loan problem started to become

---

7. The Balcerowicz plan is the popular description of the first step in the Polish transformation: a comprehensive set of measures designed to bring down inflation, impose fiscal discipline, remove price distortions, free internal markets, and open up the Polish economy; see Kierzkowski, Wellisz, and Okolski (1993).

8. Newly established private banks were rather small and their expansion was rather slow in the beginning of the 1990s. Fast privatization of state-owned banks was also not possible at that time, so reform of state-owned banks was a must for the success of macroeconomic reform (Wyczański and Golajewska, 1995).

9. The English translation of the law can be found in Montes-Negret and Papi (1997).

10. Kawalec, Sikora, and Rymaszewski (1994), written by the major authors of the program, describe the details; Gray and Holle (1996a, 1996b) and Montes-Negret and Papi (1997) present some evaluation of the program's results; and Borish, Long, and Noël (1995) put it into some comparative perspective.

apparent. A major group of state-owned banks went through a special auditing procedure, where they were required by the minister of finance (acting as an owner) to identify doubtful and loss loans and to set up new workout units responsible for those portfolios. An important part of that exercise was a formal obligation to find persons that did not have ties to the banks concerned to head these units as well as to fill supervisory positions at the board level. Those new units were then responsible for selling those loans or restructuring them according to a special set of procedures. Restructuring—if it was not to endanger the capital adequacy ratio of banks—required recapitalization, done by the government through a special issue of long-term bonds. Another important feature of the program was its incentive structure for banks. Bad loans (unless sold) were kept on banks' books with the intention of keeping banks actively engaged in the process of monitoring and restructuring enterprises. In addition, the amount of recapitalization was not tied to the collection of bad debts, but rather to the continued good performance of the restructured portfolio. Enterprises thought too big to fail were handled separately, so banks were given incentives to behave with purely commercial goals in mind. This notwithstanding, some features of the program placed restrictions on the banks: they were not allowed to extend new loans to debtors with previous bad loans unless restructuring had been completed and a new business plan presented and approved, and a strict deadline for completing restructuring was imposed. At the same time, prudential regulations were strengthened, particularly capital adequacy and provisioning rules and limits on ownership concentration ratios.[11]

Lessons from Experience

Are there any lessons about corporate governance from the Polish program of the early 1990s? First, most analysts seem to value the program outcomes for the banking sector more highly than the outcomes for its debtors. Gray and Holle wrote that "the outcome . . . is decidedly mixed."[12] On one hand, the program helped banks to build their institutional capacity and pressed

11. Initially, prudential norms were introduced as central bank governor regulations; changes introduced into the banking law in 1992 strengthened their legal basis and made them more comprehensive; see Mondschean and Opiela (1997, pp. 21–22).

12. Gray and Holle (1996a, p. 32).

Figure 7-1. *Nonperforming Loans in Poland as a Share of Total Loans,*
1991–97

Percent

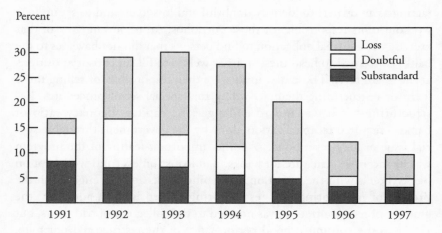

Source: National Bank of Poland.

them into closing unviable firms. Thanks to the program, the Polish banking system went through significant modernization and, as Montes-Negret
and Papi wrote, in 1996 it already resembled that of a modern market economy.[13]

Second, the results of the program for the enterprise sector were perceived as being somewhat positive, but the level of enterprise restructuring
was lower than the program's promoters had envisaged. That was because
banks concerned themselves primarily with restructuring financial conditions rather than forcing enterprises to undertake fundamental management and operational changes.[14] Nevertheless, if one were to look at some
simple performance measures, such as the ratio of nonperforming loans
and the number of uncreditworthy enterprises, there was definitely substantial improvement in the 1991–97 period (figures 7-1 and 7-2).

Another, more general conclusion can be drawn from the story presented here so far. The restructuring program adopted in Poland substan-

13. Montes-Negret and Papi (1997).
14. Mondschean and Opiela (1997, p. 22). However, banks more active in debt-for-equity swaps
and other aggressive restructuring forms suggested that the tax system and some government agencies'
interventions were major reasons for that; see Pawlowicz (1994, 1995).

Figure 7-2. *Number of Uncreditworthy Enterprises*

Number

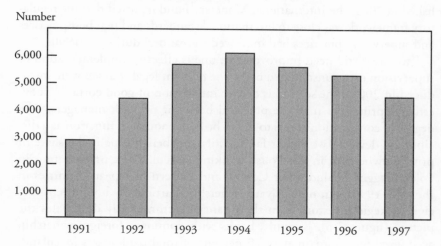

Source: National Bank of Poland.
Note: Number measured as of the end of the year.

tially changed bank behavior, and those changes could be thought of as a basis for a more active role to be played by banks in corporate governance. At the same time, by strengthening the institutional capacity of banks to identify and monitor the quality of their customers, the EBRP indirectly but positively influenced the corporate governance of debtor enterprises.

There is, however, a strong suggestion in the literature, which I fully share, that the success of banks, as loan suppliers in the monitoring and control of enterprises, depends crucially on whether banks themselves are subject to effective control.[15] Two major dimensions of this control are the quality of prudential regulation and effective banking supervision and the discipline exerted by competition within the banking system.

The present situation in these two areas in Poland may be summarized as follows. The major driving force behind changes in the prudential framework in Poland has been the process of accession to the European Union and the need to adopt a legislative framework compatible with EU standards. I am probably too biased to assess (objectively) the degree of success in this area, but—luckily for me—Poland was part of the Financial

15. Dittus (1994, p. 47); Baer and Gray (1995, p. 40).

Stability Assessment Program in 2000, and in a formal assessment published in 2001, the International Monetary Fund reported that the regulatory framework was close to international standards and that best practices and supervisory practices had improved a great deal during the 1990s.[16]

Two areas still need improvement: one is effective implementation of supervision on a consolidated basis (the relevant legal changes were introduced in 2001); the second is deeper integration of good corporate governance principles into the practical behavior of bank managers. The degree of competition seems to me to be high enough to function as a disciplinary device. Two major facts justify this belief. One is the share of private ownership in the Polish banking system. Bank privatization in Poland lagged behind other Central and Eastern European countries in the early 1990s, but now private ownership, particularly holdings by foreign strategic investors from the financial sector, clearly dominates the picture (figure 7-3). Recently, banks with dominant foreign ownership accounted for approximately 70 percent of total bank assets in Poland. Moreover, both the geographical structure of this capital and the degree of concentration indicate that bank competition does not seem to be in danger of diminishing.

Conclusions in a paper with a title like this one should simply answer the question posited by the title—in this case, how can banks exert better governance over corporations. A very brief answer, based on the Polish experience, might be: banks may be an important part of the corporate governance framework, even when their role is limited to debt supply, if their own corporate governance is good. Major factors improving the quality of their corporate governance are a consistent and transparent prudential framework, effective banking supervision, and a high level of competition within the banking sector, with the last element being strongly supported by privatization.

This notwithstanding, it still would be impossible for banks to play any role in corporate governance without effective insolvency procedures, bankruptcy law, laws on creditor rights, and the like. In the beginning of its transition process, Poland managed to overcome the shortcomings of the inherited legal framework in this area by designing a special program (the EBRP). However, for long-run success, the modern legal framework for the exit process is an indispensable part of the corporate governance

16. IMF (2001).

Figure 7-3. *Private and Foreign Ownership in the Polish Banking System*

Percent

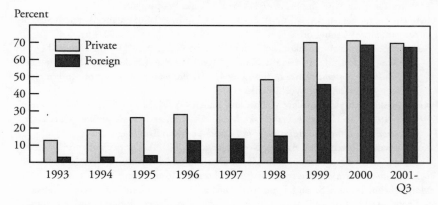

Source: National Bank of Poland.

system and a must for the successful role played by banks within this framework.

References

Allen, Franklin, and Douglas Gale. 2000. *Comparing Financial Systems.* MIT Press.

Baer, Herbert, and Cheryl W. Gray. 1995. "Debt as a Control Device in Transitional Economies: The Experiences of Hungary and Poland." Policy Research Working Paper 1480. World Bank, Washington.

Berglöf, Erik, and Ernst-Ludwig von Thadden. 1999. "The Changing Corporate Governance Paradigm: Implications for Transition and Developing Countries." Paper presented at the annual World Bank Conference on Development Economics, Washington (www.ssrn.com).

Borish, M. S., M. F. Long, and Michel Noël. 1995. "Restructuring Banks and Enterprises. Recent Lessons from Transition Countries." World Bank Discussion Paper 279. World Bank, Washington.

Dittus, Peter. 1994. "Corporate Governance in Central Europe: The Role of Banks." BIS Economic Papers 42. Bank for International Settlements, Basle.

Edwards, Jeremy, and Klaus Fischer. 1994. *Banks, Finance and Investment in Germany.* Cambridge University Press.

Gray, Cheryl W., and Arnold Holle. 1996a. "Bank-Led Restructuring in Poland. An Empirical Look at the Bank Conciliation Process." Policy Research Working Paper 1650. World Bank, Washington.

————. 1996b. "Bank-Led Restructuring in Poland. Bankruptcy and Its Alternatives."
Policy Research Working Paper 1651. World Bank, Washington.

IMF (International Monetary Fund). 2001. "Republic of Poland: Financial System Stability
Assessment." Washington.

Kawalec, Stefan, Slawomir Sikora, and Piotr Rymaszewski. 1994. "Dealing with Bad Debts:
The Case of Poland." In Gerard Caprio, David Folkerts-Landau, and Timothy Lane,
eds., *Building Sound Finance in Emerging Market Economies*. Washington: International
Monetary Fund and the World Bank.

Kierzkowski, Henryk, Stanislaw Wellisz, and Marek Okolski. 1993. "The Polish Economy
1989–1991." In Henryk Kierzkowski, Marek Okolski, and Stanislaw Wellisz, eds., *Stabilization and Structural Adjustment in Poland*. London: Routledge.

Kokoszczyński, Ryszard, and Andrzej Kondratowicz. 1993. "Banking, Credit and Monetary
Policy." In Henryk Kierzkowski, Marek Okolski, and Stanislaw Wellisz, eds., *Stabilization and Structural Adjustment in Poland*. London: Routledge.

Mondschean, Thomas S., and Timothy P. Opiela. 1997. "Banking Reform in a Transition
Economy: The Case of Poland." *Economic Perspectives* (Federal Reserve Bank of Chicago)
(March/April): 16–32.

Montes-Negret, Fernando, and Luca Papi. 1997. "The Polish Experience with Bank and
Enterprise Restructuring." Policy Research Working Paper 1705. World Bank,
Washington.

Pawlowicz, Leszek, ed. 1994. "Restrukturyzacja finansowa przedsiębiorstw i banków.
Pierwszy raport z badań" (Financial restructuring of enterprises and banks. First research
report). IBnGR, Gdańsk.

————.1995. "Restrukturyzacja finansowa przedsiębiorstw i banków. II raport z badań"
(Financial restructuring of enterprises and banks. Second research report). IBnGR,
Gdańsk.

Polański, Zbigniew. 1995. *Pieniądz i system finansowy w Polsce. Lata 1982–1993 (Money
and the Financial System in Poland 1982–1993)*. Warsaw: PWN.

Staniszkis, Jadwiga. 2001. *Postkomunizm (Postcommunism)*. Warsaw: slowo/obraz terytoria.

Tamowicz, Piotr, and Maciej Dzierżanowski. 2001. "Wlasność i kontrola polskich korpo-
racji (Ownership and Control of Polish Corporates)." IBnGR, Gdańsk (www.ibngr.edu.
pl/pfcg.htm).

Wyczański, Pawel, and Marta Golajewska. 1995. *Polski system bankowy 1990–1994 (Polish
Banking System 1990–1994)*. Warsaw: Friedrich-Ebert Stiftung.

KHALID SHEIKH 8

New Imperatives in
Risk Management:
A Commercial Bank's
Perspective

A BANK'S ABILITY TO measure, monitor, and steer risks comprehensively is becoming a decisive parameter for its strategic positioning. Risk management should be seen against four major developments: the rapidly changing supervisory environment; increasing global competition between banks, together with technical progress, which changes the financial intermediary role in many areas; the growing complexity of risk, correlated risks, concentration of risks, global linkages, and complex structured products; and the need for transparency and management information systems, particularly after the debacles of Enron, UPC, and Kirch.

These driving forces clearly indicate that risk management should be included at an early stage in a bank's strategic process. The integration of risk into the strategic function is a recognition that each business within the bank can add value to the strategic planning process by managing its portfolio within existing risk appetites of the specific line of business and the firm as a whole. The same principles also apply roughly to countries to the extent that they are perceived as a large incorporation.

Why Risk Management?

The financial crises in Asia and more recently in Argentina and Turkey and the corporate failures of Enron and Kirch have once again illustrated how important it is for banks to develop a systematic, homogeneous, and objective method for setting criteria, whether they be qualitative or quantitative, to analyze, evaluate, and discriminate among risks—not only among traditional ones, but, more important, among new types of risks!

Modern risk management tools and philosophies have emerged over the past two decades in response to the growth of systemic risk and a strong increase in volatility in interest rates and exchange rates. Interestingly, however, there is still no single measure that captures all risks. The need to develop such a framework is not a new phenomenon. On the contrary, for many centuries different parties have tried various means to safeguard their investment. The earliest form of security can be traced back to Hebrew bankers in ancient Babylon whose network of spies and couriers throughout the world alerted the bankers on the likely victors of wars and feuds, thereby allowing bankers to avoid undue risks. Failure to take such precaution occasionally had serious repercussions; had the bankers of fourteenth century Florence understood risk (especially political risk), they might not have suffered the massive losses that followed upon their loans to Edward III of England when he invaded France at what became the beginning of the Hundred Years' War.

The shaping of the modern political risk insurance industry (and in many ways the first constructive way to manage risks) can be traced to the end of the nineteenth century, when the private risk insurance market was centered in the city of London and institutions of private international insurance were developed. This market operated, with little intervention or competition from the government, to reduce risks associated with foreign trade and investment by providing specialized forms of political risk insurance.

The lesson learned from the examples is that despite the maturing of insurance markets and their participants, certain risk features reappear in different business cycles and in different settings. This recurrence raises several questions: Do market participants (banks, export credit agencies, pension funds, multilaterals) have a clear notion of the evolution of risks? How do these risks correlate to business cycles? And why are we unable to detect the occurrence of these risks at an early enough stage to be able to formulate preemptive policies?

Shifting Forms of Crises

Part of the answer can be found in the breed of crises, which has shifted from crises based on fundamentals to those based on expectations. Before the 1980s the main risk was sovereign risk because the public sector was the only borrower both domestically and internationally, and because foreign direct investment in emerging economies was rare. Moreover, the international financial market itself was in an embryonic stage.

At the start of the 1980s trade flows between emerging and developed economies were unsubstantial, but began to gather more momentum as international capital grew increasingly available. Oil-rich countries channeled their dollars to countries in deficit. Emerging market governments could borrow at cheap terms, which led to overlending and a rapid buildup of foreign debt. To fight the escalating inflation, the United States government tightened its monetary policy. The resulting transition from inflation to disinflation in the world economy ignited a severe crisis as funds that were borrowed when inflation was high and real interest rates low or even negative were no longer cheap in an environment of lower inflation and high real interest rates. In addition, many borrowers were confronted by an adverse psychological shift in the credit markets. As a consequence debt service obligations rose faster than the growth in export revenues. Ultimately, sovereigns went into default, and lenders were confronted with transfer and inconvertibility risk.

The weak state of the financial system and regulatory regime in both developed and developing countries led to financial fragility. Major U.S. banks encountered difficulties; because their portfolios were not sufficiently diversified and they had a large uncovered exposure in emerging markets, they had a high proportion of nonperforming loans. In addition, there was a lack of sound prudential supervisory systems.

During the 1990s the sources and forms of private capital flowing to emerging markets expanded and became more diversified. These flows represent a range of market participants that were not important sources of financing in earlier periods, including asset management companies, insurance firms, and pension funds.

Another noteworthy development during this period was an increase in the participation of the private sector in infrastructure development. Before the 1990s infrastructure services such as telecommunications, electricity, and waste and water treatment were generally believed to be public goods, with governments being responsible for providing these services.

But insufficient investments, growing pressures on government budgets, and general concerns about inefficient service provision by the public sector resulted in a turnaround of this situation. Especially in the last ten years, with the retreat of the central government, the private sector has become more and more involved in providing financing in infrastructure. In 1986 about 7.4 percent of infrastructure financing in developing markets was lent to private borrowers. In 1995 private borrowing had increased to 70 percent of the total!

The growing participation of the private sector has led to a more complex structuring of deals as well as the use of several new financial instruments. Both developments have highlighted the number of new types of risk in financing projects for the lender, project sponsor, and borrower. It should not be forgotten that every loan requires not just a borrower, but also a lender. The borrowers who misallocated their investments share responsibility for the problems with the lenders, many of them international commercial banks, who provided them with the money. In the same line of reasoning, it could be argued that responsibility lies not just with bank supervisors in the borrowing countries, but also with bank supervisors in the lending countries, particularly if the international community feels that there is sufficient systemic risk to the global economy to warrant interventions. Indonesia and Turkey are good examples of this point.

In summary, the risks to which a bank or other lenders can be exposed can vary greatly. The risks are to a large extent determined by the structure of the deal and the parties involved. The risks could be categorized as market risk, credit risk, reputational risk, operational risk, legal risk, event risk, and institutional risk.

Another part of the answer can be found in the assumption that the interaction between borrowers and creditors has changed the transmission mechanism that triggers risk. Table 8-1 illustrates this point by showing the factors that affected cross-border risk for ten crisis-afflicted countries in the last five years.

Several hypotheses can be derived from this table. The first is that the traditional cross-border risks (inconvertibility; transferability; confiscation, expropriation, and nationalization; war and civil conflict) have by and large not materialized. The second hypothesis is that different types of risks (market risk and credit risk, for example) appear to be strongly correlated. As the counter value in local currency of many claims against Asian counterparties rose during the financial crisis of 1997, the financial stability and soundness of many counterparties fell, thus increasing the risk of nonpayment by those counterparties and ultimately the sovereign.

A related hypothesis is that countries in the intermediate stage of development, such as Pakistan and Russia, have incurred a large range of quasi-correlated risks (maxidevaluation, changes in the local legal environment, sovereign default, and official restructuring), suggesting that there are simultaneous triggers or policy sensitivities. Fourth, countries in the same region and with similar economic structures have incurred the same risks, suggesting either contagion or spillover effects, or both. Finally, it could be said that the sovereign payment defaults, corruption, massive currency devaluation, and breach of contract have been the major risk, one that could be identified at the macroeconomic level during these crises. These sovereign risks have resulted in losses or nonpayments for banks and other types of creditors.

It should be noted that risk at the sector and project levels also has ultimately translated into sovereign default either directly or indirectly. This development has created a new angle in assessing political risk, for which at this stage there seems to be insufficient cover. Examples are Pakistan's unilateral cancellation of a range of electric power agreements, the dispute over tolls for the Bangkok toll road project, and conflicts over power generation contracts in Indonesia. All three examples suggest that stability remains elusive as the role of different governments has changed.

Value of Governance for Risk Management

Risk management is perceived as a governance tool, but it is a complex exercise. The purpose of this tool is to allow the firm to bear only those risks it has accepted and to manage them in an efficient, consistent, and objective manner. The process involves identifying a measure of performance, identifying and measuring the risk exposure in relation to the performance measurement, deciding on an acceptable degree of risk exposure, and finally laying off the risk. To illustrate, suppose the objective of the firm is to maximize shareholders' value. This value fluctuates over time for several reasons such as investment strategy, international prices (foreign exchange and interest rates), and competitiveness. The risk manager sorts the fluctuations into movements related to financial prices and those unrelated to financial prices. The latter type cannot be insured against and fully

Table 8-1. *Risk Factors in Ten Recent Financial Crises*

Factor	Mexico 1994	Thailand 1997	Indonesia 1997	Korea 1997	Russia 1997	Pakistan 1998	Brazil 1998	Ukraine 1998	Romania 1999	Ecuador 1999
Inconvertibility	…	…	…	…	x	…	…	…	…	…
Transferability	…	…	…	…	…	x	…	…	…	…
Confiscation, expropriation, and nationalization	…	…	…	…	…	…	…	…	…	…
Contract frustration	…	…	…	…	…	x	…	…	…	…
War	…	…	…	…	…	…	…	…	…	…
Maxidevaluation	x	x	x	x	x	…	x	x	…	x
Corruption	…	…	…	…	x	x	…	…	…	…
Local legal problems	…	…	x	…	x	x	…	x	…	…
Embargo	…	…	…	…	x	x	…	…	…	…
Sovereign default	…	…	…	…	x	x	…	x	…	x
New money	…	…	…	x	…	…	x	…	x	x
Rollover	…	…	…	x	x	…	…	…	…	…
Foreign discrimination	…	x	…	x	…	…	…	…	…	…

Source: ABN AMRO Bank, N.V.

remain as risk, whereas the former could be covered through the use of financial instruments.

A Governance System for Managing Risk

Certainly in the aftermath of the collapse of Enron, Global Crossing, and Kirch and the financial crisis in Argentina, banks were faced with a dangerous cocktail of credit, liquidity, market, and operational risk. Each of these risks is well known, but their combined magnitude is still unknown. Enron's case shows that the fine print in credit documents is very relevant and that credit integrity in structured loans can be compromised by simple majority decisions on waivers. Liquidity is still in the market, but investors and financiers are much more discriminating as they ask: "How real is what I see and how real is what I do not see?"

ABN AMRO came to the conclusion that the risk culture was clearly compromised in overbanked bull markets that speed up the "pace of the place," allowing too many illusions and complexities to build up. The latter has three layers: the concept, its administration, and finally, run time to assess the credit. So, a thorough health check was called for, involving better due diligence and a better risk/reward balance. Simply put, the new low-hanging fruit might well be poisonous.

It is said that a financial institution bears risk if it can suffer losses. If that is true, then clearly all financial institutions and all companies are bearing risks. If they are bearing risks, they are, to some extent, managing them. Therefore, the relevant issue is not bearing and managing risks, but bearing only those risks accepted by the institution and managing them in an efficient, systematic, and objective way.

ABN AMRO's governance focused both on the bank's structure and on its business approach. This resulted in the establishment of a hierarchical committee structure. The highest (credit/market) risk decisionmaking body is the Policy Credit Risk Committee, which makes decisions concerning individual credit issues that represent the highest risk and also makes policy recommendations to the board. The board has in principle two primary objectives: to establish and maintain the framework for risk in the entire organization by approving credit policies and credit instructions; and to supervise and monitor from a portfolio management viewpoint and set strategy for the credit process.

In this system three features of governance are important, from both a counterparty and a portfolio perspective: an independent risk function; limited delegation; and an appropriate balance between decisions based on models and those based on judgment.

Independent Risk Function

Two approaches can be followed in establishing the risk a financial institution bears. First, each business unit can manage and control all risks derived from its own transactions. In that situation, the global risk of the institution is the result of decentralized decisions taken without homogeneous criteria and by nonspecialized units. In this context, the overall institution risk cannot be either measured or monitored.

Second, the institution can manage and control its risks by distinguishing credit risk from market risk. Under our system, commercial units manage credit risk, and the bank's financial department manages the market risk. However, the overall management is integrated by means of rules and policies that all managers should follow. In addition, these rules and policies are enforced through a system of measurement and control.

In this system, there is a hierarchy of credit committees, beginning at the lowest level with a committee for each main line of business in the bank that has limited approval authority for decisions regarding risk and ending with a policy committee that has overall responsibility. These specialized units must set risk limits for all commercial units and the financial department; define rules and parameters to measure the risks, supervise compliance of all bank units with risk policies and procedures, and immediately report any deviations from the risk standards to top management. Top management should also make the decisions when the inevitable trade-offs between market risk and credit risk arise.

Limited Authority

Although it may seem somewhat antiquated, the independent risk function is strengthened by giving these credit committees limited approval authority. That is, each of the committees may not make decisions on risks involving more than a specified amount. The structure has proven to be effective. Committee members abstain from participating in decisions when they are incapable of providing objective advice. Because they are independent of the bank's commercial units, they avoid biased decisions. Moreover, their specialization allows them to assess the specific risk objectively.

Perhaps most important is the collective learning process. Because of cross-fertilization within and between risk committees, they learn from each other, revise their "views of the world," and generate a decision superior to what each individual could have achieved. The main risk facing any financial institution is its own people. Only staff with expertise should participate in the process of controlling and managing risks. The risk function requires staff with a wide range of knowledge (finance, statistics, econometrics, accounting, trading) and different knowledge profiles (front office, back office, risk control, risk measurement).

Striking a Balance between Models and Basics

Another feature of the learning process is finding a balance between the model-based and judgment-based approaches, as a model cannot give conclusive answers in the twilight zone with regard to expected and unexpected loss. Qualitative assessments are in this case a condition sine qua non.

Our experience suggests that quantitative models capture the interaction between risk, net revenue, and return on economic capital in a consistent way and are more transparent and easier to use than full scientific models. Nevertheless the bank should not become an uncritical slave to the model outcomes. Business decisions are taken by accountable individuals who have a large historical memory. Thus, the model can provide guidance, but management should overrule that guidance if there are good reasons to do so. Hence, our governance on the business side is characterized by paying more attention to our own internal rating systems, critically examining our large one-obligor exposures, and examining carefully our clients with low credit ratings and determining whether we should actually exit certain of these accounts if the outlook is not good. We also insist that both client coverage and loan product people be far more probing in their discussions with clients. Finally, we make sure that our compensation packages are consistent with our core principles and business principles.

Challenge Ahead

The challenge ahead is to enhance governance structures for strategic risk and business continuation. Regarding strategic risk, the argument is that a bank can find itself trapped in long-term commitments made in the past. As a result changes in client performance or migration in the bank's own portfolio can create a situation where there is no easy exit. At this stage we are unable to determine a proper price for this particular risk. In a lesson learned after 9/11, business continuation boils down to hedging backup risk.

Another challenge is the new Basel Banking Committee's Capital Adequacy Framework. Many banks have made significant strides to comply with the early recommendations of the new framework. With this framework regulatory and economic capital will move conceptually close. This raises the issue whether there will be room for both regulatory and economic capital, in the sense that banks' management of their operations will be based on a capital flavor that is distinct from regulatory capital. At present, however, the jury is still out on many issues of the framework, which leads to the notion of an uneven playing field, and as a consequence uncertainty with regard to the effectiveness of governance.

How Can Banks Exert
Better Governance
on Corporations?
The Korean Experience

THE CHALLENGES FACING the financial sector in Poland and Korea show remarkable similarities, presumably because the financial sector plays a disciplinary role in allocating resources in any advanced economy, as Dr. Kokoszczyński observes in chapter 7. The two countries are similar in the sense that their financial sectors are moving quickly to take up this role.

But there are some dissimilarities as well, in my view, mostly due to the fact that private corporatism has been much stronger in Korea. This has posed a slightly different set of challenges for the Korean financial sector compared with those facing the Polish sector, although the challenges are fundamentally the same. I focus here on three main dissimilarities between the two systems.

Omnipresence of Chaebol in Korea Put Them
beyond the Control of Banks

Just as in Poland, the Korean banking sector has played only a passive role in providing money to the real sector. Throughout the compressed development period between the 1960s and the late 1980s, Korean banks were merely a pipeline for channeling money, either deposited by households or borrowed from outside, to the corporate sector, based on a grand plan for the country's economic development set by the government.

The government selected a few entrepreneurs who had demonstrated their eagerness to invest in the government's list of high-priority areas, and banks were guided to lend to them on relatively cheap terms. In this process, so-called *chaebols,* large, family-controlled conglomerates, emerged, and their economic power was almost invincible by the early 1980s: they produced almost 30 percent of gross domestic product and used more than half of the financial lending available in Korea.

To induce these chaebol-controlled enterprises to go public, the government set an environment under which ownership of the chaebols was almost unchallengeable. Hostile takeovers were prohibited by law. Banks were not allowed to own more than 10 percent of any publicly listed company. Financial investors could invest in a company's stock but only for the purpose of portfolio investment. They were not allowed to exercise voting power because of the "shadow voting rule." At the same time, minority shareholders' rights were virtually nonexistent. There were no checks and balances on the behavior of family owners in chaebol-controlled enterprises.

With no threat to their ownership, chaebols expanded their businesses by overstretching cross-ownership of affiliates within a group. Before the 1997 financial crisis, a typical chaebol family was able to control its entire group with less than 10 percent ownership. These small stakes made owner families even more aggressive risk-takers in expanding their business through debt financing. If their new businesses succeeded, they could accumulate even greater wealth under their control. Even if they failed in the new venture—the possibility of which they perceived as almost nil because they believed the government would not allow that to happen—their losses would be small compared with the assets they controlled. Guarded against threats to their ownership, they did not need to listen to calls for higher dividends from other shareholders.

Being major creditors to chaebols, banks should have played a critical role in governing their activities, but they were no match for the chaebols' rising economic power. Although most commercial banks were privatized by the mid-1980s, they continued to provide lending to chaebols without proper risk assessment. In fact, banks regarded lending to chaebols as one of the safest investments, reasoning that the loans were backed by cross-guarantees from the chaebols' affiliates. They too believed the chaebols as a group were too big to fail.

Financial supervision was also very weak before the 1997 crisis. The main criterion for determining when corporate loans were nonperforming was simply whether their interest payments had not been made for more than six months. This was too easy a test for any chaebol affiliates to circumvent as they could always rely on other affiliates within their group, even if their financial shape was dire. Because the banks themselves were well aware of this, they favored chaebols over unaffiliated small and medium-size firms in their lending decisions. Under these circumstances, strengthening financial supervision alone would have been insufficient to turn the tide of banks' favoritism away from the chaebols.

Mindful of the banks' weakness regarding the chaebols, the government introduced various direct control mechanisms to hold chaebols' increasing economic power in check. These included placing a ceiling on banks' lending to individual chaebols, setting a limit on the chaebol affiliates' cross-guarantee of their borrowings, and introducing a ceiling on cross-ownership among chaebol affiliates. But even with these somewhat draconian measures against them, chaebols' appetite for expansion did not come to a halt, and that led to high indebtedness in the Korean corporate sector.

Corporate Restructuring in Korea Required More than Financial Restructuring

Again, just as in Poland, financial crisis provided a good opportunity for banks to secure their influence on the governance of their clients through bank-led corporate restructuring. In doing so, financial institutions themselves had to go through a painful restructuring process, just as Polish institutions did during their crisis period.

Some of the Korean banks were liquidated, and those that survived with the injection of public money had to restructure to implement strong conditionalities laid out in memorandums of understanding signed with financial supervisory authorities. In this process, employment in the financial sector was cut by one-third, with the number of financial institutions being reduced nearly in half.

Financial supervision was also greatly strengthened. Under the "forward-looking criteria" system, Korean financial institutions are now obliged to judge nonperforming loans by their borrowers' future capability to service the loan, not by their current status. The system ensures that financial institutions monitor their clients' financial performance closely.

The framework of bank-led corporate restructuring is very similar to that in Poland. Banks were advised to set up work-out units responsible for their nonperforming loans. An out-of-court-settlement arrangement, known as the "work-out scheme," was provided in which creditor banks exercised hands-on influence over a company's restructuring plan in return for debt restructuring.

For those big conglomerates protected by the "too-big-to-fail" mystique, where banks were reluctant to impose restructuring on their own, some kind of government intervention was needed. The government urged the top five chaebols to make covenants with their main banks to the effect that they would carry out their own restructuring plans to meet the target ratio of 200 percent debt to equity within two years. The implementation of the restructuring plans was closely monitored by the main banks on a quarterly basis, and a lack of implementation was subject to a three-stage collective disciplinary action by creditor banks: interest penalties; no new lending; and withdrawal of existing loans.

These were powerful tools in restoring banks' proper role in monitoring family owners of big businesses. However, they were not sufficient to hold in check the growth-oriented business decisions of family owners. Shareholders needed to be allowed to play their intended role in a company's corporate governance.

That is why the issue of corporate governance has been highlighted in Korea more than in Poland in overcoming the financial crisis. I will not go into details, but I would like to note that corporate governance issues in Korea have extended beyond minority shareholders' rights to include issues from accounting to disclosure.

The corporate insolvency system has been another key area in Korea's corporate restructuring. Through the process of revisions to some laws, financial creditors, like banks, are now able to play a much more active role in restructuring companies that show signs of stress.

With these improvements in corporate governance in place, the Korean government has now embarked on withdrawing previously introduced direct control mechanisms over chaebols.

Privatization of Banks Is an Important Task Ahead, but Bank Ownership Does Matter More in Korea

Dr. Kokoszczyński stressed that banks themselves need discipline before they demand better governance from corporations. He rightly singled out good supervision of banks and competition among banks as disciplinary devices. In doing so, he noted the advantage of substantial foreign ownership in the Polish banking sector.

I do not dispute his position but would like to point out that foreign ownership alone cannot be a panacea. Foreign investors bargain hard for low prices, and the lack of effective competition from domestic strategic investors may hinder successful foreign ownership.

It is true that in the process of resolving Korea's financial crisis, foreign ownership was substantially increased. The First Korea Bank, the largest corporate lender before the crisis, is now called New Bridge, with 51 percent foreign ownership. As of the end of 2000, foreign ownership accounted for 34 percent of the remaining sixteen national commercial banks.

But Seoul Bank, which the government had committed to sell along with First Korea as part of the IMF program, failed to be sold. Although it may sound paradoxical, limiting potential bidders only to foreigners was counterproductive in promoting foreign ownership. In recognition of a lack of competition, foreign bidders asked for seemingly excessive bargain terms that were very difficult for the government to accept politically. The government has also had to come to terms with the reality that even the First Korea Bank deal with New Bridge is now heavily criticized domestically for its bargain price.

And yet, the government is determined to reprivatize commercial banks that were inevitably nationalized during the financial crisis. Currently government's ownership is around 35 percent, but major commercial banks that previously dealt with corporate loans are now under full government control. Although the government has stayed away from running these banks, it has been suspected of intervening in the corporate restructuring these creditor banks have required of their client firms. The government knows too well that the only way to avoid this unsubstantiated but detrimental suspicion of intervention is to return these banks to complete private ownership. Reprivatization will also be a way to recover public funds that were injected into these banks.

In doing so, the government is now facing a dilemma. Mindful of the strong power of chaebols, the government introduced a stringent limit on the ownership of commercial banks when it embarked on the bank privatization program in the early 1980s. No individual was allowed to own more than 4 percent of the shares of any commercial bank. Thanks to this restriction, the ownership structure of Korean banks was widely dispersed before the crisis.

There were some exceptions to allow for foreign participation, and these exceptions have been extensively used to promote foreign ownership during the crisis period. As things are beginning to return to normalcy, this type of reverse discrimination against domestic investors is increasingly difficult to defend. Furthermore, Korea's own experience in the 1980s shows that dispersed ownership in an extreme form may not be good for the efficiency of bank management and may even provide room for government intervention. On the other hand, the government still needs to be concerned about the possibility that a commercial bank may fall into a private vault for a chaebol.

Of course, strengthening prudential regulation, including a "fit-and-proper-test," would be a formidable means of installing a firewall guarding the soundness of banks' asset management from potential intervention from their industrial shareholders. In fact, the Korean government has made a big push in this direction over the past few years, but it is still uncomfortable with leaving bank ownership vulnerable to influence from industrial capital.

A fine balance needs to be struck here. The government has decided to increase the ownership ceiling from 4 percent to 10 percent in return for a tightening of prudential regulation to make connected lending subject to tighter scrutiny.

Conclusion

Can banks exert better governance on corporations? Dr. Kokoszczyński's answer is yes, although it is qualified with the condition of good corporate governance. I would like to note that this qualification is very important to the extent that the answer could be changed to the negative. According to the Korean experience, banks cannot replace good corporate governance. Banks' supervisory role is limited if sound governance is not ensured in the corporate sector in the first place.

Once an effective system for good corporate governance is in place, banks certainly can help their corporate clients do a better job of implementing the system. But in doing so, they need to look after their own backyard first; namely, governance in the banking sector itself.

Dr. Kokoszczyński touched upon this issue by referring to effective banking supervision and the high level of competition in the privatization process. But I believe the issue is much more complicated than this. As the Korean experience strongly suggests, the ownership structure of banks is certainly another dimension worth further study.

L. L. TSUMBA

CASE
STUDY

How Can Banks Exert
Better Governance
on Corporations?
The Zimbabwe Experience

IN SEEKING TO answer the question of how banks can exert better governance on corporations, this paper looks at recent experience in Zimbabwe and the Southern African Development Community (SADC) and compares those with the experience in Poland. The paper considers what constitutes corporate governance from both a macroeconomic and a microeconomic perspective. It articulates the differences in approaches taken by Poland and Zimbabwe on this problem, highlighting the nature, strengths, and limitations of the Polish Enterprise and Bank Restructuring Program (EBRP), especially the bank conciliation agreements, as well as the approaches taken in Zimbabwe to improve corporate governance within the banking sector. Finally, the paper details recent corporate governance initiatives that have been undertaken in Zimbabwe and the SADC region.

There is no consensus on whether banks are able to or should even be expected to impose good governance behavior on enterprises with which they do business. What is clear, however, is that no bank is able and willing to underwrite poor corporate performance because such behavior also impacts negatively on its own viability and survival.

Nature of Corporate Governance

Corporate governance depends on the quality of economic, regulatory, fiscal, institutional, and judicial structures, which in turn are influenced by a given country's political disposition.[1] The state does, of course, execute its functions through various bodies, a process that naturally gives rise to rent-seeking behavior. The quality of a country's legal traditions and institutions also affects the prospects for economic and financial development through the enforcement of contracts and property rights.[2] There has been a renewed focus in recent times on political structures as determinants of the degree of the financial sophistication of a given country.[3] The group in power tends to design policies and institutions that guarantee self-entrenchment and self-enrichment at the expense of financial deepening and financial development. If the ruling class stands to benefit from free markets, it will enact laws and create institutions supportive of competitive markets. For very personal reasons as well, centralized or autocratic political systems will, in contrast, tend to be intolerant of competition, transparency, and accountability and are therefore bound to retard, rather than encourage, financial development.

Similar conclusions can be drawn regarding the origins and driving force behind colonialism, empire building, and territorial conquest. In countries where settlers paid little regard to equity, the rule of law, and contract enforcement insofar as these affected the indigenous population, postindependence rulers have tended to exploit the established institutions to their own advantage and profit.[4]

There is a need, therefore, to create an environment where stakeholders, be they shareholders, citizens, or other interested parties, are assured that "the goings-on" are not detrimental to their own political and financial interests. For the state, this assurance takes the form of checks and balances

1. As defined by Zingales (1997, p. 2), governance has to do with "the exercise of authority, direction, and control." In this context, one can refer to governance of a transaction, contract, institution, or nation. Governance is, therefore, essential at both the micro- and macroeconomic levels. Shleifer and Vishny (1997, p. 738) and Beck, Demirgüç-Kunt, and Levine (2001) provide sound evidence on the linkages between law, politics, and finance.

2. For an in-depth analysis, see La Porta and others (2000), who have looked at these linkages in detail. Beck, Levine, and Loayza (2000) as well as Levine, Loayza, and Beck (2000) also provide valuable empirical evidence.

3. Chirozva (2001) traces the evolution of the Zimbabwe Financial System since 1892, providing evidence that historical developments affected the prospects of financial development.

4. Beck, Demirgüç-Kunt, and Levine (2001, p. 23).

as reflected by the separation of powers: judiciary, executive, and legislature.[5] For state-owned enterprises, the objective is the same, with the additional requirement that while functional appointments are determined by market practice, the appointment of chairmen, chief executive officers, and board members is the responsibility of the executive or his delegate. Confirmation of the appointments by the legislature is an effective check and injects the requisite transparency.

A group of sophisticated shareholders provides checks and balances in the private sector. Without sophisticated shareholders, good governance of a corporate body is impossible. Sophisticated shareholders often demand external auditors, on the presumption that external auditors are independent arbiters and presumably hard to compromise, precisely because they are from the outside.[6]

In the wake of the Enron saga, however, the question must now be raised regarding the effectiveness of such arrangements in an emerging market setting such as Zimbabwe, which is characterized by a less sophisticated investing public, a paucity of generally available financial information, and a monopoly of financial knowledge and skills by a limited number of people.

Governance structures do, of course, cascade down from the state to the private sector. Poor results in some countries arising from experiments with privatization have taught the world that in the absence of adequate institutional structures, privatization of state-owned enterprises will not lead to sustainable economic development, because governance issues have a significant effect on the creation of value, its control, and distribution. At the microeconomic level, good corporate governance improves strategic direction. It attracts outside investment; sets standards of transparency, accountability, and probity; and promotes integrity as well as high standards of corporate citizenship.

Corporate governance is, therefore, often and rightly defined as the ways in which suppliers of finance assure themselves that they will receive a fair return on their investment.[7] Banks, as significant creditors, have vested interests in enforcing sound corporate governance on their corporate borrowers. In general, banks enforce sound corporate governance by screening

5. The standard is the American arrangement, which, with some variation, has been emulated by most democracies.

6. This presumption does not seem to have stood the test of time given the unfolding Enron debacle.

7. Shleifer and Vishny (1997, p. 737).

Figure 1. *Categories of Sources of Finance among Companies*

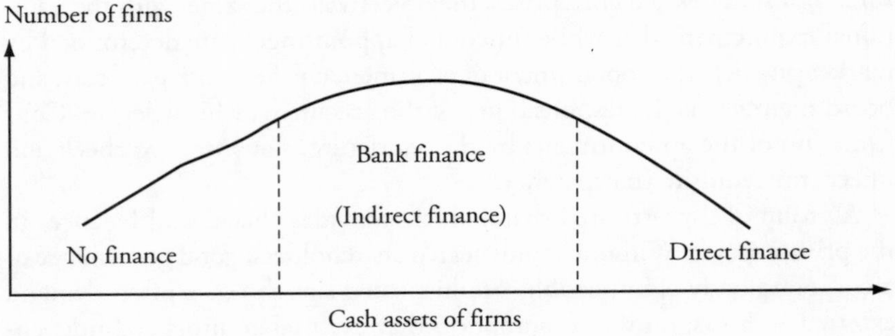

Number of firms

Source: Freixas and Rochet (1997, p. 185).

projects to be funded. They monitor performance and enforce lending clauses. Before granting loans, they ask for project proposals, statements of financial condition, and resumes of senior management; examine the shareholding structure; and review the borrowers' records to establish accomplishment. Borrowers are routinely required to submit periodic management accounts as part of the monitoring process. All of these steps are, of course, very desirable.

Sound corporate governance may also be brought about through the capital markets. Mechanisms used will correspond to ways in which corporations raise funding. Enterprises typically fall into three groups depending on their ability to secure funding, which in turn is determined by a company's capital endowment and reputation.[8]

Figure 1 depicts the relationship between capital endowments and the ways corporations raise funding. Small companies cannot afford the cost of borrowing and have no known reputation that enables them to access capital markets directly. The smallest companies, therefore, receive no external funding. Medium-size companies tend to make the greatest use of bank finance, while large companies can attract funding in capital markets.

This pattern has fundamental implications for small economies and for many developing countries such as Zimbabwe, where small and medium-size enterprises are considered the major engine of economic development.

8. See Holmström and Tirole (1997, p. 674) on capital endowment; Freixas and Rochet (1997, p. 185) on reputation.

In Zimbabwe and the SADC region as a whole, for example, more value arises from sound corporate governance through banks than through capital markets. This is because in most cases, only a few companies would normally be listed on a country's stock exchange.

Comparative Corporate Governance Experiences: Poland and Zimbabwe

Poland and Zimbabwe obviously have very different political histories and institutional arrangements. The most obvious distinction is that Poland was once a full-fledged socialist country, while Zimbabwe has always been a mixed economy.

Under socialist governance arrangements, the state in theory owns all productive resources. Banks channel state funds and provide no competent monitoring role or guarantee of efficiency. In Poland, a state monobank system, essentially a large "accounting firm," was dismantled only in January 1989, with nine state-owned commercial banks created in its stead.

By contrast, privately owned banks in Zimbabwe date back to 1892. Successive governments, however, allowed private enterprises to coexist only with a heavy dosage of official controls. In theory, one would expect Zimbabwe to have better corporate governance structures than Poland, as Zimbabwe has had a longer experience with a market economy. Furthermore, because Zimbabwe's legal system is based on common law, which theoretically is supposed to provide better contractual protection than the civil law system in Poland, one would expect that corporate governance would be more advanced.

Poland introduced macroeconomic reforms in 1990 that involved the removal of price controls and subsidies, devaluation, and a partial floatation of the currency. Today Poland stands out as one of the most successful open transition economies. Change has provided Poland with "a window of political opportunity" to change its entire socioeconomic system through the institution of a new legal framework and a corporate governance regime supportive of market-based economic activity. The reform program, however, coincided with the collapse of trade links with other Eastern European countries that participated in Comecon, or the Council of Mutual Economic Assistance. As in Zimbabwe, poverty reduction was a key concern in Poland at the onset of the economic reforms. Poland would, however, appear to have overcome these difficulties. The economy has grown at an annual average of 5 percent since

1992, while inflation declined from 70 percent in 1991 to less than 10 percent by 1998.[9]

In Zimbabwe the reverse has occurred. Inflation is currently at about 113 percent, and the economy has shrunk. The private sector in Poland now accounts for 70 percent of economic activity, while in Zimbabwe the private sector share of the economy increased by 9 percentage points in the last ten years. In Zimbabwe, 70 percent of the population is classified as poor, compared with around 24 percent in Poland.[10] The poor in Poland have access to unemployment and social assistance programs for poverty alleviation. There are no unemployment benefits in Zimbabwe to assist the poor.

To redress colonial imbalances, Zimbabwe embarked on ambitious egalitarian policies upon its independence in 1980. From 1980 to 1990 Zimbabwe's economy was characterized by an extensive system of controls on wages, prices of goods and services, foreign trade, foreign exchange, and credit and interest rates, as well as on free health services and education. These controls and regulations had far-reaching implications for the role of banks and the private sector in relation to corporate governance. The Economic Structural Adjustment Programme (ESAP), which operated from 1991 to 1995, dramatically transformed the economy from a quasi "command" economy to a market-based economy. Notwithstanding this, the transition to a market economy was stalled by 1999. In 2000 Zimbabwe reverted to some aspects of a command economy.

Nature of Corporate Organizations in Zimbabwe and Their Governance

Corporate activity in Zimbabwe is based on common law, with some Roman-Dutch influences. Corporate law is embodied in the Companies Act (1951) and the Zimbabwe Stock Exchange Act (1996). All companies, whether private or public, are subject to the Companies Act. Voting rights are based on the one-share, one-vote concept. The registrar of companies and the minister of justice are empowered to investigate alleged violations of this act.

The Zimbabwe Stock Exchange (ZSE), a corporate body established by an act of Parliament, has extensive regulatory powers. It is the second

9. Okrasa (2000).
10. Zimbabwe has a population of 13 million, compared with 39 million in Poland.

largest stock exchange in Sub-Saharan Africa, after the Johannesburg Stock Exchange. The ZSE is a self-regulating authority under the direction of the Ministry of Finance. An exchange committee supervises its work. The minister of finance appoints two members of the committee, while the stockbrokers appoint five to seven members. Each member of the committee holds office for a renewable one-year term. The minister of finance has power to appoint investigators to examine the committee for any alleged misconduct.

Governance of Corporations: Poland and Zimbabwe

Mr. Kokoszczyński discussed Polish reforms, which increased the capacity of the banking sector to influence real activity through credit and monetary channels, as well as through corporate governance. In fact, the Polish Enterprise and Bank Restructuring Program (EBRP), introduced in 1993, is considered one of the most innovative programs ever implemented in the transition economies. The program was designed to facilitate the restructuring of banks and companies, and to foster sustainable economic and political reforms. Banks were given quasi-judicial powers to enforce out-of-court loan work-out agreements, known as bank conciliation agreements (BCAs), with financially distressed companies. Bank work-out departments had to be staffed with experts from outside the bank, who were represented in the bank at board level, to ensure transparency and accountability. Initiatives to sell or swap debt for equity were meant to inject new skills, ideas, management styles, and technology into beneficiary companies. The creation of an optimal mix of "insider" and "outsider" shareholders was an excellent move. Active shareholders rely on "voice," unlike passive shareholders who rely on "exit" as a way of disciplining company management.[11] The sale of debt also enabled banks to rid themselves of nonperforming loans without getting involved in complicated court processes.

Critique of the Polish EBRP

When contrasted with the insider privatization prevalent in Russia, for example, the Polish BCA had many attractive features. In Russia, insider

11. Gray (1996, p. 3).

privatization was blamed for rampant asset stripping and looting.[12] The Polish privatization approach was slower than approaches adopted in Russia and the Czech Republic, however. BCAs benefited large companies, at the expense of small and medium-size enterprises. Most of these companies in Poland relied on interenterprise sources of finance, rather than on bank loans.[13] In practice, the BCA process involved the removal of delinquent loans from bank balance sheets to a governmental "resolution" agency. At least one set of critics argued that "the reform program focused heavily on working out bad debts, but that it did little to correct deficient lending procedures."[14] Weaknesses in traditional bankruptcy procedures were not addressed, limiting the development of financial intermediation and contract enforcement. In general, however, the BCA was a successful program.

Governance in Zimbabwe

In Zimbabwe, governance by banks has gone through two distinct phases. Banks operated under a semi-command economy from 1980 to 1990. Corporate governance, while still important, was not given the attention it deserved. Monetary policy and banking supervision functions were carried out in a low-key fashion as the controls in place ensured that risks were kept at the very minimum. Obviously, the controls also implied a significant opportunity cost in terms of important banking activities that were not undertaken.

Although the central bank undertook only minimal supervision, it is not surprising that no banks failed during this period. Bank viability and profitability were guaranteed. There was no dynamic and meaningful competition in the financial sector. Low and negative real interest rates, which characterized the 1980s, underwrote economic activity. There was no incentive for efficient cash flow and cost-effective management systems.[15] Corporate governance was not a material issue for banks, as their clients were guaranteed profit under a cost-plus pricing formula. Not surprisingly

---

12. Black, Kraakman, and Tarassova (1999).
13. Montes-Negret and Papi (1996, p. 24).
14. Gray and Holle (1996a, p. 6).
15. Chimombe (1983) documents collusive pricing and several interlocking directorships among financial intermediaries, which further curtailed the ability of banks to impose sound corporate governance principles on banks.

banks had no incentive, therefore, to insist on sound corporate governance practices.

The financial sector reforms introduced in 1991 entailed the removal of market segmentation and facilitated the entry of more institutions into the sector. Trade liberalization was also designed to move the economy away from quantitative import controls toward a fully market-based system. Historically, the import control system, which had flourished over the previous three decades, had bred and sustained an inefficient and monopolistic private sector, which hardly paid any attention to sound corporate governance.

As a result of these reforms, there was increased reliance on the role of market forces. This forced banks to revalue their loan portfolios, because their clients were no longer guaranteed a profit. Banks had to develop appropriate methods for loan origination, administration, monitoring, and review. In this environment, companies were now required to submit accurate and reliable financial information if they wanted to obtain access to loan facilities.

The problem of nonperforming loans is, however, more evident in locally owned banks. Because of stiff competition, such banks are often not able to influence the management of enterprises they lend to, which, of course, reduces their ability to exert effective corporate governance.[16]

In deserving cases, the Reserve Bank of Zimbabwe has permitted bank restructuring, curatorship, and regulatory forbearance approaches to resolving institution-specific banking problems. Bank restructuring has involved the creation of loan work-out departments, which are responsible for the bad loans and legally separate from the good assets. Two large commercial banks were rehabilitated successfully through this approach.

Ideally, independent personnel should have staffed the "bad book departments," as was the case in Poland. That would have promoted transparency, accountability, and good corporate governance. The Reserve Bank of Zimbabwe has, however, not hesitated to remove incompetent managers from troubled banks. In 1999 the Reserve Bank took over management and ownership of a building society that was facing imminent collapse. Another merchant bank was placed under curatorship. New investors have now been identified to take over that institution.

In Zimbabwe banks have tended to place great emphasis on security. Collateralized lending has thus reduced the incentive for corporate governance

16. One merchant bank has failed because of this, and its failure resulted in adverse repercussions on most indigenous financial institutions in the country.

and market discipline. In addition, subsidized credit schemes, targeted at previously disadvantaged small and medium-size enterprises, have increased the level of moral hazard. Banks are sometimes not concerned about corporate governance issues in such instances, however, because lending tends to be guaranteed by the state.

To complicate matters, shareholders in Zimbabwe, as in emerging markets elsewhere, are generally not sophisticated. They do not attend meetings, and those that attend fail to ask meaningful or pertinent questions. And as long as a company is making a profit, shareholders place less reliance on external auditors for additional financial information. Unlike developed countries, which have high concentrations of skills in government departments, civil services of developing countries, such as Zimbabwe, tend not to be as well endowed in this regard. For this reason such countries are unable to bring the required supervision to bear.

The legal framework in Zimbabwe needs to be improved to ensure that banks play a more active corporate governance role. Due to sociopolitical considerations, laws and regulations, particularly those relating to bankruptcy, are difficult to enforce. Even where collateral is available, it is not easy for banks to realize such collateral. Repayment of government-guaranteed loans tends to be a protracted process.

Current regulations, however, do permit banks to control enterprises through share ownership, where this involves debt for equity swap arrangements. Experience does show, however, that ownership of corporate shares by banks helps to reduce moral hazard by influencing the investment strategy, by bringing about management change sooner than bankruptcy laws allow, and by increasing the lender's ability to closely monitor the borrower's behavior.[17]

While the number of Zimbabwe banks has almost trebled over the last ten years, the level of competition has not been commensurate with this development. Numbers alone do not necessarily create high levels of competition. In theory, competition is supposed to result in a fall in the price of financial services or in an increase in the variety and quality of services provided at a given price. Falling spreads between deposit and lending rates indicate competitive forces at work. In Zimbabwe, however, wide spreads for the entire bank industry have continued to be a contentious issue ever since economic reforms were introduced, while the price of services has tended to rise rather than fall.

17. Dittus (1994, p. 400).

One school of thought holds that wide interest rate spreads reflect the relatively high level of nonperforming loans, caused by unfavorable macroeconomic conditions, such as declining economic growth and high and volatile inflation, interest, and exchange rates. The other school counters that the high spreads between deposit and lending rates reflect the lack of competition. To support this view, it is argued that the level of competition, relative to savings, is moderate as evidenced by a high degree of bank concentration and limited access by residents to foreign banking services.

Opening the banking sector to foreign ownership is clearly one way of addressing the problem of concentration. Such a development would complement the privatization program still under way. Increased competition would also provide incentives for banks to exert better governance and improve the efficiency of enterprises to which they lend.

Corporate Governance Developments in Zimbabwe

Banks cannot be expected to provide effective corporate governance unless they have competent governance structures themselves. The Reserve Bank of Zimbabwe has taken concrete steps to encourage the adoption of sound governance practices at every banking institution.

On-site examination was introduced in 1996. The primary focus at inception was on commercial and merchant banks. On-site examination of nonbanking institutions, which include discount houses, finance houses, and building societies, commenced in 1998. Risk-based examinations were introduced in 2001. The supervisory plan under this structure is tailored to the institution's risk profile. Consolidated supervision was introduced in 2002. There are also plans to bring more nonbank financial institutions under this coverage because the Reserve Bank believes that a broader scope of supervision is essential to ensure the safety and soundness of the entire financial and corporate system.

There is no doubt that on-site examinations have improved the effectiveness of banking supervision in Zimbabwe. It has allowed examiners much greater access to actual bank documents and records. Supervisors can make more informed judgments about the financial condition of the supervised banks and, by extension, their corporate clients. In this way, it is possible for the central bank and the banks it supervises to know the real condition of their clients. When this supervision is done well, the soundness of the financial system is assured.

Under the banking act enacted in 2000, the Reserve Bank of Zimbabwe now has a strong legal basis for supervising banking institutions. It should be noted that the licensing function has been retained as a government policy issue, although the Registrar of Banking Institutions is required by law to secure the concurrence of the Reserve Bank of Zimbabwe before approving an application for a banking license.

Under the new legislation, banking institutions are required to disclose material information with respect to risk management and risk exposures. In this connection, banking institutions must publish financial statements every six months for the information of the public. This has helped significantly in instilling discipline and good corporate governance among the banking institutions. A policy dealing with troubled and insolvent banks was also introduced in 2001. This policy provides a benchmark for early identification and prompt response to banking problems. This in turn has been reinforced by the requirement that banks and their boards of directors, accompanied by their external auditors, attend an annual review of their operations at the Reserve Bank of Zimbabwe. This has, of course, improved governance in a very visible way.

Other Corporate Governance Initiatives

The King Report on Corporate Governance issued in South Africa in 1994 was the first code of conduct published on the continent and followed on the heels of the Cadbury Report, issued in the United Kingdom in 1992.[18] Concerted efforts to enhance corporate governance have been made in Zimbabwe in recent years, partly encouraged by international social and economic developments. The Institute of Directors of Zimbabwe (IODZ)

18. The King Report was revised in 2001. The revised code identifies seven chief characteristics of good corporate governance, namely discipline or commitment to governance; transparency; accountability; board members' independence; responsible management; fairness in dealing with stakeholder interests; and response to social issues. The code was entirely a private business initiative spearheaded by the Institute of Directors of South Africa. (IOD). The King Committee referred to the Cadbury Report, and received support from the Johannesburg Stock Exchange; South African Chamber of Business; South African Institute of Chartered Accountants; the Chartered Institute of Secretaries and Administrators; the South African Institute of Business Ethics; and various business organizations. The Cadbury Report focused primarily on financial reporting, accountability, and the responsibilities of executive and nonexecutive directors.

has naturally spearheaded the campaign to adopt principles popularized in the Cadbury and King reports.

Zimbabwe has received technical assistance to enhance its corporate governance from the International Finance Corporation, the African Management Services Company, and the Government of Denmark. A multipronged approach has also seen the adoption of *The Principles for Corporate Governance in Zimbabwe: Manual of Best Practices.*[19]

High-profile scandals in government and the private sector have also galvanized support for good corporate governance. Valuable insights have also been drawn from the Principles for Corporate Governance in the Commonwealth, issued by the Commonwealth Association for Corporate Governance in 2000, and from the Principles of Corporate Governance, issued in 1999 by the Ad Hoc Task Force on Corporate Governance of the Organization for Economic Cooperation and Development.

Other initiatives have been made through the Pan African Consultative Forum on Corporate Governance, the United Nations Economic Commission for Africa, the African Development Bank, African Union, the Common Market for Eastern and Southern Africa, SADC, and ECOWAS (Economic Community of West African States). In Southern Africa, Malawi, South Africa, Zambia, and Zimbabwe have introduced codes of corporate governance. Ghana and Nigeria have led similar efforts in West Africa, while Morocco and Egypt have done the same in North Africa. The private sector, through the respective institutes of directors and stock exchanges, have been actively involved in the promotion of good corporate governance.

In Kenya the Private Sector Corporate Governance Trust has pioneered corporate governance. The adoption of good corporate governance principles in 1999 has resulted in the separation of the posts of chairman and managing directors at state-owned institutions such as the National Bank of Kenya. The government-appointed position of executive chairman has been abolished in order to minimize opportunities for political patronage, including the influence of permanent secretaries, ministers, and politicians.

19. Whereas implementation of good corporate governance principles is voluntary in Zimbabwe, the revised King Report also incorporates important corporate governance themes such as risk management; effectiveness of internal controls; assessment of the board performance, the chief executive, and individual board members; and assessment of other nonfinancial issues such as stakeholder interests. Financial reporting standards are also being developed to cover small enterprises, which are exempted from complying with International Accounting Standards.

In Zimbabwe, two corporations, Anglo-American and Delta, have led by example by developing in-house corporate governance manuals. Vibrant civil society groups have, as a result, encouraged government and companies to adopt fundamental principles of good corporate governance in the public interest as well.

The primary responsibility for good corporate governance, however, rests with the board of directors and senior management. In Zimbabwe listed companies are expected to have at least four directors. Banks must have a minimum of five directors, at least three of whom must be independent nonexecutive directors.

Zimbabwe encourages disclosure and transparency through adoption of international accounting standards; external audits; and dissemination of essential information in line with international best practices. By addressing the judicial framework, composition of the board, role of auditors, contract enforcement, stakeholder participation, accountability, and transparency, corporate governance is improved.

The aim of these efforts is to improve wealth generation and efficiency in both the private and public sectors. Corporate governance is, therefore, an essential tool for improved efficiency, prosperity, economic growth, and social progress. Sound corporate governance is, of course, characterized by transparency and accountability, while poor corporate governance is associated with rent-seeking behavior affiliated with crony capitalism, characteristic of many developing countries.

Concluding Remarks

The foregoing suggests that if banks are governed well themselves, they can be relied on to exert sufficient pressure to ensure that corporates are properly governed too. The combination of increased competition in the financial sector and an increasingly effective banking supervision function has provided the necessary incentives for such a development. There is room for improving Zimbabwe's legal framework, particularly, as it relates to enforcement of contracts, bankruptcy laws, and other regulations to ensure that banks effectively execute this very important function.

Whatever a country's general economic standing, poor corporate governance manifests itself in several ways. On the one hand, public officials often fail to make the distinction between public and private resources. On the other, the private sector is often associated with excessive greed, conspicuous consumption, and "get-rich-quick" schemes. These things, of course, suggest that banks will tend to overlook the very requirements of good corporate governance. Banks are, however, better placed—and should be relied on and encouraged—to spearhead programs aimed at improving such governance.

These programs should strive to ensure that both shareholders and company directors measure up to their responsibilities. Information dissemination, however, has a cost, which someone must bear. The cost is higher in emerging economies, such as Zimbabwe than in developed countries. Expenditure incurred in promoting good corporate governance should, however, be viewed as an investment. Indeed, the sooner such investments are made, the higher the medium- to long-term benefits that will accrue to society as a whole.

References

Beck, Thorsten, Asli Demirgüç-Kunt, and Ross Levine. 2001. "Law, Politics, and Finance." Working Paper. World Bank (January).

Beck, Thorsten, Ross Levine, and Norman Louisa. 2000. "Finance and Sources of Growth." *Journal of Financial Economics* 58 (1): 261–330.

Black, Bernard, Reinier Kraakman, and Anna Tarassova. 1999. "Russian Privatisation and Corporate Governance: What Went Wrong." Working Paper 178. Stanford Law School.

Chimombe, Theresa. 1983. "The Role of Banks and Financial Institutions in the Accumulation and Reinvestment of Capital in Zimbabwe." M. Phil. thesis, University of Zimbabwe.

Chirozva, Gift. 2001. "Financial Intermediation and Economic Performance in Zimbabwe." Master's thesis, Edith Cowan University, Western Australia.

Dittus, Peter. 1994. "Corporate Governance in Central Europe: The Role of Banks." Economic Papers 42. Bank for International Settlements. Basel. August.

Freixas, Xavier, and Jean-Charles Rochet. 1997. *Microeconomics of Banking*. MIT Press.

Gray, Cheryl W. 1996. "In Search of New Owners: Lessons of Experience with Privatisation and Corporate Governance in Transition Economies." Policy Research Working Paper 1595. World Bank, Washington.

Gray, Cheryl W., and Arnold Holle. 1996a. "Bank-Led Restructuring in Poland: An Empirical Look at the Bank Conciliation Process." Policy Research Working Paper 1650. World Bank, Washington.

———. (1996b) "Bank-Led Restructuring in Poland: Bankruptcy and Its Alternatives." Policy Research Working Paper 1651. World Bank, Washington.

Holmström, Bengt, and Jean Tirole. 1997. "Financial Intermediation, Loanable Funds, and the Real Sector." *Quarterly Journal of Economics* 112: 663–91.

La Porta, Rafael, Florencio Lopez-de-Silanes, Andrei Shleifer, and Robert Vishny. 1997. "Legal Determinants of External Finance." *Journal of Finance* 52: 1131–50.

La Porta, Rafael, Florencio Lopez-de-Silanes, Andrei Shleifer, and Robert Vishny. 2000. "Investor Protection and Corporate Governance." *Journal of Financial Economics* 58: 3–27.

Levine, Ross, Norman Loayza, and Thorsten Beck. 2000. "Financial Intermediation and Growth: Causality and Causes." *Journal of Monetary Economics* 46: 31–77.

Montes-Negret, Fernando, and Papi Luca. 1996. "The Polish Experience in Bank and Enterprise Restructuring." Policy Research Working Paper 1705. World Bank, Washington.

Okrasa, Wlodzimierz. 2000. "The Dynamics of Poverty and the Effectiveness of Poland's Safety Net (1993–1996)." Working Paper. World Bank, Washington.

Shleifer, Andrei, and Robert W. Vishny. 1997. "A Survey of Corporate Governance." *Journal of Finance* 52 (June): 737–81.

Zingales, Luigi. 1997. "Corporate Governance." NBER Working Paper. National Bureau of Economic Research, Cambridge, Mass.

PART IV

Governance Issues and the Capital Market

SALLY BUXTON
MARK ST. GILES

9

Governance of Investment Funds

INVESTMENT FUNDS ARE characterized by the International Organization of Securities Commissions (IOSCO) as "collective investment schemes" (CISs). They are savings vehicles that have three main characteristics: contributions from investors are pooled; the pooled funds are professionally managed; and risk is diversified by purchasing in a range of investments. Collective investment schemes are also required to value their portfolios at market value, and their assets are held by custodians. All these characteristics are also shared by many defined-contribution pension schemes—for instance, those based on the Chilean model, where members' contributions buy units in the scheme at net asset value. Thus many of the governance issues highlighted in this paper also apply to defined-contribution pension schemes, whose operation closely resembles that of CISs, though additional limitations such as accessibility and qualifications for preferential tax treatment also apply.

Table 9-1 illustrates quite clearly the dominance of investment funds in the relatively more developed markets, where the funds are used primarily to mobilize savings to finance commerce and government and to provide a form of saving for retirement. The United States, probably primarily because of the role mutual funds play in retirement provision, has achieved investment fund assets representing over 50 percent of gross domestic

Table 9-1. *Total Net Asset Value of Publicly Offered Open-End Investment Funds Worldwide, 1987–2001*
Millions of U.S. dollars

Year	United States	Europe	Rest of world	Total
1987	769	307	n.a.	1,076
1988	809	419	n.a.	1,228
1989	981	542	n.a.	1,523
1990	1,066	760	405	2,230
1991	1,393	902	413	2,709
1992	1,643	1,001	447	3,091
1993	2,070	1,241	683	3,994
1994	2,155	1,380	692	4,228
1995	2,812	1,549	752	5,113
1996	3,526	1,789	897	6,212
1997	4,468	2,040	845	7,354
1998	5,525	2,739	1,002	9,265
1999	6,846	3,210	1,379	11,436
2000	6,965	3,284	1,610	11,859
2001[a]	6,975	3,183	1,582	11,739

n.a. Not available.
a. Data through end of September.

product (GDP), whereas in Europe this figure is only 25 percent.[1] In emerging markets—in most cases in the transitional economies of central Europe and the former Soviet Union—funds have also been used to transfer state ownership of assets to the private sector through privatization. As we explain, the way that each of these objectives should be realized is quite different, even though each is accomplished through a collective investment scheme. The expectation that a variety of desirable aims can be achieved through ill-defined operational structures is an all-too-common case of muddled thinking, the outcome of which is that none of the objectives will be achieved.

1. OECD (1998).

Types of CIS Governance Structures

Three governance structures for collective investment schemes are common in both industrial and emerging markets. These are

—The investment company, a specialized form of company that has directors with a fiduciary responsibility to look after the interests of investors.

—The trust, made by trust deed between a management company and a trustee, where the trustee has the fiduciary responsibility to look after the interests of investors.

—The contractual fund, where investors contract with a management company to manage their investment as part of a pool and where the interests of investors are protected by a combination of contract law, fund law and regulation, and the actions of the depositary, which plays a quasi-trustee role.

Each of these structures has essentially two operational variants: open-end funds, which are required to redeem their shares, units, or participations from investors and consequently have variable capital; and closed-end funds, which are not required to redeem their shares, units, or participations and consequently have fixed capital. Closed-end funds are often listed on stock exchanges.

Of the three main forms, the investment company is by far the most predominant if measured by the total value of funds thus constituted; this is almost entirely because U.S. investment companies account for 58 percent of the total value of collective investment schemes worldwide. However, the trust and contractual types are predominant if measured by the number of funds thus constituted. We estimate that more than 60 percent of the approximately 53,000 open-end collective investment schemes established in the world at the end of the third quarter of 2001 were of either the trust or the contractual form.

It should also be noted that in emerging and transition countries (and some industrial countries), open-end investment companies are hardly known at all; that is largely because they conflict with joint stock company laws, which do not usually permit companies to issue and redeem their own shares continuously. Even in Britain, where the investment company form is now permitted after a long period of debate, these companies function not under British company law, which still does not permit continuous issue and redemption of a company's shares, but under the European

Communities Act of 1972. A further problem for investment companies is taxation: all too often investment companies are taxed as if they were ordinary companies, which makes their returns subject to two or sometimes even three levels of taxation. One reason for the predominance of contractual funds in many emerging markets is that they are not taxed because they are not legal persons (unlike companies or trusts). A discussion of the governance of collective investment schemes in emerging countries, therefore, should not place undue emphasis on the U.S. model of the open-end investment company, because as effective as it has proved in practice, the U.S. model is not an option in many developing, emerging, and transition countries.

Among countries in which the contractual form is most commonly found are most members of the European Union, almost all transition countries of Eastern Europe and the former Soviet Union, most of Latin America, and those countries of North Africa and the Middle East that have a civil code background, such as Egypt, Morocco, and Tunisia. Countries in which the trust form is the most common are almost all the countries of the former British empire that have some features of the common law tradition, including countries of the developing world with enormous populations such as India, Nigeria, and Pakistan, and countries that have significant collective investment fund industries but smaller populations, such as Hong Kong, Malaysia, and Singapore. Australia has introduced a variant of the trust form.

In Japan and Korea collective investment schemes are also predominantly a hybrid of the trust and contractual forms, called investment trusts, although both have recently started experiments with the investment company form. Interestingly, China has also adopted a preliminary model that looks rather like the trust form, perhaps because of the influence of Hong Kong. Collective investment schemes are in their infancy in China, however, and the form may change.

Thus, nearly 85 percent of the people in the world either invest in or may only be able to invest in either the trust or contractual form of collective investment schemes rather than in open-end investment companies. So, given that the U.S. investment company model is not available to many legislators and regulators, we look at the potential conflicts of interest that exist between those who promote and manage the trust and contractual— as well as corporate—forms of collective investment schemes and those who invest in them, and at ways in which these conflicts may be resolved or at least contained.

Conflicts of Interest within Collective Investment Plans

> The collective investment sector is characterized by complex agency relationships as well as asymmetry in market power and information. The risk is present that some participants in the collective investment process will abuse agency relationships.[2]

This comment, made by John K. Thompson and Sang-Mok Choi, neatly summarizes the fact that collective investment schemes are subject to a wide variety of conflicts of interest that may arise between fund investors and fund management firms (henceforward referred to as fund *operators*, following the IOSCO nomenclature). These conflicts take three broad forms:

—The desire of the operators to make as much profit as possible from their activities in managing the schemes. For example, in general, the operators' commercial interest dictates that charges made to the fund and the fees earned from it are as high as possible. The investors clearly wish that these charges should be as low as possible, since the charges made to the fund will reduce the return that the fund earns for them.

—The desire of the operators to enlarge the funds under their management not only by an increase in value resulting from investment returns, but also by selling more units or shares or participations. This desire may lead operators to misrepresent past returns and to make promises about future returns or even manipulate fund valuations to attract more investors (and thus increase fund management fees) or to indulge in high-pressure sales methods with a view to convincing investors to invest with them.

—Worst of all, because it is potentially the most damaging, is the temptation for operators to use the substantial funds under their management, information about whose investments is asymmetrically in their favor, to benefit themselves or their affiliates at the expense of the investors.

No One Governance Structure Clearly Protects Investors' Interests Better than Others

Measured by incidence of scandals reported to and reviewed by IOSCO, incidence of conflicts and breaches identified by regulators are evenly distributed among all types of legal and operational structures throughout

2. Thompson and Choi (2001, p. 9).

the world, with no major concentration of breaches within any one structure or in any one country.[3] Thompson and Choi's exhaustive examination of fund governance structures concludes:

> The OECD countries have used a variety of governance structures in the CIS sector. The fact that very few countries have had any crises in the CIS sector and that CIS have become major repositories of wealth would suggest that existing governance mechanisms are adequate and that public confidence is high. At the same time the fact that fraud and misallocation of funds occurred in several European countries before the introduction of adequate legal frameworks and that a serious systemic crisis arose in Korea, where adequate standards were not effectively enforced, provides evidence that such safeguards are needed. At the same time, once a body of acceptable standards has developed and governance structures matured to the point where those assigned an oversight role can compel participants to apply those standards, it becomes very difficult to demonstrate that any particular system provides better investor protection than others.[4]

In industrial markets, the net governance outcome of most permitted fund structures is broadly the same. The board of directors, trustee, or depositary of the fund essentially supervises the day-to-day conduct of the fund management firm, while the regulator sets entry requirements and standards of conduct for these entities. The regulator, in effect, delegates much of the day-to-day responsibility for ensuring compliance to these "supervisory" bodies; this is realistic and practical since they see more of the day-to-day activity of an operator than a regulator possibly can. In many ways, a trustee or a depositary may be more effective than fund directors because they see each and every securities transaction carried out by an operator on behalf of the fund at the time or very shortly after it occurs, whereas directors meeting perhaps every other month or even less frequently may receive only summaries of activity and those a fairly long time after the event.

It might be argued that pressure for an operator to perform is arguably stronger where the directors of a corporate fund or trustee of a unit trust

---

3. *Conflicts of Interest of CIS Operators,* May 2000, IOSCO Report of the Technical Committee. See also www.iosco.org.

4. Thompson and Choi (2001, p. 5).

have the power, in the final analysis, to dismiss and replace the operator. The exercise of the power of directors, however, is problematic both because even independent directors could be subject to capture by operators (see below) and because in some cases directors are not independent anyway. In the unusual structure of open-end investment company permitted in the United Kingdom, for example, the management company is permitted to be the single "authorized corporate director" of a fund, without the inclusion of any independent directors, and so is unlikely to sack itself. Many observers in the United States and the United Kingdom regard this provision as a weakening of investor protection and a setback to good governance. However, its proponents point out, rightly, that operators have little room for exploitation because the rules of operation of the fund are set out in advance, with any major changes requiring a vote of investors, and because the operators will suffer loss of business if they fail to achieve fund objectives.

The capacity of a board of directors or a trustee to dismiss or replace a management company does not really exist in the case of the contractual form of fund (although the regulator can and may assume powers to replace management firms in this case). However, no more and no fewer scandals have been associated with this form of fund than with those that arguably have a stronger governance structure in terms of powers of the directors or trustees of corporate or trust funds and stronger voting rights for fund investors.

The degree of investor rights also does not appear to make a critical difference in governance forms. While it is true that investors in corporate and trust funds have voting rights at annual or extraordinary general meetings that give them powers that contractual fund investors generally do not have, getting fund investors to actually participate in such votes is very difficult indeed (voting response rates of less than 1 percent are not uncommon), so these rights are not necessarily a strong governance factor. Regrettably, investors in funds prove relatively inert when it comes to voting, possibly because they would not have invested in funds had they wished to be active investors on their own behalf.

There is no doubt that a higher incidence of scandals occurs among funds in emerging markets than in industrial markets, but here again they occur in a variety of governance structures with no clear correlations visible. Privatization funds in Central and Eastern Europe had large numbers of scandals. In some countries, notably members of the Commonwealth of Independent States, we estimate that 75 percent or more of such funds have vanished over time because of change of status, mismanagement, or theft. Most privatization funds were structured as closed-end investment companies since that was the only legal form available at the time. As a result, weaknesses in corporate law and regulation of companies and securities markets had a double effect on these funds, which not only were companies themselves, but invested in other companies. In the only country where more than one fund governance structure was permitted for privatization funds—the Czech Republic, where both corporate and contractual funds participated in the second privatization wave—there are no statistics indicating that any larger or smaller number of scandals arose within the one structure or the other.

In many of the countries of Central and Eastern Europe, however, a second generation of funds that attract cash investment—virtually all of them contractual rather than corporate in nature—is beginning to develop successfully. The governance structures and rulebooks applied to these funds in many cases broadly parallel those in developed markets, often because of the need for *acquis communautaire* based on their desire for accession to the European Union (table 9-2).

The Key to Good Governance

If specific governance structures are not the key to good governance of collective investment schemes, what is? The answer is "reputational risk," as identified by Julian Franks and Colin Mayer.[5] This argument goes as follows. Large, often internationally known institutions that offer funds to their customers cannot afford to be seen to fail. If they are seen to fail, they will lose their reputation and as a consequence their business.

Thus two pressures are brought to bear: the need to be seen to operate a collective investment business profitably and successfully; and the need to put things right in the event problems arise. An illustration of this is the high-profile fund scandal that arose in 1996 when Deutsche Bank, owner of the British investment bank Morgan Grenfell, discovered that the manager of three Morgan Grenfell European funds had artificially pumped up prices of units in those funds by manipulating the values of securities in the portfolio. Deutsche Bank acted decisively to protect its reputation, and

5. Franks and Mayer (2001).

Table 9-2. *Development of Investment Funds in Central and Eastern Europe and the FSU, December 31, 2001*
Number, unless otherwise indicated

Country	Management companies	Closed-end funds/PIFs	Open-end funds	Total value of funds (millions of U.S. dollars)
Croatia	19	9	14	384
Czech Republic	35	10	68	2,086
Estonia	6	0[a]	20	170
Hungary	21	95[b]		2,514
Poland	16	14	97	2,979[c]
Russia[d]	27	3	51	430
Slovakia	9	54	33	165
Slovenia	20	37	18	1,538
Total	153	521		10,266[e]

Source: Cadogan Financial, securities commissions, trade associations, and CIC, Russia.
a. All privatization funds voted to liquidate.
b. Predominantly open-end funds.
c. Does not include asset value of privatization funds (known as National Investment Funds).
d. Figures are for first ten months of 2001 only.
e. For comparison, the total UK open-end fund sector was worth around this figure in 1982.

resolution of the problem is believed to have cost it nearly $700 million. It is worth noting that in the early stages of the scandal, approximately 8 percent of total assets under Morgan Grenfell's management were withdrawn; this trend subsequently reversed.

Reputational risk counterbalances the argument that directors, trustees, or depositaries of funds cannot be truly independent because fund management firms often select them. This symbiotic relationship means directors, trustees, or depositaries may be deemed unlikely to take punitive action against the fund managers of the funds for which they act, since that would amount to biting the hand that feeds them; conversely, the management company is unlikely to choose directors, trustees, or depositaries who will be awkward.

However, in developed markets any director, trustee, or depositary seen to have failed to take action against a dilatory or, worse, noncompliant or fraudulent fund management company would suffer penalties (in addition

to applicable legal or regulatory penalties) that are, in themselves, a sufficient deterrent. Fund directors, for example, are unlikely to be reappointed
by fund investors, or chosen as directors of other funds, and will thus lose
well-paid and prestigious posts. Trustees and depositaries may lose clients,
the funds which they are servicing will contract, and their fees, which are
often partly based on a percentage of net asset value of the fund, will
decline. Moreover, because trustees and depositaries are likely to suffer
damage to their reputation, they are unlikely to be appointed to other
funds and will therefore be unable to replace or augment their income.
They may also be subject to personal legal action by fund investors for
damages if it can be established that losses have occurred as a result of their
negligence.

Moreover, in developed markets, failure of a fund operator to perform
its duties well or properly will bring the penalty of loss of assets under management, reduction in fee income and consequent contraction of profit.
This will affect profit share and bonuses for staff and in extreme cases may
even force the management company to seek a merger or takeover by
another management company.

Elements of Effective Pressure
for Good Governance: Transparency

We believe that lack of transparency and disclosure is the key inhibitor of
growth of investment funds in emerging markets—markets that frequently
have good regulatory standards and reasonably effective regulators, but
where funds still fail to develop satisfactorily. Would-be investors in funds
in those markets have little or no idea whether funds exist. Actual investors
may be unable to find out whether their fund is performing well or badly
either absolutely or relatively and are thus unable to form judgments as to
whether they should buy, sell, or hold. Investors are thus unprepared for
the bad times, when poor returns come as a nasty shock and cause disillu-
sion. The world is littered with examples of countries in which investment
fund industries started in bullish times and promised much to investors
but then almost disappeared when investors realized that funds could incur
losses as well as gains.

In industrial markets, by contrast, the wide availability of information
ensures that most failures are clearly visible and will attract comment,
which in turn creates pressure to improve performance either by changing

the investment strategy, the individual fund manager, or the fund management company, or by reducing fees.

Accessibility of Information

Contrast, for instance, the availability of information about funds in, say, the United Kingdom, with the information available in Russia. The only place in Russia where information is available about all fifty-one investment funds operating in the last quarter of 2001 is the website of the Collective Investment Centre. These data are available only because the regulator, the Russian Federal Commission on Securities Markets, requires disclosure in this way. The only other sources of information are the operators of the funds and media articles. There is no independent statistical comment or analysis. Few investors in Russia are likely to be prepared to expend the considerable time and money required trying to find out about the available investment funds.

By comparison, in the United Kingdom, lists of all funds available could be found in at least two daily newspapers, through the regulator, through trade associations, through specialist financial publications aimed at the public and at professionals, and on a multiplicity of websites, many of which provide a broad range of comparative fund data mostly focusing on costs and performance. The information is easily available at little cost.

Clarity of Purpose and Objective

A further issue relating to funds is clarity of definition as to the purpose and permitted investments of categories of funds and the degree of risk associated with these investments, all of which need to be understood by potential investors before they invest. This problem affects funds not only in emerging markets, but in some more developed markets as well.

THE CASE OF JAPANESE MONEY MANAGEMENT FUNDS. A good example of the problems in this area concerns the so-called "money management" funds in Japan. These were misleadingly sold as higher-yielding substitutes for bank accounts, an attractive proposition in a country in which interest rates on deposits hover around zero. What investors had not realized was that the higher yields were only being obtained by lengthening the maturity of the portfolio and increasing its risk. Substantial holdings of Enron bonds and Argentinean Samurai bonds in some of these funds caused a drop in net asset values and precipitated panic redemptions, which resulted in a loss of 60 percent of assets invested in those funds (totaling 12 trillion yen) in the space of two months at the end of 2001.

The run on these funds was led, it is thought, by insiders and professionals using their knowledge of fund assets, which was not available to ordinary investors. In a classic case of opaque and asymmetric information flows, these investors exited, causing the better-quality assets to be sold to meet the redemptions and leaving the ordinary investor, again, bearing the brunt of the fallout. Two problems seem to have been key: a lack of rules for the type of assets that money market–style funds should have held in order to maintain the capital value invested; and failure to disclose the risks associated with the actual fund portfolios. Investors were thus unable to make informed choices.

PRIVATIZATION FUNDS IN CENTRAL AND EASTERN EUROPE AND THE FORMER SOVIET UNION. Another recent example of lack of clarity of purpose involves the funds that participated in the mass privatizations undertaken in many of the countries of Central and Eastern Europe and the former Soviet Union in the 1990s—funds that were neither fish nor fowl. These privatization funds were initially designed to be "fish"—that is, they were to be as much like the highly diversified, relatively low risk collective investment schemes offered to the public in developed markets as possible, since they were to be offered to a public that was unaccustomed to dealing with investments and since it was assumed that domestic capital markets would develop rapidly. Like "fish," the funds were permitted to hold only 5–10 percent of any one company's shares. Unfortunately, the funds could not successfully operate like the CISs in developed markers because the shares they owned were not as easy to buy and sell as are shares in developed markets, where funds exert performance pressure by selling the shares of failing companies. Company law was also generally weak, so the only way for a fund to exert pressure on a company to perform better was essentially to take a larger stake in it, which funds were not permitted to do.

Equally, although the privatization funds had to invest in illiquid assets, which were all that was available, they were not designed as "fowl"—venture capital funds, which are specifically designed to invest in companies whose shares are not listed or traded, but which are higher risk and therefore less suitable for investment by members of the public. These funds, recognizing the need to exert control over the companies in which they invest—because they are unable to sell their shares easily—take larger stakes in companies and have precautionary side agreements that ensure that in the event stated targets are not achieved, the fund gains a higher level of control and can force necessary changes to be made. In addition, in developed markets these funds generally provide other forms of financing to companies whose shares they buy; but since privatization funds lacked cash, they were unable to fulfill this role.

In other words, the advice of foreigners to privatizing governments was based at least partly on overly optimistic assumptions about how quickly a market economy could develop, which would have enabled the funds to sell and buy investments in the market and allow fund investors to benefit from efficient management of the portfolio. As it also turned out, the regulatory regimes and the ability of regulators either to impose standards on the enterprises that had been privatized or on the funds that invested in them were inadequate for the task. Thus greed and self-interest flourished, and investors in privatization funds generally saw no return at all.

However, it is arguable, in our view, whether permitting privatization funds to hold larger stakes would necessarily have improved their ability to exert governance pressures on companies and therefore improve their performance. The evidence indicates that funds' management often retained the majority of benefits from investing in companies for themselves, frequently selling stakes for almost nothing to affiliated entities who then resold the stakes at a large profit. Thus the ability to hold larger stakes would simply have increased the affluence of fund affiliates, rather than improving fund performance. Abundant evidence from a range of former Communist bloc countries in the early stages of privatization shows that even outsiders holding large stakes in companies were made almost powerless by incumbent management or their affiliates who diluted outsider holdings or, worse, deprived outside investors of potential returns through transfer pricing. There is no evidence that funds allowed to hold larger stakes would have been better able to resist such tactics.

In any event, many funds were vehicles through which individuals affiliated with local governments and industries perpetuated the control of those entities and never intended to bring pressure to bear on investee companies to perform better. Moreover, these funds lacked the money to fight the long and expensive court cases that some Western venture capital funds investing in such companies have had to undertake to protect their minority positions (this is also a factor in developed markets, where few fund investors and fund management firms would be prepared to finance such public-spirited endeavors).

In addition, the experience of Western-financed venture capital funds in transition countries is that few companies welcome outside shareholders, even those with cash that will help to finance development, because they fear loss of control or disclosure of confidential data that might attract the attention of unwanted predators or authorities (for example, tax inspections instigated by firms wishing to take over the unlucky recipient). It is therefore likely that companies would have resisted venture capital investment by privatization funds. As a result, most successful venture capital investments in many transition countries have been in completely new start-ups rather than in existing companies, something that privatization funds had neither the mandate nor the money to do.

Unleashing forces of raw capitalist endeavor thus led to the hollowing out of funds' assets and the plundering of value and created an environment in which the greed of managers proved to be stronger than the forces that should have been in place to hold them in check. It must be pointed out that such outcomes are not only a feature of transition and emerging markets. The recent exposure of a whole range of major governance scandals, of which Enron in the United States and Marconi in the United Kingdom are only two examples, has made it inappropriate for those in developed countries to be too pious on the subject.

Apart from the obvious fraud and dishonesty, which permeated privatization processes in many countries, it is equally important to understand that, in our view, there was no external pressure on the managers of these funds to perform. For one thing, funds faced no danger of commercial loss of business, since they had already attracted vouchers for investment; funds were closed-end so investment could not be withdrawn. Managers whose objectives were genuine did not hold enough shares to force less scrupulous managers and insiders to act responsibly. There was no "opportunity cost," because most funds had no intention of developing a longer-term fund management business, which would require confidence building. No information on the funds' performance was disclosed publicly, so it was impossible for any investor to compare one fund's results with another. (In Russia, even the regulator could compile lists of licensed investment funds only by visiting regional regulators' offices and offices of the funds themselves; although funds were required to report quarterly to the regulator, few of them ever did.) Fund shares were often not required to be listed or traded, and prices were not disclosed where transactions did occur; as a result investors had few opportunities to sell and no reference prices to guide them. Although many fund investors complained (those who had vouchers stolen from one Russian fund demonstrated outside the regulators' offices, and as a result the fund was assigned replacement vouchers as compensation), the poorly financed courts and regulator were vulnerable to capture by the funds.

Thus most privatization funds were neither fish nor fowl and their objectives were not clearly defined. Operating mainly as conventional funds with minority interests, they did not have the shareholding power necessary to come to grips with poor management of the enterprises themselves. Neither could they operate as conventional diversified funds, since the markets were insufficiently developed to provide liquidity and transparency. In this lack of clarity of purpose were the seeds of their failure.

Information Content

In developed markets, regulators require a minimum level of disclosure of information about collective investment schemes. Generally regulators want to see the prospectus or offering document of the fund, which must clearly state the risks associated with the structure of the fund as well as the assets it invests in; an annual report including the details of the fund's performance during the past year, the fund's portfolio, and an audited financial report; and regular publication of net asset value of the fund share or unit, with clear rules as to how such values are calculated.

In emerging markets, disclosure of much of this information is weak, and investors often do not understand the risks associated with the fund they have invested in, nor do they understand that it is unlikely that performance claims can be substantiated.

The case of Korea is instructive in this respect. The main problem that arose within Korean investment funds was that they were marketed to the public as quasi bank accounts, implying that the capital invested was secure. In fact, most of these funds, in order to offer competitive rates of interest, were investing in longer-term bonds, which increasingly put at risk the maintenance of that capital value. Managers also transferred older bonds with higher interest rates out of existing funds' portfolios (at cost, since bonds were only required to be valued at cost at that time) into the new funds to give these new funds a flying start, thus stripping value from existing investors in order to attract new ones. As a result, Korean investors were being churned out of existing funds into new funds. Disclosure was limited, with the new funds being "sold" on their interest rates, with some degree of "promise" of future returns. The assets in which the funds invested were rarely disclosed.

The Daewoo collapse in July 1999 exposed the weakness of this invest-ment and operational strategy. The fact that assets were valued at cost, rather than marked to market, meant that redemptions were being allowed at prices that were diluting the assets of continuing holders; when Daewoo defaulted, there was a massive shortfall in assets. The government took action to prevent a systemic collapse, at substantial cost to the Korean tax-payer. However, the action seems to have been successful, since it has led to revision of legislation and regulation and better enforcement of it. Also new types of funds with a better governance structure and greater trans-parency have been introduced and are developing successfully. The lesson has been learned.

Effectiveness of Disclosure

Where disclosure is effective, and investors understand the nature of the risk they are taking, they are less likely to panic and withdraw money from funds, and thus runs on funds and systemic risk are less likely to arise. A good example of this is the response of American mutual fund investors to the extraordinary events of September 11, 2001: while new purchases of equity funds were down by around one-third from $98 billion in August 2001 to $68 billion in September, redemptions from equity funds were actually lower in September than in August: $96 billion compared with $103 billion.[6] The outflow from equity funds totaled $30 billion, but that amount was less than 1 percent of total equity funds under management of $3 trillion; and less than 0.5 percent of the total value of U.S. mutual funds of $6.4 trillion at the end of September 2001. Compare this with the Japanese money management fund scandal, where just under a quarter of total funds under management was redeemed.

Elements of Effective Pressure for Good Governance: Ease of Exit from Funds

In developed markets, the incompetent will ultimately be driven out of business by commercial pressures. If investment funds fail to attract and keep enough investors, and as a result to make money, they will have to

---

6. Investment Company Institute data "Trends in Mutual Fund Investing," September 2001. See www.ici.org.

shut down—or sell out. This is a much more effective discipline than regulatory pressures because it directly affects the pockets of the owners of investment management companies. For pressure from exit to be effective, however, investors not only must have the information on which to base their decisions, but also must have the means to implement those decisions by withdrawing their money from the fund or by selling its shares.

In Developed Markets

In open-end funds in developed markets, steady withdrawal of money from a poorly performing fund, through a redemption of shares or units, progressively reduces the size of the fund and hence the fees to management companies. This loss of revenue provides a powerful incentive for a firm to improve performance, halt the decline in the funds' value, and start once again to attract new money from which to earn higher fees; failure to improve performance will cause the management company to go out of business or to be taken over.

In the case of a closed-end fund, this exit can be achieved only by finding a buyer in the market for the seller's share in the fund. If the fund is performing poorly, there will be few buyers, and discounts (the amount by which the share price is lower than the net asset value per share, expressed as a percentage of that value) on that fund's share will be larger. In developed markets, this poor performance will lead to one of three results: directors of the fund will seek to replace the management company; investors will press for a liquidation of the fund or its conversion into an open-end fund in order to be able to extract their investment at full net asset value; or the fund itself may become vulnerable to a takeover bid. In any of these ways the management company will suffer sometimes potentially catastrophic loss of revenues, so it has an incentive to improve its performance.

Directors of funds do exercise such powers, as has been illustrated in the recent case of the Edinburgh Investment Trust, a $1.5 billion U.K.-based closed-end investment company, whose recent performance had been poor. A planned merger between its management company and a larger asset management business was called off after the directors of the fund indicated that they were proposing to invite a competitive tender for the future management contract, income from which formed a significant proportion of the income of the management company that wished to merge.

Thus in developed markets, investors very quickly become aware of problems within a fund or its operator and can act rapidly and decisively upon information received. Fund operators are aware of this and must act to protect their reputation; otherwise their businesses can be severely damaged.

In Emerging Markets

Easy exit from either open- or closed-end funds in emerging markets is not as straightforward. Open-end funds are required to hold highly liquid and well-diversified portfolios to facilitate the investment and disinvestment of constant inflows and outflows of money. Often, however, emerging markets lack a sufficient range of liquid assets to accommodate such funds. In addition, emerging markets are by their nature more volatile, and assets that have been liquid may become illiquid overnight and remain so for some time (take, for example, Russian markets after August 1998 when the ability to trade in a range of ten fairly liquid and some fifty less liquid stocks vanished overnight). There may also be a lack of instruments to facilitate the operation of highly liquid funds, such as money market funds. The difficulty of operating open-end funds in many emerging markets means therefore that the commercial pressure applied by "ease of exit" does not come into play.

The popularity of open-end funds internationally, however, is highly dependent upon the ease of entry and exit from such funds. For example, in the United States, where entry and exit is easy, most investments are in open-end funds; the total value of closed-end funds is just 2 percent of that of open-end funds. In the United Kingdom, which has one of the largest closed-end fund markets in the world, the total value of such funds is generally between 20 percent and 30 percent of the total value of open-end funds.

Closed-end funds are able to hold illiquid assets because they do not have to raise liquidity to meet redemptions. They are therefore highly suited to emerging markets and have frequently been used as vehicles for privatization in Central and Eastern Europe. But they are difficult to exit from where there is no proper market in the shares of the fund itself—as was certainly the case in most privatizing countries.

An interesting exception is the Polish National Investment Funds (NIFs), which were required to be listed and traded and where there has been greater transparency, even if the funds themselves may not have performed as well as was hoped. It is also interesting that many of these NIFs have major foreign institutional involvement at the management company level, so reputational risk is also potentially higher in relation to these funds.

Conversion from Closed-End to Open-End Funds

In the Czech Republic, former privatization funds have been required to become open-end, presumably to improve the ability of investors to exercise their choice to exit, thus making the managers subject to resulting pressures to perform. If a fund's assets are liquid—that is, if they are easily bought and sold in the market without the transactions substantially affecting market prices—the fund can easily function as an open-end fund and sell assets to meet any demand for redemptions.

In developed markets conversions of closed-end funds to open-end funds are permitted only if the assets of the converting fund can meet the liquidity requirements of open-end fund regulation and thus are able to be sold easily to meet redemptions, which are likely to be substantial where the majority of holders have voted for such a conversion.

Mandating that closed-end funds convert to open-end funds when the converting funds hold illiquid assets has various dangers, especially in emerging markets.

—Professionals and insiders usually will get out first.

—The best assets will be sold to meet these earlier redemptions, and poorer assets will be left to less well-informed investors.

—The fund will be a "forced seller" of its remaining assets if other investors wish to redeem.

—Professionals and insiders will exploit the forced seller situation, and the prices obtained are likely to be low.

—Some assets will be unsalable, and remaining investors, unfairly, will be unable to realize any value from the fund.

—Scandals may ensue.

In our view, the best way to address the "easy exit'" need in emerging markets is to ensure that all closed-end funds are listed and not to attempt any conversions to open-end funds unless a wide range of reliably liquid assets is available.

Effective Pressure for Good Governance: Fair Competition

In developed markets fund management firms compete under clear and fair rules, which are equitably applied. Transparency ensures that failure to compete honestly and effectively will be visible and will have consequences in terms of loss of business.

In emerging markets, however, the basis of competition is often poorly established, and playing fields are rarely level. Regulators may be subject to capture and may permit entry to the market to those who do not meet regulatory requirements and may bring it into disrepute, damaging reputable businesses; or regulators may enforce requirements arbitrarily, favoring some competitors over others. The incentive to compete honestly on performance is low in such markets.

Because most investors are unwilling to invest in such arbitrary markets, the opportunity cost of the inability of a fund's management to attract more assets is low, and the disincentives to misbehavior are correspondingly low. Under such circumstances the investment fund industry is unlikely to play its part in the financial sector.

Enhancing the potential for fair and open competition, and ensuring transparency and accountability of regulatory decisions could also improve the quality and fairness of regulatory decisionmaking, provided that regulators have suitable protection from vexatious litigation.

The classic case here is that of the Unit Trust of India (UTI) Scheme 64, known as US-64. Since its establishment in 1964, Unit Trust of India has been a state monopoly. It was not subject to the regulation of the Securities and Exchange Board of India, it did not publish net asset values, and its portfolio was not fully disclosed. The price of units for sale and redemption was "smoothed" so that market volatility would not worry its 20-odd million relatively unsophisticated investors. By July 2001, however, following a steep fall in the Indian market, the price of US-64 units had come so far adrift from their net asset value that UTI was offering to redeem units at a premium of nearly 40 percent to the real net asset value. Once the Indian press got hold of this fact and published advice to everyone who held units in US-64 to get out while the going was good, the dilution effect of the resulting wave of redemptions caused UTI to have to suspend dealings in US-64 altogether. The problem is still in the process of being resolved.

The only good outcome is that UTI's share of the market in relation to privately sponsored and managed unit trusts has fallen; by the end of 2001, the public and private market shares were nearly even. (The private funds were first permitted in the early 1990s and may buy and redeem only at net asset value calculated in accordance with a standard formula that is regularly disclosed.)[7] Thus the playing field has been leveled, and

---

7. Association of Mutual Funds in India (AMFI), see www.amfiindia.com. Also, Securities and Exchange board of India (SEBI), see www.sebi.gov.in.

disclosure with resulting vigorous competition is proving to be a force for good governance.

Lessons for Emerging Markets

The OECD paper on governance of collective investment schemes neatly summarizes the issue:

> Adequate disclosure enhances the capability of investors to undertake independent scrutiny. In cases where inadequate governance procedures are in place or where standards are not observed investors can take legal action or lodge complaints with regulators. Perhaps most importantly, any practice that leads to diminished returns to investors will lead to a decline in funds under management. Particularly in advanced competitive markets, this is the sanction most feared by CIS operators. . . . The two basic factors that enhance the capability of the market to monitor operators are the degree of competition among suppliers and the access of investors to information. In most markets competition is growing markedly—a powerful factor in aligning the interests of investment managers and CIS promoters with those of investors.[8]

Our belief is that it is the lack of fair competition, reliable disclosure, and transparency in many emerging markets that is the root cause of lack of confidence in funds and therefore of the cause of failure of investment fund sectors. In our view, the most important function of law and regulation—both of funds and of capital markets generally—is to ensure fair competition, full disclosure, and transparency. This is far more important than drawing up detailed and prescriptive regulation. The concern with process rather than outcomes, which can become an obsession with many regulators, can lead to a heavy supervisory approach that, in the end, amounts to mere "box ticking." Regulatory overkill may simply add to expense and complexity, which may even inhibit the growth of collective investment funds. It takes little account of the power of rigorous market scrutiny to act as a governor of the behavior of fund operators and as a protective shield for investors.

---

8. Thompson and Choi (2001, p. 5).

Our recommendations are, therefore:

Developing Collective Investment Fund Regulatory Regimes

—Place priority on identifying the desired results rather than on developing procedures.

—Utilize the fund governance form (company, contractual, trust) that best suits the local legal and fiscal environment.

—Establish additional, clear regulatory standards and apply them fairly and consistently, with a particular emphasis on handling conflicts of interest.

—Clearly define permitted types (open, closed) and categories of funds (for example, securities, money market, balanced, fund of funds) and set clear investment limitations for each category; define venture capital–type funds as "specialist" and higher risk and restrict investment to professional or sophisticated investors.

—Define rules that establish the basis for valuation of all forms of assets that may be held by funds; require all funds to use the same valuation basis.

—Set clear rules for marketing of funds to investors that seek to prevent misrepresentation of funds and abusive sales practices.

Transparency

—Educate the public about funds and their risks and rewards.

—Make sure basic information on funds and operators is cheaply and easily accessible and that its availability is widely known. Lists of licensed funds and operators should be widely available and updated regularly.

—Stimulate the development of data providers on funds, particularly those providing comparative performance and cost information or ratings type services.

—Encourage development of a cadre of financial journalists and commentators on funds and provide training for them.

—Encourage development of specialist financial publications for retail investors.

—Encourage the development of financial advisers.

Disclosure

—Set detailed requirements for information to be disclosed in fund prospectuses, particularly the risks associated with the structure of the fund and the assets in which it proposes to invest.

—Require a prospectus to be made available to all investors before they invest.

—Set detailed requirements for information to be included in annual audited fund reports, including the assets held by funds and those acquired or disposed of in the period.

—Require reports to be sent to all fund investors and made available to potential investors.

—For open-end funds require regular publication of fund net asset values per unit or share or participation in at least one widely read publication.

—For closed-end funds require regular publication of prices per share or unit or participation; as well as regular publication of net asset values per share or unit or participation in at least one widely read publication.

Ease of Exit

—Do not permit creation of open-end funds in very volatile or barely liquid markets: disaster will ensue.

—Do not require closed-end funds to become open-end funds unless their assets are liquid and diversified enough to sustain the conversion.

—Require closed-end funds to be listed.

—When designing privatization funds, create "general purpose public funds" and give them access to better-quality assets, such as holdings of companies for which strategic investors are sought, particularly utilities, and that are likely to be liquid and profitable; differentiate these general purpose public funds from the more specialized, venture capital–style funds that entail higher risk.

Competition

—Do not set high entry barriers that will reduce competitive pressures.

—Do not set high capital requirements that may allow only the rich and powerful to enter the market, increasing risks of regulatory capture; fund management is not a capital-intensive business, and investors assume all the investment risk (which must be properly disclosed).

—Ensure transparency of regulatory decisionmaking, subject to protections against vexatious litigation.

References

Franks, Julian, and Colin Mayer. 2001. "Risk and Regulation in European Asset Management." Oxford Economic Research Associates, Oxford (www.oxera.co.uk).

OECD (Organization for Economic Cooperation and Development). 1998. *Institutional Investors Statistical Yearbook.* Paris.

Thompson, John K., and Sang-Mok Choi. 2001. "Governance Systems for Collective Investment Schemes in OECD Countries." Financial Affairs Division Occasional Paper 1. Organization for Economic Cooperation and Development, Paris. April.

CALLY JORDAN
MIKE LUBRANO

10

How Effective Are Capital Markets in Exerting Governance on Corporations?

The German government yesterday announced broad voluntary guidelines for publicly traded companies on the management of their businesses, citing the collapse of the US company Enron as a warning sign. . . . Herta Daubler-Gmelin, justice minister, argued that while the code contained no sanctions for non-compliance, "the capital market will provide very effective sanctions" for those that chose to ignore it.

NEWS STORY, *Financial Times*, FEBRUARY 27, 2002

Common rules for corporate takeovers have become a test for Europe's capacity to reform itself. Thanks to the conservatism of German business and the refusal of the Berlin government to look beyond narrow political interests, it is one that Europe is likely to fail. Despite the eye-catching call for greater disclosure of executive pay, Germany's new voluntary code, published yesterday, does little to nudge German corporate governance towards a more investor-friendly model.

EDITORIAL, *Financial Times*, FEBRUARY 27, 2002

IT HAS BECOME A truism that the pressures of the capital markets will improve the governance of corporations; equally, that improvements in corporate governance will promote development of the capital markets. However, the relationship of the capital markets to corporate governance is neither simple nor linear; rather, it is more in the nature of a complex feedback loop, a dynamic process responsive to many factors. One of those factors, law, is the delivery mechanism. How effective capital markets are in exerting governance over corporations is in part a function of how effective the legal rules are through which the markets operate.

This paper looks at a set of corporate governance initiatives and innovations driven by capital markets that have been undertaken in emerging markets in recent years and tries to draw some tentative recommendations about their effectiveness. Throughout the paper we examine the dynamic between public legal rules (legislation, regulations, judicial enforcement) and private legal rules (contracting, adherence to voluntary standards, enforcement through arbitration and market discipline) and their relationship to several other factors that have been identified as significant in the development of financial markets. The events of the last fifteen years rival the South Sea Bubble and tulipmania in focusing popular attention on the operations of the capital markets and corporations, for a number of intriguing reasons examined elsewhere. There have been spectacular market surges and market failures, accompanied by a panoply of regulatory and private sector responses. The intensity of the activity and its consequences have raised fundamental questions about how capital markets in particular, and financial systems in general, grow and develop and about the role of corporate actors in that development.

There are still more questions than answers. As Bratton and McCahery wrote in 1999:

> In these globalizing times, corporate law's leading question is whether one or another national corporate governance system (or component thereof) possesses relative competitive advantage. . . . Related questions about competitive advantage and convergence to best practice come up in domestic policy discussions in many countries. Concern about local firms' performance in international markets turns attention to alternative governance practices identified in international comparisons: If competitive advantage lies elsewhere, then domestic practice should be reformed to follow the international leader. An extensive body of studies addresses these questions, identifying and

evaluating national variations in management and financial practices, industrial organization, and corporate and securities laws. Unfortunately, even as these descriptions become thicker and more cogent, answers to the bottom-line questions respecting competitive advantage have become more elusive and convergence predictions have become more qualified.[1]

With respect to public legal rules, there are some beacons shining through the thicket of discourse, speculation, and experimentation. Legal rules and legal families do matter. Political structures matter. History—the way legal concepts have been introduced—matters. Legal concepts are not indiscriminately interchangeable components of legal systems. Forces of convergence and divergence in legal rules operate selectively.[2]

La Porta, Lopez-de-Silanes, Shleifer, and Vishny were among the first to turn the spotlight on the relationship of legal rules and development of financial matters: "Because legal origins are highly correlated with the content of the law, and because legal families originated before financial markets had developed, it is unlikely that laws were written primarily in response to market pressures. Rather the legal families appear to shape the legal rules, which in turn influence financial markets. . . . [L]egal rules do matter."[3] In a comprehensive literature review, Bratton and McCahery noted that La Porta and his colleagues looked to the two main legal traditions in developed economies, the Anglo-American common law tradition and the continental European "civil," or Roman-Germanic, legal tradition, to conclude that the level of legal enforcement and the origin of the legal rules correlated to the level of development of both equity and debt markets. Measures of investor protection appeared superior in common law countries and translated into more vibrant equity markets.[4]

The implication, that common law systems are superior in fostering sophisticated financial systems, was bound to sow controversy and did not go long unchallenged.[5] Rajan and Zingales were among the first to contest this view:

---

1. Bratton and McCahery (1999).
2. On each of these points, see, respectively, La Porta and others (2000); Rajan and Zingales (2001); Pistor (2000), and Pistor and others (2000); Bratton and McCahery (1999); and Jordan (2000).
3. La Porta and others (2000, p. 3).
4. Bratton and McCahery (1999).
5. Rajan and Zingales (2001).

First, it does not seem that legal or cultural impediments to financial development are as serious as one might have concluded from recent literature. Somewhat facetiously, one does not have to have the good fortune of being colonized by the British to be able to have vibrant financial markets. However, the main impediment we identify—the political structure within the country—can be as difficult to overcome as more structural impediments. Nevertheless, our second main implication is that to the extent a country can be coaxed to be open, it makes it less easy for domestic incumbents to retard financial development.[6]

Both viewpoints are significant and not necessarily incompatible; each identifies a major determinant in the functioning of financial markets, the legal rules, or more precisely, the legal family or tradition to which they belong, and the political structures that create, support, or possibly undermine them. Legal rules, or more precisely again, public legal rules, are the product of and dependent upon political action.

This debate, and the related one of convergence or divergence in corporate governance systems, caught the eye of Katharina Pistor, then a comparative legal scholar at the Max Planck Institute in Hamburg, who wrote:

> There is a lively debate in the corporate governance literature about these alternative patterns of institutional development and in particular about the role of law for convergence or divergence of corporate governance systems. Proponents of the divergence, or path dependence, hypothesis argue that even if the corporate law was harmonized across countries, other legal rules (tax laws, codetermination legislation, etc.), and institution constraints (financial structure, existing ownership structure of firms), or simply political considerations would stand in the way of convergence. The opposite view holds that convergence is likely to take place once the main regulatory obstacles are removed. The economic forces towards success, they suggest, are the same all over the world. Both views regard legal institutions as important for promoting or hindering convergence, but differ in their assessment of the propensity of a particular body of law, such as corporate law, to achieve this goal.[7]

6. Rajan and Zingales (2001).
7. Pistor (2000).

Pistor's conclusion: "a simple convergence story does not do justice to the complexity of legal change."[8]

Intrigued by the complexity of legal change, Pistor went on to look at "legal transplants" or the "transplant effect." How do legal concepts from one system fare when transplanted to another? Pistor argued that the manner of transplantation is significant; the extent to which a "foreign" legal concept has been voluntarily introduced or embraced (as opposed to imposed, for political or other reasons) is a predictor of effectiveness, she wrote.[9]

The proliferation of legal transplants has in part been driven by the promotion of "international standards" in both capital markets and corporate governance, an important indicator, it is often held, of convergence of legal rules. International standards have not been picked out of thin air, however; their legal origins can be traced back to national systems, predominately systems based in common law. Gauging the effectiveness of convergence to these standards becomes a more complex matter.

There is yet another twist to the convergence-divergence debate. The forces of convergence and divergence operate contemporaneously, but selectively, on different kinds of legal rules. Relatively recent statutory law in highly regulated and internationalized areas such as capital markets or banking regulation is sensitive to the forces of convergence. Older, more established bodies of law, statutory or otherwise, are more "path dependent," more resistant to change and absorption of "foreign elements." Corporate or company law, largely a product of the nineteenth century, is an example. The more basic the legal concept, the longer its roots and, arguably, the more impervious it is to the forces of convergence. Concepts of contract, status, and property law, for example, reach back hundreds and thousands of years.

Moreover, legal rules are part of legal systems; legal rules are interdependent within their system. Capital market rules interact with corporate law rules, which themselves are grounded in notions of contract, status, and property. Legal rules that, in theory, should have been effective at one level could be disabled because of conflicts or incompatibility at another level. Much of the grief that has ensued in the aftermath of the mass privatizations of the 1990s can be attributed to the indiscriminate mixing and matching of legal rules, a process of transplantation that resulted in dysfunctional or

8. Pistor (2000, p. 46).
9. Pistor and others (2000).

imbalanced feedback loops. The corporate governance systems could not support the functioning of the capital markets; nascent or ailing capital markets collapsed or declined; without the disciplines of the capital markets, corporate governance systems did not respond. This is not the whole story, of course, but it is a part of it.

Although the academic work has focused more on public legal rules than on private legal rules, the questions at the heart of the debate apply equally in the context of private rulemaking. Are some systems of private rulemaking superior to others? Are these private systems on a path toward convergence? Is private rulemaking path dependent? How effective can various mechanisms of private rulemaking and enforcement be within the overall system of public and private law? To what extent can private rulemaking mechanisms be imported or transplanted between systems?

Whether one is talking about public or private legal rules, or both, in the end the question is "What works?" Clearly, we are nowhere near the point where we can give definitive answers. Form, however, appears to be as important as substance when it comes to fashioning effective legal rules. And form also appears to be predictive of effectiveness, depending on the legal system in which a rule operates. Different legal traditions demonstrate different preferences for the form that legal rules take.

As the cases that follow illustrate, there has been a blossoming of public and private capital market initiatives intended to improve corporate governance. Some exciting experiments are under way. One intriguing feature of the Latin American experimentation, in particular, is the way in which public and private legal rules have been combined and mobilized to create the "quasi" public rules discussed below. But the majority of these efforts did not gather steam until after the Asian financial crisis of 1997. All we can do at this point is to begin to examine such initiatives on a systematic basis and start thinking about what combination of factors is likely to affect the success or failure of the experiments.

Interplay of Public and Private Legal Rules

The debate over the role of legal rules in capital market development and corporate governance systems has focused on public legal rules—legislation (enacted through the political process) and its enforcement through the judicial system. One conundrum noted by Pistor in transition economies is the co-existence of high-quality formal legislation (in Pistor's words, a product of "an external supply of legal solutions") and low levels of effectiveness:

> Weaknesses in the governance structure that are noted today are often attributed to weaknesses in the law, which in turn leads to new proposals for improving statutory law. The evidence of the quality of the law on the books, however, suggests that this is at best a partial story. The level of shareholder and creditor rights protection in transition economies today is higher than in many other countries. Other factors, including the dynamic of the reform process and its impact on the development of effective institutions to enforce the new law, need to be analyzed more closely to understand the remarkable difference in the governance of firms despite the trend towards convergence of the law on the books.[10]

Largely overlooked in this debate, however, is the role of private legal rules, that is, private legal rules established by contract (ex ante) and implemented and enforced (ex post) by means of various contractual dispute resolution mechanisms, including arbitration, or possibly by market discipline or "reputational hostage-taking."

As an example of the interplay of public and private rules, Professor Frank Partnoy of the University of San Diego recently presented a paper at the Brookings Institution looking at the regulation of the derivatives markets in the United States from this perspective.[11] These derivatives markets are regulated by a combination of private and public legal rules that operate ex ante and ex post (table 10-1 shows this graphically). His assessment:

> First are private *ex ante* legal rules developed primarily by the International Swaps and Derivatives Association, Inc. . . . for OTC [over-the counter] derivatives (and by various exchanges and self-regulatory organizations for exchange-traded derivatives). The recent trend has been toward increased privatization of derivatives regulation, with trading volumes shifting from exchanges to OTC transactions, and this trend is likely to continue. . . . Second are private *ex post* legal rules applied by arbitrators in disputes, particularly those of the National Association of Securities Dealers. . . . Arbitration has

10. Pistor (2000, pp. 46, 47).
11. Partnoy (2002).

Table 10-1. *Derivatives Regulation Framework*

	Private	Public
Ex-ante	Contract (ISDA)	Congress (CFMA)
Ex-post	Arbitration (NASD)	Courts (SDNY)

Source: Partnoy (2002).

numerous drawbacks, especially uncertainty, and likely will not predominate in future adjudication of derivatives disputes. . . . Third are public *ex ante* legal rules, including securities, commodities, and banking law and regulation, but also including derivatives-specific rules. Historically, public regulation in these areas has not achieved its goals; instead public legal rules too often have generated perverse incentives related to regulatory arbitrage, regulatory licenses, and regulatory competition. . . . Fourth are public *ex post* legal rules, including rulings by courts adjudicating derivatives disputes. Thus far, judges have shied from deciding important issues in derivatives disputes, and end-users of derivatives increasingly avoid litigation— even when losses are large—because of the high costs of discovery and motion practice.[12]

Partnoy's conclusion: "The recent trend to privatize legal rules applicable to derivatives is likely to continue."[13]

Private Legal Rules: Powerful and Pervasive

Private legal rules are powerful and pervasive. Contracts are at the heart of any market, and capital markets are no exception. From the central contract of purchase and sale radiates an extensive network of complex contractual relations that make the market function. The Euromarket (origi-

12. Partnoy (2002, pp. 2–3). The acronyms in table 10-1 refer to the International Swaps and Derivatives Association (ISDA), the Commodities and Futures Markets Act (CFMA), the National Association of Securities Dealers (NASD), and the federal court in Manhattan, the Southern District of New York (SDNY).

13. Partnoy (2002, p. 36).

nally the Eurobond market) is a highly successful capital market governed virtually exclusively by various forms of private legal rules. It has proven remarkably resistant to the intrusion of public legal rules.

At their origin, stock exchange listing rules for example, are private legal rules, adhered to by contractual arrangement. This, in fact, is often the main source of their weakness as a regulatory mechanism in case of market abuse; because they rely on contracts, stock exchanges ordinarily may go no further than delisting (resiliation of the contract to list) or public censure.[14] Over time, listing rules have been transformed in many cases by an overlay of public legal rules, so called "statutory backing" or subjugation to supervisory oversight, thus evolving into a form of quasi public legal rule. Contracts are also at the heart of the corporate entity. Modern U.S. legal theory looks at the corporation as a "nexus of contracts."[15] In the interest of efficiency, corporate law—the public legal rules—acts primarily to establish a standard form of contract, or a set of default rules, for the organization of corporations.[16] In private or closed corporations, the incorporators themselves, and subsequent shareholders, may vary these rules (and often do) virtually in their entirety by contract. Private companies are the predominate corporate form throughout the world, in most cases composing 99 percent of incorporations or registrations. They are creatures of contract and rely on contract, in the form of bylaws and shareholders' agreements in particular, for their operation.

The primacy of contract in the market also underpins the dominant regulatory approach to the capital markets (and therefore to corporate governance): the Anglo-American disclosure-based regimes. Why is transparency so fundamental? Because a guiding principle of the capital markets is still

14. But see the later discussion of mandatory arbitration of shareholder disputes required of companies listing on Brazil's Level 2 or the Novo Mercado.

15. Pinto and Branson (1999, pp. 115–16): "Law and economic theorists conceptualize the corporation in terms of contract law. A corporation can be viewed as a nexus of contracts through which various claimants such as creditors, workers, shareholders, and consumers enter into agreements. Private contracts are an efficient means to lower transaction costs in the agency relationship between the shareholders and managers. One can view the articles of incorporation and the bylaws as a contract between the shareholders and the managers setting out the rules governing their relationship. This private ordering through contracts allows the parties to provide rules to maximize value and minimize costs. Under this view, corporate law should provide the basic terms of these contracts (that is, default rules), but the shareholders and the managers should be allowed to change the terms, thus providing an optimal and mutually agreeable system."

16. In the United Kingdom and many Commonwealth jurisdictions, contract is still the basis of the formation of a company; the memorandum of association—the contract among the founding members—is registered to establish limited liability and legal personality.

caveat emptor, let the buyer beware, from the Roman law of the contract of sale. The nature of these public disclosure-based rules is determined by their deference to the private legal rules of the market.

What are the characteristics of contract: it is consensual, flexible, and, optimally, both self-enforcing and *independent of the political process*. Each characteristic can vary in degree, but the consensual nature of the contract is arguably its defining characteristic. Standard form contracts, rife in the securities industry, are largely inflexible, either for the sake of predictability and convenience or because of the superior bargaining power of one party, but they are still consensual. Bylaws or industry association rules are a variation on standard contracts.[17] In becoming a member of the organization or company, the member agrees to abide by the rules. Contract thus forms the basis of so-called self-regulatory organizations so prevalent in the Anglo-American securities industry.

Private legal rules, contracts, have drawbacks, of course. In the absence of agreement, there is impasse and recourse must be had to public legal rules, which are rigid, prescriptive, circumscribed, and subject to the vagaries of the political process. Nevertheless, in certain circumstances public legal rules are more effective than private legal rules.

A Framework for Rulemaking

To begin to sort out the various effects of and relations between private and public rules, we have developed a framework for rulemaking, shown in table 10-2, and then examine how several recent initiatives fit this framework. Table 10-2 takes as its starting point the two-by-two matrix of public versus private ex ante and ex post rulemaking developed by Partnoy to describe derivatives regulation. However, applying the same strict public-private dichotomy would, in our view, too dramatically oversimplify the typology of corporate governance initiatives driven by capital markets in recent years in emerging markets. Accordingly, we have added a column to provide a home for mixed private-public rulemaking. This facilitates sepa-

---

17. The derivation of the word "bylaw" is interesting in this respect. According to the *Oxford English Dictionary*, it is believed to come from the Old Norse language "byrlaw": a local custom or law of a manor or district whereby disputes over boundaries, trespass were settled *without recourse to the public courts of law* or a regulation or ordinance agreed to *by consent* in baronial court.

Table 10-2. *Corporate Governance Framework*

	Private	Quasi-private/public	Public
Ex-ante	Contract	Sponsored "voluntary" standards	Law, regulation
Ex-post	Arbitration	Special arbitral bodies	Judicial

rate treatment of those contractual arrangements that are negotiated on a case-by-case basis between companies and stakeholders as well as "prepackaged" contractual arrangements that derive from voluntary adherence to a set of standards developed by third parties (such as the government, an exchange, a corporate governance code committee, or some sort of rating entity). Likewise, insertion of a box between arbitration and judicial enforcement helps to differentiate between general commercial arbitration systems and those that may be established especially to settle disputes over adherence to particular voluntary standards.

The cases that follow describe a variety of experiments in public and private rulemaking in a set of significantly different emerging markets. The set of cases we have included is neither comprehensive nor even representative of the full range of capital market corporate governance initiatives that have been tried or may be tried. Rather, we believe that by analyzing a set of recent initiatives that includes elements that might fit into each of the boxes in table 10-2, some useful observations can be drawn. Accordingly, the cases cover instances of "pure" legal reforms, optional listing standards, "pure" issuer-investor contracting, government-sponsored "voluntary" codes, a mandatory disclosure regime, and the use of ratings.

Of course, the diagram remains simplistic in that it is static and does not capture the ebb and flow between private and public legal rules. Many of the initiatives we have examined incorporate one or more ex ante or ex post elements that may not fit neatly into a single box. This is probably evidence both of the ingenuity of the innovators and of the value of utilizing a mix of public and private legal rulemaking in the capital markets to address issues of corporate governance.

Case 1: Legal Reforms in Latin America

When corporate governance issues become popular fodder for the national press, as they have in both industrial and emerging markets, it is unusual for national legislatures to remain completely quiescent. Falling most squarely into the right-hand column of table 10-2 are the numerous reforms of company law and capital market legislation undertaken in the emerging markets over the past five years. In Latin America alone, high-profile amendments to the legal and regulatory framework have become law in the four major markets: Argentina, Brazil, Chile, and Mexico.[18] At least one smaller market, Colombia, is considering similar legislation.

Scandals, the Impetus for Reforms

The reforms of Latin American company and securities laws were typically conceived in the aftermath (or sometimes during the course) of scandals in the public securities markets involving perceived inequitable treatment of shareholders. In Chile the managers and controllers of the power company Enersis managed to secure fully one-third of the total price paid for control of the company in return for an economic interest in the company of far less than 1 percent. The shareholders of TV Azteca in Mexico took up arms after its controlling shareholder used the company as a virtual bank to finance his purchase of cellular licenses (after publicly insisting that he would never do such a thing). Investors in a series of Brazilian and Argentine companies were forced to accept "low-ball" offers from controlling shareholders who decided to delist the companies. Brazilian shareholders (most of them holders of nonvoting "preferred" shares of such companies) felt themselves unfairly frozen out of transactions in which control of the company was sold by those holding a majority of the voting shares.

As the case studies that follow demonstrate, capital market participants of one sort or another almost always undertook private initiatives in the area of corporate governance, either simultaneously or immediately following

18. Chile, December 2000 (mandatory tender offers, pension fund-nominated directors, class actions, special procedures and board committees for transactions with affiliates, and director responsibility); Argentina, June 2001 (mandatory tender offers, audit committees, shareholder rights); Mexico, June 2001 (nonvoting shares, independent directors, code compliance disclosure); Brazil, November 2001 (mandatory tender offers, accounting standards, board representation for minority voting and nonvoting shareholders, voting procedures, legal authorization for arbitration).

the amendment of the legal framework. One problem with legislated reform is its general applicability to all companies similarly situated (for example, all listed companies must comply with all legislation pertaining to corporate governance). Not surprisingly, the recent spate of Latin American legislative initiatives failed to enjoy the unanimous support of the business community. Typically, established firms with proven track records in the market or with dominant positions in the equity indexes were less enthusiastic about having to disclose additional information to shareholders or allowing outsiders onto their boards. Controllers fought doggedly against mandatory tender offer triggers that would have forced them to share control premiums with minority shareholders. During the reform debates, it became evident that many listed Latin American companies (including some blue chips) no longer thought of the public securities markets as a potential source of new capital. Rather, a fair number of them anticipated selling control to larger national or, more often, international competitors (in transactions precisely like those to which the tender offer reforms were designed to apply) and thus were indifferent to the prices at which their securities currently traded in the markets. To the controllers of such companies, any strengthening of the tender offer regime was anathema.

Not all securities issuers or potential issuers were resistant. A handful of listed firms voluntarily amended their charters to incorporate some of the elements of the legislative reforms in advance of their passage. Several companies in Brazil negotiated tag-along rights for minority voting shares and even nonvoting shares before the legislated reforms were passed in 2001. A major Mexican company was the first firm there to adopt the Mexican code of best practices in a (so far unsuccessful) effort to turn around its reputation for trampling on minority shareholder rights. The less resistant firms typically expect heavy capital-raising requirements in the short to medium term.

In the end, the final measures approved by the respective legislatures and executives in Latin America were more-or-less watered-down versions of what was initially proposed to the legislature. Chile's reformers were perhaps the most successful, but even there, majority shareholders were permitted to suspend the application of the law's mandatory tender offer provisions for three years. Mexico's legislation delegated authority for setting the parameters of the mandatory tender offer rule to the banking and securities regulator, which after much delay was able to issue strong mandatory bid rules in early 2002. Brazil's very comprehensive legislative initiative was the subject of extensive horse-trading in the legislature. In the end, the mandatory tender offer requirement for nonvoting shares and the provisions that would have given minority shareholders control over fiscal boards had to be dropped.

Early Results: Mixed

The promoters of the recent legislative initiatives in Latin America and in emerging markets elsewhere clearly hoped that by mandating greater transparency, providing shareholders with better tools to ensure equitable treatment, and beefing up judicial enforcement, the reforms would have a salutary effect on the development of capital markets. In the case of the Latin American reforms, it is certainly too early to make any definitive judgments about the long-term impact on access to and cost of capital, new offerings, liquidity, securities prices, or company performance. Two or three more years must pass before there is enough solid data to test the hypothesis that the reforms helped reduce the overall "governance discounts" in the respective markets, and resulted in more access to capital at lower cost. (One prominent analyst, however, already asserts that the Brazilian legal reform shifted the balance of power in Brazilian companies positively for minority shareholders and recommended that investors buy minority voting shares in Brazilian firms.)[19]

Short-term anecdotal information presents a mixed picture. Clearly, the supporters of reform have succeeded in focusing the attention of companies, managers and directors, institutional investors, and the general public on the importance of corporate governance to the health of the capital markets (and by extension, the pension savings regimes). Although it is hard to judge just how much the legal reforms encouraged the development of private contractual arrangements discussed elsewhere in this paper, recent experience supports the conclusion that legal reforms can have the effect of accelerating the development and adoption of complementary or supplementary private contractual mechanisms (see the discussions of Brazil and Colombia, below).

The reforms have clearly been no panacea. In no case was there an immediate rise in equity prices that might have reflected a reduction in the

---

19. Deutsche Bank Latin America Strategy, November 5, 2001.

governance discount as a result of passage of the reforms. Controversial delistings and changes of control accelerated during 2001 and continue today. It may be that controllers have tried to "get while the getting is good" before the legal reforms were in place (and during the grace period before Chile's mandatory tender offer regime goes into effect). Nor does the impetus created by the legal reforms for voluntary private contracting appear to be uniform. In Chile all public companies have duly constituted the conflicts committees required by the legislation, and growth companies, firms with American depository receipt programs (ADRs), and those with large pension fund stakeholdings have begun to improve their overall practices. However, Santiago's tightly knit community of senior managers and directors has not experienced an epiphany. There has not been a general blossoming of interest in restructuring corporate boards to make them more effective watchdogs of shareholder interests. Privately led efforts (with support from the government) to develop a best practices code for Chilean companies have so far fizzled.

Case 2: Stock Exchange Listing Rules: Brazil's Novo Mercado

The New York Stock Exchange requirements for independent directors and audit committees are often cited as an example of the positive role that self-regulatory organizations in the securities markets can play in improving corporate governance standards. However, before the mid-1990s, many stock markets in both developed and emerging markets resisted calls to impose higher standards on shareholder rights or board composition. Not surprisingly, this resistance was grounded in a concern that listing rules that exceeded minimum requirements of local company law might discourage new listings, particularly by start-up, founder-controlled companies. Most established listed companies were also less than anxious to change their practices. As with legislation, listing rules can suffer from the "one size fits all" problem. That is, all issuers are usually required to meet the same minimum standards, so the old guard resists.

Born of Need and Disappointment

The Novo Mercado initiative of the Sao Paolo Stock Exchange (BOVESPA), conceived in late 2000, traces its roots to the efforts to reform Brazilian company and securities legislation, discussed in Case 1. The initiative represents a quasi private effort to make up for the perceived shortcomings of legislative reform by creating a common mechanism to encourage voluntary adherence to appropriate standards, and providing specialized private dispute resolution. BOVESPA's leadership conceived the Novo Mercado at a time when two trends particularly worrisome for a stock exchange were evident. First, market capitalization and trading volumes in the public equities markets were contracting dramatically; and second, efforts to enact comprehensive corporate governance reform in Brazil were encountering strong political resistance, as described in Case 1, of the kind identified by Rajan and Zingales.[20]

By the end of the 1990s, the weaknesses of the Brazilian capital market were painfully evident. In 1999 and 2000 there were no IPOs, few new issues by companies already listed, and a growing number of delistings. Liquidity was drying up for all but the largest companies as trading volumes declined. Another ongoing challenge for BOVESPA was a shift of trading in shares of the largest Brazilian companies to the ADR market in New York. While these disturbing trends were attributable to many factors, one of the more important was the perception by domestic and international investors that corporate governance practices of Brazilian companies were generally poor and legal protections inadequate (particularly those dealing with minority shareholder rights).[21] BOVESPA decided that perception called for some sort of response.[22]

The compromises that were made in the course of legislative consideration of the initial reform bill guided the content of the Novo Mercado listing rules. BOVESPA recognized that the well-understood and objectively determinable shortcomings of existing law that were not successfully addressed by the legal reforms could provide the basis for a voluntary rules-based response. BOVESPA's initiative can properly be called a "privatization" of part of the legal reform process.

---

20. Rajan and Zingales (2001).

21. McKinsey Emerging Market Opinion Survey (www.mckinsey.com/knowledge/articles/pdf/emergingmarketsurvey2001.pdf).

22. The president of Brazil's securities commission took a leading role in the effort to reform the company and securities law precisely because he shared the view that while improvements in corporate governance of Brazilian companies would not by themselves effect a recovery of the equity market, they were a necessary condition.

Different Strokes for Different Folks

The Novo Mercado is a listing segment of BOVESPA for companies that choose to commit themselves to the highest standards of corporate governance by contracting to follow a stricter set of rules.[23] In addition, BOVESPA created two intermediate listing segments, the Special Corporate Governance Level 1 and Level 2. The listing rules for Levels 1 and 2 also require higher corporate governance standards than existing norms, but they are not as strict as the requirements of "full" Novo Mercado. Companies remain free to list under BOVESPA's old rules, which simply require compliance with Brazil's company and securities laws. Therefore, companies listed on BOVESPA can now choose among four listing segments, in ascending order of corporate governance standards: the old market, Level 1, Level 2, and the Novo Mercado.[24]

By committing themselves to higher standards of corporate governance, companies that join the Novo Mercado hope that investors will respond by placing higher valuations on these companies' securities—reducing the general "corporate governance discount" applied to Brazilian firms.[25] The creation of the Level 1 and 2 segments was a bit of an afterthought. Under pressure from their base of existing listed companies, BOVESPA had to offer something that would allow such companies to avoid appearing indifferent to investor concerns.[26]

23. (www.novomercadobovespa.com.br/english/index.htm).

24. The idea of creating a separate set of listing rules within an established stock market was taken from the German Neuer Markt. However, an important difference is that the Neuer Markt was designed for companies from the technology, media, and telecom sectors, whereas the Novo Mercado is intended for all companies wishing to demonstrate adherence to the highest standards of corporate governance, regardless of their industrial sector.

25. The most exigent of the Novo Mercado's rules is that companies may not issue nonvoting shares. The other main rules require that public shares be offered through mechanisms that favor capital dispersion; that the company maintain a free float equivalent to 25 percent of the outstanding stock; that the same financial terms offered be to controlling shareholders in the transfer of the controlling bloc must be extended to all shareholders (tag-along rights); an obligation to make a tender offer at an objectively determined "economic value" share price should a decision be taken to delist from the Novo Mercado; that a single one-year term for the entire board of directors be established; that the annual balance sheet be made available in accordance with accepted international accounting practices; and that quarterly reports be improved (consolidated financial statements were required).

26. Level 2 has almost all the same rules as the Novo Mercado; the notable exception is that Level 2 companies may still issue nonvoting shares. Level 1 relates mainly to transparency and disclosure, rather than shareholder rights. It is doubtful whether a company's adherence to Level 1 shows a real improvement in its corporate governance; adoption of Level 1 standards is better viewed as a first step toward more substantial changes.

Novo Mercado and Level 2 companies, but not Level 1 companies, must settle disputes using the Market Arbitration Panel. (In anticipation of the Novo Mercado, the Brazilian legal reforms described in Case 1 explicitly strengthened the legal standing of voluntary arbitration, making the enforcement of arbitral awards easier.) Obviously, the establishment of the Market Arbitration Panel reflects market doubts about the effectiveness of the Brazilian judiciary to deal with shareholder disputes in a fair and expeditious manner.[27]

Any Takers?

Since BOVESPA launched its corporate governance initiative, several public and quasi public entities have taken supportive action. BNDES, the Brazilian national development bank, has a simple formula for offering progressively lower interest rates on loans to companies that follow the requirements of Level 1, Level 2, and the Novo Mercado. The pension fund regulator allows pension funds to invest a larger proportion of their assets in companies listed on Level 1, Level 2, or the Novo Mercado, creating another incentive for companies to move to these listing segments.

The early results of BOVESPA's corporate governance initiative have been less than spectacular—a result that is explained almost entirely by the dismal economic scenario and market conditions prevailing in Brazil since 2001. The listing rules were officially launched in December 2000, but it was not until February 2002 that Companhia de Concessões Rodoviárias (CCR), a highway concession manager, became the first company to make an IPO on the Novo Mercado. As of April 2002 CCR remained the sole Novo Mercado company. Meanwhile, nineteen companies have joined Level 1, but none have joined Level 2 (although several have announced their intention to move to Level 2 in the near future). By focusing on transparency and disclosure issues, rather than on shareholder rights, Level 1 was envisaged as a stepping-stone to Level 2. However, the list of companies that have joined Level 1 includes several companies with doubtful corporate governance credentials; these companies are willing to disclose the information required to meet Level 1 standards but may have little intention or incentive to continue to Level 2.

---

27. The Market Arbitration Panel appears to represent a significant shift of power to shareholders and is reported to be perhaps the greatest single obstacle to persuading companies to adhere to Level 2.

Case 3: Ad Hoc Contracting in Brazil before and after the Reforms

Every time a company issues securities, it enters into a set of voluntary explicit and implicit contracts with investors concerning the company's governance. The company's charter, the terms of the securities, and any representations made in the marketing materials amount to explicit contracts, usually enforceable in law. Other understandings between issuers and investors—for example, that the company's voluntary governance practices will be in line with evolving market standards and expectations—may be more subtle (and less easily enforced). As investors in emerging markets have become more conscious of the shortcomings of governance during the debates over legal reforms, direct negotiation between investors and companies with respect to the governance practices of companies seems to have become more common, another example of Partnoy's observation on the trend toward "privatization" of legal rules. Two recent Brazilian IPOs (initial public offerings), one for ADRs issued before passage of the legal reform and the launch of the Novo Mercado, and another that was the first listing on the Novo Mercado, may illustrate this tendency.

Issuer-Investor Negotiations over Tag-Along Rights

Ultrapar is a large Brazilian liquefied petroleum gas and petrochemicals distribution company. Its 2001 total sales amounted to almost $1 billion.[28] As of March 1, 2002, its market capitalization exceeded $460 million.[29] Ultrapar decided to test the international market in 1999, offering non-voting shares to U.S. investors through a sponsored ADR program listed on the New York Stock Exchange. The company had a solid reputation in Brazil for professional management and comparatively good treatment of shareholders. Although descendents of the founder still held the largest block of Ultrapar equity, day-to-day control of the company had long been entrusted to a cadre of professional managers, many of whom had come to hold substantial amounts of shares themselves, mostly locked up in trusts set up as part of their long-term compensation packages.

28. Currency is in U.S. dollars unless otherwise specified.
29. Ultrapar's annual report is available at www.ultra.com.br.

Despite Ultrapar's history of good shareholder relations, potential investors in the international offering expressed concerns about the prospective treatment of holders of ADRs in the event of a change of control of the company. Prior to the "road show" for the offering, neither the company nor its underwriters seems to have anticipated the investors' reaction. Given the existing control arrangement in the company (the descendants of the founder and senior management holding a majority of voting shares and a fair amount of the nonvoting shares as well) and the nature of the industry, it was reasonable to expect a merger or takeover in the future, at which point a fair amount of the value of the company would be realized. Under existing (and still current) Brazilian company and securities law, there was no requirement that a purchaser of a controlling interest offer to purchase the nonvoting shares, so ADR holders might be left out in the cold. The potential investors wanted "tag-along" rights, entitling them to sell their shares at the same price as the controllers and secure an equal share of the control premium.

After a certain amount of back-and-forth among the company, its underwriters, and investors, Ultrapar's chairman verbally committed to amend the company's charter *after the offering* to grant all nonvoting shares tag-along rights (something he could ensure, given the combined voting power of the founder's descendants and the management team). This undertaking was apparently credible enough to permit the offering to go forward. The ADRs were indeed successfully placed in October 1999. Investors and intermediaries felt that the company's reputation for fair dealing was sufficient "collateral" to assure that the chairman would make good on his promise. It may also have been understood that there was something of a community of interest between the investors and the management group, since the latter would have a direct interest in a higher share price once their shares of the company were released from the trust arrangements. Ultrapar did indeed amend its charter at its next general meeting of shareholders in March 2000.

Issuer-Investor Negotiation over Conflicts of Interest

The very recent case of CCR is similarly one of investors demanding protections that go beyond those required by law. Indeed, it is an example of investors and the company contracting for the whole gamut of protections and enforcement: the benefits of the Brazilian legal reform (Case 1), the Novo Mercado protections and arbitration (Case 2), and additional ad hoc arrangements tailored to the company's special circumstances and investor concerns.

CCR is the result of the merger of a set of Brazilian highway concession managers. Its initial shareholders were Brazilian civil engineering companies (who build highways) together with a Portuguese construction contractor. The objective of its equity offering in the domestic market in early 2002 was to deleverage the company and establish a base upon which to finance expansion (that is, the purchase of new concessions). The company's controllers intended to sell a large minority interest (up to 49 percent) in the company. From the start, they committed that CCR would meet all the qualifications for Novo Mercado—including one-share, one-vote; tag-along rights; international accounting standards; independent directors; and arbitration of shareholder disputes. In fact, CCR proved to be the first company to achieve a Novo Mercado listing. However, given the controllers' potential conflict of interest (together they represented most of the country's highway construction industry), investors insisted on protections going beyond those of the Novo Mercado requirements. Discussions focused on special procedures for approval of contracts between the company and the controllers. CCR's management is reported to have originally offered to empower a majority of the independent directors to order an appraisal (fairness opinion) in the case of any transaction in excess of $1 million reals (US $450,000) between the company and affiliates. In the end, the company had to go beyond this, agreeing that *any single director* could demand such an independent appraisal. This provision was duly incorporated into the company's charter and described in the final prospectus for the offering. The $300 million real (US $135 million) offering was successfully concluded in late January 2002.

Ad Hoc Contracting: Alive and Well

Ultrapar and CCR show that ad hoc contracting on corporate governance between issuers and investors is possible and practiced in Brazil. Ultrapar's experience was well known in Brazil and certainly contributed to the thinking behind, and the eventual content of, BOVESPA's Novo Mercado rules. Institutionalized contracting arrangements such as Novo Mercado can grow out of shared experiences with ad hoc contracting. At the same time, the CCR case demonstrates that institutional mechanisms such as Novo Mercado can also be supplemented by ad hoc arrangements that take the "packaged" institutional arrangement as a basis upon which to build an appropriate company-specific governance structure credible in the markets.

Case 4: "Voluntary" Codes in Mexico, Russia

The understanding most practitioners have of a national code of best practices is that of a set of voluntary standards of corporate behavior produced by some sort of grouping of representatives from the private sector, government, academics, and market participants. However, in some emerging markets, it has been the government that has taken the lead role—either "push-starting" the effort or arranging for it to be carried out almost entirely by organs of the state (or persons handpicked by the authorities). The Mexican Code of Best Corporate Practices, adopted in 2000, and the Russian Code of Corporate Governance, adopted in 2002, provide illustrations of each approach.[30]

Mexico: Push-Starting a Code

In the aftermath of the Mexican banking sector collapse of 1995–96, it was apparent that the financial system had done precious little to promote corporate governance among securities issuers and borrowers. The evident lack of transparency and accountability in the corporate sector greatly complicated the process of financial system resolution, contributing to the more than $100 billion cost of the bailout of Mexico's banking system. In late 1999 the Comision Bancaria y de Valores (CNBV), Mexico's banking and securities supervisor, launched an initiative to draft a code of best practices for public companies. Mexico's Business Coordinating Council (the umbrella group including most national corporate and financial sector associations) was tapped to coordinate the private sector's contribution to the effort, and it selected well-known academics and representatives of the legal community to participate. The result was a set of guidelines focusing largely on the quality of financial information and disclosure and on the composition and functioning of boards of directors. The code requires the boards of public companies to establish finance, compensation, and audit committees; a majority of directors on the audit committees must be inde-

---

30. For Mexico, see Business Coordinating Council, *Codigo de Mejores Practicas Corporativas* (www.cce.org.mx). For Russia, see (www.fedcom.ru).

pendent of management and controllers. From the start of the process, it was expected that public companies would be required to disclose periodically the extent to which their practices are in compliance with the code. Soon after publication of the code, the CNBV issued a regulation requiring such periodic disclosure.

Russia: The Heavy Hand

Russia's new code of corporate governance had a more dirigiste provenance than Mexico's. The idea to draft some sort of code of practices was launched by the chairman of the Russian Federal Commission on Securities Markets (FCSM) in late 2000. A committee selected by the FCSM was assigned the task of preparing a final code within a year. Although informational public meetings were held during the first half of 2001, the discussions at these meetings had little actual impact on the drafting process. As initially conceived, the code was to be a (quite lengthy) compendium of existing law, regulation, and FCSM interpretation, as well as "recommended" practices not necessarily grounded in the existing legal and regulatory framework. An early draft of some of the code's chapters indicated that the document would not likely be very clear about which of its provisions were restatements of existing law, which represented FCSM interpretation of the existing framework, and which were to be regarded as merely hortatory.

Throughout the course of preparation of the code, the FCSM gave the market every indication that instead of establishing general guidelines of behavior as most national codes do, the Russian code would be quite prescriptive concerning the conduct of shareholders' meetings, voting of shares, composition and activity of supervisory and management boards, financial accounting and audit, internal controls, and other aspects of corporate governance. The FCSM chairman made repeated public statements to the effect that the code would provide Russian companies with guidance on how the authorities would be enforcing the country's company and securities legislation. Although the chairman announced that the code drafting process was formally completed in December 2001, copies were not made available until two months later.

Prospects for Effectiveness and Enforcement

What is the significance of a "voluntary" code that is issued, for all intents and purposes, by the regulator? Should such a code be placed toward the right column of table 10-2—legal prescriptions to be enforced in the courts (or through administrative action)—or toward the left column? Or should it be regarded as a mix, with ex ante characteristics of legislation, but with enforcement left mostly to private means? The ultimate answer in any particular case probably depends largely on the approach that the regulator takes to enforcement and that the courts take to interpretation. Regulators that push-start the code-drafting *process* but not its content or enforcement (as in Mexico) may accelerate the emergence of appropriate benchmarks for good governance—if the process is inclusive. However, if the regulator construes its code as akin to a law or regulation, particularly in an environment where judicial oversight of executive action is weak (as in Russia), then the code may come to be regarded as law. This may have important implications for compliance. In such a case, as with most laws, companies may come to regard minimum formal compliance as the goal, with perhaps negative consequences for development of more voluntary initiatives and even for the development of public discourse on the topic of corporate governance.

Case 5: Disclosure Regime in Colombia

Both industrial economies and emerging markets have experienced a virtual flood of national codes of best practices and independently conceived "codes" or "governance policies" adopted by individual companies. A not uncommon evolution has been to follow the approach taken in connection with the United Kingdom's Combined Code: a national code of best practices is drawn up by a committee representing some mix of the business community, investors, intermediaries, and government. Public companies are then required by law, regulation, or custom to disclose the extent to which their practices differ from the code. Individual private companies may formally adopt the national code as their own or devise their own set of internal policies, which may go beyond the national code in some respects and not as far in others.

Corporate Governance Activism in Colombia: A Combined Response

Very recent experience in Colombia provides an interesting example of the interrelation between public policy efforts and voluntary initiatives with respect to corporate governance. Before the end of 2000, both the public and private sectors began to focus public attention on the shortcomings of the corporate governance regime and practices in Colombian corporations. In preparing a draft capital market law for presentation to Congress, the Superintendency of Securities insisted that the legislation had to address head-on perceived problems with enforceability of shareholders' rights, transparency, board practices, and director and controller liability.[31] At about the same time, the Confederation of Chambers of Commerce launched a corporate governance project to increase awareness by Colombian companies of market expectations, an effort joined by the Stock Exchange of Colombia, which was interested in preparing unlisted companies for the public markets, and the Pension Funds Association, representing the country's principal institutional investors.[32] A benchmark national code project is in the early stages, with participation from all major private sector associations, but so far no drafts have been circulated or discussed publicly.

Superintendency of Securities Resolution 275

On May 23, 2001, Colombia's Superintendency of Securities issued Resolution 275 pursuant to its power to prescribe certain rules for issuers whose securities (both debt and equity) are to be eligible for purchase by Colombia's pension funds.[33] Perhaps because of concern that too prescriptive a rule might be resisted in practice or challenged in the courts on the grounds that it went beyond the Superintendency's statutory authority, Resolution 275 does not mandate specific shareholder protection, board practice, transparency, or enforcement provisions to be included in company charters.[34] Rather, Article 3 states that in order for a company's securities to be eligible for purchase by pension funds, the company must have "specific mechanisms" in place to ensure protection of shareholder rights and equitable treatment of investors.[35] Articles 4, 5, and 6 then require

31. Interestingly, in anticipation of further private sector initiatives, the draft law included specific legal authorization for corporate governance rating agencies.

32. Confederation of Chambers of Commerce, Corporate Governance Project (www. confecamaras.org.co).

33. Law 100 of 1993, Article 100, sections 3 and 4.

34. Article 7 of the resolution does require that companies achieve at least a 20 percent public float in their shares within four years of the resolution's effectiveness.

35. Such specific mechanisms must at a minimum cover management control and oversight, conflicts of interest, identification and disclosure of risks, the election and role of the "revisor fiscal," special audits, internal controls, requirements for minorities to be able to call a shareholders' meeting, and enforcement.

that these mechanisms be disclosed in some specificity to investors through the preparation, approval, and publication of a company-specific code of good governance.

In essence, Resolution 275 establishes a minimum disclosure regime for corporate governance for all Colombian listed companies (in practice, companies without access to the pension fund market are unlikely to achieve much liquidity in their shares or issue new securities). The companies themselves (and the market) are to interpret what the term "specific mechanisms" means, although companies will be hard pressed to avoid putting in place at least minimal measures in each of the areas specifically covered by the resolution. The resolution also injects the potential for three levels of enforcement. Judicial enforcement of company charter provisions will presumably now extend to those provisions amended by, or construed in accordance with, the provisions of the new codes (which must be approved by the board of directors and presented to the shareholder meeting). The Superintendency itself will play a role in ensuring that companies comply, at least in form, with the resolution—a role that may eventually lead to the use of the Superintendency's disclosure oversight powers to influence the content of codes and companies' compliance with them. Finally, Resolution 275's references to enforcement seem to contemplate the adoption of arbitration mechanisms for enforcement of investor rights.

Two Poles: Company Responses to Resolution 275

Although most Colombian listed companies did not formally present their codes to shareholders until the 2002 annual general meetings season, many company boards approved codes in early 2002 and made them publicly available on the companies' websites, through the media, and directly to pension funds. A number of companies appear to have opted for technical compliance. They apparently view Resolution 275 as little more than a "box-ticking" exercise and recite their existing charter provisions and practices with appropriate cross-reference to the resolution. Investors now have a clearer and more concise statement of such companies' policies and practices, but the companies themselves have made no dramatic improvements in policies or practices.

Other companies seem to have embraced Resolution 275 as an opportunity to improve their governance practices and, just as important, to communicate their commitment to good governance to current and future investors. In a number of cases, company management (sometimes with the help of outside governance consultants) drafted codes organized more along the lines of the Principles of Corporate Governance set out by the Organization for Economic Cooperation and Development (OECD), and with specific shareholder protections and transparency requirements that go beyond the general requirements of both Resolution 275 and the OECD principles. Although the codes that have been made available to the public so far exhibit a diversity of style and content, some of them clearly represent a new contract between the company and its investors in key areas of corporate governance.[36]

TAKING THE BALL AND RUNNING WITH IT: INVERSURA. The code adopted by Inversura, an insurance holding company, is perhaps the most dramatic example of the use of a Resolution 275 code by a Colombian company as a voluntary contractual and privately enforceable mechanism of corporate governance.[37] The Inversura code is organized largely along the lines of the OECD Principles of Corporate Governance (with separate chapters for shareholders' rights and equitable treatment, the role and organization of the board, and stakeholders), with an additional chapter covering ethical treatment of clients, suppliers, and government officials.

In its code, Inversura's management binds the company to a number of important shareholder protections and board practices that go well beyond the minimum requirements of Colombian law and Resolution 275. Cumulative voting is authorized, and the company is prohibited from issuing multiple voting or nonvoting equity. At least four of the ten board directors must be independent of management and controllers. The board is required to have audit, compensation, and governance committees, with the audit committee dominated by independent directors. Perhaps most significantly, the code provides that disputes between shareholders and the company will be submitted to arbitration by an outside panel, in this case the Commercial Arbitration Panel of the Chamber of Commerce of Medellin.[38]

36. Given the circumstances surrounding their birth, it is probably fair to place all the Colombian codes issued in the aftermath of Resolution 275 in the center column of table 10-2, with those of the compliance-type more toward the right (Public) column, and those with shareholder-friendly and board professional codes closer to (if not actually in) the left (Private) column.

37. Inversura is not a public company, but devised its code in anticipation of its eventual entry into the public securities markets. Its code is probably the most shareholder-friendly and board professional that we have seen from a Colombian company, although others have taken similar approaches.

38. This last provision probably puts the Inversura code, and those of any companies in Colombia that approve similar provisions, solidly within the left column of table 10-2.

PROSPECTS. Colombian institutional investors report that Resolution 275 has had positive effects on transparency. All companies who want their shares to be actively traded must publicly explain charter provisions and company policies regarding shareholder protection, board practices, and disclosure. The resolution has helped move corporate governance up the public agenda and garnered a great deal of public attention. Indeed, Resolution 275 accelerated the very active collaboration of the Pension Funds Association, the Confederation of Chambers of Commerce, the Stock Exchange of Colombia, and the Superintendency of Securities in jointly promoting best practices in corporate governance throughout the country. This degree of formal voluntary cooperation among representatives of issuers, investors, intermediaries, and government is perhaps unique in an emerging market. It is probably fair to state that one reason cooperation has been possible is precisely the lack of prescription and the opening for voluntary initiative that Resolution 275 presented to the private sector.

It remains to be seen how well companies will actually comply with their new codes and how enforceable their obligation to do so will be in the longer term. The efforts that companies have expended to comply with Resolution 275 (preparation, board approval, and submission to the annual shareholder meetings) may have the unintended consequence of discouraging later amendment of the initial "compliance-type" codes produced by less progressive companies. It will be particularly interesting to follow the development of the initial codes over the next few years. Will there be competition among issuers to adopt more shareholder-friendly provisions? Or will a certain set of minimum standards be seen as sufficient? How active a role will the pension funds themselves play in pushing issuers to do more? Will the market permanently bifurcate into one set of issuers that take a progressive stance and another interested only in bare compliance? What will be the experience with enforcement? Will recourse to the courts remain the ultimate tool for enforcement, or will actions by the Superintendency of Securities and arbitration take on greater importance? And what will the contribution be to capital market development? It will require at least a few years before any firm conclusions can be drawn.

Case 6: Ratings

Corporate governance ratings can be characterized as an implicit private contract between a company and investors, partly enforceable through private means (the left-hand column of table 10-2). The company promises to maintain certain standards of shareholder treatment, board practices, and transparency, and the institution producing the rating determines whether the company is upholding its part of the bargain. (The rating may involve a combination of scoring the company on its charter and practices and evaluating its relative position within the market.) If the company fails to maintain its rating, the company is penalized by reputational damage and, in theory, a consequent decline in the market value of its securities.[39]

Certain corporate governance factors (notably the quality of transparency, internal controls, and auditing) are (or should be) important components of credit rating. But unlike the case of credit rating, a set of viable business models has yet to emerge for conducting ratings of corporate governance on a stand-alone basis. Instead, both developed and emerging markets are still in a "let a thousand flowers bloom" period. This is not the place to canvas corporate governance rating efforts worldwide. Rather, we merely note some of the more recent efforts with which we have become familiar in our work in emerging markets and provide some preliminary observations (and, perhaps, speculations).

Deriving Ratings from Voluntary Code Efforts

In some markets, sponsors of corporate governance codes have looked to ratings as a way of promoting adherence by companies to the provisions of such codes. Code sponsors tend to conduct rating exercises at their own expense and based on fully public information. The Stock Exchange of Thailand (SET) is collaborating on a ratings methodology linked to the Thai Code of Best Practices issued in 1999.[40] SET's strategy at this point is to produce a first round of confidential ratings and relative rankings of listed companies to be divulged on an individual basis.[41] Certain other markets in East Asia are currently debating whether to follow Thailand's example.

---

39. As in the case of credit ratings, failure to maintain a corporate governance rating could conceivably trigger default under loan agreements, or make the company ineligible (or less eligible) for investment from some sources (such as pension funds).

40. Stock Exchange of Thailand, "The SET Code of Best Practice for Directors of Listed Companies," 1998 (www.set.or.th).

41. Initially, each company will be told only its own score and its ranking relative to the other listed companies. A second round of ratings will be made public after companies have had a chance to react to the initial ratings by conforming their behavior more closely to the code.

The drafters of the first published corporate governance code in Poland, the Gdansk Institute for a Market Economy (GIME), a respected Solidarity-affiliated think tank, produced a set of ratings for a subset of companies on the Warsaw Stock Exchange earlier this year. GIME intends to publish a fuller set of ratings later in 2002. Ironically, GIME's code is not supported by the Warsaw Stock Exchange, which has initiated its own code-drafting effort, with the collaboration of market participants and issuers. WSE, or the Polish securities regulator, is expected to require that each listed company disclose on an annual basis the extent of its compliance with the WSE-sponsored code rather than with GIME's.

National shareholder rights groups have also undertaken rating initiatives. One of the best-known of these groups, Russia's Institute for Corporate Law and Corporate Governance (ICLG), initiated a ratings service in early 2001, after an extended period of consultation with local and international experts to arrive at an appropriate methodology. ICLG is a nonprofit institution that makes its basic company ratings public. However, it also maintains a fee-based subscription service for investors, which provides much more detailed information on the corporate governance of individual Russian listed companies. ICLG clients may also contract for in-depth corporate governance reviews of particular companies in which they are considering an investment. Although some ratings are conducted with the cooperation of the subject company (and some are clearly not!), ICLG receives fees solely from investors.

In Search of a Viable Business Plan

For-profit commercial services that rate corporate governance in emerging markets appear still to be searching for a business model that will prove viable in the long term. Some of these efforts are operated in close association with general equity research and analysis; examples include CLSA in Europe and Deutsche Bank Alex Brown, which recently launched a global effort based in New York. Standard & Poor's Corporate Governance Rating Service, although so far active in only a few markets, intends to operate as a stand-alone business. As in the case of its credit ratings business, S&P expects its customers to be mostly the rated issuers themselves; the results will usually be published, as is the case for its equity research services. S&P hopes that companies with good governance will use an S&P rating as a vehicle to attract investors. S&P also hopes that its reputation for careful analysis and integrity will make such ratings credible in the markets, despite the fact that the rating is paid for by the issuer.[42]

In contrast, a new company, Governance Metrics International, seeks to provide investors with corporate governance ratings for companies across entire markets both in developed and developing countries. Although its service has not yet been launched, Governance Metrics's sponsors have developed a methodology that incorporates evaluation of company-specific and country-specific data to produce scores that they contend can be compared between companies in the same market and across markets. The service is intended for institutional investors with large portfolios in a variety of markets. The scorings will not be made public. Nonetheless, were such a model to prove economically viable, it is likely that enough elements of the methodology would become well enough known in the markets that some companies would take steps to improve their governance in ways that would likely result in higher scores.

What Flowers Will Produce Fruit?

Each of the approaches to corporate governance ratings described above has its virtues and limitations. How effective any one system of ratings can be as a system of private contracting depends on a variety of factors, including quality of methodology, perceived impartiality, comparability of ratings between companies and across markets, and breadth and depth of coverage. Clearly at this stage some players in the market think there is a future for corporate governance ratings. A better indicator of the future of corporate governance ratings would be their inclusion in loan covenants, in legal investment rules (for example, pension funds), and in the formulation of market indexes.

Implications for Capital Markets and Corporate Governance

Although it is too soon to make definitive judgments about what works, several general observations can be made about the role of private and

---

42. The S&P business model may result in incomplete coverage of each market since only a handful of companies are likely to take on the expense of securing a rating in any given emerging market.

public legal rules in promoting the development of capital markets and enhancing the governance processes of corporations.

—Private legal rules are important.

—Different legal traditions have different balances in terms of the effectiveness of private or public legal rules.

—A predictor of effectiveness of any particular governance mechanism may be its form (private, public, or quasi public legal rule) and the legal tradition in which it operates.

—Public policymakers should anticipate and encourage private and quasi public legal rules that complement and reinforce public legal rules of corporate governance.

—The optimal content and mix of mechanisms in any market depends on a variety of factors. Some of the most effective mechanisms may be found in these intermediate forms, quasi public legal rules, enforceable by private means.

Private Legal Rules Are Important

The regulation of capital markets and governance of corporations have been very much an Anglo-American debate over the last several years; not surprisingly, the governance mechanisms that have proliferated recently find their origins in Anglo-American law and practice. Although the debate surged into public prominence ten to fifteen years ago, corporate governance has been the daily bread of lawyers and accountants for a hundred and fifty years. Over that time, fairly standardized private legal rules developed and were inserted into negotiated partnership contracts, shareholder agreements, and private company bylaws to balance and protect the ongoing economic interests of participants and, if necessary, provide for exit from the enterprise and for dispute resolution without recourse to the courts. In commercial matters the courts were a last, and undesirable, resort.

Particularly in the United States, these contractual governance mechanisms were transformed into legislation, or public legal rules, applicable often on a default basis to private or closed corporations.[43] Such mechanisms included cumulative voting to ensure board representation for minority shareholders, tag-along rights in cases of change of control, puts

43. That is, nonmandatory; consistent with their consensual, contractual origins, they would operate unless otherwise specified by contract or corporate constitution; see the Revised Model Business Corporations Act (1984).

and calls in various circumstances to provide an exit, valuation mechanisms to determine economic interests, disinterested voting techniques to deal with conflicts of interest, buyout or appraisal mechanisms triggered by certain events; arbitration and nonjudicial dispute resolution. Some of these contractual governance mechanisms were adapted and crossed over to the realm of public corporations; their outlines, for example, can be seen in the 1964 Williams Act in the United States, the source of U.S. tender offer rules.

These contractual governance mechanisms, or private legal rules, figure prominently, in different forms, in the Latin American case studies. Private legal rules, or contracts, are important in and of themselves, but they are also important in two other respects. Private legal rules generate market-tested solutions that can, over time, provide the basis for public legal rules of greater general applicability. And, as Partnoy observed, public legal rules may migrate back to the private sector in search of a more effective form of implementation.

Different Legal Traditions Have Different Balances

Even within the common law tradition, there are significant differences between the two main branches of the tradition, the English (now Commonwealth) tradition and the American. The American common law tradition branched off more than two hundred years ago at the time of the American Revolution and in some interesting respects has greater affinities with the continental European civil law tradition than with the English common law.

The American and English traditions share a heavy reliance on ex post public legal rules: the courts. As every common law student learns, for reasons reaching back to the English medieval court, there is no right without a remedy. This heritage persists and endows procedural elements of the law and the judicial system in common law countries with great importance.

In the English common law, the importance of judicial action continues to dominate even statutory law, the ex ante public legal rules. The English common law system demonstrates to this day a surprising aversion to ex ante public legal rules. Large and complex swathes of English law have never been legislated, but instead have developed through case law. Trust law, from which the concept of "fiduciary duties" derives, is a prime example; the fundamental principles remain judge-made. The American legal tradition shows no such aversion to the use of legislation; in this, its proclivities are more in line with continental European legal traditions. It is no accident that the United States has a uniform commercial code (or a bankruptcy code, or any number of other state and federal codes).

As for the continental European legal tradition (which serves as the basis for the legal systems of much of the non-Commonwealth world), its defining characteristic is the importance of written law, particularly as embodied in the great nineteenth century civil and commercial codes. If in the common law world there is no right without a remedy, then in the continental European tradition, there is no right without a written law. A second, related characteristic of continental European law, virtually unknown in the United Kingdom, is the hierarchy of law: with the constitution at the top, followed by codes, then statutes, and then regulation. Like a game of cards, a civil or commercial code provision will always trump a provision in specialized legislation.

Form and Legal Tradition May Predict Effectiveness of Governance

The same governance mechanism may take different forms and the form in which it will be most effective may be determined by the legal system in which it operates. La Porta and others are correct; legal families do matter. Pistor is correct; the manner in which a legal concept is introduced or transplanted matters. And the form that a rule takes matters. Some of the otherwise "inexplicable" failures of the waves of capital markets and corporate governance initiatives can be traced, in part, to a failure to recognize the importance of these observations.

Here are three concrete examples of some of the most popular governance mechanisms (voluntary codes, cumulative voting, and class actions) that may not survive transplantation to another legal system because they are an inappropriate form of rule.

VOLUNTARY CODES OF CORPORATE GOVERNANCE. Voluntary codes have been probably the most popular corporate governance mechanism of the 1990s, proliferating around the world irrespective of legal tradition, corporate ownership patterns, or level of development of the capital market. They trace their immediate origins to the Cadbury Report issued in the United Kingdom in 1992. Subsequently revised, it is currently known as the "Combined Code."[44]

---

44. Committee on Corporate Governance, "The Combined Code," London, 1998.

The most significant feature of the Combined Code is that it is not written law, but rather a "voluntary" code. Now, in the continental European tradition, a voluntary code is an oxymoron. A code, according to the *Oxford English Dictionary,* is a written body of laws so arranged as to avoid inconsistency and overlap.

So if it is not legislation, what kind of creature is the Combined Code? The *Oxford English Dictionary* gives a variant meaning of the word *code* as "a set of rules on any subject, *esp.,* the prevalent morality of a society or class; an individual's standard of moral behavior." A code in the United Kingdom, in other words, is one of the weakest forms of private legal rule, if that—no more than a set of guidelines without even the binding force of contract that a set of industry association rules might possess by virtue of contractual membership obligations.

The questions then become: why this choice of form, and how effective can the Combined Code possibly be. To deal with the second question first, reasonably effective in the United Kingdom, all other things being equal. Remember, this is a country that relies on unwritten parliamentary conventions in lieu of a written constitution and that has a respectable, if now fraying, tradition of the use of moral suasion as a regulatory technique. The Combined Code is not the only voluntary code; the U.K. City Code on Takeovers and Mergers is not written legislation, as many people think, but also a voluntary code.

As to why this choice of form, the answer is more elusive. It is not as though the United Kingdom were emulating an existing voluntary code. Several of the substantive recommendations of the Cadbury Report (the use of audit, remuneration, and nomination committees, for example) are taken directly from the listing rules of the New York Stock Exchange. These listing rules we would characterize as quasi public rules: their binding nature derives from contract, but their substance is subject to regulatory oversight of a public agency, the Securities and Exchange Commission. The use of audit committees by companies listed on the New York Stock Exchange is not a pious wish; it is a requirement.[45]

45. The origins of the audit committee requirement can be traced to 1975 and the new Canada Business Corporations Act, which made audit committees mandatory for federal public companies. The interesting twist here is that, although inspired in many respects by the U.S. Model Business Corporations Act, the Canadian legislation was also subject to the beneficent influences of the Quebec Civil Code (itself at that time based largely on the French Napoleonic Code), in terms of legislative approach and drafting techniques, and with its continental European bias in favor of written law, ex ante public legal rules. So, one rule, three different but related manifestations.

The question remains: why did the Cadbury Report take the form of a voluntary code? The usual virtues of private legal rules can be cited: flexibility, responsiveness, sensitivity to industry specific concerns and considerations. The peculiar British aversion to written legislation also shines through. Yet even subtler forces may be at work in influencing the form of these rules.

The Cadbury Report focused on the composition and responsibilities of boards of directors. The directors of English companies, like their American counterparts, are subject to fiduciary duties derived from very ancient legal concepts of trust law. Early nineteenth century English businesses, predating the various companies laws enacted over a period of several decades, were organized as trust vehicles with what would now be the role of the directors being assumed by trustees. Trustees were subject to strict fiduciary duties of fair dealing, impartiality, and accountability, which because of a quirk of medieval history, were enforced by a separate ecclesiastic court system, the Courts of Equity. Because fiduciary obligations are triggered whenever ownership of property is separated from its management, these duties carried over to boards of directors because of the separation of ownership and management of corporations resulting from the shareholder-director structure. Enforced by the Courts of Equity (literally, "the court of fairness"), fiduciary duties are suffused with moral righteousness. What more appropriate vehicle could there be than one establishing "a standard of moral behavior," a voluntary code.

While a voluntary corporate governance code might work well in the United Kingdom, how effective is it likely to be elsewhere? Would voluntary codes transplant to continental European law systems or to the complex hybrid legal systems of Asia (legal families matter). The saga of the new Russian code of corporate governance, described above, is indicative of the confusion and muddle (is it law/is it not) that can result from dropping a voluntary "code" into an essentially continental European system that does not recognize the concept.

Voluntary Codes and Corporate Governance

Here is where the capital markets may, ironically, be having a perverse effect on the governance of corporations. International capital markets have been so dominated in recent years by Anglo-American law and practices that the spillover into local laws and practices, regardless of legal tradition, has been inevitable, if uneven. Some of this spillover may be ineffective because the mechanisms introduced are incompatible with the underlying legal system (fiduciary duties, for example) or conflict with civil or commercial code provisions (in which case, the newer elements are simply trumped by the older code or even constitutional provisions that are higher in the legal hierarchy).

Other mechanisms, and voluntary codes may be among them, may in fact be detrimental to improving corporate governance. By deliberately introducing an ineffective, but internationally recognized, corporate governance delivery mechanism, political interests may divert attention from approaches that would in fact be more effective, but equally, more disruptive to the cozy corporate and political status quo.[46]

Given all this, how effective is the voluntary corporate governance code in Germany (referred to at the beginning of this article) likely to be? Perhaps the editorial writer at the *Financial Times* was justified in expressing skepticism about prospects for change. At the same time, as ineffective as such a mechanism may be domestically in raising levels of corporate governance, it may have an important signaling effect in the international markets. To the extent that corporations participate in the international capital markets (and that may be only a tiny fraction of a country's corporations), other more effective corporate governance mechanisms would be engaged (foreign listing rules, compliance with U.S. securities laws and regulations, for example). Where there is little interest in international capital markets, there may be little interest in triggering the signaling effect of introduction of a domestically inappropriate, but internationally recognized, corporate governance mechanism.[47]

CUMULATIVE VOTING AND CLASS ACTIONS. Second only in popularity to voluntary codes of corporate governance has been the introduction of cumulative voting mechanisms and class actions in emerging and transition economies. Both procedural mechanisms originated in the United States and are designed to enhance minority shareholder representation at the board level and to promote management accountability. Public

---

46. See Rajan and Zingales (2001) on the signifcance of political structures as impediments to development of financial systems.

47. Tunisia, for example, with a very "pure" French civil law tradition, has recently introduced a new corporate law designed to improve various aspects of governance, but has little interest in a voluntary code of good corporate governance or judicially oriented shareholder remedies (ex post public legal rules). As one Tunisian legal expert explained, the concepts are inconsistent with the legal tradition, which prefers structural adjustments to the corporate law (ex ante public legal rules). To the extent that Tunisian corporations have little interest in participating in international capital markets (nondomestic activity is more likely to be focused on France and Italy), there is little need to send a signal to the international capital markets.

investors in the capital markets can use these mechanisms to influence corporate governance directly.

Again, the primary virtue of such governance mechanisms is their signaling effect to international capital markets. U.S institutional investors recognize the signal: the domestic market has become aware of and taken up the corporate governance debate. As an effective means of promoting better governance in the corporate sector domestically, however, cumulative voting and class actions are likely to prove disappointing. They are the wrong form of legal rule for most of the legal systems in which they have been transplanted, and they may have been implemented by the wrong method, that is, imposed rather than adopted voluntarily.[48]

The introduction of cumulative voting and class actions in Korea provides an example. The Korean legal system has been strongly influenced by German models, via Japan; it demonstrates a preference for ex ante public legal rules, written law, and structural mechanisms within its corporate law that create, in theory, a balance of power among the constituents. Procedural rules and reliance on ex post public legal rules, judicial recourse, are limited in their effectiveness in Korea, as they are in the Japanese and German legal systems.

Cumulative voting originates in private legal rules (corporate charters or bylaws) as a procedural mechanism, and a cumbersome one at that, to allow minority shareholders to pool their votes and thus ensure some degree of representation on the board of directors in the absence of a statutory right to direct representation. It was a compensatory mechanism to override the principle of majority rule, whereby a majority shareholder could elect an entire slate to the board. In the United States, cumulative voting passed from private legal rule to statutory formulation, becoming a mandatory feature in many state laws. Over time, however, with a shift to more management-friendly corporate laws in the United States, cumulative voting started to slip back into the realm of private legal rules; it remained a feature of corporate statutes, but was made optional in most states. German corporate law, in contrast, has long provided a statutory mechanism to ensure that certain constituencies have direct representation on supervisory boards.

In the aftermath of the 1997 Asian financial crisis, Korea acted quickly to try to reestablish confidence in its markets; among other actions, waves of corporate law reforms were enacted, some at the suggestion of the inter-

---

48. Adoption of cumulative voting and class actions has often been highly recommended or otherwise "imposed" by international financial institutions. See Pistor (2000).

national financial institutions. Cumulative voting provisions were among the reforms, but they were of the weak, or quasi public, variety. They were not mandatory and could be bypassed in the corporate charter. Although Korean academics had raised questions about the effectiveness of these optional or default rules, international advisers assured them that this was the modern formulation in the United States. The result: Korean corporations moved quickly, and predictably, to neutralize cumulative voting rules by charter amendments, rendering the statutory but nonmandatory rules ineffective. Wrong rule; wrong form.

Class actions are even less likely to be effective in most transitional or emerging markets. At least with cumulative voting, there is a chance of developing rules that could work in the context of corporate legislation to which they were not native. Class actions, however, fall squarely into the category of ex post public legal rules, dependent upon the existence of an experienced judiciary, an extensive network of other procedural rules, an active body of litigation professionals, and a general populace with a litigious bent. They are procedural rules in the great common law tradition of "no right without a remedy." Class action provisions dropped into the corporate law of transitional or emerging market economies are virtually always dead on arrival. There are no procedural rules or institutions to support them.

Private and Quasi Public Rules Should Complement Legal Rules of Corporate Governance.

The relationship of private legal rules and public legal rules is not necessarily static (as in the Partnoy matrix) but rather a more fluid continuum with intermediate forms. In nearly every case we have studied, efforts to improve corporate governance in an emerging market involved simultaneous or sequential initiatives in the public and private sectors. Brazil's response to the challenge seems to be the most vibrant in this regard, with a great deal of activity at the public legislative level and among quasi public entities like BOVESPA, accompanied by positive examples of ad hoc contracting at the corporate level. In addition, the fully private Brazilian Institute of Corporate Governance has played an important part in the dialogue, developing a voluntary code of best practices and an active training program for companies and corporate directors.[49] As described earlier,

---

49. The Brazilian Institute of Corporate Governance's code of best practices and calendar of trainings can be found at www.ibgc.org.br.

public legal reforms anticipated private efforts like BOVESPA's Novo Mercado and reinforced the legal status of private arbitration.

Colombia probably represents the clearest example of public and private policymakers recognizing the value of complementary public and private legal efforts. Almost from the start, the quadrilateral of the securities regulator, the Confederation of Chambers of Commerce, the stock exchange, and the pension funds association engaged in active consultation and cross-support. There is little doubt that this collaboration accelerated corporate governance's visibility as a key issue in the development of capital markets in that country. The Superintendency of Securities' draft capital markets law anticipates the development of corporate governance rating services and shareholders' associations. The result in Colombia may in the end involve the same set of public and private mechanisms that have emerged in Brazil—legal reform, changes to listing rules, a national code of best practices, and more active ad hoc contracting. However the relative scope and importance of each element is likely to be different.

In the other countries covered by the cases, the interrelation of public and private law efforts has been less prominent (and less successful), but still evident. Active institutes of corporate governance with leadership from both issuers and investors have emerged in Argentina and Thailand. Two Russian groups established director institutes in 2001, one perhaps more closely associated with government, the other more distant. An aggressive private sector response to the corporate governance challenge has been less evident in Chile and Mexico, both countries that have historically had exceptional access to international capital markets. It is possible that this has encouraged complacency among blue chip companies with active ADR programs. The peculiarities of the pension fund regimes in each country may also have contributed to complacency. The rules governing Chile's long-established and large pension industry create incentives for funds to mimic each other's portfolios; Mexico's industry is still nascent and invested almost exclusively in government securities.

Although the legal reforms already undertaken do not seem to have yet produced the effects their supporters hoped they would, there appears to have been a qualitatively better early response from companies in countries like Brazil and Colombia where quasi public and private legal mechanisms were anticipated by policymakers. Accordingly, one of the tentative lessons of recent experience with capital market corporate governance efforts is that policymakers should anticipate complementary private sector initiatives and do what they can to make the public legal framework accommodate them. However, policymakers cannot be expected to be able to predict with any certainty the kinds of quasi public and private initiatives that will emerge or be successful. The cases we have studied yield no template of how best to fill in the spaces in table 10-2. Policymakers would thus be wise to retain the flexibility to reinforce effective quasi public and private law initiatives as they emerge.

It would also be surprising if even within a single market the effective combination of mechanisms remains static. While emerging markets are currently in a period of experimentation in this area, the landscape of mechanisms will undoubtedly change as some prove more effective and adaptable to new circumstances than others. Policymakers need to follow developments carefully and retain the flexibility to respond when necessary to encourage and accommodate effective private rulemaking.

Optimal Content and Mix of Mechanisms in Any Market Depend on Many Factors

The emerging markets we have studied differ importantly in ways that go beyond the existing legal framework and historical legal tradition. Key market characteristics that almost certainly affect the trajectory of public and private corporate governance initiatives and their prospects for effectiveness include:

—*Relative adequacy of existing practices.* Are the salient problems objectively determinable (such as a lack of tag-along rights, too many nonvoting shares, application of substandard accounting rules, uncertain rules for protection of minority shareholders in delistings) or more subtle (poor audit quality; lackluster boards; managers, boards, regulators, and investors in conflict)?

—*Number, size, and industry of public issuers.* Is there a clubby atmosphere among controlling shareholders and corporate executives, or are there multiple centers of entrepreneurialism, competing aggressively in the financial markets (and perhaps in the political sphere as well)?

—*Number, size, and nature of principal investor groups (institutional, pensions, international).* How well are the investors themselves governed? Are there distortions in their incentives or conflicts of interest that limit the extent to which they are profit-maximizers?

—*Resources of the enforcement mechanisms (courts, regulators, existing alternative dispute resolution).* What enforcement agents are realistically in the best position to see that contracts are performed, standards observed, and regulations complied with?

Markets are idiosyncratic. Indeed, the importance (and even the presence) of the economic actors involved in public debate over reforms and private initiatives is a function of the characteristics of the market. In the interest of encouraging further examination, analysis, and debate among scholars and practitioners, we offer some tentative observations:

—Standardized private rulemaking (and dispute resolution), such as the Novo Mercado, probably works best when there is general agreement on the set of objectively determinable deficiencies that exists within the legal framework and governance practices, and when there are a reasonably large number of issuers and investors (such that no single issuer or investor is likely to set the standards itself and negotiate directly).

—Private standard setting of any type (be it listing rules, voluntary codes, or rating criteria) is likely to have the most immediate impact on the IPO market, as such standards provide investors with a common negotiating position.[50]

—Ratings may be a more valuable tool for encouraging better practices where the number of issuers is relatively small, so that a larger portion of the market can actually be rated and thus provide good comparatives. However, a large enough set of investors (local pension funds or international investors) is likely required to make the exercise viable from a business perspective. This paradox leads us to suspect that devising a viable business model for ratings will be problematical for some time.

In this early stage it is hard to make any definitive conclusions about what specific guidance the recent experiments in public and private law in emerging markets can provide those interested in improving the corporate governance practices of companies in such markets. However, their early popularity and some encouraging results from the initiatives in Brazil, Colombia, Thailand, and elsewhere lead us to suspect that there is likely to be space in many emerging markets for intermediate forms of quasi public legal rules, enforceable by private means (such as special listing segments,

---

50. A prominent Latin American policymaker once told a group of foreign institutional investors after a meeting with local CEOs whose companies had already achieved access to the public securities markets, "one day this market will have companies with good governance, but it won't be the companies run by the guys you just met."

ratings, and other types of benchmarking, and investment disclosure regimes). Indeed, some of the most effective mechanisms may be found in these intermediate forms.

References

Bratton, William, and J. McCahery. 1999. "Comparative Corporate Governance and the Theory of the Firm: The Case against Global Cross-Reference." *Columbia Journal of Transnational Law* 38: 213–97.

Jordan, Cally. 2000a. "Experimentation in Capital Markets Regulation." International Organization of Securities Commissions, Montreal.

———. 2000b. "Law Matters: Corporate Governance Legal Reforms in Asia and Their Implications for the ECA Countries." Paper presented to the World Bank, September. Washington.

La Porta, Rafael, and others. 2000. "Investor Protection and Corporate Governance." *Journal of Financial Economics* (October–November).

Partnoy, Frank. 2002. "ISDA, NASD, CFMA, and SDNY: The Four Horsemen of Derivatives Regulation." *Brookings-Wharton Papers on Financial Services,* edited by Robert E. Litan and Richard Herring, pp. 213–52.

Pinto, A., and Douglas Branson. 1999. *Understanding Corporate Law.* New York: M. Bender.

Pistor, Katharina. 2000. "Patterns of Legal Change: Shareholder and Creditor Rights in Transition Economies." EBRD Working Paper 49/2000. European Bank for Reconstruction and Development.

Pistor, Katharina, and others. 2000. "Economic Development Legality and the Transplant Effect." Working Paper 410. The Davidson Institute.

Rajan, Raghuram G., and Luigi Zingales. 2001. "The Great Reversals: The Politics of Financial Development in the 20th Century." NBER Working Paper 8178. National Bureau of Economic Research, Cambridge, Mass.

GREGORIO IMPAVIDO 11

Governance Issues in Public Pension Fund Management: Preliminary Considerations

W ORLD LABOR FORCE coverage by publicly managed pension schemes is estimated at approximately 800 million, or roughly one-third of the total world labor force. Of this 800 million, about 49 percent are covered by mandatory, publicly managed defined-benefit, pay-as-you-go plans, while 32 percent are covered by partially funded schemes. The rest of the work force is covered by a mix of public defined-benefit and private defined-contribution plans. Only 10–15 percent are covered by public and/or private defined-contribution schemes.[1] In mature economies with flat demographic pyramids (that is, with a larger ratio of older to younger residents) such as Italy, Poland, and Slovenia, universal coverage is the norm, and public pension spending can reach 15 percent of gross domestic product (GDP), while gross implicit pension debt can be as high as 400 percent of GDP. Aging of the population is bound to increase pressure on countries to reform their pension systems, and so far, at least twenty-five countries have adopted reforms and many others are in the process of formulating serious reform proposals. Table 11-1 compares the

The author is grateful to Bob Litan, Olivia Mitchell, Alberto Roque Musalem, Robert Palacios, and Michael Pomerleano for useful comments. This paper reflects the views of its author, not necessarily those of the affiliated institution. The author is of course responsible for any errors.
    1. Palacios and Pallares (2000).

Table 11-1. *Pension Fund Reserves in Select Countries*

Partially funded defined benefit[a]		*Centrally managed defined contribution*[b] *(provident funds)*		*Privately managed defined contribution*	
Country	*Percent of GDP*	*Country*	*Percent of GDP*	*Country*	*Percent of GDP*
Egypt	33.1	Malaysia	55.7	Switzerland	117.0
Sweden	32.0	Singapore	55.6	Netherlands	87.3
Japan	25.0	Sri Lanka	15.2	United Kingdom	74.7
Jordan	16.9	Kenya	12.1	Australia	61.0
Mauritius	13.1	Tanzania	9.4	Chile	45.0
Philippines	11.2	Swaziland	6.6	Denmark	23.9
Gambia	11.1	India	4.5	Argentina	3.0
Canada	11.0	Nepal	4.0	Colombia	2.9
Belize	10.5	Indonesia	2.8	Peru	2.1
Ghana	9.4	Brunei	2.4	Poland	1.1
Morocco	8.7	Zambia	0.7	Uruguay	1.0
Switzerland	7.1	Uganda	0.6	Bolivia	1.0
Korea	7.0			Mexico	0.5
Tunisia	6.9			Kazakhstan	0.5
Swaziland	6.6			Hungary	0.4
Jamaica	5.7			El Salvador	0.3
Costa Rica	5.4			Croatia	0.0
United States	5.0			Sweden	0.0
Yemen	4.0			Hong Kong	0.0
Honduras	3.5				
Senegal	1.6				
Ethiopia	1.4				
Algeria	1.2				
Chad	0.5				
Namibia	0.4				
Paraguay	0.4				

Source: Palacios and Pallares (2000).
a. Partially funded means with not enough assets to meet liabilities according to actuarial calculations.
b. Centrally managed means managed by one unique asset manager within the scheme.

ratio of reserves to GDP for publicly managed pension funds with that of privately managed funds.

The issue of management is relevant to some sixty-two public pension plans.[2] The investment performance of these schemes has been mixed, to say the least, with many funds obtaining negative real rates of return over

2. Palacios (2001).

an extended period of time. Investment performance is obviously of central importance if accumulated assets are used to meet pension obligations. This is especially true in developing countries, where these schemes represent a large share of retirement income for covered workers.[3]

Governance of public pension funds should also be relevant to a wider and diversified audience:

—Pension fund managers, to the extent that their remuneration is linked to performance, are likely to be interested in understanding the variables that influence the return on their portfolios.

—Participants in public pension schemes are likely to be interested in knowing the risks to which they are exposed.

—Policymakers and pension reformers are likely to be interested in addressing the design of pension schemes, governance issues, and performance as well as in improving the performance of public pension funds as part of their effort to instill financial and fiscal discipline throughout the economy.

—Academicians are likely to be interested in analyzing the aspects of governance in the private sector that are transferable to public schemes.

This paper begins with evidence from the literature linking the performance of public pension funds with their governance. It then focuses on governance issues of the pension governing body, indicates the need to distinguish between the governance of public and private pension funds, and presents governance practices in select countries. Finally, it draws some conclusions and highlights some lines for future research.

Governance and Performance

A relatively large body of literature underlines the importance of governance for the performance of public pension funds.[4] For instance, Iglesias and Palacios observe, "The worst returns are produced by publicly managed

3. From a social policy point of view, one could argue that the issue of fund management is not a high priority in countries (African countries, for instance) where the covered labor force is, on average, only 10 percent of the total labor force. It could also be argued, however, that if existing governance structures are not improved, the more important problem of poverty during the retirement age will be difficult to address.

4. The text refers to four main pieces of work: Ambachtseer (2001) focusing also on private pension governance, Iglesias and Palacios (2000), Mitchell and Hsin (1997), and Useem and Mitchell (2000). Further references can be found in Mitchell (2000b), included in the reference list at the end of this chapter.

Figure 11-1. *Correlation between Average Real Return on Public Pension Assets and a Governance Index*

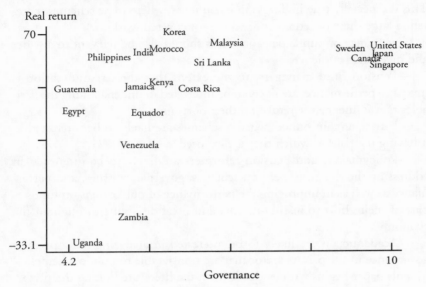

Source: Iglesias and Palacios (2000).

pension funds in countries with poor governance records."[5] Figure 11-1 illustrates this statement by plotting the average real return on public pension assets for twenty developing and developed countries against a governance index.[6] The relationship is highly nonlinear, with rapidly diminishing (but positive) marginal returns to governance levels. In other words, countries like Uganda could improve the rate of return on public pension assets considerably by making very limited improvements in governance practices.[7] For many of these countries, investment returns on public pension funds are often below bank deposit rates and almost always below the growth of per capita income.

Factual evidence also links this poor performance to undue political interference in the investment decision of public funds. Governments have often imposed on financial intermediaries explicit social and developmen-

5. Iglesias and Palacios (2000, p. 35).
6. See Iglesias and Palacios (2000) for details.
7. Notice, however, that the relationship presented does not imply causality, just correlation.

tal objectives that undermine their financial viability. When explicit mandates are absent, governments have often relied on their powers of coercion to ensure sufficient demand for their debt to finance public expenditure or demand for other securities to finance well-connected entrepreneurs and public enterprises. Sometimes regulations require commercial banks to meet reserve and liquidity requirements by holding government paper. Other times, and in both developing and developed countries, commercial banks, insurance companies, and pension funds, as well as social security funds, are required to invest in government bonds—sometimes in specially issued nonmarketable instruments with substantially below-market yields. Many countries impose a minimum quantitative floor for public pension fund assets to be invested in government paper, and politicians are often allowed to have a say in the investment policy of social security funds.[8] Obviously, these policies can greatly reduce the credibility of the macroeconomic stance in countries with a poor record of economic discipline.

Even countries without explicit social mandates for pension funds often limit investment of those assets abroad, with the implicit rationale that local savings should be used to develop the local economy. Is localization of investments justified? Should exchange controls be applied to contractual savings? Fontaine surveys the Chilean experience with foreign investment of pension funds and concludes that there are no good macroeconomic reasons to treat international investment of pension funds differently than

---

8. In the Philippines, the Social Security System (SSS) and the Government Service Insurance System (GSIS) are "offered" tax-free government bonds that remain tax free to the extent that they are not subsequently traded, effectively forcing the two social security institutions to hold these assets until maturity. In Singapore, the Central Provident Fund is required to invest a large share of its assets in nonmarketable government securities; and only until recently this share was 100 percent. In the Philippines, the SSS and the GSIS were often instructed to provide direct lending to industries to which commercial banks refused to lend. In Mexico as well as in the Philippines, a large share of pension contributions have to be invested in housing, INFONAVIT and Pag-IBIG, respectively. The real returns on the assets of these "specialized" institutions have been rather disappointing (Impavido, Musalem, and Vittas 2001). Also, as discussed in Mitchell (2001a), the Malaysian Employee Provident Fund was used to keep insurers solvent, and the Korean Pension Fund was forced to lend two-thirds of its assets to the Ministry of Finance for "social" purposes. The Korean investment companies (mutual funds) have received loans from the Central Bank with the mandate that they support the stock market. Many social security plans in Africa are required to invest in mortgage loans and often asked to be direct developers. The Alaskan Retirement System lost around $80 million from its housing investments (mortgages and real estate) when the price of oil fell and with it the value of properties and the ability of borrowers to repay the loans. In the second half of the 1990s, the National Social Security Fund of Tanzania (NSSF) was investing in personal loans and in huge residential and commercial buildings despite financial guidelines from the central bank requiring that social security funds be used to purchase liquid assets.

local investment.[9] In other words, foreign investment of pension funds should be subject to the same (*mutatis mutandis*) rules of diversification applied to domestic investments. Indeed, policymakers should allow foreign investment of public pension schemes in order to diversify away from local risks. Countries that need to impose foreign investment restrictions on the stock of contractual savings assets (public or private) because of balance of payments concerns are countries that have an unstable macroeconomic environment. These countries need to give priority to economic stabilization while developing pension funds.

In a work of a different flavor (and focusing on private pension funds), Ambachtseer also finds that organizational performance is strongly correlated with governance indicators. Fifty private pension fund executives were asked to list the most important "drivers" of organizational performance (table 11-2). Six out of the eleven performance drivers identified are statistically significant at the 5 percent level and belong to the category of good governance.[10]

Useem and Mitchell use two surveys of U.S. state and local pension systems carried out in 1992 and 1993 to show that the way public pensions are governed has an impact on investment strategies and how assets are invested.[11] This, in turn, directly affects fund performance. Governance variables include indicators that are related to the structure of public pension governing bodies as well as rules that guide their oversight of fund assets. These variables are regulatory restrictions on international investments, independent performance evaluation, board composition and size, and responsibility of the board for setting investment policies and for choosing investments. Variables related to the investment strategies used are step dummies for the use of tactical investment, external fund management and some internal fund management, and the share of equities in total asset portfolios.

Table 11-3 shows that, in general, governance variables explain a large share of the variability of the investment strategy variables. However, not all governance indicators are always individually significant. Restrictions on international investment are highly significant in explaining whether funds

---

9. Fontaine (1997). Only in March 1990 were pension funds allowed to invest abroad, almost ten years after the pension reform. At that time regulation allowed foreign investment of up to 3 percent of the portfolio in fixed-income securities issued by low-risk countries and banks. In 1995 investment in foreign shares was allowed with a limit of 12 percent of the total portfolio.

10. Ambachtseer (2001).

11. Useem and Mitchell (2000).

Table 11-2. *Drivers of Organizational Performance*

Governance

My governing fiduciaries have good mechanisms to understand and communicate with plan stakeholders.[a]

My governing fiduciaries do a good job of balancing overcontrol and undercontrol.

Our fund has an effective process for selecting, developing, and terminating its governing fiduciaries.

My governing fiduciaries and related committees use their time efficiently (focused and do not waste time).

There is a high level of trust between my governing fiduciaries and the pension investment team.

There is a clear allocation of responsibilities and accountabilities for fund decisions between the governing fiduciaries and the pension investment team.

Planning and management

I can describe our vision of where we should be in the future.

I can describe our fund's strategic positioning (how we provide better value to stakeholders than alternatives).

I can describe our resource plan (obtaining and optimally utilizing the required human, financial, and information technology resources).

Developing our asset mix required considerable effort on the part of myself and the governing fiduciaries, and it reflects our best thinking.

Operations

My organization uses its time efficiently (well focused and does not waste time).

Source: Ambachtseer (2001).

a. Governing fiduciaries are members of the governing body.

adopt tactical investment strategies or invest a higher share of assets in stocks. Nevertheless, governance indicators are not significant in explaining the decision of pension funds to use internal, external, or a combination of internal and external asset managers. Independent performance evaluation is highly significant at explaining all of the investment strategy variables except the decision to outsource all asset management. Finally, the number of governors appears to be associated with a larger share of asset portfolios in stocks, but the presence of plan members' representatives has little significant impact on any of the investment strategies.

Useem and Hess obtain similar results using surveys of U.S. state and local retirement systems conducted during the 1990s.[12] They identify seven

---

12. Useem and Hess (2001).

Table 11-3. *Impact of Governance on Public Pension Investment Strategies*

Explanatory variables: Governance policy	Tactical investment	Equities as percentage of total	All external management	Some international management
Investment restrictions	−1.44 (0.46)**	−7.59 (2.34)**	−0.41 − (0.39)	−0.24 (0.33)
Independent performance evaluation	−1.60 (0.38)**	14.08 (2.34)**	0.55 (0.41)	1.48 (0.38)**
Board purview				
Board sets asset allocation	1.88 (0.40)**	3.97 (2.64)	0.75 (0.42)	−0.41 (0.37)
Board is responsible for investment	−0.12 (0.37)**	1.59 (2.15)	−0.11 (0.36)	0.05 (0.30)
Board composition and size				
Number of governors	−0.54 (0.57)	0.63 (0.31)*	−0.11 (0.05)*	0.09 (0.04)*
Plan participants as a percentage of governors	0.14 (0.66)	−4.28 (3.97)*	−1.23 (0.70)*	0.67 (0.58)*
R^2 or log-likelihood/ concordant pairs	209/82.2 percent**	0.226**	219/76.7 percent*	293/62.1**

Source: Useem and Mitchell (2000).

Note: ** $p < 0.01$, * $p < 0.05$. Regressions are based on 254, 243, 215, and 235 retirement systems, respectively; linear regression for equities is as a percentage of total; logistic regression is for other variables. Standard errors are in parentheses.

determinants of governance that are consistently associated with seven key investment strategies, as shown in table 11-4.

Although governance indicators have a direct impact on investment strategies, Useem and Mitchell do not find a direct impact on performance, measured as the annual rate of return on assets one year later and shown in table 11-5. Only investment strategy variables are found to explain a relatively large variability of fund performance, and these results do not change when controls for investment risk and portfolio size are taken into consideration (regression 2).

Indeed, two of the investment strategy variables—equity and international investing—are associated with higher fund performance the following year, with a coefficient that is significantly different from zero at less

Table 11-4. *The Most Important Single Governance Determinant of Key Investment Strategies*

Investment strategy	Most important governance determinant
Allocation of funds into equities	Independent performance evaluation
Placement of funds in equity indexes	Board responsible for investments
Long-term investing	Board responsible for setting asset allocations
Tactical investing	Governors elected by plan participants and investment restrictions
External management portfolio	Number of governors
At least some international investing	Independent performance evaluation
Investor activism	Governors elected by plan participants
Social limiting	None
Economic targeting	None

Source: Useem and Hess (2001).

than 1 percent level of significance.[13] From this analysis, the authors conclude that governance of public pension funds affects performance only indirectly by determining key investment strategies; these strategies are associated, in turn, with higher performance.

Finally, Mitchell and Hsin use a survey of 201 U.S. pension systems conducted in 1991, covering 269 separate retirement plans, to link governance and information disclosure variables with funding levels or with practices and performance.[14] The governance and information disclosure indicators used are pension board composition, board management practices, and reporting requirements and assumptions. As shown in table 11-6, they find that composition of public pension boards is significantly associated with performance.[15] They explain the negative association by the fact that these representatives make more conservative investment decisions than do representatives of other boards. However, they do not conclude that retiree

13. A nonquantified selection bias may partly explain the results obtained. Useem and Mitchell (2000) note that data on all variables were available for only half of the plans surveyed. Plans providing full information were found to have the same average performance but higher shares of equities and foreign assets in their portfolios than plans providing only partial information.

14. Mitchell and Hsin (1997).

15. This is contrary to the findings of Useem and Mitchell (2000), who find that representation of plan participants is not significantly correlated with performance, while Mitchell and Hsin (1997) find that participation of retirees on public pension boards is negatively correlated with performance.

Table 11-5. *Impact of Governance on Public Pension Fund Performance*

Explanatory variable	Dependent variable: Rate of return on assets	
	(1)	*(2)*
Governance policies		
Investment restrictions	−0.23 (0.59)	−0.16 (0.59)
Independent performance evaluation	0.81 (0.67)	0.43 (0.72)
Board purview		
Board sets asset allocations	−0.72 (0.71)	−0.48 (0.76)
Board is responsible for investments	0.18 (0.51)	0.43 (0.55)
Board composition/size		
Number of governors	−0.08 (0.06)	−0.15 (0.07)*
Share of plan participants	−1.16 (10.6)	−1.16 (1.07)*
Investment strategies		
Tactical investing of assets	1.69 (0.65)**	1.25 (0.69)**
Equities as a percentage of total assets	0.07 (0.02)**	0.07 (0.22)**
External management of all assets	0.58 (0.58)**	0.71 (0.58)**
International investment of some assets	2.17 (0.52)**	1.87 (0.56)**
Other controls		
Investment risk[a]		0.05 (0.09)
System assets (ln)		0.41 (0.30)
Multiple R^2	0.38**	0.41**

Source: Useem and Mitchell (2000).

Note: ** $p < 0.01$, * $p < 0.05$. Regression is based on 104 retirement systems; linear regression is for return on assets. Standard errors are in parentheses.

a. Standard deviation of annual return on assets for 1988–92.

participation on pension boards is to be avoided or discouraged. Finally, they find that the presence of independent evaluation is not correlated with performance.[16] This last result is probably due to the presence of the reporting frequency variable, which tends to offset the expected positive impact of independent performance evaluation.[17]

In summary, governance has a significant impact on public pension performance. The literature surveyed finds that inconsistent performance is

16. This finding, too, is contrary to Useem and Mitchell (2000).

17. The regulatory requirement to invest locally in-state (INSTATE) has a significantly negative impact on 1990 performance. Localization of investments is one of the practices often used in developing countries to "develop" the local economy; this is often thought to explain poor performance because it sacrifices appropriate diversification of the portfolio.

Table 11-6. *Determinants of Public Pension Fund Investment Returns*

Explanatory variable	Dependent variable	
	1990 return	Five-year average return
Pension board composition		
BDELAC	–0.01 (0.02)	–0.02 (0.01)
BDELRT	–0.17 (0.07)**	–0.002 (0.05)
Pension management practices		
ADINVST	–0.34 (0.89)	–1.24 (0.58)**
INVINHS	0.80 (1.36)	0.60 (0.92)
TOP10MG	–0.49 (1.32)	–0.32 (0.86)
TOP10*EXT	–0.08 (1.78)	1.03 (1.17)
Pension investment practices		
INSTATE	–0.08 (0.04)*	–0.02 (0.02)
PRUDMAN	0.83 (1.20)	0.33 (0.84)
STKMAX	–0.03 (1.18)	0.57 (0.86)
Pension reporting practices		
INDINVPF	–1.16 (1.00)	–0.57 (0.68)
FREQVAL	0.70 (0.54)	0.13 (0.56)
R^2	11.3	12.4
Number	158	132

Source: Mitchell and Hsin (1997).
Note: ** $p < 0.01$, * $p < 0.05$.
Both models also include a constant term as well as controls for plan type, plan size, and the fraction of the plan assets held in bonds and stock. Standard errors are in parentheses. Mitchell and Hsin (1997) give the following definitions of variables used: BDELAC, fraction of pension boards elected by active employees (percent); BDELRT, fraction of pension boards elected by retired employees (percent); ADINVST, administrative costs charged to pension investment income; INVINHS, investment staff of pension portfolio partly (or fully) managed in-house; TOP10MG, some investments handled by top-ten money managers; TOP10*EXT, plan investments handled exclusively by top-ten money managers; INSTATE, fraction of pension investment that must be directed in-state; PRUDMAN, pension board required to act according to "prudent man" rule; STKMAX, maximum limitation on assets in the pension portfolio; INDINVPF, use of independent investment performance evaluations; and FREQVAL, frequency of independent investment performance evaluations.

associated with indicators of poor governance. However, a direct link between governance and investment performance cannot be established with U.S. data, although governance indirectly affects performance by determining key investment strategies. A few results are contradictory, such as the impact of the size and composition of the board. Other results are more clear-cut, such as the fact that independent performance evaluation is associated with better investment policies and that frequent performance evaluation is not significantly associated with performance. Evidence for developing countries—some empirical, most factual—clearly indicates that the poor governance (that is, the inability to isolate fund management from political risk) is an important determinant of poor performance. Further research is clearly needed, especially to identify in developing countries those governance elements or mechanisms that are necessary to improve public pension fund management and hence performance.

Toward a Definition of Governance Standards for Public Pension Funds

This section makes a preliminary attempt to define the elements of good governance necessary for public pension schemes. The discussion is based on the empirical and factual evidence presented earlier as well as on key concepts imported from the literature on governance of private pension funds. Limitations of this approach are also highlighted.

The term *governance* refers to the manner in which an institution is governed and regulated, its method of management, or its system of regulations. In the context of pension funds (public or private), governance assumes a more specific connotation; it refers to the manner in which authority or power is exercised to fulfill duties and obligations to a constituency or stakeholders. With respect to a public pension fund, authority is vested in the administrator (for example, the governing body or the state), and the constituency consists of the beneficiaries. Duties and obligations should be specified by law or in the trust agreement, plan document, and other related documents (custodial, investment management, and insurance contracts). In summary, good governance is a function of the responsibilities and accountabilities of key groups in the organization, as well as of the presence of qualified and trustworthy staff to discharge those responsibilities.

This definition makes governance endogenous and raises several major issues: the definition of a public pension plan, the definition of stakeholders in public pension plans to which key groups are accountable, the definition of the manner in which the governing body is elected and exercises its power, the definition of responsibilities of the governing body, and the way in which the governing body is made accountable. These issues are addressed in the remainder of this section.[18]

18. See Impavido (2002) for a more detailed analysis of governance practices in select countries.

What Is a Public Pension Plan?

The issue of what makes a pension plan "public" is rather complicated. A unique metric that classifies all existing pension funds into public or private is difficult to devise. This paper categorizes public pension funds as funds with publicly centralized management and, hence, with governments as important stakeholders.[19]

Despite the obvious difficulty of defining what is public in pension plans, their raison d'être is identical to that of private pension plans: that is, the provision of an affordable and sustainable retirement income.[20] For this to be achieved, the plan should have no other objectives. The objective or mission should be clearly stated to facilitate the adoption of measurable goals against which the performance of the plan and of its governors and administrator can be measured. It should not include social and developmental objectives, as is often the case in developing countries.

The Canadian legislated requirements draw a sharp distinction between the investment mandate of the Canada Pension Plan Investment Board (CPPIB) and that of public funds in many other nations. For example, unlike pension funds in Japan, Korea, and the United States, the CPPIB is required to make funds available to the government only if it is decided that a bond portfolio is to be built, and the CPPIB has not yet built one. Furthermore, the CPPIB is not required to make loans to state-owned firms, it is not required to make social investments, and it is not used to implement economic development policy, as occurs in many other nations, including Iran, Japan, and Sweden.[21]

The Norwegian Government Petroleum Fund, although strictly speaking not a public pension plan, invests abroad because of diversification

---

19. We recognize that the categorization of public versus private pension funds can be controversial. This issue warrants a more detailed analysis than is possible here.

20. Holzmann and others (2002) advocate that retirement income should be adequate, affordable, sustainable, and diversified. Adequate refers to both the absolute level of income (preventing old-age poverty) as well as the relative level of income (replacing life-time earnings enough to smooth lifetime consumption). Affordable refers to the financing capacity of individuals and the society. Sustainable refers to the current and future financial viability of different plans. Diversified refers to the source of financing of old-age income: unfunded through contributions of the working population and funded through the returns on assets and their divestment from a diversified financial portfolio. These characteristics apply to both the retirement income system as a whole and to individual plans or schemes. Indeed, affordability and sustainability should be attained at the level of individual plans, while adequacy and diversification should be attained at the level of the retirement income system as a whole.

21. MacNaughton (2001).

concerns.[22] The fund invests 100 percent of assets abroad in an attempt to diversify national wealth away from petroleum. Indeed, the rationale behind the diversification is multifaceted: the fund should not constitute a second budget for the government; and petroleum activity already yields substantial foreign currency, forcing appreciation of the local currency. Furthermore, if foreign reserves were not allowed to accumulate, a real appreciation of the currency would take place, and production input would be encouraged to move away from less productive sectors of the economy. Finally, eventual depreciation following real appreciation would result in misallocation of resources, as predicted in what is known as Dutch disease.

The Namibian Government Institution Pension Fund (GIPF) has no social mandate to invest in targeted industries, and investment regulation aims to achieve liquidity and diversification of risk. Foreign investment is allowed. However, at least 35 percent of pension fund assets must be invested within the borders of Namibia, while foreign investment is restricted to a maximum of 15 percent of total assets. This excludes South Africa, where, at present, the GIPF invests 55 percent of its assets.

In Ghana, the Social Security and National Insurance Trust (SSNIT) also aims to maintain the financial viability of the plan. Investment managers are required to invest in safe assets with adequate yield and liquidity. Rules for asset diversification are followed to ensure that an optimal funding ratio is maintained and that long-term rates of return are secured for the fund. However, the fiduciary responsibility of governors toward beneficiaries is compromised because the SSNIT investment policy includes a social and developmental mandate in housing finance, student loans, and industrial estates. Although returns on these assets were not reported, Dei comments that the student loan scheme has become a burden for the SSNIT.[23] Loans are provided to poor students at a subsidized interest rate up to a university education. Loans are repaid through social security contributions, and repayment can take up to ten years. The number of students has increased considerably, but postgraduate unemployment has also increased. Since loans are indexed to inflation, their value also has increased considerably. Finally, the government delays the payment of interest subsidy to the SSNIT.

---

22. The fund was established by law in 1990. The inflow to the fund is represented by the annual surplus of the central government account. The fund is not formally a pension fund, but the government uses it to manage the budget surplus or deficit.

23. Dei (2001).

A similar judgment can be made for the National Pension Fund (NPF) of Korea and the Indian Employee Provident Fund (EPF). The objectives of the Korean NPF are to achieve long-term financial stability, contribute to economic and social development, and increase beneficiaries' welfare.[24] Until recently, the NPF implemented this policy by lending to the government at nonmarket rates, purchasing nontradable government bonds, and imposing minimum deposit requirements. The Indian EPF has no formal social mandate, but according to Rao, the fund seeks to ensure the complete safety of employees' funds and confidence in the system, channel funds to the government sector, and pay a reasonable return to the employee.[25] Since the EPF is a multipurpose fund, it also lends to plan participants for housing purposes.

Finally, the Central Provident Fund (CPF) of Singapore also has many objectives besides retirement. It administers schemes covering housing, medical savings accounts, and cursory education and permits extensive pre-retirement withdrawals for investment in real estate, financial assets, and even gold and commodities. Several accounts are set up for specific needs. The housing account, for example, can be used to purchase a house, which is the predominant expense for most members.[26] A medical account is used to pay for hospital services, certain outpatient services, and catastrophic health insurance premiums, which cover between 20 and 40 percent of the average hospital bill.

Who Are Public Pension Stakeholders?

The understanding of who are public pension stakeholders allows us to identify to whom the authority charged with administering the system should be accountable. The key stakeholders in any pension system are the participants: that is, current contributors. In addition, other stakeholders can have vested interests in the design and operation of the system, such as

---

24. Han (2001).

25. Rao (2001). Despite the absence of an explicit social mandate, the allowance of drawdowns on assets makes it seem that providing adequate return to all employees is not an official objective. The EPF permits withdrawals for specific purposes, such as housing, major medical expenses, children's education, and marriage. Many contributors make use of this ability. In fact, almost everyone who buys a house uses the provident fund to do so. The same is true in Singapore.

26. Thirty percent of contributions go toward funding this account.

retirees (especially when the system is unfunded and provides insurance for longevity risk) as well as other beneficiaries, such as survivors and dependents. Since participants are the central stakeholders of all pension systems, Western trust law holds that a pension plan must be managed solely in their best interests.[27]

The government is a legitimate stakeholder in any public pension system. Indeed, public pensions can be compared with other public goods, and the government, as plan sponsor, has a keen interest in how the plan works, how expensive it is to run, and how the pension assets perform (to the extent the plan is funded). Indeed, public pension obligations are contingent liabilities of the government. Other public agencies could have vested interests in the design and operation of the system, depending on the role that existing regulations give to these agencies. These could include, for instance, legislative bodies and regulators, tax authorities, investment managers, and other entities charged with budgeting in the public domain.[28]

Finally, taxpayers and general lenders to governments are natural stakeholders of any public pension system. Taxpayers and lenders are the ultimate source of financing used to make good on underfunded promises of a pension in publicly managed defined-benefit, pay-as-you-go plans.

Key Groups: The Governing Body

Governance elements should apply to all key groups in a pension plan: the governing body, management, and junior staff.[29] The governing body is the entity with the highest level of governance authority as defined by the terms of the law or other regulations. In Western common law, it usually takes the name of board of directors or board of trustees, while in French-speaking countries, it takes the name of *conseil d'administration*. Its identification should be independent of any nominal label, but strictly related to its role and responsibilities.

STRUCTURE AND QUALIFICATIONS. In many countries the governing bodies of public pension funds are populated with representatives of inter-

27. This holds for private sector employees under the U.S. Employment Retirement Income Security Act and also applies in the United Kingdom.

28. In the United States, for instance, the Internal Revenue Service plays a key role in determining what pension contributions may be set aside on a pretax basis and in allowing the inside buildup to be similarly tax free until the payout phase (Mitchell 2001a).

29. Indeed, the importance of these three groups is underlined in Ambachtseer and Ezra (1998), who define them as governing, management, and operational fiduciaries.

ested parties. These parties usually include the government as plan sponsor or employer, some form of representation of private sector employers, and some form of representation (usually unions) of contributors. For instance, the governing body of the Korea National Pension Fund follows this model. The Fund Operating Committee—the governing body—is composed of twelve representatives of the insured and seven government representatives.[30] However, two specialists are also on the board: the presidents of the Korean Development Institute and the Korean Institute for Health and Social Affairs.[31]

Another example of a public pension plan with a representative board is the Central Provident Fund of Singapore. The CPF board is composed of twelve members with representation from the government, employers, employees, and professionals. A key challenge for the CPF is to ensure that competent and independent governors are appointed to the board.[32] As of today, no piece of legislation requires the appointment of qualified and independent governors who operate in a prudent manner in the sole interests of beneficiaries.

The Namibian governing body is composed of nine members, three appointed by the office of the prime minister, three appointed by recognized labor unions, and three appointed by the Public Service Commission.[33]

Finally, the governing body of the Indian Employee Provident Fund is composed of thirty-seven members.[34] The chief executive officer of the EPF is also on the board of governors, breaching the principle of separation between governing and managing fiduciaries.

In general, due to the absence of proper incentive mechanisms in the appointment procedures of governors, these tripartite boards can be

---

30. The twelve representatives of the insured include three representatives of the employees, three representatives of the employers, and six representatives of farmers, fishermen, and other rural beneficiaries. The composition of the Committee for National Pension Fund Operation (NPFO) was changed in 1998 as part of a reform of the National Pension Fund. The minister of health replaced the minister of finance as chairman, and the number of members was increased from eleven to twenty. The members include the vice ministers of finance, agriculture, industry, and labor, the president of the National Pension Corporation (which administers the NPF), three representatives of employers and employees, respectively, six representatives of farmers, fishermen, and the self-employed, and two pension experts.

31. Han (2001).

32. Asher (2001).

33. Hango and Jensen (2001).

34. Rao (2001).

directed by fiduciaries not necessarily fit and proper for their role. Indeed, the main concern about tripartite boards is their lack of independence. In many developing countries the politicization of representatives on the board often means that funds are invested imprudently and not necessarily in the interest of beneficiaries, but rather in the interest of the sponsor's other public policies. Even in more developed countries, it is possible to link the difference in performance between private sector pension funds and public pension funds to the composition of their respective boards of governors. Mitchell and Hsin argue that a possible reason explaining why the investment portfolios of U.S. public plans yield consistently lower rates of return than portfolios of private sector pension funds is that the two sets of funds operate under different rules.[35] Private sector funds are managed by professional and qualified governors with a clear economic mandate, while public pension funds are managed by staff responding to economic as well as political pressures. The governing body of public funds typically is composed of eight members: three elected members (usually active employees), three appointees (often appointed by the state governor), and two ex officio members (such as the state treasurer or superintendent of schools). Thus the better performance of private pension funds is hypothesized as being a result of the professional nature of their governing fiduciaries. Mitchell and Hsin then test this hypothesis on a sample of 168 public employee retirement systems using dummies for the presence of active employees and retired beneficiaries on the governing body. They find that the presence of retired beneficiaries on the governing body is associated with lower returns and conclude that either the type or the inappropriate selection of governors negatively affects performance.

Hence, two questions become relevant. First, what are the appropriate qualifications for governors? Second, how can independence of governors from political power be ensured?

Prudence (and logic) should demand the following from a governor of a pension plan:

—Governors should understand financial markets, risk management, and actuarial principles.

—Governors should be prepared to study and understand the promise and policies of the pension plan.

---

35. Mitchell and Hsin (1997) analyze the governance structure and performance of public employee retirement systems, which are established by state and local governments for individuals such as teachers and other school employees, police and firefighters, judges, and other civil servants.

—Governors should clearly understand their conflicts of interest and commit to resolve them in favor of the plan's beneficiaries.

—Governors should enunciate and follow an appropriate code of conduct, behave only in an ethical fashion, and clearly understand their fiduciary duties.

—Finally, some basic criteria should be used in selecting governors so that persons without the moral status required by the position are excluded. Thus governors should not have been convicted of any criminal offense or have received significant civil penalties in relation to the administration of a pension plan or its governing body. They should not have been involved in insolvent or bankrupt companies.

MacNaughton discusses how these standards are achieved in Canada.[36] The twelve members of the board of the Canada Pension Plan Investment Board are selected for their investment and business expertise in areas such as economics, accounting, actuarial science, finance, investing, banking, and business in general. The requirement for relevant expertise and experience is set out in legislation. This is quite different from most of the public pension funds around the world, which typically are governed by nominees or representatives from government, unions, and employers.

To ensure that the appointed governors are both qualified and independent from management and the sponsor of the plan (the government in case of publicly managed pension plans), a transparent and credible mechanism is needed for appointing and electing them. This should be an open and transparent process in which the sponsor consults independent bodies, such as the parliament or other expert committees.

The process for nominating the directors of the CPPIB provides a good example of how to depoliticize the nomination process of public pension plan governors.[37] In Canada the federal finance minister and the finance ministers for the nine participating provinces appoint a nominating committee. Each government nominates one committee member. The

---

36. MacNaughton (2001).

37. MacNaughton (2001). Independence from political interference is also achieved by having two separate juridical persons for the Canada Pension Plan (CPP) and the CPP Investment Board (CPPIB). The CPP is the exclusive responsibility of the federal and provincial governments. Through the CPP, these governments are responsible for the design, administration, and funding policy of the plan. For example, they set contribution rates, and determine the benefits, with the federal government actually collecting contributions and paying benefits. The CPPIB is a separate Crown corporation with the only mandate being to invest funds transferred from the plan. The CPPIB has no policy or administrative responsibility for the plan itself. Not only is it governed and managed independently of the CPP, but it also is governed and managed independently of governments.

federal finance minister chooses the committee chair from among chief executive officers of private sector companies. The committee identifies a set of qualified (as previously defined) prospective candidates from across Canada. The committee must agree on the list of qualified candidates, which is referred to the federal finance minister. The federal finance minister then consults with his provincial counterparts on the proposed names and appoints directors from the list of nominees recommended by the arm's-length committee. The federal finance minister also appoints the chair of the CPPIB, but again, in consultation with provincial finance ministers and also in consultation with the directors already appointed. Once appointed, the directors serve a three-year term, renewable three times, for a maximum of twelve years. The CPPIB chair can serve a fourth term, for a total, potentially, of twelve years. No director may be removed from the board during his or her term of office other than for cause. This means that, during any three-year period, no one can be removed from the board for any reason other than illegal or immoral conduct.

Finally, an appropriate balance should be sought on the number of governing fiduciaries. A large number of governors could ensure independence from government if they are appointed outside the ranks of civil servants. However, a small number of governors usually ensures that the work is done because it reduces the incentive of individual free riding on the contributions of others. The number of governors should be limited to maximize effectiveness of the board.

ROLE AND RESPONSIBILITIES OF THE GOVERNING BODY. A pension business should be governed and monitored by individuals who have accepted the responsibility of keeping the stakeholders' objective for the business clearly in mind. Hence, pension governors should be responsible for the performance of the fund. They may not necessarily be required to devote their full time and attention to the pension plan's affairs, and they are not expected to manage the plan on a daily basis. However, they are expected to oversee the business and affairs of the plan. Ongoing management of large plans should be delegated to a senior manager or group of managers who are responsible to and report to the board on a regular basis. In other words, "governing" functions and responsibilities should be clearly separated from "managing" functions and responsibilities. Different individuals should belong to each of these groups.

The law of fiduciary duty should define the responsibilities of governors. Legally, governors should act as owners of the assets (to ensure accountability) and on behalf of the beneficiaries and must exercise the care, skill, and diligence of a prudent person in carrying out their duties. Fiduciary obligations normally extend, but not exclusively, to the following:

—Complying with legislative requirements,

—Communicating to members their rights and entitlements,

—Ensuring that actuarial valuations are performed for defined-benefit plans,

—Ensuring that required contributions are remitted to the plan in a timely manner,

—Ensuring that funds are prudently invested,

—Ensuring that the payment of benefits is correct, timely, and in accordance with terms of the plan and the law, and

—Ensuring that the level of funding is appropriate; this element is likely to be different from private sector pension funds because taxpayers (and other lenders) are the ultimate source of public pension funds.

The objectives of governors should be clearly included in the relevant sets of regulations. For instance, the Canadian legislation sets two main objectives for the governors of the Canada Pension Plan. First, governors are to manage the cash transferred to them in the best interests of the contributors and beneficiaries. That means that currently monies must be invested in the best interests of about 16 million people. Second, governors are expected to maximize investment returns without incurring undue risk of loss. Furthermore, they are not to conduct any business that is inconsistent with these two objectives.[38]

In meeting their fiduciary obligations, pension governors should decide the main goals and policies for the fund. These could include and exceed the following:

—Deciding how much balance sheet risk is acceptable and what returns are targeted for given levels of risk.

—Hiring or firing the organization's chief executive officer.

—Approving the business plan.

—Monitoring outcomes versus target expectations and establishing a system of compensation linking the economic objectives of the plan to the remuneration of management.

The governing body can be divided into separate committees with separate responsibilities, such as for investment, auditing, human resources and compensation, and governance. Government bodies should have a

38. MacNaughton (2001).

process for evaluating their own performance and that of their committees. In particular, the investment committee should establish both an investment policy and an implementation policy covering issues such as asset allocation and active versus passive management.

Management fiduciaries should be responsible for the day-to-day operations and execution of the policies established by the board, and they should be bound by their fiduciary responsibility. They should be constituted as independent from the board but still report to the governing body through a chief executive officer. This procedure is typical of large funds. However, smaller funds might decide to outsource specific functions, such as asset management, to external providers in an effort to reduce the large sunk costs of many aspects of pension fund management. Notwithstanding the outsourcing arrangements, integrated management is essential. Even though oversight is separated from management, the presence of a chief executive officer ensures that the pension fund is managed as an integrated business entity.

In meeting its fiduciary obligations, the operational management should assemble the necessary human and operational resources. It should define a strategy for meeting the investment targets and identify tactics for implementing that strategy. It should develop systems to measure the success of the strategy and tactics. It should advise the governing fiduciaries on balance sheet risk policy. It should analyze and report outcome versus target policy and investment performance to the governing body.

In summary, the governing body should represent the best interests of the stakeholders. For public pension plans, these stakeholders include, among others, the government, plan participants, beneficiaries, taxpayers, and eventually other government agencies. The responsibility of the board should be to review and approve the policies and strategies, provide oversight of management, and compensate management according to its performance. Management should be responsible for all aspects of the ongoing operation of the organization within the approved policies, strategies, plans, and budgets. It should implement policies, strategies, annual business plans, and budgets and present them to the board for approval.

ACCOUNTABILITY AND INFORMATION DISCLOSURE. Without a system of accountability, governance cannot be improved. In general separation between ownership and management dictates that the governing body should report to the plan stakeholders and that management should report to the board. This principle should be supported by a strict system of internal controls that regulates the activities of fiduciaries and by commitment to public transparency and reporting.

For private sector pension funds, accountability for governance functions is particularly important to allow the supervisory authority and members and beneficiaries of the plan to sanction or discipline the governing body in case of bad management. The legal basis for accountability is personal liability. Insurance for personal liability can further ensure the ability of the pension fund to recover losses in case of mismanagement. Compulsory insurance of this liability is rare among industrial countries, the United States being an exception. Most industrial countries, however, do hold members of the governing body accountable under the law for their actions and decisions with regard to operation of the pension fund.

Accountability is more difficult to establish for public pension funds than for private ones, largely due to differences between the two types of plans. For instance, public pension plans do not have a supervisory authority, with Costa Rica being a special case.[39] They also have a very large number of stakeholders. One of these stakeholders is the government, which sets financial and fiscal policies directly affecting the extent to which governors and the fund can perform. Accountability of public pension governors is limited by the fact that many of the parameters against which their performance should be measured are outside their control. Investment regulation, contribution rates, and funding policies are often established by law and may be inconsistent with the fiduciary responsibilities usually attributed to governors of private pension funds. Personal liability of truly independent governors should be established. However, the local legislative framework may inhibit the development of such a concept for public figures. Also, it may be difficult, if not impossible to insure the personal responsibility of governors of large public pension funds.[40]

If personal liability cannot be established, governors should be made accountable to an independent body representing all stakeholders. Should this representative body be the same governing body or should it be an

---

39. The Namibian GIPF can be considered another special case as it is currently supervised. However, in Namibia there is no public pension plan per se. Around 400 pension plans are registered under the 1956 Pensions Funds Act. These cover around 120,000 members of the 500,000 economically active population. The GIPF covers about 70,000 of these 120,000 members.

40. In the United States, governors of the Thrift Savings Plan are exempted from personal liability because during the legislative process it was established that personal liability could not have been insured in the private sector.

external one? Stakeholder representation is guaranteed in tripartite governing bodies, but experience has shown that this type of representation is often highly politicized, which undermines accountability. Does a tripartite governing body meet all the standards of governing bodies in private plans that are needed to establish proper accountability? These include independence, absence of politicization, fit and proper tests, transparent and monitored standards and process for nomination, fixed period of appointment, removal with due cause, and so forth. The literature has not yet provided a definitive answer. Before more information is made available on the strengths and weaknesses of tripartite governing bodies, experience suggests that stakeholder representation should be sought elsewhere. The local legislature seems to be the strongest candidate for this role.

In fact, the need to promote disclosure seems to support the choice of parliament, or the national legislature, as the external and independent entity to which the governing body of the public pension fund should be accountable. Indeed, since accountability is limited in public pension funds, transparency and information disclosure become even more important than for private pension funds. But information disclosure should not be limited to the parliament alone. All members of the pension plan should receive information on the objectives of the fund, its strategy for achieving the stated objectives, and the rights of plan members. This information should be stated in a simple format that is easy to understand. Changes in these objectives or rights should be reported to members and beneficiaries in a timely manner. Relevant aspects regarding the means of achieving the objectives should include the composition of the governing body, its committees, their mandates and objectives, contribution rates and benefit schedules, investment strategy of the pension fund, level of funding, and other relevant aspects of the financial accounts. Plan participants should receive, when appropriate, periodic statements reporting accrued benefits and performance of the pension fund. They should also receive information regarding conflicts of interest and remuneration of key fiduciaries.

Two other functions should be instituted to ensure accountability: auditing and custody. Although auditing can be provided internally, it should also be provided externally. The financial activities of the fund should be audited on a regular basis. The auditor should be required to verify that the fund activity complies with all relevant regulations. The auditor should also conduct a periodic actuarial evaluation of liabilities and provide an analysis of funding levels. Obviously, custody should be provided externally only by an independent financial institution. The main function of the custodian is to carry out securities movement and control. The assignment of custody responsibility to an entity other than the asset manager is an efficient way to ensure the physical and legal integrity of the assets and to oversee the transactions of the asset manager. For public pension plans, an ideal custodian could be a truly independent central bank.

These internal controls and disclosure rules are commonly in place in plans with a good system of governance. The Canadian CPPIB, for instance, imposes tight controls on the personal investing of directors and employees. Directors and employees are required to clear trades before executing them for their personal accounts and to report on their investment activity on a regular basis. Also directors and employees are required to disclose in writing any real or potential conflicts of interest and to take appropriate steps to ensure that the interests of the CPPIB and of its contributors and beneficiaries cannot be deliberately or inadvertently compromised. In assessing these matters, both real and perceived conflicts are taken into account. The idea is to avoid the possibility that CPPIB employees will use confidential information for their personal financial benefit or for any other inappropriate purpose. This is important for building and maintaining public confidence in the integrity of the CPPIB staff and the CPPIB itself.

Additional checks and balances are also in place for the same purpose. They include the appointment of an independent, outside accounting firm to review the CPPIB operations and record and to report directly to the audit committee; a procurement policy covering the selection of outside organizations and suppliers; an external custodian selected through a rigorous process of due diligence; and the determination of signing authorities and limits to protect cash and portfolio assets. These checks and balances illustrate the range of policies that the CPPIB has adopted in an effort to earn and nurture the public trust.

The CPPIB also has a strong commitment to public transparency and reporting. A report is published annually and is distributed to the federal and provincial finance ministers. The report includes audited financial statements; a statement of corporate governance practices that sets out the duties, objectives, and mandate of the board of directors; the board's committees and their composition, mandates, and activities; the decisions of management requiring the board's prior approval; the procedures in place for the board to assess its own performance; and the directors' expectations with respect to management.

The CPPIB is required by law to include in the annual report a discussion of the objectives for the past year and how these have been met as well as objectives for the coming year. Annual returns for the Canadian, international, and total portfolios are calculated and disclosed. This information is also provided in an annualized format so that Canadians can compare recent performance with long-term performance. The fund is required to disclose the total compensation of the top five officers, as well as the total compensation of the directors and executive officers. All of this is presented and discussed in the federal Parliament and the provincial legislatures, and it is made available to all interested Canadians.[41]

The Namibian GIPF also generally complies with these principles of accountability and disclosure. The pension act requires the use of external auditors. An investment consultant, who advises the board and the investment committee on the selection of asset managers and also the investment strategies and policies, is also used. The board has an audit committee. However, actuarial evaluation of liabilities and analysis of funding levels are not done externally. Even if external procurement were made, the Namibian regulation would prevent the GIPF from using the services of firms not incorporated in Namibia.

The Irish National Pension Reserve Fund has included in its statute all regulations on disclosure applying to Irish private pension plans. These include a requirement for a detailed annual report with information focusing on expenses and charges, investment performance, and clear statements on how investment performance compares with the investment strategy and objectives. Valuations of the fund have to be made at regular intervals, and both independent evaluations and independent assessments of the investment performance must also be made. Finally, there are requirements for an annual audit of the accounts by the comptroller and auditor general (the senior auditor in the state).

Conclusions

This paper has sought to provide initial consideration of the importance of governance in public pension fund management, to advocate the development of governance guidelines tailored to the public nature of these funds, to underline the necessity of implementing these guidelines in developing

---

41. In fact, the annual report is sent to all members of the parliament and legislature, to stakeholder groups, such as trade unions, pensioner associations, business associations, economic and social policy research groups, universities, and every public library in Canada.

countries where the largest share of retirement income is provided by public pension funds, and to identify lines of future work and research to support the development of such guidelines.

The empirical literature on the relationship between governance and public pension fund performance, based largely on U.S. data, indicates that governance determines key investment strategies that, in turn, affect performance. These results are also supported by evidence in developing countries—some empirical, most factual—clearly indicating how the absence of good governance (that is, the inability to isolate fund management from political intervention) is an important determinant of poor performance. Few detailed results are so clear. For instance, independent performance evaluation is clearly associated with better investment policies, while excessively frequent performance evaluation is not significantly associated with performance. However, other detailed results are not so clear. For instance, it is not clear what impact the size and composition of the board have on performance, although consensus is building that governors should be fit and proper and not too numerous. Further research clearly is needed, especially to identify the governance elements or mechanisms that are necessary to improve public pension fund management and hence performance in developing countries.

Governance clearly matters. On the one hand, the importance of governance for private pension funds has been stressed for quite a long time now. In Canada, the Pension Investment Association of Canada (PIAC), the Association of Canadian Pension Management (ACPM), and the Office of the Superintendent for Financial Institutions (OSFI) have all developed independent guidelines for governance. The Canadian Standing Senate Committee on Banking, Trade, and Commerce issued a report on the governance practices of institutional investors in November 1998, which included a recommendation that pension plans in Canada adopt industry best practices with respect to plan governance. Specifically, the committee recommended that plan administrators adopt one of the PIAC, ACPM, or OSFI guidelines and report annually to pension plan members, setting out how they comply with or exceed the adopted guidelines and explaining why they do not comply if they choose not to do so.[42] On the

---

42. Because the three guidelines issued by PIAC, ACPM, and OSFI in the past few years contain many common principles, these organizations have formed a Joint Task Force on Pension Plan Governance. Its purpose is to develop a common set of principles for pension plan governance and a guide for plan administrators to conduct an assessment of their governance practices.

other hand, the development of governance guidelines for public pension funds has lagged behind, probably because of the cross-national nature of the debate. Only a handful of countries are active in this area.

Nevertheless, consensus is building on the following statements:

—The sole objective of public pension funds should be to provide affordable and sustainable retirement income.

—Governors should be independent from political power and fit and proper for their role.

—The law of fiduciary duty should define the responsibilities of governors.

—Governors should be made accountable for the performance of the fund.

—Independent performance (investment, audit, actuarial, and other) evaluations should be conducted by external and independent entities on a regular basis.

—Outside experts should be used regularly in the definition and implementation of fund policies.

—Finally, internal controls should be established to avoid conflicts of interest.

Beyond this, proper guidelines are needed to implement these concepts and to develop a satisfactory list of governance elements for public pension fund management. To attain this objective, an exhaustive survey of governance practices in both developed and developing countries should be carried out. It is possible that the design of this exercise will be modified with time, given the endogenous nature of the guidelines one would like to develop. The starting point could be a list of governance elements derived from considerations made in this paper.

Research is clearly needed on several topics. There is a need to identify what governance elements are relevant for, and specific to, public pension plans that are not relevant for private pension funds. There is a need to identify what governance elements are linked with performance specifically in developing countries. There is a need to identify what good practices of governance can be used to improve the performance of public pension fund management in developing countries and how these can be implemented.

Finally, there is a need to establish a network of public pension fund managers responsible for the development of these guidelines.

References

Ambachtseer, Keith P. 2001. "A Framework for Public Pension Fund Management." Paper presented at the 2001 World Bank Public Pension Fund Management conference, Washington. (www.worldbank.org/finance/).

Ambachtseer, Keith P., and D. Don Ezra. 1998. *Pension Fund Excellence: Creating Value for Stakeholders.* John Wiley and Sons.

Asher, Mukul. 2001. "Managing National Provident Funds in Malaysia and Singapore." Paper presented at the 2001 World Bank Public Pension Fund Management conference, Washington. (www.worldbank.org/finance/).

Dei, Henry. 2001. "Public Pension Fund Management in Ghana." Paper presented at the 2001 World Bank Public Pension Fund Management conference, Washington. (www.worldbank.org/finance/).

Fontaine, Juan A. 1997. "Are There (Good) Macroeconomic Reasons for Limiting External Investments by Pension Funds? The Chilean Experience." In Salvador Valdés-Prieto, ed., *The Economics of Pensions: Principles, Policies and International Experience.* Cambridge University Press.

Han, Sung-Yun. 2001. "National Pension Fund in Korea." Paper presented at the 2001 World Bank Public Pension Fund Management conference, Washington. (www.worldbank.org/finance/).

Hango, Primus, and Andrew P. Jensen. 2001. "National Pension Fund in Namibia." Paper presented at the 2001 World Bank Public Pension Fund Management conference, Washington. (www.worldbank.org/finance/).

Holzmann, Robert, and others. 2002. "Understanding the World Bank's Position on Pension Reform: Issues and Open Questions." World Bank, Washington.

Iglesias, Augusto, and Robert J. Palacios. 2000. "Managing Public Pension Reserves. Part I: Evidence from the International Experience." Social Protection Discussion Paper 3. World Bank, Washington.

Impavido, Gregorio. 2002. "On the Governance of Public Pension Fund Management." World Bank, Washington. Mimeo.

Impavido, Gregorio, Alberto R. Musalem, and Dimitri Vittas. 2001. "Contractual Savings Development in Countries with a Small Financial Sector." Policy Research Working Paper 2841. World Bank, Washington.

MacNaughton, John. 2001. "Principles and Practices of Governance for Public Pension Funds." Paper presented at the 2001 World Bank Public Pension Fund Management conference, Washington. (www.worldbank.org/finance/).

Mitchell, Olivia S. 2001a. "Issues in U.S. Public Pension Management." Paper presented at the 2001 World Bank Public Pension Fund Management conference, Washington. (www.worldbank.org/finance/).

———. 2001b. "Re-designing Public Sector Pensions in Developing Countries." World Bank, Washington. Mimeo.

Mitchell, Olivia S., and Ping-Lung Hsin. 1997. "Public Sector Pension Governance and Performance." In Salvador Valdés-Prieto, ed., *The Economics of Pensions: Principles, Policies and International Experience.* Cambridge University Press.

Palacios, Robert J. 2001. "Managing Public Pension Reserves: Experience and Prospects." Paper presented at the 2001 World Bank Public Pension Fund Management conference, Washington. (www.worldbank.org/finance/).

Palacios, Robert J., and Montserrat Pallares. 2000. "International Patterns of Pension Provision." Social Protection Discussion Paper 9. World Bank, Washington.

Rao, Nagashwar. 2001. "Public Pension Fund Management in India." Paper presented at the 2001 World Bank Public Pension Fund Management conference, Washington. (www.worldbank.org/finance/).

Useem, Michael, and David Hess. 2001. "Governance and Investment of Public Pensions." In Olivia S. Mitchell and Edwin C. Hustead, eds., *Pensions in the Public Sector.* University of Pennsylvania Press.

Useem, Michael, and Olivia S. Mitchell. 2000. "Holders of the Purse Strings: Governance and Performance of Public Retirement Systems." *Social Science Quarterly* 81 (2): 489–506.

R. THILLAINATHAN

Malaysia's Employees Provident Fund and Its Governance: A Critical Review

THIS PAPER DISCUSSES the adequacy and performance of Malaysia's Employees Provident Fund (EPF) and its governance. The adequacy of the EPF as a retirement scheme and as a financial performer is reviewed in the context of the EPF's design as a provident fund, the regulations to which it is subject, the underdeveloped domestic financial markets within which it has to operate, and its governance arrangements. The real returns generated by the EPF since its inception in 1951 are very respectable by the standards of other developing countries. But the EPF's management practices pertaining to accounting, performance measurement, and dividends declared depart significantly from best practices that apply to a private sector fund manager. This shortcoming is distorting behavior and causing malgovernance.

The failure to run the EPF on a portfolio basis (by restricting its exposure to portfolio risk and not business risk) and in the best interests of its members has also raised serious governance issues. Members of the governing boards of the EPF, which include its board of directors and an investment panel, may not be adequately qualified to run a retirement scheme. But they are now more independent of the government, the scheme sponsor, thanks to a lengthening of the term of their appointment from two to three years. Contributors to the EPF, however, are in no position to discipline the governing boards against bad management because they have no say on the matter. Furthermore, the oversight responsibility of the governing boards over management is not clearly specified, and many parameters are outside their control.

This situation is compounded by the fact that the chief executive officer (CEO) is appointed by the minister of finance as are members of the two governing boards. Furthermore, the CEO is a full-time appointee, whereas the governing board members serve only part-time. The well-placed position of management vis-à-vis the governing boards was abundantly clear when the chairman of the board and the CEO of the EPF were one and the same person during the 1990s.[1] Personal liability of a governing board member is also not well established in law, possibly because board members are treated as "public figures." The Ministry of Finance is the regulator and supervisor of the EPF but does not have the requisite expertise to do this job, especially given its many other equally important job functions.

Where the regulator and the regulated are both government bodies, as in the case of the ministry and the EPF, the regulator has been less able or willing to go public with criticisms of the regulated. Moreover, there has always been a "conflict of interest" between the ministry as EPF's regulator and the government as the biggest borrower from the fund. Specifically, there is a conflict of interest to the extent that government spending benefits all Malaysians, but only private sector employees are mandated by law to contribute to EPF's pool of "forced" savings.

An Overview of Provident Fund and Pension Schemes in Malaysia

There are two types of retirement schemes for employees in Malaysia. One is akin to a defined-contribution plan run by the EPF for employees of the private sector.[2] The other is a defined-benefit plan run by the government pensions department for employees in government service.

---

1. Until the late 1980s the secretary-general of the Ministry of Finance was the chairman of the EPF.

2. A provident fund arrangement is akin to a defined-contribution plan, but the contribution rate is mandatory and the investment decision is exercised by the fund while the contributor bears the risk. This is a potentially explosive arrangement. The government has addressed this problem in a less than optimal manner by guaranteeing a minimum return of 2.5 percent a year and by mandating the portfolio in which the funds can be invested.

Malaysia's EPF, which was established in 1951, is the oldest provident fund scheme in the world. The fully funded scheme can be considered one of the most successful provident funds in the world, but it is subject to certain constraints within which it has to operate. These constraints are imposed by the nature of provident funds themselves, by regulation, and by Malaysia's financial markets, which are underdeveloped.

The pension scheme for government employees has been partially funded starting in the late 1980s. The corporatization and privatization of many government entities, such as those in the utility sector, has led to a migration of employees from the defined-benefit plan to the defined-contribution plan.

More than 40 percent of the country's labor force is not likely to be covered by a retirement scheme. Active contributors to the EPF amounted to 4.78 million in 1999, or 52 percent of the labor force of 9.18 million. Only 6.2 percent of the labor force may have been covered by the government pension scheme.[3] The contribution rate is set at 23 percent of salary (with the employer contributing 12 percent and the employee contributing 11 percent).

Key Issues and Proposals

The EPF has assets in excess of $50 billion.[4] In relative terms, the EPF is one of the largest asset management companies in the world, with the ratio of its assets to Malaysia's gross domestic product above 50 percent. The EPF's investment management is centralized and its investment portfolio is mandated. At least 70 percent must be invested in Malaysian Government Securities (MGS), investment in domestic equities cannot exceed 25 percent, and investment in global or emerging market equities or bonds is not permitted. But the Ministry of Finance has waived the investment required in government securities (on a year-to-year basis) because of a

---

3. Of 961,100 government employees in 1999, only 393,134 were classified as active members of the EPF. A substantial proportion of the rest may be classified as inactive members of the EPF. Government employees begin contributing to the EPF upon employment but are enrolled in the pension plan only after a minimum period of service. The inclusion of pensionable government employees partly accounts for the EPF's total membership of 9.54 million in 1999, which was above the labor force of 9.18 million.

4. Currency is given in U.S. dollars unless otherwise noted.

Table 1. *EPF: Real Dividend Rates, Five-Year Averages, 1956–2000*
Percent

Year	Dividend rate	Rate of inflation	Real dividend rate
1956–60	2.80	0.40	2.40
1961–65	4.80	0.50	4.25
1966–70	5.70	1.40	4.29
1971–75	6.10	7.40	−1.30
1976–80	7.30	4.50	2.75
1981–85	8.30	4.66	3.84
1986–90	8.20	1.96	6.24
1991–95	7.90	3.96	4.04
1996–2000	6.80	3.18	3.60

Source: Bank Negara Malaysia (1989, 2001); EPF (1991).
Note: The five-year dividend rate and rate of inflation have been computed as a simple average of the annual data.

shortage of those instruments. The EPF is thus overinvested in short-term instruments (and underinvested in marketable securities) (table 2) and suffers from a massive duration mismatch, given the clamor for the payment of a higher fixed dividend.

The EPF's existing arrangement for the investment and pooling of risk offers no protection to a retiring contributor against market or longevity risks.[5] Taking the case of market risk, for example, the risk-bearing capacity of the young contributors to the EPF (as measured by volatility) is higher than that of the older groups of contributors, but the EPF's investment program (with respect to asset allocation) makes no distinction between each age groups. Therefore, the young end up with an investment program that bears too little risk (that is, they are underinvested in equities), and the old with too much risk. This anomaly has to be rectified.

Market risk can be addressed by investing a contributor's retirement fund in less volatile assets as he nears his retirement age. But the retiree still faces the problem of smoothing his income or consumption after his retirement. A well-developed market in annuity products can address the market and longevity risks faced by retirees, but only up to a point. And the

5. An in-depth analysis of the current state of the EPF and the required reforms are given in Thillainathan (1999a; 2000), who benefited greatly from a reading of Modigliani and Muralidhar (1998a; 1998b).

Table 2. *EPF'S Asset Allocation, Selected Years*
Percent

Asset class	1985	1990	1995	2000
Malaysian Government Securities (MGS)	86.3	79.2	40.4	34.5
Loans and debentures (corporate bonds)	7.0 (0.0)	8.2 (0.7)	17.7 (6.0 +)	20.5 (9.4)
Equity	3.3	2.2	11.9	21.2
Property	0.0	0.0	0.4	0.7
Money market instruments	3.4	10.5	29.5	23.1
Total	100.0	100.0	100.0	100.0
Total in Malaysian ringgits, billions	23.9	45.6	96.6	179.1

Source: Bank Negara Malaysia (2000); Sallehuddin bin Mohamed (1996); "The EPF Remains Resilient in Challenging Times," *The Sun*, December 2, 2001.

market in annuity products is still extremely underdeveloped in Malaysia because of overregulation and overprotection of the insurance and fund management industries.

Moreover, the EPF may not provide as much for retirement as its contributors are expecting. The EPF began as a retirement fund. Today contributors are also allowed during their working years to withdraw up to 40 percent of their accumulated savings to finance housing, education, and health needs. With the increase in withdrawals for these purposes (table 3) and declining returns, there may be a shortage of savings for financing one's retirement living.[6] A case might therefore be made for an increase in the contribution rate, an increase in the retirement age, or a restriction on withdrawals.[7]

The solution is not to curb withdrawals for big-ticket items such as housing and education.[8] Contributors save during their working years and dissave in retirement. They will experience volatility in their consumption (for example, on health spending) and investment (for example, on purchase of

6. Under certain assumptions, Zainal Abidin (2002) has calculated that with only 60 percent of one's contributions going into the retirement fund, the replacement income after retirement is expected to be 25–30 percent of a retiree's final salary before retirement.

7. The retirement age has remained unchanged at 55. In 1950 the life expectancy at birth was 55 whereas now it is around 75 (Zainal Abidin, 2002).

8. However, there is little or no case for permitting withdrawals for the purchase of PCs, a program that would be more costly to administer and more open to abuse.

a home and children's education).[9] An optimal retirement plan must help smooth this consumption over the life cycle by letting contributors draw on their accumulated funds or borrow against their future retirement contributions so that they can minimize the incidence of oversaving and inequities.[10]

At the least, however, a member's retirement fund (which is held in the EPF's Account One) should be managed differently from a member's savings balances (held in Accounts Two and Three), which are earmarked for housing, education, and health. The retirement fund in Account One is a long-term fund whereas the multipurpose savings fund in the other two accounts is a short-term or a medium-term fund. Accordingly, the asset allocation criteria for the two funds should be different. A higher proportion of the retirement fund must be invested in equities, while a greater share of the multipurpose fund is invested in bonds and money market instruments. No distinction is currently made, however, in the management of the two funds.

The short supply in quality marketable securities of domestic origin bolsters the argument for segregating the funds by different accounts and by different age groups. Given this short supply, there is also a need to review the current policy on valuation of assets as well as on allowing retired individuals to keep their funds in the EPF and not to withdraw them upon retirement. The fact that wealthy individuals are keeping their retirement funds in the fund suggests that they are happier with the returns they can receive there than with those they would receive investing the funds on their own.

An Analysis of the EPF's Performance

The data on the nominal and real dividend rates paid by the EPF are given in table 1. The real dividend was positive and significantly above 3 percent

9. With the increasing privatization of the health industry and increasing life spans, a case can also be made for a public insurance program to meet medical expenses especially in old age. Compulsory coverage through the EPF may be the best answer but with deductibles to minimize the problems of adverse selection and moral hazard.

10. A high mandated contribution rate and restrictions on withdrawals can be inequitable to the extent that a contributor is forced to borrow from a bank his own EPF savings that have been recycled to the bank and at a disadvantageous rate, as is or as has been the case in Malaysia.

Table 3. *EPF: Contributions, Withdrawals, and Investments, 1990–2000*
Malaysian ringgits, billions

Year	Contributions	Withdrawals[a]	Accumulated contributions[b]	Accumulated investments[c]
1990	4.14	1.74	46.18	45.64
1991	4.92	1.97	52.84	52.00
1992	6.32	1.76	61.71	60.86
1993	7.38	2.21	71.91	71.53
1994	8.79	2.59	83.99	83.31
1995	10.32	3.16	97.54	96.60
1996	12.90	3.64	114.19	115.22
1997	14.52	5.64	130.86	107.42
1998	16.50	8.71	145.89	145.81
1999	18.41	7.37	156.93	163.80
2000	20.95	10.40	167.49	181.51

Source: Bank Negara Malaysia (2001).

a. Withdrawals include the permitted withdrawals of 30 percent of one's accumulated fund at age 50.

b. Annual figures include dividends but exclude members' contributions with fund management institutions.

c. At book value.

a year throughout the 1980s and 1990s. During this period the EPF's asset composition shifted dramatically (see table 2).

The real returns generated by the EPF are indeed creditable. Because of the increase in the shares of equity and loans in recent years and weaknesses in the EPF's accounting policies, the data on returns have become less reliable. Adherence to best practices would require the equity portfolio to be marked to market and the loan portfolio to be subject to an impairment test (regarding the carrying value of the loans and the recognition of interest income). The EPF's annual report, however, shows the equity investments being carried at cost—despite a more than 40 percent fall in the level of the index from its high in 1997, a sizable buildup in the EPF's equity investments in the period before the crash, and payment of dividends only out of realized gains. Unrealized gains and losses are not taken into account in the EPF's performance measurement or in the dividends declared. This may have led to the selling of winners and the hoarding of losers, to "outperformance" in the near term, and to a deterioration in the long-term quality of the investment portfolio. Because of these factors, the market value of the equity portfolio is likely to be about 50 percent of its carrying value.

The EPF's annual report is also conspicuous for its failure to mention its accounting policy on loan classification (unlike banks, which are required to follow central bank guidelines on such matters). However, as many of the EPF's loans are backed by government or bank guarantees and as the central bank has to date not reneged on the guarantee obligations even of a failing bank, it is unlikely that the underlying quality of the EPF's loan portfolio has deteriorated significantly. Recently, talk has been increasing about protecting retail depositors through a deposit insurance scheme and letting large depositors, such as the EPF, deposit at their own risk. Such a move would mean that the credit quality of the EPF's portfolio would not be guaranteed through recourse to a bank. It has been suggested that given the decline in the interest rate environment, the appreciation in the EPF's bond portfolio is likely to offset any fall in the market value of its equity portfolio.[11]

By statute the EPF is still required to invest up to 70 percent of its funds in Malaysian Government Securities. This it was able to do until the late 1980s because the federal government was a big borrower in the domestic debt market. The government began to privatize in the late 1980s, however, and by the mid-1990s, it was running a budget surplus. The captive demand for, and short supply of, government securities led to depressed yields, which adversely affected EPF contributors. Fortunately, the government has given a waiver on a year-by-year basis and has not insisted that the EPF comply with the letter of the law for its investments in government securities. If it had done so, even the outstanding supply of MGS would not have been adequate for the EPF to meet its legal requirement. The sort of governance issues raised by this requirement for the EPF to finance the national development effort is dealt with later in this paper.

---

11. However, under the current best practice, an institution such as the EPF that is holding its bond portfolio to maturity is not required to mark to market its investments in bonds (except in circumstances where there has been a permanent impairment in the underlying quality of the credit of any bond issuers). But the EPF allows sizable withdrawals from its funds for several purposes, and the interest rates on those bonds can increase from their current low levels. Therefore, it is in the interests of contributors that EPF mark its bond portfolio to market.

The Adverse Impact of EPF's Inappropriate Policies

The EPF's investment and accounting policy should be adapted, if necessary on a phased basis, to conform to international best practice. The reformed investment policy should allow the EPF to invest its funds on a portfolio basis and in marketable securities to maximize its returns and to minimize volatility (one-fourth to one-third of these funds should be invested in global and regional securities, but these overseas investments should be phased over a period of ten years), to reap the benefits of diversification, and to overcome the short supply of marketable securities of domestic origin. The EPF should also be required to mark its portfolio to market (if necessary, over a three-year time frame) and should benchmark and evaluate the performance of its portfolio in relation to the performance of the market, as well as realized and unrealized gains and losses.

Unless the EPF follows such a reformed investment policy, it is likely to continue to suffer from the following weaknesses:

—Underinvestment in equities because of a possible bias toward capital preservation (although equity is the best asset class for a long-term pension fund).[12]

—Differing treatment of contributors because of differences in the timing of their withdrawals (with the existing rules favoring the wealthier or more savvy contributors).

—A tendency to sell its winners (to book the realized gains so that dividends can be declared) and keep its losers. This practice can lead to a deterioration in the quality of the investment portfolio in the long run.

—Vulnerability to undesirable external influences in the decisions it makes and hence to weak governance practices.

Current Governance Arrangements and Practices in Malaysia

From the 1990s the EPF has been managing its funds largely, but not solely, in the best interests of its members.[13] The Ministry of Finance and the governors and managers of the EPF still believe that the fund has a

12. This point was demonstrated by Siegel (1994).
13. The key issues in the governance of the EPF are taken up in Thillainathan (1999b), who benefited from a reading of Gilbertson (1999).

development role to play in general and that it cannot ignore the implications of its activities on the country's development. One widely accepted position is that domestically generated funds should only be used to invest within and for the further development of the country. Therefore, overseas investments by the EPF require government approval on a case-by-case basis, and approval has seldom been given. To date the EPF does not have the government's approval to allocate a proportion of its funds for investment in overseas equities and bonds. This restriction has been a serious constraint on the fund's efforts to maximize its returns and minimize its risk, especially given that the size of the fund is huge relative to the size of Malaysia's domestic financial markets.[14] The EPF is also now expected to play a role in the development of the domestic fund management industry as well as to create job and training opportunities in fund management for Malaysians in general and Malays in particular.

Many pension and provident funds in the developing world are governed by a "tripartite" board of directors composed of representatives from the government, employers, and employees. In Malaysia the board of a fund such as the EPF has been extended to include an additional group of representatives, namely, one drawn from the ranks of professionals. More interestingly, this board, which is appointed by the Ministry of Finance, is responsible for monitoring all matters related to the fund's management except its investment activities. Those are overseen by an investment panel, which is made up of a member from the Ministry of Finance, one from the central bank, and three professionals, with the fund's chairman and chief executive officer as ex-officio members. The members of the panel are appointed by the Ministry of Finance and are accountable to it and not to the fund's board.[15]

From the preceding discussion, one can infer that in Malaysia the investment activities of the major retirement fund are governed more by specialists and not by representatives of employers and employees. Typically, the

14. Currently, the size of the EPF funds is about one-third the size of the market capitalization of the Kuala Lumpur Stock Exchange (KLSE). Assume 50 percent of the EPF funds are allocated to investment in the KLSE or domestic equities. This would make the EPF a 15 percent shareholder in each listed company, too large a position to allow it to play the role of a passive portfolio investor. The problem is compounded by the fact that the EPF is now choosing to observe the "Syariah" principle based on Islamic law in its investing activity although at least 50 percent of the funds belong to members who are not Moslems. Such a restriction would further increase EPF's shareholding in each of the permitted companies.

15. The funds of the Social Security Organization (SOCSO) and the Pilgrims Funds management board are also managed by an investment panel.

specialists have been drawn from the banking and accounting profession, and unless they have been long-standing members of the EPF investment panel, they are likely to have only a cursory understanding of financial markets, risk management, and actuarial principles. Nor are they likely to have a proper understanding of the intricacies of pension and provident fund management. Furthermore, even if they are in a position to exercise the care, skill, and diligence of a prudent person in carrying out their duties, in Malaysia, as elsewhere in the developing world, their account-ability "is limited by the fact that many of the parameters against which their performance will be measured are outside their control."[16]

A fund governor not only has to be qualified, but he also has to be inde-pendent of management and the sponsor. The current part-time nature of the EPF's member on the investment panel means that he has oversight, but not management, responsibilities. Moreover, because the CEO is also a member of the panel and is appointed by the Ministry of Finance rather than the board, there is no sharp demarcation between "governing" and "management" functions and responsibilities. It has been suggested that for governors to be independent, the government, as the sponsor of the fund, has to "create a transparent and credible mechanism for appointing and electing them," with independent bodies, such as the Parliament or other expert committees, consulted on the appointments by the sponsor.[17] The only EPF position that the Ministry of Finance solicits advice on is that of a director of the board. Appointments to the EPF's board and investment panel are made by the finance ministry without any formal consultation.

Members of the EPF investment panel are required to declare their interests in and abstain from voting on any interested party transactions with respect to the EPF's lending activities. But members of the investment panel are not required to clear trades before executing them for their per-sonal accounts or to report on their investment activity on a regular basis.

Good governance requires that the governing board be held accountable for its actions and that its members be held personally liable. Accounta-bility is a problem in the case of the EPF. The contributors are in no posi-tion to sanction or discipline the governing body against bad management because there is no competent supervisory authority, there is a very large number of stakeholders, and many parameters are outside the board's con-trol. Personal liability of the EPF's investment panel members, as "public"

---

16. Impavido (2002). See also the chapter by Impavido in this volume.
17. Impavido (2002).

figures, is also not a well-accepted norm or well established in law. Such public figures are viewed as providing national service on a part-time basis and at a nominal fee, making it more difficult to hold them personally liable for their public actions under the law. However, public figures in Malaysia have been successfully prosecuted for actions involving a criminal breach of trust.

Before the governors of the EPF can be held accountable for their actions, the accounting framework for the reporting of financial results must be satisfactory. As already observed, the EPF's current accounting practices do not adhere to best practices of the private sector in the fund management industry. With the collapse of the market for financial assets after mid-1997, the decision of the government to continue to measure the carrying value of EPF's assets at cost and not at market value has led to an overstatement of its financial performance. Moreover, as noted earlier, the use of inappropriate accounting policies is distorting investment behavior, which is not only weakening the quality of the fund's investment portfolio, but also benefiting contributors who make early withdrawals at the expense of the remaining contributors.

EPF and Its Purpose

The goal of a provident fund must be clearly articulated to avoid a conflict between the interests of the contributors and that of the government as the regulator. A government's development goals can often constrain the investment choices of a provident fund and increase its risk exposures.[18] It is now increasingly accepted that the activities of EPF should be geared to further the interests of contributors and not to promote development. It is also accepted that there should be no disparity (at least outwardly) in the treatment of contributors.[19] As recently as the late 1980s, however, the government and the EPF's fiduciaries were not as clear about the fund's goals.

18. Restrictions on international diversification and bias for investments in domestic assets or for doing business with domestically controlled companies or banks reduce returns and increase risks. The new regime of exchange control that requires prior government approval for overseas investments is likely to increase these biases.

19. The EPF (along with the central bank) extended special loans, at below market rates, to MBSB to finance MBSB's low-cost housing program. As MBSB had other shareholders and as only a few EPF contributors were fortunate to be beneficiaries of the housing program, there was no justification, on

Even now the EPF's funds can be used only within the country and the so-called "development goals" of the EPF keep cropping up. For example, the EPF is now expected to play a role in the promotion of Malaysia's fund management industry.

Special problems come up in governance and performance when a provident fund acts as a business investor rather than as a portfolio investor. To illustrate these problems, let us see what would have happened if the EPF had ventured into the business of property development.

Given the success of Singapore's Housing Development Board (HDB) and its Central Provident Fund in promoting housing development and home ownership, it has been suggested from time to time that the EPF should create a housing development board, either directly or through its subsidiary, the Malaysian Building Society Berhad (MBSB).[20] The EPF acceded to these calls in the mid-1990s but with restraint, agreeing to undertake a handful of low-cost housing schemes. Had the EPF promoted a full-blown housing development organization through its investing and lending policy, it might then have been biased to lend only to those home purchasers who wanted to buy the houses it had developed. The EPF would have been taking not only a lending risk but also a business risk. The alternative is a competitive situation where the EPF lends housing funds to the many who are free to buy from any developer or in any location. That will expose the EPF only to the lending risk. By remaining free to lend the funds it plans to allocate to housing to buyers who are free to buy houses from any developer, or to channel its funds by buying loans originated by many financial institutions without regard to who the developer is (as is being done by Cagamas Berhad, a mortgage corporation), or to invest in the mortgage bonds issued by Cagamas, the EPF assumes only the lending risk and is better able to maximize returns and reduce its vulnerability to undesirable external influence in its decisionmaking. The EPF can play a meaningful role in the provision of housing finance, but the government and EPF have been generally wise in not letting the fund assume a major role in housing development.

The EPF's experience with the running of its only subsidiary, the MBSB, amply illustrates the need for a pension fund to take only portfolio risk and

---

efficiency or equity grounds, for the EPF to extend such loans to MBSB at below market rates. Accordingly, such subsidized loans have been discontinued since the 1990s.

20. The EPF took over controlling interest in the MBSB from the federal government in the 1970s.

avoid assuming any business risk. In the mid-1990s, soon after the appointment of a new chief executive officer, the MBSB strayed away from its core activity of providing housing loans and started actively marketing bridge finance to developers of commercial properties and acquisition finance to speculative developers for the purchase of land with "development" potential for the construction of houses. It obtained funding for these activities not from the EPF, but from depositors (as it had the authority to take such deposits) and from revolving credit lines marked out by banks. The speculative nature of this activity and its unstable funding base drove the MBSB into a liquidity and solvency crisis in the aftermath of the Asian financial crisis in mid-1997.

The central bank strictly prohibits the lending of money for the purchase of land. But the MBSB was not subject to this prohibition as it was outside the central bank's purview. Some senior managers of the EPF may have aided the management of the MBSB in its aggressive move into these nontraditional activities. There was little or no oversight by the EPF's governing boards partly because of the divided responsibilities of its board of directors and investment panel and partly because the investment panel was not responsible for supervising the EPF's subsidiary.[21]

Where the EPF has become a substantial or controlling shareholder (as in the MBSB and STAR, a light rail company and an associate of the EPF), its senior management has ended up devoting a disproportionate share of its time in running such companies. This was readily evident with respect to MBSB, STAR, and the joint ventures EPF undertook for low-cost housing development. The EPF's shareholding interest in these companies or ventures was only a fraction of 1 percent of its total funds, but its managers spent far more than 1 percent of their time working with these businesses. Running a business is very different from investing on a portfolio basis. To have the right focus, the EPF should invest only on a portfolio basis.

---

21. MBSB's CEO in the mid-1990s submitted his five-year business plan to the EPF investment panel soon after his appointment. But the plan was severely criticized by some members of the panel because of its radical departure from MBSB's core activity and because of its failure to address MBSB's unstable funding source. The panel itself was very guarded in increasing the EPF's exposure to MBSB, except to refinance its housing loans on a secured basis. No business plans were submitted to the panel subsequently, nor did the panel receive any progress reports on MBSB's business activities. That happened only in the late 1990s and in response to searching questions from the panel on MBSB's request for new lines of credit. It took the panel many weeks to establish the extent of MBSB's foray into speculative lending and the very poor quality of its loan portfolio.

Conclusion

Good governance requires qualified and independent governors who can be held accountable and liable for their actions. Existing weaknesses in the governance framework of public sector pension and provident funds in Malaysia have resulted from weaknesses in the regulatory, supervisory, and accounting frameworks. A reform of the accounting and auditing framework of a provident fund can ensure that the measurement and reporting of the performance of such a fund adheres to best practices. That will minimize distortion in the behavior of a fund's fiduciaries. Public opinion can also be mobilized to pressure the government to change those governance practices that make for poor performance. If fund performance is overstated through the use of poor accounting policies, governance practices—difficult to change in normal circumstances—will be even more difficult to change. So in any reform of governance practices of pension and provident funds, priority should be given to reforming the accounting framework, and the fund should be audited by an external auditor from the private sector who can then be held liable for negligence or fraud.

References

Bank Negara Malaysia. Various years. *Annual Report*. Kuala Lumpur.
———. 1989. *Money and Banking in Malaysia*. Kuala Lumpur.
———. 2001. *Monthly Statistical Bulletin*. Kuala Lumpur.
Employees Provident Fund. 1999. *Annual Reports and Statistics*. Kuala Lumpur.
Gilbertson, Kristin. 1999. "Governance of Pension Plans." Paper presented at a conference on "Recent Trends in Institutional and Pension Fund Investment Management in Asia," organized by the World Bank and Hong Kong Monetary Authority in Hong Kong, October 11–13.
Impavido, Gregory. 2002. "Governance Issues in Public Pension Fund Management: Preliminary Considerations." World Bank, Washington. March.
Ministry of Finance, Government of Malaysia. 2002. *Economic Report 2001/2002*. Kuala Lumpur.
Modigliani, Franco, and Arun Muralidhar. 1998a. *A Taxonomy of Pension Reform Issues: The Case of Social Security*. MIT. August.
———. 1998b. *Latin American Pension Reforms: Prescriptions for Disaster*. MIT. August.
Sallehuddin bin Mohamed, Tan Sri. 1996. "The Employees Provident Fund: Asset Management and Implications to the Ringgit Bond Market." Paper presented at a conference on the "Ringgit Bond Market: Institutional Investors' Role and Perspectives," Kuala Lumpur, October 1.

Siegel, Jeremy J. 1994. *Stocks for the Long Run: A Guide to Selecting Markets for Long-Term Growth.* New York: Irwin.

Thillainathan, R. 1999a. "Pension and Financial Market Reforms in Malaysia: The Agenda and Why One Depends on the Other." Paper presented at a conference on "Recent Trends in Institutional and Pension Fund Investment Management in Asia," organized by the World Bank and Hong Kong Monetary Authority in Hong Kong, October 11–13. A revised version of this paper was presented at a "Workshop on Pension Fund Reforms," organized by the Asian Development Bank Institute in Singapore, November 8–13, 1999.

———. 1999b. "Employees Provident Fund and Governance Issues." Paper presented at a conference on "Recent Trends in Institutional and Pension Fund Investment Management in Asia," organized by the World Bank and Hong Kong Monetary Authority in Hong Kong, October 11–13.

———. 2000. "Pension and Financial Market Reforms and Key Issues on Governance—with Special Reference to Malaysia." Paper presented at a Pension Fund Management Workshop organized by the Employees Provident Fund in Kuala Lumpur, August 14–15.

Zainal Abidin, Mohd Kassim. 2002. "Retirement Benefits: The Malaysian Perspective." Paper delivered at a seminar organized by the Securities Industry Development Center and the Malaysian Economic Association, August.

ALVARO CLARKE DE LA CERDA

CASE
STUDY

How Capital Markets
Exert Governance
on Corporates:
Experience in Chile

Among the elements that must be considered in implementing an
effective corporate governance regulation are the legal rules, legal history, legal systems, political forces, and forces of convergence and divergence at work in the country. The Chilean legal system is based on civil
law, or Roman legal tradition, with written law being the main source of
the legal framework. As a consequence, rights and duties must be clearly set
down in the law in order to have a compelling force. Conventional wisdom
in Chile implies that one can do what the law allows one to do. In contrast,
under the British common law tradition, a person is allowed to do anything the law does not forbid. These two approaches need different coherent and comprehensive legal frameworks. Whether a country follows civil
law or common law tradition, the fundamental principle is the development of a coherent legal framework, one that avoids imposing external
solutions that are incompatible with the legal tradition and culture of a
country.

La Porta, Lopez-de-Silanes, Shleifer, and Vishny have compared different legal systems and their relation to the financial markets, finding that
countries whose laws originate in the common law have more developed
capital markets. As they observed, "Countries whose legal rules originate in
the common law tradition tend to protect investors considerably more

than do the countries whose laws originate in the civil law."[1] Although these researchers have not gone unchallenged, they have made an interesting contribution to the understanding of different legal systems and to the comprehension of their weaknesses and strengths in the development of capital markets.

Pistor, Raiser, and Gelfer have made a great contribution by studying the relationship between the effectiveness of the legal framework and market development. They find that "an important constraint on financial market development is the absence of effective legal institutions. Our regression analysis shows that legal effectiveness has overall a much higher explanatory power for the level of equity and credit market development than [does the] quality of the law on the books."[2] From this they conclude that legal systems, including corporate governance systems, cannot simply be transplanted from one country to another and be effective.

For example, in the British legal tradition that rests on private rules, best practice codes have been very successful, but in the Chilean legal tradition that rests on public rules, best practice codes may not be successful. In short, there is no common solution to improving corporate governance regulation.

Governance Framework in Chile

The corporate governance scheme and the tender offer process in Chile have been included in the public laws; this is the so-called ex ante approach. The legal framework rests on public rules and institutions. As a consequence, the law constitutes the frame that defines the attitude and interaction among the private agents.

The need for a capital market system that adequately protects minority shareholders and that allows for increasing market liquidity and transparency led the Chilean government to undertake the development of a new law, which was approved in December 2000. Among other provisions, this law improves corporate governance practices through the formation of audit committees, the regulation of operations between affiliated parties, and the upgrading of rights of holders of American depository receipts (ADRs) to the same level as common shareholders in Chile.

The regulation on tender offers allocates the corporate premium to all shareholders on an equal basis. The operational flexibility that the law gives

1. La Porta, Lopez-de-Silanes, Shleifer, and Vishny (1998).
2. Pistor, Raiser, and Gelfer (2000).

to mutual and investment funds is intended to increase market liquidity and its depth.

Corporate Governance Standards

A top priority for the Chilean government has been the development of adequate corporate governance standards. The new law seeks to maximize corporate value by bringing together the interests of insider and outsider parties. This convergence is designed to prevent insiders from selling a corporation's assets at prices different from those prevailing in the market and from transferring corporate business opportunities. The law also seeks to avoid potential damage to minority shareholders, by clearly defining the responsibility of those who participate in management. The major clauses of the law provide for equal rights among ADR holders and common shareholders on all matters including equity issues. These rights include:

—Proportionate voting rights in shareholder meetings;

—Preemptive rights in new capital issuance;

—Withdrawal rights if certain conditions arise.

These provisions should reassure foreign shareholders that their rights are duly protected under Chilean law.

Transactions between Affiliated Parties

One of the most controversial issues in all companies is transactions between affiliated parties. Legislation that adequately protects minority shareholders encourages participation, improves transparency and liquidity, and reduces the discount that affects these shares. The major provisions that regulate transactions between affiliated parties are the following:

—If a transaction involves substantial amounts, the company board of directors must decide whether or not it meets market conditions.

—If the board of directors is unable to reach a decision, it may, with the abstention of the interested director, approve or reject the proposal to avoid a potential conflict of interest; alternatively the board can designate two independent evaluators. The evaluators' reports must be available to shareholders and to the board of directors during a twenty-day working period.

—Shareholders who represent at least 5 percent of the outstanding shares can request an extraordinary meeting to make a decision about the transactions between affiliated parties.

These provisions allow for transparent resolution of transactions between affiliated parties, avoiding damage to minority shareholders.

Audit Committees

The establishment of an audit committee represents a significant step toward the development of improved corporate governance practices, encouraging better internal monitoring. Moreover, the new law requires that a majority of the members of audit committees be independent directors.

The primary functions of audit committees are to review financial statements, propose external auditors and risk-rating agencies, review salaries and compensation plans paid to management, review transactions between affiliated parties, and perform other functions as established in the company's bylaws or authorized by the action of the board of directors or a shareholders' meeting.

Withdrawal Rights

The law broadens the criteria that give rise to withdrawal rights to protect investors in matters that may be against their best interests. Withdrawal rights can be applied when 50 percent of more of the company's assets are sold or given as collateral or when a controlling group acquires more than two-thirds of outstanding shares.

Class Actions

Any loss of net worth as a consequence of an infraction of a law or company by-law gives any shareholder or group of shareholders who represent at least 5 percent of the outstanding shares, or any director, the right to sue a party for compensation on behalf of the company. The possibility to sue on behalf and for the benefit of the company gives all shareholders a greater capacity for protecting their rights.

Tender Offer Standards

Tender offers represent one of the most important corporate events affecting capital markets not only because they involve a change in company control and, therefore, of company management, but also because they allow minority shareholders to participate in the dynamics of the market and benefit from subsequent changes. For this reason, it is most important that minority shareholders have a clear regulatory framework that protects their rights when property changes occur. If the change in control takes place to the disadvantage of minority shareholders, not only are their interests harmed, but the market also is harmed due to the resulting loss of confidence, which leads to diminished participation in company shares and greater stock discount rates.

To provide greater protection for minority shareholders, the new law establishes that whenever a change in corporate control takes place, a public bid must offer prorated acquisition of all stocks; exceptions to this rule are made in the event of equity issuance, mergers, acquisitions as a result of death, or forced transfers. A corporate controlling group wishing to make a transfer need not make a prorated offer for all stock if the premium gained is not substantially higher than the market price (10–15 percent, established annually by the Chilean securities and insurance regulator), if the payment is made in cash, and if the stock has low liquidity. If these three conditions are not simultaneously followed, the change in control must be prorated.

Additionally, to develop a more transparent market, the law requires prior notice of several kinds of action. For example, the intention of obtaining a controlling interest must be announced at least ten working days before the acquisition takes place or as soon as negotiations begin or information and documentation related to the company is distributed. Majority shareholders who hold 10 percent or more of a company's outstanding shares must report their subsequent acquisitions whether these are intended to obtain control of the company or are only a private financial investment.

Each director must submit a report concerning his or her personal opinion on the suitability of the tender offer for shareholders. The directors must make known their relations with the controlling party and the bidder, as well as any interest they may have in the transaction. Such reports must be made available to the public together with the prospectus. Furthermore, the law establishes that when a controlling shareholder accumulates more than two-thirds of a company's stock, he or she must make a tender offer for the remaining shares. This clause seeks to protect minority shareholders from very high concentrations of property, which may reduce liquidity and therefore confine shareholders.

Conclusion

The changes incorporated by the law promulgated in December 2000 will aid the Chilean capital market in enhancing market liquidity and efficiency. The law will improve price setting, avoid property concentration, and lower stock discount rates. In addition to the changes described above, other legal provisions were introduced, including the elimination of the one-year holding period and the removal of capital gains taxes on foreign investors. Those legal amendments along with economic stability and a solid economic base differentiate and highlight Chile as a model for other countries in Latin America. Consequently, we can expect to have a strong rebound in foreign investment in Chile.

The Chilean legislation has incorporated the corporate governance rules taking into account Chile's history and tradition and focusing on developing a coherent legal framework. Moreover, the effectiveness of the law rests on strong institutions. A long tradition of strong public institutions has developed a solid confidence in their work and operations. The courts and the government agencies (such as the SVS, the Chilean securities and insurance regulator) have had an active role enforcing and overseeing compliance with the law. The high level of formal legislation and the effectiveness of institutions permit designing an efficient contract that converges to the best practices in corporate governance.

Finally, an open economy requires the incorporation of international practices such as corporate governance principles, accounting standards, tender offer procedures, clearing and settlement systems, and other practices necessary for Chile to compete effectively in a globalized world. Investors need a common language to be able to understand and trade in different countries. As a consequence, Chile has incorporated these practices in its legal framework to maintain its competitive advantage over other emerging economies.

References

La Porta, Rafael, Florencio Lopez-de-Silanes, Andrei Shleifer, and Robert Vishny. 1998. "Law and Finance." *Journal of Political Economy* 106 (6): 1113–55.
Pistor, Katharina, Martin Raiser, and Stanislaw Gelfer. 2000. "Law and Finance in Transition Economies." *Economics of Transition* 8 (2): 325–68.

PART V

*Summaries of
Breakout Sessions*

12

Reports to the Plenary Session

THE CONFERENCE AT which the papers in this volume were presented had an unusual degree of participation by conference participants. After the authors of a series of papers on a similar topic summarized their findings, they answered questions from the participants. These papers and the discussion that followed then were used as background for a series of breakout sessions where smaller groups of participants discussed particular issues in greater detail. Each of the breakout groups elected its own chairperson to report back to the full conference.

What follows are the summaries of those reports, written by each chairperson. The topics include the governance of banks by regulatory agencies (David Carse); governance exerted by the capital markets (John C. Coffee Jr.); governance of the accounting and legal professions (Karl Ernst Knorr); and governance of investment and asset management companies (Mark St. Giles).

David Carse: Governance of Banks by Public Agencies

Banking regulators are not the only public officials that should be involved in ensuring good corporate governance within banks; securities market regulators can enforce discipline and market conduct rules, deposit insurance corporations set the regulations for deposit insurance and the generosity of those rules, and the government itself establishes the overall legal framework for corporate governance within economies, particularly the effectiveness of insolvency legislation.

It is difficult to reach general conclusions on bank governance or apply lessons learned from one economy to another. Banking regulation must be debated on a country-by-country basis. For example, the American corporate model is of a board of directors composed of mainly independent, nonexecutive directors backed by the threat of shareholder class action. The Securities and Exchange Commission is a strong securities market regulator. While that system may work reasonably well in the United States, it is not perfect (it did not prevent the Enron crisis, for example), and it cannot be transplanted uncritically to other countries, especially those that do not share similar legal, regulatory, and corporate cultural traditions.

Banks are a special class of companies for two important reasons: problems in one bank can quickly spread to others, thus causing a banking crisis; and banks have fiduciary responsibility for managing people's money. These factors help make the case for special corporate governance rules for banks that do not apply to other types of companies within the economy, although this view is not universally shared. Some suggested examples of such special rules, however, are additional disclosure requirements for banks because their activities are opaque; changes in the number of independent directors of banks; and mandatory rotation of auditors. Prudential requirements that regulators impose upon banks help foster good corporate governance and protect the financial position of banks. For example, minimum capital requirements not only provide a buffer in case of losses, but also help to foster good governance by ensuring that the owners of banks have a stake in their sound and efficient operation.

Regulatory forbearance can be and has been a major problem, however, particularly in relation to state-owned banks. Before the banking crisis in Turkey, banking resolution was in the hands of the Turkish treasury. Specifically, the treasury owned, regulated, and borrowed from the banks, creating major conflicts of interest, which contributed to the financial crisis there. If regulators are unable to enforce their regulations on state-owned banks, then they lose credibility. Therefore good governance of the regulators themselves is very important. Nonetheless, prompt corrective action that sets performance standards for the regulators may not be the solution.

This is because a rule-based approach creates the possibility of loopholes. Moreover, it is always possible for the regulators to turn a blind eye to the kinds of indicators that they should be looking at.

Forbearance by external auditors is also a problem and indeed they have failed to spot a number of banking crises. Regulations relating to auditing, such as the mandatory auditor rotation that has been introduced in Singapore and elsewhere, may be able to help. But the number of internationally recognized audit firms is very small, and all of them have had problems in the past. Moreover, new auditors tend to miss bank troubles early in their tenures, so mandatory rotation could result in a deterioration of audit quality.

A more direct approach to corporate governance, such as the system adopted in Hong Kong, would examine how the board of directors operates and interacts with senior management. In Hong Kong during the Asia crisis, the boards of directors of a number of troubled banks essentially were missing in action. In response, regulators required bank boards to have a minimum number of independent members and to meet a minimum number of times during the year. Regulators also monitored the attendance record of individual directors.

Disclosure should involve aligning three types of information: the information that banks need for their own risk management processes, the information made available to supervisors, and the information that is to be publicly disclosed. Regulatory forbearance is likely to be minimized by the maximum possible disclosure of information to the public.

Our discussions revealed skepticism about the view set out in the Caprio-Levine paper that foreign entry can help to foster good corporate governance by increasing the competitive pressure on domestic banks and by facilitating transfers of knowledge and skill. Several participants argued that foreign entry can be very dangerous for small, open economies whose domestic banks are weak. The net result of such entry can be the failure of domestic institutions, leaving much of the economy underserved as the foreign banks cherry-pick only the good customers.

In addition, although widely dispersed ownership can exacerbate the principal-agent problem, concentrated ownership sometimes can be even worse. For example, during the Asian crisis there was widespread looting of banks by the majority owners in countries such as Indonesia.

John C. Coffee Jr.: Capital Markets' Governance of Corporations

At least three fundamental problems must be dealt with in any effort to transplant an Anglo-American system of corporate governance to much of the rest of the world, especially in emerging market and transition economies. One difficulty is that in countries and sectors of the world characterized by concentrated ownership, an active takeover market—the most effective part of the Anglo-American system of discipline—is not likely to materialize quickly. Second, counting upon independent directors is unrealistic in economies where majority shareholders are the norm. Third, enforcement systems such as class action suits are not easily transportable to other countries where judicial traditions are different and where the legal system is likely to resist novel transplants.

What then can be done to ensure good corporate governance under these conditions? A number of suggestions were advanced during the breakout session. One possible solution would require approval from a majority of the minority shareholders for certain kinds of fundamental transactions, particularly self-dealing transactions involving controlling shareholders. While "majority of the minority" voting can lead to holdouts and other problems, it may give realistic protection to shareholders. In addition, independent appraisals by investment banking firms could be triggered by the request of a defined percentage of the minority shareholders to approve transactions.

Another suggestion is to introduce specialized legal decisionmaking bodies for corporate legal issues. Such bodies would render it unnecessary to train all judges in corporate law, as administrative lower judges could handle certain kinds of recurring and less significant disputes. In addition, specialized corporate or securities courts with judges who have had special training would handle a limited range of cases.

A form of mandatory arbitration could be achieved through provisions in corporate charters. For example, the Novo Mercado in Brazil mandates that listed companies must resolve disputes between the minority and controlling shareholders through a mandatory arbitration system.

A British Companies Act approach would obligate the controlling shareholder to buy out the remaining shareholders at a fair price once shareholding crosses some threshold. However, some stock exchanges would not allow the majority shareholder to hold more than 75 percent, out of the fear that liquidity would be destroyed.

Although legislation to implement any one or all of these changes would very likely face significant obstacles and vested interests, other points of leverage might succeed. For example, new forms of securities markets with very high listing standards such as those in Germany and Brazil could work, although it appears that demand for this kind of high-disclosure, high-quality exchange in transitional economies may be limited.

Cross-listing on U.S. exchanges also could represent a desirable form of regulatory competition that would give adequate protection to minority shareholders. At present, the firms that cross-list tend to have superior earnings growth possibilities, high leverage, and prospects for superior market valuations (higher Tobin's qs), even before they cross-list. These firms appear to be willing to pay the price of surrendering some private benefits of control accruing to their controlling shareholders in order to gain from a higher stock valuation.

Yet another approach for strengthening corporate governance would establish special eligibility standards for pension funds. In particular, pension funds could be limited to investing only in those local companies that have certain corporate governance standards. In this manner corporate governance standards are moved from the listing process to the regulatory body having control over the pension funds.

Problems similar to those that came to light during the Enron affair in the United States are surfacing in other countries, where debt rating agencies and securities analysts also face serious conflicts of interest because they provide both consulting and investment banking services. Hence, it would be desirable to have independent ratings agencies assess the quality of corporate governance of private companies. Perhaps "buy-side" analysts working for institutional investors could perform this duty.

Special problems arise in other circumstances, notably when state-owned financial institutions are only partially privatized. When this occurs, the state tends to continue to interfere in the operations of the institution, making political appointments and blocking certain board activities. In addition, in certain cases, central banks have excused largely privatized financial institutions from filing securities disclosures, creating conflicts with securities regulators.

Participants in the breakout group generally agreed on the importance of best practice standards and the development and growth of local institutional ownership. At the same time, no fears were expressed about foreign portfolio investors, pension funds, or mutual funds, although some concerns were raised about local investment funds being under the control of financial holding companies, which can lead to conflicts of interest where the financial institution has business relationships with certain corporate clients in which the investment fund may hold shares.

Karl Ernst Knorr: Effective Governance of the Accounting and Legal Professions

Well before Enron, the accounting profession had been taking steps to promote the use of internationally accepted standards, not just for reporting, but also for auditing—especially for transnational firms. With regard to reporting, the momentum clearly is toward the international standards set by the International Accounting Standards (IAS) board . For example, the European Union had decided to adopt IAS standards for all listings starting in 2005. The United States, however, continues to adhere to U.S. Generally Accepted Accounting Principles. Either these two standards will coexist, or some effort will be made to harmonize the two.

With respect to auditing, no global regulator has yet to emerge. In its absence, a Forum of Firms has been formed, consisting of thirty of the world's largest accounting firms, to promote a system of self-regulation to enforce the compliance of auditors with internationally accepted auditing standards. The forum has been established under the auspices of the International Federation of Accountants (IFAC). The aim of the forum is to implement a global assurance program to certify the quality of audits of transnational firms. The audits of the auditors, so to speak, could be carried out by individuals working for a separate entity, not necessarily for the firms themselves (although it would be desirable to draw somehow on the experience and expertise of the participating firms). The forum has not yet decided on the precise institutional arrangement.

Questions of independence arise regarding relations between management and auditors. One solution is to have shareholders and the audit committee choose the auditor, as is now the case in Germany.

Another area of concern grows out of the pursuit of both audit and nonaudit work by the same firms. The profession is aware of this concern, and accepts that internal and external audits should be separated in order to maintain the independence of the auditor. However, prohibiting auditors from performing any consulting work deprives them of the opportunity to utilize the knowledge they gain through auditing. In part for this reason, the European Commission has ruled that the combination of tax work and audit-related services should not be prohibited. If concerns about the mixing of audit and nonaudit work remain, perhaps they are best handled through listing requirements of the exchanges, rather than through government regulation.

Mark St. Giles: Asset Management Companies and Governance

The governance issues relating to investment management companies can be viewed from two perspectives: the governance of investment management and investment funds themselves, and the corporate governance activities in which the funds engage to ensure the efficient operation of the companies whose shares they hold. In addition, a specialized type of asset management company—the bank workout AMC—has been developed in recent years in several countries, especially in Asia, to deal with troubled assets inherited from weak or insolvent banks.

In the governance of funds, independent custody is crucial to prevent the fund manager from stealing or fraudulently converting the fund's assets. The fund custodian or trustee should have some kind of fiduciary role to assure investors that the fund is being managed in accordance with the terms of the prospectus and the objectives on which the fund is established. It is not clear, however, whether a single corporate trustee is more or less desirable than a set of individual trustees. Individual trustees or directors might be subject to capture by the individual or entity who appoints them, because they may be unwilling to "bite the hand that feeds them."

Risk and risk control within investment management are important issues for rapidly emerging types of pension schemes, which are in effect collective investment schemes. Chile already has such systems, while Croatia, India, and other countries are considering them. In the countries that have collective investment plans, there are more participants in these schemes than people who have bank accounts. A continuing, unresolved issue is how to explain to investors the risks to which they are exposed—and whether the risks should be quantified in some fashion or just explained verbally.

In mandatory pension schemes, millions of people are being forced to invest to provide for their retirement. These pension holdings for many people are their most important asset. This is a reason for constraining the investment freedom of pension fund managers—specifically, to some minimum percentage in safe assets, such as government or high-quality corporate bonds—to ensure they do not place their beneficiaries at undue risk. As the funds mature and managers gain experience, the permitted portfolio compositions could be allowed to vary.

To what extent should fund managers engage actively in governance of the firms whose shares they hold—in other words exercise voice rather than exit? This question is not easily resolved. Breakout participants pointed out that fund managers tend to vote with corporate managers, and when they are dissatisfied with companies whose shares are actively traded in liquid markets, they tend to sell. But in other circumstances, where markets for shares are not deep, the participants urged fund managers to take a higher profile on governance issues.

With respect to investments in countries breakout participants urged fund managers not to exercise moral judgments (except in the case of so-called "ethical" funds that have other objectives), but rather to make decisions solely on the basis of investment criteria since their primary duty is to serve the interests of plan participants.

Meanwhile, asset management companies that are used as bank workout vehicles may be desirable and necessary to cleanse dirty balance sheets and bankrupt banks, thereby helping to restore confidence in banks and the economy as a whole and attracting investment back into the economy. Nonetheless, placing no time limit on the AMCs to work out the assets that were entrusted to them could allow the assets to deteriorate in value. Accordingly, AMCs should be subject to strict time limits or sunset periods. Of course, asset workouts can cause social and economic dislocations, especially if corporate operations are interrupted. But participants felt it better to work out the problems quickly than to have them fester for long periods.

Contributors

Sally Buxton
Cadogan Financial

Gerard Caprio Jr.
World Bank

Jeffrey Carmichael
Australian Prudential Regulation Authority

David Carse
Hong Kong Monetary Authority

Won-Dong Cho
Ministry of Finance and Economy, Korea

Alvaro Clarke de la Cerda
Superintendency of Securities and Insurance, Chile

John C. Coffee Jr.
Columbia Law School

David C. Cooke
Barents Group, KPMG Consulting

Udaibir S. Das
International Monetary Fund

Gregorio Impavido
World Bank

Cally Jordan
World Bank

Daniel Kaufmann
World Bank

Karl Ernst Knorr
BDO Deutsche

Ryszard Kokoszczyński
National Bank of Poland and University of Warsaw

Ross Levine
University of Minnesota

Robert E. Litan
Brookings Institution

Mike Lubrano
International Finance Corporation

Michael Pomerleano
World Bank

Marc Quintyn
International Monetary Fund

Y. V. Reddy
Reserve Bank of India

Khalid Sheikh
*Group Risk Management Corporate
    Center, ABN AMRO*

V. Sundararajan
International Monetary Fund

Mark St. Giles
Cadogan Financial

R. Thillainathan
Malaysian Economic Association

L. L. Tsumba
Reserve Bank of Zimbabwe

Shang-Jin Wei
International Monetary Fund